SELF, SOCIAL IDENTITY,
and PHYSICAL HEALTH

RUTGERS SERIES ON SELF AND SOCIAL IDENTITY

Volume 1   *Self and Identity: Fundamental Issues*

Volume 2   *Self, Social Identity, and Physical Health: Interdisciplinary Explorations*

RUTGERS SERIES ON SELF AND SOCIAL IDENTITY   *Volume 2*

SELF, SOCIAL IDENTITY, and PHYSICAL HEALTH

Interdisciplinary Explorations

Edited by

Richard J. Contrada

Richard D. Ashmore

New York   Oxford
Oxford University Press
1999

Oxford University Press

Oxford   New York
Athens   Auckland   Bangkok   Bogotá   Buenos Aires   Calcutta
Cape Town   Chennai   Dar es Salaam   Delhi   Florence   Hong Kong   Istanbul
Karachi   Kuala Lumpur   Madrid   Melbourne   Mexico City   Mumbai
Nairobi   Paris   São Paulo   Singapore   Taipei   Tokyo   Toronto   Warsaw

and associated companies in

Berlin   Ibadan

Library of Congress Cataloging-in-Publication Data
Self, social identity, and physical health : interdisciplinary
explorations / edited by Richard J. Contrada, Richard D. Ashmore.
   p.   cm.—(Rutgers series on self and social identity ; v. 2)
Papers from the Second Rutgers Symposium on Self and Social
Identity held in 1997.
Includes bibliographical references and index.
ISBN 0-19-512730-7; ISBN 0-19-512731-5 (pbk.)
1. Medicine and psychology—Congresses.   2. Health behavior—
Congresses.   3. Self—Congresses.   4. Identity (Psychology)—
Congresses.   I. Contrada, Richard J.   II. Ashmore, Richard D.
III. Rutgers Symposium on Self and Social Identity (2nd : 1997)
IV. Series.
R726.5.S46   1999
610'.1'9—dc21   98-20149

9 8 7 6 5 4 3 2 1

Printed in the United States of America
on acid-free paper

Norman B. Anderson, Ph.D.
Office of Behavioral and Social Sciences Research
National Institutes of Health

Foreword

It was a pleasure for me to have been invited to participate in the second Rutgers Symposium on Self and Social Identity. The topic for the 1997 symposium—Self, Social Identity, and Physical Health: Interdisciplinary Explorations—unites two of my interests and goals as the first director of the Office of Behavioral and Social Sciences Research (OBSSR) at the National Institutes of Health (NIH). First, exploring the relationship between the self, social identity, and physical health is an example of a more *integrated* approach to health research that my office wishes to advance. The philosophy of the OBSSR is that scientific advances in the understanding, treatment, and prevention of disease will be accelerated by a more integrated approach to research—one that recognizes the manifold connections between psychosocial, behavioral, and biological functioning (Anderson, 1995; OBSSR, 1997). Figure F.1 (OBSSR, 1997) illustrates these connections, and shows how constructs such as the self and social identity (which I place in the behavioral, sociocultural, and environmental box) may interact with biological processes to affect illness. It also shows that the presence of health problems may in turn have profound ramifications for the self and social identity.

The conference's focus on *interdisciplinary* research corresponds to a second major goal of the OBSSR. To achieve a more integrated approach to health research, scientific collaborations across disciplines are crucial. Although the success of single-discipline research is undeniable, this approach to health research may also be somewhat limiting

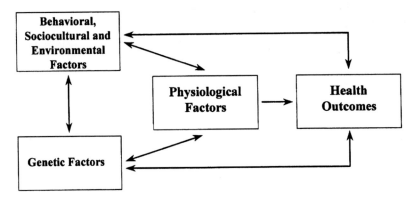

FIGURE F.1. Factors affecting health.

because, although the disciplines concerned with health research may be separated conceptually, methodologically, and administratively, the processes about which they are concerned are inextricably linked. In other words, the social, behavioral, and biological processes that affect health are interdependent. Failure to conduct research across disciplinary lines often precludes the discovery of these interdependent processes. In a sense, the distinctions between scientific disciplines have been reified as if the compartmentalization of the health sciences reflects a corresponding compartmentalization of the origins of human illness. A substantial body of research demonstrates the manifold connections across the "levels of analysis" of health science. Research that integrates these levels represents one of the next great frontiers in the health sciences, with the potential to accelerate advances in both basic and clinical research and in public health. The hallmark of such integrated, multilevel research is interdisciplinary collaborations, which use the expertise of several disciplines to address complex health issues. I would like to briefly outline the concept of multilevel research and some of the principles on which it is based.

The Concept of Levels of Analysis

The concept of levels of analysis is not new to the health sciences. For example, it has been applied quite productively to cognitive and behavioral neuroscience, where both theoretical models and empirical findings have emerged (Churchland & Sejnowski, 1988; Fodor, 1968; Koob & Bloom, 1988). Cacioppo and Berntson (1992) have provided one of the most detailed overviews of the concept of multilevel analyses in their discussion of the interdependence of social psychological and neuroscience research. The success of this approach in neuroscience research suggests that it might be a useful heuristic in other areas of the health science enterprise. In fact, an integrated, multilevel approach to research may represent a unifying framework for all of the health sciences.

Anderson (1998) has outlined one potentially useful way of categorizing the various levels of analysis in health research: the social/environmental, behavioral/psychological, organ systems, cellular, and molecular. Each contains a large number of indices that have been used to study specific health outcomes or pathogenic sociobehavioral or biological processes. Some of these indices are shown in Table F.1. The social/environmental level includes such variables as stressful life events, social support, economic resources, neighborhood characteristics, and environmental hazards. The behavioral/psychological level may include emotion, cognition, memory, dietary practices, stress coping styles, and tobacco use. The organ systems level of analysis includes the cardiovascular, endocrine, immune, and central nervous systems and their outputs. On the cellular level, variables include receptor number and sensitivity, dendritic branches, synapse number, and electrical conductance. Finally, the molecular or genetic level includes such variables as DNA structure, proteins, mRNA, and transportation factors.

The determination of which indices fall within which levels of analysis is admittedly somewhat arbitrary. The point, however, is that the majority of research in the health sciences occurs within a single level of analysis, closely tied to specific disciplines. Even when scientists from different disciplines are working together on the same problem, theirs is not always *multilevel* research. This type of interdisciplinary research focuses on a single level of analysis, with no exploration of influences from higher or lower levels on the problem of interest. Even though the single-level approach has made important contributions at each level, knowledge produced at one level has not always been used to inform research at other levels. Moreover, the science in some areas has progressed to a point where a more integrated, multilevel approach to research design and analysis could pay dividends.

Processes and Principles of Integrated Multilevel Research

In discussion of an integrated, multilevel approach to social psychological and neuroscience research, Cacioppo and Berntson (1992) state that "analysis of a phenomenon at one level of organization can inform, refine, or constrain inferences based on observations at another level of analysis and, therefore, can foster comprehensive accounts and general theories of complex psychological phenomena." That is, *interpretation* of findings from single-level research might benefit from consideration of relevant factors from other levels. Applied to health sciences research

TABLE F.1. Some Indices of Various Levels of Analysis

Social/ Environmental	Behavioral/ Psychological	Organ Systems	Cellular	Molecular
Stressful life events	Emotion	Cardiovascular	Receptor number	DNA structure
Social support	Memory	Blood pressure	Receptor sensitivity	Proteins
Sociocultural groupings	Learning	Heart rate	Cell number	mRNA
Economic resources	Diet	Ejection fraction	Dendritic branches	tRNA
Family environment	Exercise	Occlusion	Synapse number	rRNA
Neighborhood characteristics	Smoking	Endocrine	Cortical reorganization	Proto-oncogenes
Environmental stimulation & enrichment	Alcohol intake	Catecholamines	Electrical conductance (e.g., cell firing)	Transcription factors
Environmental hazards	Drug abuse	Cortisol		Second messengers
	Perception	ACTH		Translation factors
	Stress appraisal and coping	GH		
	Language	Insulin		
	Personality	Immune		
	Aggression	Lymphocytes		
		Phagocytes		
		Cytokines		
		CNS		
		Evoked potentials		
		Cortical weight		
		Blood flow		
		Metabolic rate		
		ANS		
		SNS		
		PNS		

more generally, an integrated, multilevel approach involves two types of processes. The first, following Cacioppo and Berntson, involves the use of findings from one level of analysis to inform, refine, and constrain inferences from observations at another level of analysis. This process might be thought of as "multilevel model or hypothesis development." Here, the objective is a more complete conceptualization of the phenomenon of interest through multilevel models or hypotheses that necessitate the incorporation of findings from other levels. The researcher is asking, What are the variables at higher or lower levels of analysis that might influence or be influenced by the phenomenon that I am studying? The second process logically follows the first and involves the simultaneous study of a phenomenon across levels of analysis to foster a more comprehensive understanding of the determinants of health outcomes or pathogenic processes. The second process is epitomized by integrated, multilevel, cross-disciplinary research designed to test well-articulated multilevel models or hypotheses.

Several principles and a corollary of multilevel research have been proposed (Cacioppo & Berntson, 1992) that may be adapted for the broader domain of health research. These include the principles of parallel causation, convergent causation, and reciprocal causation, and the corollary of proximity. Each of these concepts is defined below.

The Principle of Parallel Causation

The principle of parallel causation holds that each level of analysis may contain risk factors for a single health outcome or pathogenic process (Figure F.2). Each of these risk factors may be sufficient, but not necessary, for the prediction of outcomes or processes. For example, in the prediction of coronary heart disease (CHD), social-level risk factors include socioeconomic status and social support; behavioral-level risk factors include physical inactivity and smoking; and organ systems–level risk factors include low-density lipoproteins and hypertension. Each level of analysis contains variables that alone are sufficient to account for a significant proportion of the variance in CHD, though no particular level is necessary for the prediction of CHD.

The Principles of Convergent and Reciprocal Causation

With convergent causation, a convergence or interaction of variables from at least two levels of analysis leads to a health outcome or pathogenic process (Figure F.3). Thus, variables within a single level may be necessary, but not sufficient, to produce an outcome. Here, factors from one level of analysis affect factors at another level, and this cross-level causation ultimately influences outcomes. The principle of reciprocal causation is similar to that of convergent causation, but posits

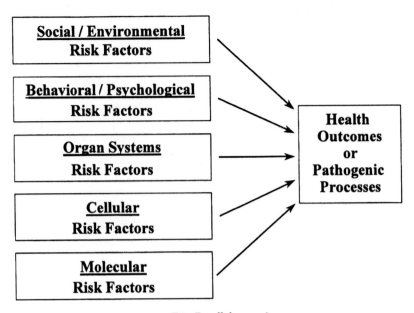

FIGURE F.2. Parallel causation.

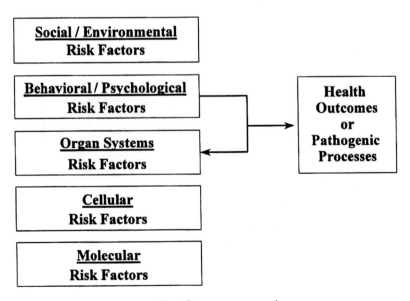

FIGURE F.3. Convergent causation.

bidirectional influences across levels, involving negative and positive feedback loops (Figure F.4). For example, the initiation of cigarette smoking (behavioral level) in adolescents may be strongly tied to such social and environmental factors as peer influences and advertising (convergent causation); smoking behavior in turn could later affect biological processes leading to a biological addiction (convergent causation); and this biological addiction contributes to the maintenance smoking behavior (reciprocal causation). Thus, the behavior of smoking leads to biological changes that further serve to maintain this behavior. The principles of convergent and reciprocal causation are the foundations of integrated, multilevel research in that they highlight the critical importance of interactions across levels of analysis in fostering more complete accounts of health phenomena.

The Corollary of Proximity

This corollary holds that the mapping of elements or variables across levels of organization increases in complexity as the number of intervening levels increases (Cacioppo & Berntson, 1992). That is, research aimed at exploring interactions between variables at adjacent levels of analysis will typically be less complex than that examining variables at nonadjacent levels. This is true because events at any level of analysis (e.g., the cellular level) can be influenced by events within the same or at adjacent levels (e.g., organ systems level), which in turn

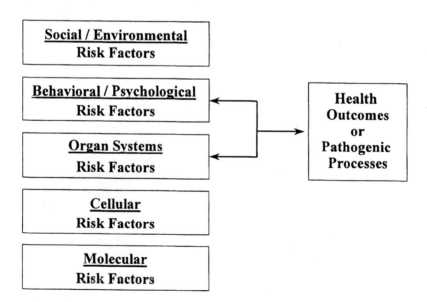

FIGURE F.4. Reciprocal causation.

may be affected by events at the next level organization (e.g., behavioral level). This added complexity does not preclude research across multiple levels but suggests that an incremental approach may be the most useful (Cacioppo & Berntson, 1992). Churchland and Sejnowski (1998) voiced a similar perspective:

> The ultimate goal of a unified account does not require that it be a single model that spans all levels of organization. Instead, the integration will probably consist of a chain of models linking adjacent levels. When one level is explained in terms of a lower level, this does not mean that the higher level theory is useless or that high-level phenomena no longer exist. On the contrary, explanations will coexist at all levels.

Numerous examples of multilevel research exist in such fields as cognitive neuroscience, psychoneuroimmunology, behavioral cardiology, developmental psychobiology, psychosocial oncology, and behavior genetics. Treatment approaches based on a multilevel perspective are emerging for health problems such as cancer, heart disease, depression, asthma, diabetes, and arthritis. As I stated earlier, I believe that research that integrates the various levels of analysis represents a new frontier in the health sciences, with the potential to accelerate advances in both basic and clinical research and in public health. Interdisciplinary, multilevel research on the self, social identity, and health is an important contribution to this perspective. I congratulate the conference organizers for their vision in crafting such a timely theme for this symposium and for choosing speakers whose contributions have effectively highlighted the scientific opportunities that exist in research on the self, social identity, and physical health.

References

Anderson, N. B. (1998). Levels of analysis in health science: A framework for integrating sociobehavioral and biomedical research. *Annals of the New York Academy of Sciences, 840,* 563–576.
Anderson, N. B. (1995). Integrating behavioral and social sciences research at the NIH. *Academic Medicine, 70,* 1106–1107.
Cacioppo, J. T., & Berntson, G. G. (1992). Social psychological contributions to the decade of the brain: The doctrine of multilevel analysis. *American Psychologist, 47*(8), 1019–1028.
Churchland, P. S., & Sejnowski, T. J. (1988). Perspectives on cognitive neuroscience. *Science, 242,* 741–745.
Fodor, J. A. (1968). *Psychological explanation.* New York: Random House.
Koob, G. F., & Bloom, F. E. (1988). Cellular and molecular mechanisms of drug dependence. *Science, 242,* 715–723.
Office of Behavioral and Social Sciences Research. (1997). *A strategic plan for the office of behavioral and social sciences research.* NIH Publication No. 97-4237.

Preface to Volume II

The initial volume of the *Rutgers Series on Self and Social Identity* examined fundamental theoretical issues. It was organized around contrasting perspectives and critical contexts. The concept of self as a multiplicity was contrasted with a unitary conception, and views of self and identity were presented that emphasized their personal or social aspects. Self and identity then were examined in relation to the contexts of history, culture, and American society at the end of the twentieth century. The volume noted major themes emerging from the first hundred years of scientific research on self and identity and defined current challenges.

This second volume of the *Rutgers Series* explores self and identity in relation to another area of study, namely, the social and behavioral analysis of physical health and illness. The concepts and methods of social and behavioral sciences have increasingly become part of the paradigm for basic research and intervention aimed at understanding and controlling physical health problems. Health scientists and practitioners in many disciplines now accept the important role played by social, psychological, and behavioral factors in the development and prevention of major diseases, in the impact of sickness and disability, and in medical treatment. Concepts such as psychological stress and coping, social support, and disease-prone personalities have attracted the attention of practicing physicians and biomedical researchers, and few would dispute the implications for physical health of behaviors such as cigarette smoking, unsafe sexual practices, and noncompliance with medical regimens.

This volume poses the question: Would it be fruitful to engage in an explicit and deliberate examination of self and identity in relation to social and behavioral aspects of physical health and illness? Both self and identity, and health and illness, involve interactions between personal and social systems usually described at different levels of analysis. Thus, it may be useful to consider self and identity constructs as a means of conceptualizing the interplay between person- and social-level systems involved in the development and treatment of physical health problems. Chapters by John Kihlstrom and Lucy Canter Kihlstrom and by Margaret Lock begin this exploration by considering self and identity as they relate to systems—psychological systems and health care systems operating at the level of the individual's illness experience (Kihlstrom and Canter Kihlstrom) and the larger cultural and political systems operating at the societal level (Lock).

Many of the essential aspects of self and identity are social, including our beliefs about what others think of us, and our perception of differences between members of those groups with whom we do and do not identify. And the fundamentally social nature of human beings is both the basis for conflicts and tensions that lead to health-damaging psychological stress and a source of comfort, support, and understanding in times of stress. It follows that self and identity may offer a lens through which we may gain a better understanding of the social origins of psychological stress and the social resources and processes involved in coping with stress. In this volume, David Williams, Michael Spencer, and James Jackson examine race and ethnicity as social categories whose involvement in the production and moderation of psychological stress may reflect the operation of self- and identity-related factors. James Pennebaker and Kelli Keough then discuss findings indicating that the disclosure of thoughts and feelings associated with traumatic stressors enhances well-being through processes that involve the reorganization of self and identity.

Major health problems, including the chronic diseases that are currently the leading sources of death in the United States, typically do not erupt suddenly. They often emerge as a result of processes that develop slowly over years, even decades. In many instances, these processes may reflect the influence of broad patterns of psychological and behavioral activity that increase exposure to health-damaging events and conditions over significant periods of time. In this volume, Suzanne Ouellette considers the merits of conceptualizing enduring personality patterns that have been associated with physical health problems in terms of psychological structures and processes involving self and identity. Jeanne Brooks-Gunn and Julia Graber then examine self and identity in relation to patterns of sexual activity that often are initiated during the adolescent years and may contribute to disease risk.

During the course of this century, shifting disease patterns, improvements in public health practices, and advances in medical technology have increased the likelihood of a significant period of survival following serious illness. As a result, greater attention is being given to the impact of disease on social, emotional, and physical functioning. This work has, in turn, led to growing recognition that quality of life in illness, rather than merely reflecting degree of organic damage or dysfunction, is also influenced by social and psychological factors. In the last section of this book, Howard Leventhal, Ellen Idler, and Elaine Leventhal use several distinct but interrelated concepts of self and identity to conceptualize the social and psychological processes whereby the person experiences and manages serious illness. Kathy Charmaz then provides an historical perspective and critique of the sociological concept of sick role, before turning to the story and the act of storytelling as a means of understanding self and identity in sickness.

This volume is based, in part, on the Second Rutgers Symposium on Self and Identity, held in April 1997. The two-day symposium was attended by hundreds of researchers, practitioners, and students from the social, behavioral, and health sciences. Both the formal talks and commentaries and the informal discussions they generated provided a strong indication that concepts of self and identity can fruitfully be examined in relation to the current paradigm for the study of social and behavioral aspects of physical health and disease. We hope that this volume captures, and stimulates further examination of, some of the many exciting possibilities presented at the symposium.

Piscataway, New Jersey   R. J. C.
June 1998   R. D. A.

Acknowledgments

We are indebted to numerous individuals and organizations for the guidance and support they provided as we conceptualized and carried out the Second Rutgers Symposium and created this volume. We thank you all. We apologize if, in the comments that follow, we inadvertently fail to mention any of you. Because we were helped in so many ways, by so many people, over so lengthy a period of time, we would be surprised if there were no omissions.

Our initial thanks must go to the symposium speakers/chapter authors. These individuals were selected because they are distinguished scholars and researchers in their fields of study. Although all have examined *either* self/identity *or* health/illness in their work, we believe that few, if any of them, would characterize that work as involving a focus on self/identity *and* health/illness. Nonetheless, all the contributors accepted the challenge to extend their perspectives, either by using their knowledge of self and identity to examine health/illness, or by examining the health-related phenomena in which they were interested from a self/identity perspective. And, judging from the quality of the symposium presentations and the final chapters appearing in this book, we can report that each of the speakers/authors met that challenge. In addition, during the course of realizing our visions of both the symposium and this volume, the speakers/authors held to a demanding production schedule, much of the time accepting our feedback, the rest of the time showing why it clearly would be better if they did not, and all of the time displaying levels of patience, perseverance, and professionalism that made the entire venture as enjoyable as it was intellectually satisfying. Each of you has our heartfelt thanks.

Next, we wish to thank our publisher and series editor, Joan Bossert. Joan has been an invaluable source of guidance and support since she first received the proposal for the *Rutgers Series*.

There are many to thank for sharing ideas about the topic of self/identity and physical health, for suggesting speakers/authors, and for providing comments on chapter drafts. These include series coeditor, Lee Jussim; members of our editorial board, who provided valuable feedback on initial and revised proposals; and a host of others, including Norman Anderson, Andrew Baum, David Glass, Peter Guarnaccia, Dan Hart, Alan Horwitz, Ellen Idler, Howard Leventhal, David Mechanic, Ann O'Leary, Timothy Smith, Shelley Taylor, Peggy Thoits, and Neil Weinstein. The input we received from these individuals played a major role in shaping both the structure and content of the symposium and this book.

Throughout the entire process culminating in the production of this volume, we have benefited from suggestions and assistance from faculty, staff, students, and administrators of Rutgers, The State University of New Jersey. The following members of the Rutgers University community were particularly helpful: Steven Lione, Thelma Collins, and the staff of the Rutgers Continuing Education Center; Joanne Aguglia of the Douglass College Center; Rosemary Manero and her colleagues in the Rutgers Dining Service; Rae Frank, Bonita Holt-Griffin, Anne Sokolowski, and Alison Smith, all with the Department of Psychology, who exhibited patience and good humor in their extremely efficient handling of day-to-day tasks and deadline pressures.

Other members of the Rutgers community must be singled out for special thanks. The first is Charles Flaherty, chair of the Department of Psychology, for his support and encouragement and for making departmental staff and other resources available for our use. Second, we are extremely grateful to members of the doctoral program in Social Psychology, faculty and students alike. Members of the Social Psychology Program served as hosts for speakers, helped with symposium registration, transported speakers to and from airports and train stations, directed traffic between symposium sessions, and helped conduct myriad other essential tasks. Third, we thank the following members of the Rutgers community for their generous financial assistance: Joseph J. Seneca (Vice President for Academic Affairs), Richard F. Foley (Dean, Faculty of Arts and Sciences), David Mechanic (Director, Institute for Health, Health Care Policy, and Aging Research), Charles F. Flaherty (Chair, Department of Psychology), and the Rutgers Research Council.

We are also grateful for grants from the National Institutes of Health (MH/AG57108) and from the Fetzer Institute that supported both the Second Rutgers Symposium and the production of this volume.

To all those who provided financial assistance, we would like to point out that your support did more than make the symposium and this book possible—it also allowed us to hold the symposium without the need for registration fees or other charges. Thus, your generosity made both formal and informal aspects of the symposium accessible to a larger and more diverse audience than would otherwise have been the case.

Contents

Contributors   xxiii

1

INTRODUCTION: Self and Social Identity: Key to Understanding
   Social and Behavioral Aspects of Physical Health and Disease?   3
      Richard J. Contrada / Richard D. Ashmore

PART I / Self, Social Identity, and Systems Affecting Health and
   Health Care

2

Self, Sickness, Somatization, and Systems of Care   23
      John F. Kihlstrom / Lucy Canter Kihlstrom

3

The Politics of Health, Identity, and Culture   43
      Margaret Lock

PART II / Self and Social Identity in Stress, Coping, and Physical
   Disease

4

Race, Stress, and Physical Health: The Role of Group Identity   71
      David R. Williams / Michael S. Spencer / James S. Jackson

5

Revealing, Organizing, and Reorganizing the Self in Response to Stress
and Emotion   101
James W. Pennebaker / Kelli A. Keough

PART III / Self-Related Personality Structures, Identity
Development, and Disease-Related Behavior

6

The Relationship between Personality and Health: What Self and
Identity Have to Do with It   125
Suzanne C. Ouellette

7

What's Sex Got to Do with It? The Development of Sexual Identities
during Adolescence   155
Jeanne Brooks-Gunn / Julia A. Graber

PART IV / Influences of Illness on Self and Identity

8

The Impact of Chronic Illness on the Self System   185
Howard Leventhal / Ellen L. Idler / Elaine A. Leventhal

9

From the "Sick Role" to Stories of Self: Understanding the Self in
Illness   209
Kathy Charmaz

10

CONCLUSION: Self, Social Identity, and the Analysis of Social and
Behavioral Aspects of Physical Health and Disease   240
Richard D. Ashmore / Richard J. Contrada

Index   257

Contributors

Norman B. Anderson, Office of Behavioral and Social Sciences Research, National Institutes of Health, Building One, One Center Drive, Bethesda, MD 20892. E-mail: norman.anderson@nih.gov.

Richard D. Ashmore, Department of Psychology, Rutgers University, 53 Avenue E, Piscataway, NJ 08854-8040. E-mail: ashmore@rci.rutgers.edu.

Jeanne Brooks-Gunn, Center for Children and Families, Teachers College, Columbia University, 525 W. 120th Street, New York, NY 10027. E-mail: brooks-gunn@columbia.edu.

Kathy Charmaz, Department of Sociology, Sonoma State University, Rohnart Park, CA 94928. E-mail: charmaz@sonoma.edu.

Richard J. Contrada, Department of Psychology, Rutgers University, 53 Avenue E, Piscataway, NJ 08854-8040. E-mail: contrada@rci.rutgers.edu.

Julia A. Graber, Center for Children and Families, Teachers College, Columbia University, 525 W. 120th Street, New York, NY 10027. E-mail: jag51@columbia.edu.

Ellen Idler, Institute for Health, Health Care Policy, and Aging Research, Rutgers University, 30 College Avenue, New Brunswick, NJ 08903. E-mail: idler@rci.rutgers.edu.

James S. Jackson, Department of Psychology and Research Center for Group Dynamics, Institute for Social Research, University of Michican, Ann Arbor, MI 48106. E-mail: jamessj@umich.edu.

Kelli A. Keough, Department of Psychology, University of Texas, Austin, TX 78712. E-mail: keough@psy.utexas.edu.

John F. Kihlstrom, Department of Psychology, University of California, Berkeley, CA 94720-1650. E-mail: Kihlstrm@cogsci.berkeley.edu.

Lucy Canter Kihlstrom, Institute for Personality and Social Research, MC 5050, University of California, Berkeley, CA 94720-5050. E-mail: lucyck@uclink4.berkeley.edu.

Elaine A. Leventhal, Department of Medicine, Robert Wood Johnson Medical School, UMDNJ, New Brunswick, NJ 08903-0019. E-mail: eleventhal@umdnj.edu.

Howard Leventhal, Institute for Health, Health Care Policy, and Aging Research, Rutgers University, New Brunswick, NJ 08903. E-mail: howardl@rci.rutgers.edu.

Margaret Lock, Department of Social Studies of Medicine and Department of Anthropology, McGill University, Montreal, Quebec H3G 1YG Canada. E-mail: cy61@musica.mcgill.ca.

Suzanne C. Ouellette, Social/Personality Psychology, CUNY Graduate Center, New York, NY 10036-8099. E-mail: souellet@email.gc.cuny.edu.

James W. Pennebaker, Department of Psychology, University of Texas, Austin, TX 78712. E-mail: pennebaker@psy.utexas.edu.

Michael S. Spencer, School of Social Work, University of Michigan, Ann Arbor, MI 48106. E-mail: spencerm@umich.edu.

David R. Williams, Department of Sociology and Survey Research Center, Institute for Social Research, University of Michigan, Ann Arbor, MI 48106. E-mail: wildavid@umich.edu.

SELF, SOCIAL IDENTITY,
and PHYSICAL HEALTH

Richard J. Contrada
Richard D. Ashmore

Introduction

Self and Social Identity: Key to
Understanding Social and Behavioral Aspects
of Physical Health and Disease?

It is a bit risky to characterize a specific topic in the social and behavioral sciences as having entered a period of sustained activity. Even long-standing enthusiasm for a concept or subject matter can fade unexpectedly in the face of empirical inconsistencies, theoretical cul-de-sacs, or methodological difficulties, to say nothing of the vagaries of research funding. Yet, we have little hesitation in describing the two main topics of this volume—(1) self and social identity and (2) social and behavioral aspects of physical health and illness—as research areas whose current high levels of activity and productivity are likely to remain constant, if not intensify, in the foreseeable future. Over the past few decades, each of these topics has become a firmly established focus of investigation.

A riskier proposition is identifying in advance areas of study that, with increased investment, would produce the greatest dividends. Most predictions of this sort are bound for disconfirmation, if only by virtue of their sheer number and mutual incompatibility. Moreover, depending on the manner and style with which they are presented, projections and exhortations about certain research topics deserving greater attention can be off-putting, appearing either presumptuous and strident or perfunctory and formulaic. Nonetheless, we would like to make the case for the merits of a focused examination of self and social identity constructs in relation to social and behavioral aspects of physical health/illness. Our view is that the interface of these two domains offers exciting opportunities for theoretical and empirical advancement.

Accordingly, the purpose of this volume is to explore that interface as a means of stimulating and guiding research that asks two inter-related questions: Should the conceptual and methodological tools emerging in the study of self and identity form major elements of the paradigm for understanding social and behavioral factors in physical health and illness? How can the study of social and behavioral aspects of physical health and illness contribute to knowledge about self and identity?

For background, we begin this chapter with brief characterizations of the current status of social and behavioral research on self and identity and on physical health and illness. Then we examine the conceptual foundations of social/behavioral approaches to physical health and disease and identify their points of connection with concepts of self and identity. We subsequently describe the organizational structure of the volume and present an overview of the specific topics addressed in the chapters that follow.

Self and Identity in the Social and Behavioral Sciences

The concepts of self and social identity,[1] important to psychology at its inception, have undergone a revitalization in that discipline (Ashmore & Jussim, 1997a). William James (1890) first introduced the self as a major determinant of psychological phenomena and as a tractable topic of empirical research. He differentiated the self as subject (agent or process) from the self as object (content or structure), referring to the former as the "I," or self-as-knower, and the latter as the "Me," or self-as-known. Since then, multiple diverse lines of psychological research and theory have used self and identity concepts in seeking to understand human thought, feeling, and action (Ashmore & Jussim, 1997b; Banaji & Prentice, 1994; Markus & Herzog, 1991). Concepts of self and identity also appear in early sociological (e.g., Cooley, 1902; Mead, 1934) and anthropological (e.g., Hallowell, 1955; Radin, 1920) writings and are now subjects of renewed interest in those disciplines (in sociology, see Gecas, 1982; Gleason, 1983; Scheibe, 1985; in anthropology, see Fogelson, 1982; Holland, 1997; Whittaker, 1993). Self-related concepts are crucial in accounting for interrelationships between the individual and larger sociocultural institutions and systems. Self and identity, as important constructs in social and behavioral research, ought to be useful in facilitating understanding of those social and behavioral factors associated with physical well-being and disease. More specific support for this premise can be found in the core assumptions underlying recent developments in the health and medical sciences.

Social and Behavioral Aspects of Physical Health and Illness

Over the past two decades, the multidisciplinary field of *behavioral medicine* has been formally recognized in response to increasing productive involvement of social and behavioral scientists in efforts to understand physical health and disease (Matarazzo, 1980, 1982). Within behavioral medicine, *behavioral health* refers to an interdisciplinary specialty concerned with health maintenance and disease prevention in healthy individuals, and *health psychology* refers to the involvement of the discipline of psychology in physical health and disease (Matarazzo, 1980, 1982). There is now widespread recognition that the study of many significant physical health problems can be enlightened by psychosocial and behavioral perspectives. Research guided by this view has uncovered new risk factors for physical disease (Adler & Matthews, 1994), delineated physiologic pathways to explain linkages between psychological factors and disease states (Cohen & Herbert, 1996; Krantz & Manuck, 1984), identified psychological processes that can facilitate or undermine medical treatment (e.g., Leventhal, Meyer, & Nerenz, 1980), and led to behavioral interventions that can improve physical health, modify the course and outcome of illness, or prevent disease (e.g., Bracke & Thoreson, 1996).

Research in behavioral medicine and its subfields addresses a wide variety of questions concerning health and illness, including those about illness prevention/health promotion, psychosocial epidemiology, etiology and pathogenesis of disease, medical diagnosis, treatment, and rehabilitation. Although diverse theoretical frameworks and models necessarily have been used to guide these various research agendas, much of the work reflects the *biopsychosocial model*, a focus on *mechanisms*, and a *systems perspective*. As discussed below, translation of these three sets of principles into specific theoretical and empirical activity often involves psychosocial structures and processes concerning self and identity. Although self/identity constructs have been formally and explicitly recognized in some cases, in others they remain implicit and largely unexplored.

Conceptual Foundations of Behavioral Medicine and Concepts of Self and Identity

The Biopsychosocial Model

The *biopsychosocial* model provides a meta-theory for the study of social, psychological, and behavioral aspects of physical health (Engel, 1977, 1980). It is often contrasted with the *biomedical* model that has guided medical practice for several hundred years. The biomedical model has been faulted for its reductionist view in which illness is defined solely in terms of bodily dysfunction, its assumption of single-factor causation, its mind/body dualism, and its emphasis on disease and treatment to the relative neglect of health and health promotion. The biopsychosocial model calls for simultaneous integrated study of both macro-level and micro-level processes; assumes that health and illness are multiply determined by biological, psychological, and sociological factors; rejects mind-body dualism; and gives equal emphasis to health and illness, rather than viewing health solely as the absence of disease (Taylor, 1995).[2]

Where are self and identity within the biopsychosocial model? We think there are numerous possibilities. Consider, as a starting point, the attention given to subjective states in the holistic conceptions of health associated with the biopsychosocial model. In these conceptions, health is defined in terms of physical, mental, and social well-being as well as physical dysfunction and disability (Stone, 1979; Ware, 1992). Research on the subjective experience of health indicates that individuals' self-ratings of their physical status predict mortality, even following statistical adjustment for objective health indicators (Idler & Benyamini, 1997). In addition to predicting physical disease outcomes, the subjective experience of illness has become an important health indicator in its own right. *Quality of life*, defined as a person's evaluation of his or her emotional, physical, and social functioning, has attained a status equivalent to that of morbidity and mortality as a consideration in evaluating biomedical interventions, developing health-care policy, and monitoring health in the general population (Gill & Feinstein, 1994; Ware, 1992). These two developments suggest that perceptions, beliefs, and evaluations of the physical self—components of James's (1890) Me—contain information about disease susceptibility and disease impact not captured by standard biomedical health evaluations.

Subjective aspects of physical health emphasized by the biopsychosocial model also have implications for the role of self and identity in health-care delivery. Engel (1977, 1980) explicitly called attention to the importance of a patient's experience of illness in shaping the clinical expression of disease and in guiding decisions about proper patient care. His analysis of illness experience refers to "self image," "expectations," "goals," and "concerns" (Engel, 1980), concepts many psychologists interested in self and identity would find familiar and compatible with their own theoretical frameworks. Engel also drew upon the concepts of medical sociology, arguing that health-care practitioners need to be aware of social and psychological factors that may sustain sick role behavior in the absence of disease or that may maintain patienthood following successful biomedical treatment. Further, he discussed how inadequate or inappropriate treatment can arise when patient and doctor differ in their views of the health problem that confronts them. By introducing the latter point, Engel (1980) went beyond merely calling for attention to social and psychological factors affecting illness and treatment. He used a social and psychological analysis to derive the recommendation that the physician take account of a patient's self-perceptions, rather than allowing a patient's status as a sick person to restrict the physician's attention to bodily dysfunction—a treatment model that implicitly uses self and identity concepts.

Mechanisms of Interplay between Social/Behavioral and Health/Illness Domains

Supporting the biopsychosocial model is a large, diverse body of research concerning social and psychological aspects of various physical health problems. This work can be classified in several different ways. One classification distinguishes among social and behavioral causes, consequences, and accompaniments of health and illness. Others refer to disease categories (e.g., cardiovascular behavioral medicine, psychosocial oncology) or to general problem areas that cut across diseases (e.g., psychosocial epidemiology, etiology, medical adherence). A more analytic framework for describing the points of contact between social/behavioral and health/illness phenomena emphasizes the types of *mechanisms* or *pathways* that link these two domains (Krantz, Glass, Contrada, & Miller, 1981). For example, direct, *psychophysiological mechanisms* are closely identified with the concept of stress and involve the effects of environmental stressors and emotional states on physiologic processes that promote disease. Indirect, *behavioral mechanisms* involve actions or inactions through which a person is exposed to pathogens, such as cigarette smoking and unsafe sexual practices. *Reactions to illness* refer to psychological and behavioral responses to physical symptoms, illness, and medical treatment, which may influence the course and outcome of disease. These three types of mechanisms form the causal links between the biological and psychosocial elements of the biopsychosocial model. It has been suggested that the burgeoning of behavioral medicine research and the birth of health psychology were made possible by the transition from the mere documentation of associations between psychosocial factors and physical health to the identification of specific causal mechanisms to explain those associations (Krantz et al., 1981).

Is the utility of self and identity concepts in health science limited to their importance in highlighting subjective aspects of health and disease and in understanding the doctor-patient relationship? Or can they inform efforts to identify basic mechanisms that underlie associations between social and behavioral factors and physical health and illness?

We think self- and identity-related constructs can contribute to the understanding of causal processes that underlie physical disease as well as those instigated by its occurrence. Concepts of self and identity play an important, yet often implicit role in accounts of psychophysiological, behavioral, and illness-initiated mechanisms.

With regard to physiologic mechanisms, it is widely accepted that the ability of psychosocial events to provoke pathogenic physiological changes associated with stress and negative emotion can be explained in terms of cognitive appraisal and coping processes (Cohen & Herbert, 1996; Krantz & Manuck, 1984). Both processes involve psychological structures and processes associated with self and identity. In cognitive appraisal, the goals, competencies, valued social roles, and resources that make up the self are evaluated in relation to potentially stressful environmental events and conditions (Brown & Harris, 1989; Higgins, 1987; Lazarus, 1993; Thoits, 1991). For major stressors, cognitive appraisal can involve a look back at past selves that have been lost or changed and a look forward toward possible future selves (Charmaz, this book, chap. 9; Pennebaker and Keough, this book, chap. 5). Similarly, the process of coping with stress can be conceptualized in terms of cognitive and behavioral adjustments directed at repairing, restoring, or reaffirming a threatened aspect of self or identity (Deaux, 1992; Thoits, 1991), in addition to being either problem-focused or emotion-focused, as in the more conventional analysis of coping (Lazarus & Folkman, 1984). For example, the aggressive coping style of Type A individuals has been interpreted as a chronic effort to obtain clear evidence of self-worth to satisfy a set of exacting but vague standards for self-evaluation (Strube, 1987). Thus, both cognitive appraisal and coping—cornerstones of the stress model of the psychosocial causation of physical disease—can profitably be viewed from a self/identity perspective.

Psychosocial stress moderators, another concept central to the stress paradigm, also are amenable to conceptual analysis in terms of self and identity constructs (Ouellette, this book, chap. 6; Williams, Spencer, & Jackson, this book, chap. 4). These are personal attributes and social-contextual factors that either enhance or buffer against the health-damaging physiologic effects of stress by regulating the frequency or degree of exposure to stressors, shaping the cognitive appraisal of stressors, or influencing coping responses. In the personality domain, traits such as external locus of control and pessimistic attributional style, thought to exacerbate the stress process, can be seen as self-related because they are defined in terms of self-referent beliefs about causality (Wiebe & Smith, 1997). With regard to social moderators, the stress-buffering effects of social relationships possibly include enhanced self-esteem, identification with others, and a sense of belonging to social groups, in addition to the provision of emotional, instrumental, and informational support (Cohen & Wills, 1985; Krause & Borawski-Clark, 1994; Short, Sandler, & Roosa, 1996; Williams et al., this book, chap. 4). Thus, it would appear that, as in cognitive appraisal and coping, the nature and effects of psychosocial resources and vulnerability factors thought to be major determinants of adaptation to stress might warrant further examination in relation to self/identity constructs.

With regard to behavioral pathways linking psychosocial factors to health and illness, it is noteworthy that many health-related behavior patterns emerge during adolescence, a life stage in which identity formation is crucial (Brooks-Gunn & Graber, this book, chap. 7). Moreover, both during adolescence and beyond, health-related practices including cigarette smoking, sexual behavior, alcohol consumption, eating, and exposure to ultraviolet radiation, often reflect motives related to self-definition, self-enhancement, or the projection of a particular social identity (Dolcini & Adler, 1994; Heatherton & Baumeister, 1991, Leary, Tchividjian, & Kraxberger, 1994; Steele & Josephs, 1990). The dominant theoretical models accounting for health-related behavior and behavior change, such as the health belief model (Rosenstock, 1974), theory of reasoned action (Fishbein & Ajzen, 1975), and stages of change model (DiClemente & Prochaska, 1982), do not explicitly invoke self or social identity as major constructs. However, examination of these models reveals key predictors that involve self-referent beliefs, such as the disease susceptibility component of the health belief model and the self-efficacy construct (Bandura, 1977) that has been incorporated into health behavior models such as protection motivation theory (Rogers, 1975, 1983) and the theory of planned behavior (Ajzen, 1985). Ogden (1995) has discussed a shift in health behavior research over the past few decades from a focus on a person's perception and appraisal of external hazards, to a focus on a person's perception of himself or herself as a source of risk and perceived ability to control his or her own risky behavior. She suggests that this shift in emphasis reflects the emergence, in both lay beliefs and behavioral science models, of the implicit notion that health protection is a matter of perceptual and behavioral activity of the "self" directed at a conception of "self"—corresponding, respectively, to James's (1890) I and Me. Several authors call for further consideration of self/identity constructs in connection with health behavior models as a means of enhancing the models' ability to predict and to understand risk-enhancing and health-protective actions (e.g., Charng, Piliavin, & Callero, 1988; Granberg & Holmberg, 1990; Sparks & Shepard, 1992; Sparks, Shepherd, & Zimmermanns, 1995; Theodorakis, 1994).

Self and identity have more frequently received explicit examination in theory and research on mechanisms through which sickness and medical treatment exert psychological and social effects on the patient. One's physical health status can be profoundly important to one's conception of self, as can be the disfiguring effects of surgery and negative side effects of medication. Adaptation to physical disease and its treatment has been viewed in terms of various self and identity concepts, referring, for example, to the patient's efforts to maintain a perception of himself or herself as worthy, in control, and living a meaningful life (Taylor, 1983); to retain a coherent sense of self through fluctuations in pain, physical functioning, and mood and in the face of discontinuities in social relationships and life possibilities (Charmaz, this book, chap. 9; Leventhal, Idler, and Leventhal, this book, chap. 8); and to project an optimistic view of the future self (Fife, 1995). Interpersonal consequences of physical illness have also been conceptualized from a self/identity perspective. For example, Goffman's (1963) stigma idea involves processes whereby negative reactions to diseased and disabled individuals discredit their social identity. Like psychophysiological mechanisms and health-related behaviors, social and psychological processes instigated by physical disease and illness appear amenable to further analysis in terms of self and identity.

Systems View

In addition to the biopsychosocial paradigm, and an emphasis on mechanisms linking social/behavioral factors to health and illness, the theoretical foundations of behavioral medicine include systems concepts for characterizing the structure and functioning of a person in a sociocultural context. In discussing systems approaches to physical illness and its treatment, Engel (1977, 1980) placed "the person" at the center of a hierarchy of systems involved in health and disease, from microlevel (bodily tissues, cells, and organelles) to macro-level (doctor-patient dyad, the family, and the community). The idea that social, psychological, and physiological events reflect interacting systems is congruent with the biopsychosocial model's multilevel analysis of health and illness. It provides a matrix within which mechanisms linking social and behavioral processes to health and illness can operate (Engel, 1977, 1980).

How do self and identity fit into the systems view of the role of social and behavioral factors in physical health and disease? Here we think it possible to incorporate explicitly concepts of self and identity into midlevel conceptual frameworks that are more specific and researchable than the broad, biopsychosocial perspective, and yet have greater potential for comprehensiveness and theoretical integration than models developed for particular health problems. The model of a person as a system, in which perceptual inputs are compared to internal referents in the process of guiding goal-directed activity, is widely shared among psychological researchers interested in health and illness, despite differences in emphasis and detail (e.g., Bandura, 1991; Carver

& Scheier, 1981; Leventhal et al., 1997). However, with few exceptions (e.g., Baumeister & Heatherton, 1996; Higgins, 1997), there is an apparent disconnection between models of "self"-regulation in health psychology and the treatment of "self" by psychologists interested in self and social identity. Further examination of self-referent representations and processes, such as "possible selves" (Markus & Nurius, 1986), "evaluative selves" (Higgins, 1987), and "self-motives" (Leary, 1995), as "comparators," "operators," and other elements of cybernetic feedback systems involved in the regulation of health behavior, might well advance theory concerning both self and identity and the social and behavioral ramifications of physical health. So too might further effort to integrate an explicitly *self*-psychological, self-regulaton model with sociological and anthropological perspectives on the societal and cultural systems that influence the occurrence, treatment, and meaning of physical illness (Charmaz, this book, chap. 9; Lock, this book, chap. 3).

Organizational Structure and Contents of the Volume

The structure of this volume and its specific subtopics reflect several considerations. One is our deliberate pairing of presentations that address the same issue or theme from both an individual-psychological perspective and a social-contextual perspective. This reflects basic assumptions regarding the embeddedness of a person in a larger sociocultural context and the attendant need for both social- and individual-level analysis.

Second, the book's structure recognizes bidirectional influences between social and psychological phenomena and matters of physical health and illness. Thus, self and social identity will be examined both as causes of physical disease and as factors shaped by the experience of illness and its treatment.

Third, the volume recognizes the two general pathways through which social and psychological forces can influence physical health. One is the psychophysiological pathway that is closely identified with the concept of psychological stress. The other is the pathway through which health-related behaviors mediate the effects of social and psychological forces on physical health and disease.

Person Systems and Social Systems

Part I of this volume is devoted to a consideration of systems: person systems and social systems. As discussed before, health and illness can be viewed at the person-level in terms of the regulation and dysregulation of systems that make up an individual. At a societal level, definitions and expectations concerning health, illness, and medical treatment involve systems of language and meaning, politics and economics, and health-care delivery. Thus, sickness and its treatment can be described as a point of contact between person systems and social systems.

In chapter 2, John Kihlstrom and Lucy Canter Kihlstrom address the systems topic at the level of the individual. They define the self as a knowledge structure and discuss this conceptualization as it relates to self-regulation models that have arisen from the study of physical health. Kihlstrom and Canter Kihlstrom argue for a more deliberate and explicit examination of the "self" in self-regulation. They use the examples of somatoform disorders and medical noncompliance to illustrate how problematic interactions between a person and the health-care system may reflect mismatches between a patient's self-conception and the physician's view of that patient.

In chapter 3, Margaret Lock examines larger, "big picture" systems. Lock discusses the nature of culture as a lay, political, and social scientific construct. She also characterizes self and identity and examines their relationship to culture. Lock then describes some implications of the existence of cultural prescriptions that call for individual responsibility for one's health and draws connections between macro-level political and economic events and individual health and illness. To illustrate these issues, Lock discusses the fate of Native Canadians who are dislocated by political and economic forces and that of Greek women whose identities come under stress as a result of migrating to North America. She then shows how the aging process in women is shaped differently by features of North American and Japanese culture.

Even though these two chapters discuss systems at different levels of analysis, there are parallels. In different ways, and with different kinds of consequences, both the patient interacting with the health-care system and the member of an oppressed minority group interacting with the dominant majority must cope with discrepancies between their own self-perceptions and the views of them held by powerful others. Taken together, these two chapters illustrate how mental representations of self operate in a bidirectional manner at the point of interaction between person and social systems—at the same time that the larger culture shapes and challenges beliefs about self, illness, and medical treatment, individual differences in those beliefs determine the process and outcome of interactions between the person and social institutions such as the health-care system.

Stress and Emotion

The topic of Part II is stress and emotion. That stress and emotion affect health is an ancient idea emphasizing sometimes causal determinants inside, sometimes outside the person. It has roots in the temperaments described and linked to disease by Hippocrates and Galen (see Haggard, 1929). At the beginning of this century, relevant clinical observations in Freud's discussions of ego-threat, anxiety, and intrapsychic defenses gave rise to psychosomatic hypotheses that emphasized the role of emotional expressiveness in physical disease. The empirical study of stress and emotion as disease-producing factors can be traced at least as far back as to the research of Walter B. Cannon (1932), and was given impetus by the more formal conceptualizations and systematic empirical work of Hans Selye (1956). Selye's focus on environmental stressors and the physiologic stress response has given way to an emphasis on intervening psychological processes (Lazarus, 1966; Lazarus & Folkman, 1984).

Part II addresses from two vantage points the role of stress and emotion in the production of physical disease. In chapter 4, David Williams, Michael Spencer, and James Jackson discuss a phenomenon clearly traceable to macrosocial environmental events—race-related stress in the United States. In this discussion, Williams and his colleagues point out that stress is not randomly distributed in society and that race in the United States is a marker for increased exposure both to traditionally measured stressful experiences (e.g., bereavement, occupational stress, legal problems) and to stress in the form of unfair treatment that stems from racial discrimination. Williams and colleagues discuss racial self-esteem and racial identity as potential moderators of the health effects of stress and report new empirical findings that lend support to this approach.

In chapter 5, James Pennebaker and Kelli Keough examine the psychological processes that shape the physical health consequences of traumatic life events. In Pennebaker and Keough's analysis, self-revelation and self-referent language play key roles in a set of both intrapersonal and social processes through which the victim of trauma first recognizes the identity-implications of trauma and then attempts to reorganize the self. The phenomenon captured in this work may reflect processes that operate in a variety of natural contexts, including social-support seeking among friends and family members, psychotherapy, religious services, and Alcoholics Anonymous meetings.

As in Part I, there are areas of both convergence and complementarity in the approaches of Williams et al. and Pennebaker and Keough. The perspectives in these two chapters at first appear to differ along a societal versus individual continuum, but each, in the end, reveals a concern for the processes whereby social and psychological phenomena interact with one another. Moreover, each considers self and identity as constructs that may be crucial to understanding those interactions.

Health-Related Behavior Patterns in Personality and Development

Part III addresses connections between self and health that involve two forms of behavior patterning. One sort of behavior patterning is defined in terms of underlying psychological dispositions and involves the consistency of thought, feeling, and behavior that we think of as reflecting personality, a psychological construct whose linkages to health and disease go back to the most ancient psychological and medical observations. The second form of behavioral patterning is defined, in part, with reference to its health implications and involves overt actions and inactions through which a person influences the odds of developing physical disease. Individual behavior frequently involves choosing a level of exposure to health risks—fat grams, viruses, cigarette smoke, or one of the many other pathogens that surround us.

In chapter 6, Suzanne Ouellette discusses self and health in relation to the type of behavioral patterning typically associated with personality. Ouellette argues for an approach in which self and identity are located at one level in a multilevel view of personality. This view, which highlights social and cultural concerns, is presented not as an alternative, but as a complement to the more dominant view of personality as traits, which often highlights genetic and other biological concerns. Ouellette forthrightly discusses some of the methodological challenges that confront efforts to approach the study of health-related personality constructs from a self/identity perspective and identifies recent studies that illustrate some promising research directions in this area.

Chapter 7, by Jeanne Brooks-Gunn and Julia Graber concerns inherently health-related patterns of behavior. They review work reflecting behavioral and transitional approaches to the study of sexuality in adolescence and then examine adolescent sexuality using a self/identity framework. Their analysis explores the potential heuristic value of sexual identity as a construct that may help us in thinking about the interplay of biological maturation, psychological development, and social context that culminates in health-promoting and health-damaging patterns of sexual behavior. Through links with patterns of risky behaviors, including unsafe sex and substance abuse, sexual identities may contribute to major health problems in the United States.

Despite differences between developmental and personological perspectives, the chapters by Ouellette and Brooks-Gunn and Graber share core theoretical themes. One is the view that a self/identity approach may complement and extend, rather than replace entirely, other theoretical frameworks. Another is an emphasis on personal meaning, choice and self-control, and the embeddedness of self in social relationships.

The Impact of Physical Disease on Self and Identity

In Part IV, the causal arrow is reversed as we consider the impact of physical disease and its treatment on self and identity. Physical illness is among the most stressful experiences many people face and has an inevitability unlike most other sources of severe stress. The pain, disability, disfigurement, and actual or threatened losses associated with serious disease and its treatment can create a most unpleasant personal confrontation with our physical selves and fundamentally alter our social relationships and place in the larger society. As a result, disease, medical treatment, and interactions with the health-care system certainly can be psychologically debilitating. Yet many severely ill persons find meaning and purpose in their physical limitations and suffering, and some come to experience nonphysical aspects of themselves in a new and positive way and actually express gratitude for the opportunity for personal growth.

Chapter 8, by Howard Leventhal, Ellen Idler, and Elaine Leventhal, explores the psychological impact of chronic illness from a perspective that emphasizes the interplay between mental representations of physical disease and treatment and the content and structure of the self. In this analysis, "bottom-up" processes, originating in perceived body changes and diminished behavioral capacities, are distinguished from "top-down" processes, which involve abstract labels and expectations concerning illness, its treatment, the pre-illness self, and possible future selves. The chronically ill person's task of understanding and managing the impact of disease is seen as one that requires the selection of coping procedures that coordinate a changing view of the physical and nonphysical self with social relationships and formal systems of health care.

In Chapter 9, Kathy Charmaz addresses the question of how physical health influences self and identity by revisiting the concept of sick role. Charmaz begins by providing an historical overview and critique of the sick role concept and tracing subsequent conceptual developments that culminated in contemporary views of the self in illness. Charmaz then offers an analysis of self in illness that focuses on stories, especially narratives about self. In this analysis, Charmaz describes the act of storytelling as both a personal and social event, an expression and construction of illness experience, and a product and generator of self and identity. Charmaz concludes that the narrative approach to understanding the impact of illness on the self is a promising tool but not one without its limitations and potential pitfalls.

These two chapters differ somewhat in emphasis, with Leventhal et al. highlighting the physical self and Charmaz stressing the social ramifications of chronic disease. Nonetheless, both clearly see the need to take account of both somatic and interpersonal events, and the interactions between the two, in defining the adaptive tasks faced by chronically ill individuals. Also common to these two perspectives is an emphasis on several temporal considerations, for example, the unfolding of disease episodes and the disjunction serious illness creates in separating the pre- and post-illness self. Charmaz and Leventhal et al. appear to part company in their preferred constructs for describing the cognitive structures and processes of adaptation of self to illness. Charmaz perceives a chronically ill person as a narrator of stories, whereas Leventhal et al. perceives him or her as an experimenting lay scientist.

Conclusion

It appears to us that linkages between social and behavioral processes and physical health and disease often involve psychological structures and processes concerning self and identity. Yet, although self and identity have at times been invoked in a formal way to account for these associations, self/identity concepts very often appear implicit. By contrast, in the chapters in this volume, the authors have sought to make an explicit case for the role of self and identity in psychosocial influences on physical health and disease, health-care delivery, and social and psychological reactions to illness. Because we gave this charge to each of the authors, there are some areas of convergence between their chapters. At the same time, there is much diversity, reflecting both differences in disciplinary perspectives and the broad range of problem areas, theoretical views, and methodological approaches that characterize research in the self/identity and physical health/disease domains. If the chapters that follow stimulate researchers and scholars working in either of these domains to examine the other, this volume will have served its purpose.

Notes

1. Because "self" and "identity" have been defined in a variety of ways by different researchers, we will not impose definitions of these constructs in this chapter. The interested reader is referred to Ashmore and Jussim (1997b) for an historical overview and conceptual analysis of self and identity constructs.

2. The biopsychosocial model did not emerge, de novo, in the 1970s. Many of its elements may be found in ancient writings, and it has scientific roots in subspecialties of various disciplines (e.g., psychosomatic medicine, medical specialties in anthropology, sociology, and psychology) going back to the early part of the twentieth century (Stone, 1979).

References

Adler, N., & Matthews, K. (1994). Health psychology: Why do some people get sick and some stay well? *Annual Review of Psychology, 45*, 229–259.

Ajzen, I. (1985). From intention to action: a theory of planned behavior. In J. Kuhl & J. Beckman (Eds.), *Action control: From cognitions to behaviors* (pp. 11–39). New York: Springer.

Ashmore, R. D., & Jussim, L. (eds.). (1997a). *Self and Identity: Fundamental issues* (Vol. 1). New York: Oxford.

Ashmore, R. D., & Jussim, L. (1997b). Toward a second century of the scientific analysis of self and identity. In R. D. Ashmore & L. Jussim (Eds.), *Self and identity: Fundamental issues* (Vol. 1, pp. 3–19). New York: Oxford.

Banaji, M. R., & Prentice, D. A. (1994). The self in social contexts. *Annual Review of Psychology, 45,* 297–332.

Bandura, A. (1977). Self-efficacy: Toward a unified theory of behavioral change. *American Psychologist, 84,* 191–215.

Bandura, A. (1991). Social-cognitive theory of self-regulation. *Organizational Behavior and Human Decision Processes, 50,* 248–287.

Baumeister, R. F., & Heatherton, T. F. (1996). Self-regulation failure: An overview. *Psychological Inquiry, 7,* 1–15.

Bracke, P. E., & Thoreson, C. E. (1996). Reducing Type A behavior patterns: A structured-group approach. In R. Allan & S. Scheidt (Eds.), *Heart and mind: The practice of cardiac psychology* (pp. 255–290). Washington, DC: American Psychological Association.

Brown, G. W., & Harris, T. O. (Eds.). (1989). *Life events and illness.* New York: Guilford.

Cannon, W. B. (1932). *The wisdom of the body.* New York: Norton.

Carver, C. S., & Scheier, M. F. (1981). *Attention and self-regulation: A control-theory approach to human behavior.* New York: Springer-Verlag.

Charng, H.-W., Piliavin, J. A., & Callero, P. L. (1988). Role identity and reasoned action in the prediction of repeated behavior. *Social Psychology Quarterly, 51,* 303–317.

Cohen, S., & Herbert, T. B. (1996). Health psychology: Physiological factors and physical disease from the perspective of human psychoneuroimmunology. *Annual Review of Psychology, 47,* 113–142.

Cohen, S., & Wills, T. A. (1985). Stress, social support, and the buffering hypothesis. *Psychological Bulletin, 98,* 310–357.

Cooley, C. H. (1902). *Human nature and the social order.* New York: Scribner's.

Deaux, K. (1992). Focusing on the self: Challenges to self-definition and their consequences for mental health. In D. N. Ruble, P. R. Costanzo, & M. E. Oliveri (Eds.), *The social psychology of mental health: Basic mechanisms and applications* (pp. 301–327). New York: Guilford.

DiClimente, C. C., & Prochaska, J. O. (1982). Self-change and therapy change of smoking behavior: A comparison of processes of change in cessation and maintenance. *Addictive Behaviors, 7,* 133–142.

Dolcini, M. M., & Adler, N. E. (1994). Perceived competencies, peer group affiliations, and risk behavior. *Health Psychology, 13,* 496–506.

Engel, G. L. (1977). The need for a new medical model: A challenge for biomedicine. *Science, 196,* 129–136.

Engel, G. L. (1980). The clinical application of the biopsychosocial model. *American Journal of Psychiatry, 137,* 535–544.

Fife, B. L. (1995). The measurement of meaning in illness. *Social Science and Medicine, 40,* 1021–1028.

Fishbein, M., & Ajzen, I. (1975). *Belief, attitude, intention, and behavior.* New York: Wiley.

Fogelson, R. T. (1982). Person, self, and identity: Some anthropological retrospects, circumspects, and prospects. In B. Lee (Ed.), *Psychosocial theories of the self* (pp. 67–109). New York: Plenum.

Gecas, V. (1982). The self-concept. *Annual Review of Sociology, 8*, 1–33.

Gill, T. M., & Feinstein, A. R. (1994). A critical appraisal of the quality of quality of life assessments. *Journal of the American Medical Association, 272*, 619–626.

Gleason, P. (1983). Identifying identity: A semantic history. *Journal of American History, 69*, 910–931.

Goffman, E. (1963). *Stigma.* Englewood Cliffs, NJ: Prentice–Hall.

Granberg, D., & Holmberg, S. (1990). The intention-behavior relationship among U.S. and Swedish voters. *Social Psychology Quarterly, 53*, 44–54.

Haggard, H. W. (1929). *Devils, drugs, and doctors.* New York: Harper and Brothers.

Hallowell, A. I. (1955). *Culture and experience.* Philadelphia: University of Philadelphia Press.

Heatherton, T. F., & Baumeister, R. F. (1991). Binge eating as escape from awareness. *Psychological Bulletin, 110*, 86–108.

Higgins, E. T. (1987). Self-discrepancy: A theory relating self and affect. *Psychological Review, 94*, 319–340.

Higgins, E. T. (1997). Beyond pleasure and pain. *American Psychologist, 52*, 1280–1300.

Holland, D. (1997). Selves as cultural: As told by an anthropologist who lacks a soul. In R. D. Ashmore & L. Jussim (Eds.), *Self and identity: Fundamental issues* (Vol. 1, pp. 160–190). New York: Oxford.

Idler, E. L., & Benyamini, Y. (1997). Self-rated health and mortality: A review of twenty-seven community studies. *Journal of Health and Social Behavior, 38*, 21–37.

James, W. (1890). *Principles of psychology.* New York: Holt.

Krantz, D. S., Glass, D. C., Contrada, R. J., & Miller, N. E. (1981). Behavior and health. In the National Science Foundation's *Five year outlook on science and technology: 1981 source materials* (Vol. 2, pp. 561–588). Washington, DC: U.S. Government Printing Office.

Krantz, D. S., & Manuck, S. B. (1984). Acute psychophysiologic reactivity and the risk of cardiovascular disease: A review and methodological critique. *Psychological Bulletin, 96*, 435–464.

Krause, N., & Borawski-Clark, E. (1994). Clarifying the functions of social support in later life. *Research on Aging, 16*, 251–279.

Lazarus, R. S. (1966). *Psychological stress and the coping process.* New York: McGraw-Hill.

Lazarus, R. S. (1993). From psychological stress to the emotions: A history of changing outlooks. *Annual Review of Psychology, 44*, 1–21.

Lazarus, R. S., & Folkman, S. (1984). *Stress, appraisal, and coping.* New York: Springer.

Leary, M. R. (1995). *Self-presentation: Impression management and interpersonal behavior.* Madison, WI: Brown & Benchmark.

Leary, M. R., Tchividjian, L. R., Kraxberger, B. E. (1994). Self-presentation can be hazardous to your health: Impression management and health risk. *Health Psychology, 13*, 461–470.

Leventhal, H., Benyamini, Y., Brownlee, S., Diefenbach, M., Leventhal, E. A., Patrick-Miller, L., & Robitaille, C. (1997). Illness representations: Theoretical foundations. In K. J. Petrie & J. A. Weinman (Eds.), *Perceptions of health and illness* (pp. 19–45). Amsterdam: Harwood Academic Publishers.

Leventhal, H., Meyer, D., & Nerenz, D. (1980). The common sense representation of illness danger. In S. Rachman (Ed.), *Contributions to medical psychology* (Vol. 2, pp. 7–30). New York: Pergamon.

Markus, H., & Herzog, A. R. (1991). The role of the self-concept in aging. *Annual Review of Gerontology and Geriatrics, 11,* 110–143.

Markus, H., & Nurius, P. (1986). Possible selves. *American Psychologist, 41,* 954–969.

Matarazzo, J. D. (1980). Behavioral health and behavioral medicine: Frontiers for a new health psychology. *American Psychologist, 35,* 807–817.

Matarazzo, J. D. (1982). Behavioral health's challenge to academic, scientific, and professional psychology. *American Psychologist, 37,* 1–14.

Mead, G. H. (1934). *Mind, self, and society from the standpoint of a social-behaviorist.* Chicago: University of Chicago Press.

Ogden, J. (1995). Psychosocial theory and the creation of the risky self. *Social Science and Medicine, 40,* 409–415.

Radin, P. (1920). The autobiography of a Winnebago Indian. *University of California Publications in American Archaeology and Ethnology, 16,* 381–473.

Rogers, R. W. (1975). A protection motivation theory of fear appeals and attitude change. *Journal of Psychology, 91,* 93–114.

Rogers, R. W. (1983). Cognitive and physiological processes in fear appeals and attitude change: A revised theory of protection motivation. In J. T. Cacioppo & R. E. Petty (Eds.), *Social Psychophysiology: A sourcebook* (pp. 153–176). New York: Guilford.

Rosenstock, I. M. (1974). Historical origins of the health belief model. *Health Education Monographs, 2,* 1–8.

Scheibe, K. E. (1985). Historical perspectives on the presented self. In B. R. Schlenker (Ed.), *The self and social life* (pp. 33–64). New York: McGraw-Hill.

Selye, H. (1956). *The stress of life.* New York: McGraw-Hill.

Short, J. L., Sandler, I. N., & Roosa, M. W. (1996). Adolescents' perceptions of social support: The role of esteem enhancing and esteem threatening relationships. *Journal of Social and Clinical Psychology, 15,* 397–416.

Sparks, P., & Shepherd, R. (1992). Self-identity and the theory of planned behavior: Assessing the role of identification with "green consumerism." *Social Psychology Quarterly, 55,* 388–399.

Sparks, P., Shepherd, R., Wieringa, N., & Zimmermanns, N. (1995). Perceived behavioral control, unrealistic optimism and dietary change: An exploratory study. *Appetite, 24,* 243–255.

Steele, C. M., & Josephs, R. A. (1990). Alcohol myopia: Its prized and dangerous effects. *American Psychologist, 45,* 921–933.

Stone, G. C. (1979). Health and the health system: A historical overview and conceptual framework. In S. George, C. F. Cohen, & N. E. Adler (Eds.), *Health psychology—A handbook* (pp. 1–17). San Francisco: Jossey-Bass.

Strube, M. J. (1987). A self-appraisal model of the Type A behavior pattern. In R. Hogan & W. H. Jones (Eds.), *Perspectives in personality: Theory, measurement, and interpersonal dynamics* (pp. 201–250). Greenwich, CT: JAI Press.

Taylor, S. E. (1983). Adjustment to threatening events: A theory of cognitive adaptation. *American Psychologist, 38,* 1161–1173.

Taylor, S. E. (1995). *Health psychology.* New York: McGraw-Hill.

Theodorakis, Y. (1994). Planned behavior, attitude strength, role identity, and the prediction of exercise behavior. *Sport Psychologist, 8,* 149–165.

Thoits, P. A. (1991). On merging identity theory and stress research. *Social Psychology Quarterly, 54,* 101–112.

Ware, J. E. (1992). Measures for a new era of health assessment. In A. L. Stewart & J. E. Ware (Eds.), *Measuring functioning and well-being* (pp. 3–11). Durham, NC: Duke University Press.

Whittaker, E. (1993). The birth of the anthropological self and its career. *Ethos, 20,* 191–219.

Wiebe, D. J., & Smith, T. W. (1997). Personality and health: Progress and problems in psychosomatics. In R. Hogan, J. Johnson, & S. Briggs (Eds.), *Handbook of personality psychology* (pp. 891–918). New York: Academic Press.

PART I

SELF, SOCIAL IDENTITY, AND SYSTEMS AFFECTING HEALTH AND HEALTH CARE

John F. Kihlstrom
Lucy Canter Kihlstrom

2

Self, Sickness, Somatization, and Systems of Care

The scope of health psychology is very broad, including concerns with the promotion and maintenance of health, the prevention and treatment of illness, the psychological correlates of health and illness, the individual's relations with the health-care system, and the use of psychological knowledge in the formulation of health policy (Taylor, 1995). Perhaps because of its roots in social psychology, health psychology has focused on the sociocultural contexts of illness and health. For example, a recent review of the field (Taylor, Repetti, & Seeman, 1997) emphasized the unhealthy environment and discussed the role of such factors as race and socioeconomic status, the community, family, peer groups, work relations, and social networks in determining the level of disease-inducing chronic stress experienced by individuals, their vulnerability to mental illness, their coping skills and resources, and their health habits and behaviors. Interestingly, in all the literature in this new and exciting field, relatively little attention has focused on the role of the self in the genesis and maintenance of health and disease and in moderating an individual's health-related behavior, including his or her interactions with health-service providers.

It is true that concepts of *self-regulation* are implicit in much of the psychosocial literature on health (Carver, 1979; Carver & Scheier, 1982, 1985, 1991; Leventhal, Nerenz, & Steele, 1984). Monitoring one's own symptoms and other bodily states, whether on one's own, or by consulting a physician or using biofeedback devices, is essential to achieve and maintain good health. Only when we are aware of the discrepancy between our current state and the state we wish to attain can we engage in the kinds of behaviors that will reduce this discrepancy. This bifurcated knowledge of our current states, and of our ultimate goal states, constitutes an important aspect of self-awareness. Moreover, our motivation to engage in effective self-regulation may be determined by *self-efficacy* (Bandura, 1977, 1997), our belief that we are capable of engaging in the kinds of behaviors required to achieve the goal state in the first place, or return to it after we have drifted away. Physical disease can have a profound impact on one's *self-image*, as when scars, disfigurements, and amputations create a divergence between the current appearance of a patient's body and the way he or she remembers appearing in the past. The visible stigmata of disease, and disease-related inability to return to work or to pursue other accustomed activities, may pose a grave threat to one's *self-esteem* (Jones et al., 1984). (For detailed analyses of how physical illness influences self-related contents and processes, see Charmaz this book, chap. 9, and Leventhal, Idler, & Leventhal, this book, chap. 8).

Thus, the self plays an important role in health and illness, but most theoretical work in this area seems to rely on a rather informal, or even implicit, construal of the self and does not refer to any specific theoretical formulation. Consider, for example, the biopsychosocial model of health and illness that lies at the core of most health-psychology theory (Engel, 1977, 1980; Schwartz, 1982, 1984). The biopsychosocial model attempts to show how illness arises through the interaction of biological factors such as viruses and bacteria, psychological factors such as beliefs and coping strategies, and social factors such as socioeconomic status and social support (and how illness can be prevented by systematic attention to the same interaction). The self is somewhere in the biopsychosocial model, surely, but it is not represented explicitly anywhere in that model. Similarly, the health belief model (Becker, 1974; Rosenstock, 1966) invokes such factors as people's perceptions of their susceptibility to illness to explain their health-related behaviors, but does not otherwise talk about their beliefs about *themselves*. Even Leventhal's self-regulation theory of illness behavior, which has *self* in the title, does not invoke the self at any of its stages, except implicitly in the perception of symptoms and the appraisal of coping strategies (Leventhal & Cameron, 1987; Leventhal, Meyer, & Nerenz, 1980; Leventhal & Nerenz, 1985; Leventhal, Nerenz, & Steele, 1984). Put bluntly, if we want to entertain the concept of self-regulation, we need to know what the *self* is and what it looks like.

The Self as a Knowledge Structure

The social intelligence view of personality and social interaction (Cantor & Kihlstrom, 1987) defines the self as one's mental representation of his or her own person and personality. It is part of the repertoire of declarative knowledge on which one draws to guide his or her social interactions. In other words, the self is an organized knowledge structure representing people's own individual understandings of themselves (their appearance, their characteristic beliefs, motives, values, attitudes, and behaviors, and their typical relations with other people). In addition to this more or less abstract self-knowledge, the self also includes some reference to one's autobiographical record of events and experiences in which he or she was the agent or patient, stimulus or experiencer (Kihlstrom & Cantor, 1984; Kihlstrom & Klein, 1994, 1997; Kihlstrom, et al., 1988; Kihlstrom, Marchese-Foster, & Klein, 1997). This is especially the case for those autobiographical episodes that exemplify one's self-concept. But every episodic memory is linked to the self (Kihlstrom, 1997).

More specific descriptions of the self as a knowledge structure are derived from more general theories of knowledge representation within cognitive psychology (e.g., Kihlstrom & Klein, 1997). For example, when considering the *self-concept*, one may begin by asking how other concepts are structured in the mind and assume that the self-concept is structured similarly. Viewed as a concept, then, the self does not appear to be a monolithic mental representation composed of defining features that are singly necessary and jointly sufficient to distinguish the self from all others. Rather, it appears to be a fuzzy set of context-specific exemplars representing what one is like in each of a number of salient social contexts: with parents or with friends, at work or at home, in sickness or in health. These exemplars may be united by a principle of family resemblance, resulting in a prototypical self representing a person's most characteristic features. Or they may be unified by an overarching theory of why we seem to be the people we are, or why we seem to be one person in one kind of situation and quite another person in others (Epstein, 1973).

In a similar way, consider Schilder's definition of the *self-image* as "the picture of our own body which we form in our own mind" (1938, p. 11). That idea is very close to folk psychology, and most scientific psychologists today are reluctant to talk as if there are pictures in the head because a homunculus would be needed to view them. On the other hand, recent research on mental imagery and perceptual memory suggests that it might be quite appropriate to view the self, construed as an image, as a perception-based mental representation that stores knowledge about the visual features of one's face and body, the spatial relations among these features, the acoustic properties of one's voice, the characteristic sweep of one's gestures, and so on. People have perception-based representations of others, which allow them to recognize these others on the street or on the telephone. And they have similar perception-based representations of themselves, as well: for example, people with eating disorders often rate themselves as fatter than they really are. This is a clear indication of a conflict between self-image and reality.

Other forms of mental representation are applicable to the self. For example, Pennington and Hastie (1993) have shown that jurors organize the evidence presented to them into a story structure representing initiating events, goals, actions, and consequences. More generally, Schank and Abelson (1995) have argued that knowledge is commonly represented as stories, not as lists of facts, beliefs, and features. Accordingly, the self can be viewed as a kind of narrative, or perhaps an interlocking set of narratives, told to self and others, about where one came from, what one is doing now, and where one is headed in the future (Charmaz, this book, chap. 8; McAdams, 1997; Pennebaker and Keough, this book, chap. 5).

Last, but not least, we can think of the self as part of a large associative network of memories—a bundle of sentence-like propositions representing semantic knowledge of one's own physical and psychosocial traits and episodic knowledge of specific experiences, thoughts, and actions. This idea has been pursued most vigorously by Klein and Loftus (1993), who have used sophisticated priming paradigms to show convincingly that episodic self-knowledge is represented independently of semantic self-knowledge.

All of this is admittedly quite abstract, and if we faulted models of health and illness behavior for having little to say about the self, we could, and should, equally fault models of the self for having little to say about health and illness behavior. Thus, we turn to some psychosocial problems of health and illness and consider where the self might play a role.

The Somatoform Disorders, the Self, and Abnormal Illness Behavior

The self would seem to be particularly relevant to health and illness behavior in the problem of abnormal illness behavior. As defined by Mechanic (1962), illness behavior refers to how symptoms are perceived, evaluated, and acted upon by a patient (McHugh & Valis, 1986). As such, illness behavior is neither normal nor abnormal. On the other hand, some illness behaviors are clearly less appropriate, or less adaptive, than others (Pilowsky, 1967; Pilowsky & Spence, 1975). For example, even after receiving a satisfactory explanation of his or her symptoms, and an appropriate prescription for treatment, an individual may remain highly concerned about the state of his or her health. Or a person may become annoyed at other people's reactions to his or her illness or envy those who are healthier. Or one can retain a strong conviction that he or she is ill, even though the findings of physical exams, laboratory tests, and exploratory surgeries are negative.

Perhaps the most dramatic manifestations of abnormal illness behavior are the mental illnesses known as somatoform disorders: somatization disorder, conversion disorder, pain disorder, hypochondriasis, and body dysmorphic disorder.[1] In these syndromes, individuals complain of physical symptoms in the absence of any general medical condition that would account for these symptoms. In all these cases, physical illness is a salient feature of a person's self-presentation; in somatization disorder and malingering, physical illness seems to be a central feature of the self-concept. From a cognitive point of view, some of the somatoform disorders can be thought of as conditions in which the attribute *sick* is a central feature of the self-concept in which descriptions of the self as a sick person, and of illness episodes, are highly accessible in memory, or where the self-narrative is organized around stories of sickness. Such a characterization seems particularly appropriate to somatoform disorder, pain disorder, and hypochondriasis. But these are verbal views of the self, descriptions and narratives composed of words, phrases, and sentences that are highly convenient for cognitively oriented personality and social psychologists to study, perhaps, but not the only way to represent the self. As it happens, there is another somatoform disorder, *body dysmorphic disorder*, which permits analysis in terms of nonverbal, perception-based forms of self-knowledge.[2]

The somatoform disorders are considered *mental* illnesses, and health psychology has traditionally been concerned with *physical* conditions such as cancer and hypertension. At the same time, the somatoform disorders are mental illnesses that masquerade as physical illnesses, and they are primarily encountered, and treated, by primary-care physicians. As such, they may offer a unique perspective on how people's self-concepts and self-images are related to their health and illness behavior, including their interactions with health-care professionals and other elements of the health-care system.

The Self as Ugly Person

In body dysmorphic disorder, originally called dysmorphophobia (Morselli, 1891), a person is preoccupied or excessively concerned with imagined or exaggerated defects in physical appearance, rather than with imagined or exaggerated symptoms and sickness (for reviews, see Phillips, 1991, 1996; Phillips & Hollander, 1996). These defects cause the person significant distress and cause considerable impairments in role functioning, even though they do not exist, or are hardly noticeable by others. In body dysmorphic disorder, a person's self-image is discrepant from the way in which he or she is perceived by other people.

A recent clinical study of 30 cases found that the most frequent complaints were of imagined defects with the patients' head hair, beard growth, body hair, nose, skin (including acne and facial lines), eyes, head or face shape, body build, or bone structure; somewhat less frequent were complaints about the size or shape of body parts below the neck (Phillips, McElroy, Keck, Pope, & Hudson, 1993). The average age of onset was mid-adolescence, and the course was chronic, with new imagined defects added over time. At the time they were interviewed, most of the patients had multiple concurrent complaints. Only a small minority had any insight that their defects were imagined rather than real: for most of the rest, their preoccupation with self-image usually had the quality of an overvalued idea, whereas for a large minority, the self-image was frankly delusional. Patients in this last class might qualify for a diagnosis of another syndrome relevant to the self-image, *delusional disorder, somatic type* (de Leon, Bott, & Simpson, 1989). Almost three quarters of the patients had sought treatment from plastic surgeons, dermatologists, or dentists. Most of these requests were refused on the ground that there was nothing to treat. However, eight patients had undergone a total of 25 procedures, most of which, as might be expected, only made the symptoms worse.

At the expressly subclinical level, Fitts, Gibson, Redding, and Deiter (1989) found that 70% of college students were dissatisfied with some aspect of their physical appearance, and 28% met all diagnostic criteria for body dysmorphic disorder. Young people with body dysmorphic disorder could become overconsumers of health-care services because, for some people, troubled interactions with health-care professionals may begin with the perception of the self as ugly.

The Self as Sick Person

For some time now, we have been interested in the problem of somatization disorder, formerly known as Briquet's syndrome (Briquet, 1859; Guze & Perley, 1983). In somatization, an individual complains of multiple physical symptoms that cause significant impairment in role function, but for which there are no demonstrable organic findings or known physiological mechanisms. Onset is typically before age 30, and the multiple unexplained complaints generally persist for several years. Somatization is a common cause of absenteeism from work, and an extraordinarily large portion of physician time and effort is spent with individuals who seek medical attention, not simply because of the nature of the symptoms, but more as a result of their frequency, severity, and persistence (Kellner, 1990; Kirmayer, 1986). Somatization has been called "medicine's unsolved problem" (Lipowski, 1987).

For example, a group of patients studied by Smith, Monson, and Ray (1986a) were identified in midlife by histories of chronic illness averaging 30 years in length, including multiple unexplained symptoms and multiple hospital admissions, and major diagnostic and surgical procedures. For the population as a whole, the 1980 census indicated that the annual per capita expenditure for health care in the United States averaged $543, including $123 for physician services and $385 for hospital care. By contrast, the individuals in the somatization study sample spent, on average, $4,700 per year, including $1,721 for physician services and $2,382 for hospital charges (Smith et al., 1986a). For one patient, the quarterly average was $13,067 in charges, including 42 days in the hospital. These individuals also spent an average of seven days per month in bed (the population average for this variable is slightly less than half a day). Over half of the somatization group said that they had been "sickly" for most of their lives, and 83% claimed that they had quit work because of poor health.

Mechanisms of Somatization   In somatization disorder, there is positive evidence, or at least a strong presumption, that the person's physical complaints are linked to psychological stress or conflict (Cloninger, 1986, 1987, 1996; Guze, 1967; Kirmayer & Robbins, 1991; Smith, 1991). Somatization has frequently been defined as the tendency to experience or express psychological states as somatic symptoms (Lipowski, 1968). Thus, somatization contrasts with psychologization (Kirmayer, 1984). However, somatization should not be characterized as simply a function of the transfer of emotional distress into somatic complaints. Other mechanisms that bias perception and shape expression may be crucial to the individual's experience of self as sick (for a review, see Kirmayer, 1986).

For example, the complaints in somatization disorder may reflect the somatic component, as opposed to the subjective feeling component, of an individual's negative emotional states. That is to say, an individual under stress might be expected to have cardiovascular or gastrointestinal symptoms. In this case, however, we would expect that medical tests might reveal a physical basis for the person's symptomatic complaints (e.g., tachycardia, muscle tension, or excess gastric secretion). But this is precisely what is *not* found in somatization disorder. In somatization disorder, the person complains of symptoms that cannot be objectively confirmed.

As another example, cybernetic self-regulation theories posit that one's awareness of one's internal state is a function of control processes that monitor the availability and urgency of internal compared to external information (Carver, 1979; Carver & Scheier, 1982, 1985, 1991). This cue competition theory posits that a varied external environment will reduce attention to internal information and so will decrease reporting of somatic sensations. Similarly, individual differences in public and private self-consciousness (Fenigstein, Scheier, & Buss, 1975) will determine the degree to which one is aware of, and responds to, his or her own internal physical states. According to this point of view, individuals most likely to report multiple unexplained symptoms are less likely to experience an external environment that focuses attention away from internal states. Again, however, the cue-competition theory assumes that somatizing patients are attending to actual physical changes that should be detected by appropriate medical testing, but that has not been found to be the case in somatization disorder.

More likely, somatization tendencies arise from basic processes affecting the social construction of the self (Kirmayer, 1984, 1986; Kleinman and Kleinman, 1985). Broadly speaking, people have two means for expressing emotional distress: somatization and psychologization. In somatization, distress is referred to, and expressed by, the body; there is something wrong with one's heart, stomach, and so forth. In psychologization (which might be more appropriately labeled "psychosocialization"), there is something wrong with a person's mind and social relations. For example he or she is unhappy, his or her marriage is unsatisfactory. Medical anthropologists tell us that psychologization is something of a Western invention while somatization is closer to the norm in the rest of the world, and that this difference has to do with peculiarly Western modes of construing the self (Lock, this book, chap. 3; Shweder & Bourne, 1982). Thus, cultural factors will help determine the extent to which a person uses somatic complaints as a vehicle for emotional communication and social control. According to this point of view, because emotions are related to the bodily, as well as the social, aspects of self, somatization cannot simply be the misdirected expression of psychosocial distress. Rather, somatization may be an emphasis on one aspect of all distress (Kirmayer, 1986). It can be construed as symmetrical to psychologization—the emphasis on personal and social dimensions of suffering. Somatization and psychologization perhaps can best be understood as contrasting methods of constructing the meaning of illness that assimilate emotional experience to either the bodily or the social realm.

Yet another mechanism underlying somatization involves the very structure of the health-care system. For example, medical procedures for diagnosis and treatment maintain a focus on the body and encourage somatic attributions of symptoms (Kirmayer, 1986). In the United States, mental illnesses and disorders are still stigmatized to a relatively high degree and therefore the benefits of the sick role tend to accrue to physical illnesses rather than psychiatric or psychosomatic illnesses (Blackwell, 1967). Individuals who emphasize somatic distress may be pursuing the most direct path toward reaping the benefits that may be derived from the sick role (Charmaz, this book, chap. 9).

Somatization in Young Adults   Although somatization disorder is commonly identified during middle age, it should be noted that one of the criteria for the diagnosis is a long-standing history of multiple, unexplained medical complaints. Thus, the natural history of somatization probably begins much earlier than middle age. Indeed, somatization disorder probably begins in adolescence, or even childhood, as a person develops a mental representation of illness and its personal and social consequences and begins to incorporate "being sick" into his or her self-concept and the sick role into his or her repertoire of social behaviors. Accordingly, it seems important to develop means by which people with somatization disorder, or those at risk for somatization, can be identified early in their careers as medical patients, so that their utilization of medical services can be tracked prospectively and effective interventions can be devised.

To this end, a series of studies, conducted at a major university in the Southwest, involved a total of 2,797 undergraduate students, who completed a survey of medical problems and complaints during their introductory psychology course (Canter Kihlstrom & Marsh, 1994). The subjects were nineteen years of age on average, much younger than the typical somatization disorder patient.

For purposes of the survey, Canter Kihlstrom and Marsh (1994) constructed a medical problems and complaints (MPC) questionnaire based on the 35 symptoms considered in the diagnosis of somatization disorder, according to DSM-IIIR (American Psychiatric Association, 1987). The questions covered a variety of problems in the gastrointestinal (e.g., vomiting, nausea), cardiopulmonary (e.g., heart racing, shortness of breath), sexual (e.g., impotence, painful sex), and female reproductive spheres (e.g., menstrual pain, irregular periods); conversion and pseudoneurological symptoms (e.g., blurred vision, fainting); and pain (e.g., back pain, joint pain). The subjects were simply asked to indicate whether they had ever been "bothered" by each symptom, on a 3-point categorical rating scale. A student's somatization score was simply the number of items to which he or she gave a rating of 3 ("definitely yes"). The DSM-IIIR also requires that there be no medical explanation for the complaints, of course, but this question was omitted on the survey so that the questionnaire, intended as an initial screening device, would not become too cumbersome.

The results of these studies, conducted from 1993 to 1994, were very striking. In the first study, the 683 subjects endorsed a mean of 5.91 of the thirty-five symptoms listed. The gastrointestinal symptoms were among those most frequently endorsed, while back pain and pain in the extremities were also common. Cardiovascular symptoms were frequent in a population that is, overall, quite healthy and active. Except for dizziness, pseudoneurological or conversion symptoms were relatively rare. Menstrual symptoms were fairly frequent among the women. Women yielded significantly higher somatization scores than men, even after the four genitourinary symptoms that can be endorsed only by women were eliminated. According to DSM-IIIR, the threshold for somatization is crossed by individuals who endorse 13 or more relevant symptoms, with no restrictions on their distribution: 13% of the sample (38% of this group was male) met this criterion and were considered to be at least at risk for somatization.

In a follow-up study, a much larger sample of 1,557 subjects completed a 15-item version of the MPC based on earlier studies that validated brief screening instruments for somatization (Othmer & DeSouza, 1985; Smith & Brown, 1990; Swartz et al., 1986). The subjects identified as at risk for somatization disorder reported a higher number of medical consultations in the past year than subjects with low scores on the short MPC questionnaire. Moreover, they reported higher levels of abnormal illness behavior on a brief version of the Illness Behavior Questionnaire (IBQ; Pilowsky & Spence, 1975). Within the somatization group, there were no differences in either utilization or abnormal illness behavior between men and women. In other words, within the at-risk group, men and women were similar. These findings were confirmed in a third study employing the full 35-item version of the MPC questionnaire.

As a general finding, the National Institute of Mental Health (NIMH) Epidemiologic Catchment Area (ECA) study reported a prevalence of somatoform disorder (a broad diagnostic category including conversion disorder and hypochondriasis as well as strict somatization) of about 0.3% for women and 0.1% of the population at large (Robins et al., 1984). By contrast, about 6% of women seen in one outpatient psychiatric clinic exhibited somatization disorder (Othmer & DeSouza, 1985), and other reports from various hospital consultation and liaison services report a prevalence ranging from 2% to 8%. Among primary care physicians (i.e., specialists in family practice, internal medicine, pediatrics, and obstetrics/gynecology), unexplained medical symptoms may account for as much as 10% to 30% of patient visits. In a recent study of psychiatric disorders in primary care, Kellner (1990) found evidence of somatization disorder in about 26% of medical patients. Thus, although somatization disorder may be relatively rare in the general population, it seems to be overrepresented in various health-care settings.

Somatization can be characterized as a problem of identity: an individual identifies himself or herself as a sick person, and it is this self-concept that colors the interpretation of percepts and feelings as symptoms of disease and, ultimately, leads to vigorous, persistent requests for medical services and treatments. A physician, on the other hand, identifies that individual not as sick, but perhaps as mentally ill, an identification that the individual vehemently rejects. In other words, somatization disorder involves a fundamental conflict between an individual's self-concept, "I am a sick person," and a physician's impression of that individual, "No, you're not," or even "You're crazy." Resolving this conflict is the key to more appropriate treatment of these patients by health-care providers and more appropriate utilization of health services by individuals.

Treatment of Somatization   Individuals who suffer from somatization are difficult to treat because their self-perceptions do not match the way they are perceived by others. They think that they are physically ill and seek help from a physician or other health-care professional. That provider, in turn, will try to determine what is the matter, employing the full armamentarium of modern medicine. After numerous laboratory tests, and perhaps even exploratory surgery, the health-care professional may conclude that this patient is not ill after all. He or she may even refer this individual to a psychiatrist. The patient then interprets that referral as evidence that he or she is not being taken seriously, and the relationship spirals downward. Successful intervention requires that a physician and an individual be in the same consulting room. That is, either a physician must adopt an individual's view of self, or an individual has to change his or her self-concept.

Challenging an individual's self-concept seems an unlikely prospect, so some practitioners have adopted the strategy of embracing that self-concept. For example, Wickramasekera (1995) offers individuals with somatization disorder biofeedback and other "high tech" treatment modalities. Biofeedback at least resembles a medical treatment (after all, it is intended to help the patient control bodily processes), and therefore it communicates to the individual that the health care professional is taking the physical complaints seriously. According to Wickramasekera, this treatment focuses on physical symptoms, builds rapport in turn, and lays a foundation for additional referrals such as psychotherapy.

Similarly, Smith and his colleagues have devised a consultation-liaison procedure in which services continue to be delivered by a primary-care provider (Kashner, Rost, Smith, & Lewis, 1992; Smith, Miller, & Monson, 1986; Smith, Monson, & Ray, 1986b). Instead of being referred to a psychiatrist or other mental-health practitioner, individuals with a diagnosis of somatization disorder who are first seen in primary care settings are scheduled for regular physical examinations by their general practitioner every four to six weeks. This is intended to make contact with a physician independent of symptomatic complaints. The physician, in turn, is discouraged from going further than the routine physical. For example, special diagnostic tests or hospitalization are not ordered unless they are clearly indicated by the physical exam. He or she is also encouraged not to tell individuals that their symptoms are "all in their head." Rather, as with Wickramasekera's biofeedback procedure, the physical examination is intended to communicate that an individual's self-perception as sick is being taken seriously.

Results of an initial randomized controlled study showed a clear advantage for the new approach, with health-care charges declining by about 50% over 18 months, mostly due to the controls on hospitalization (Smith et al., 1986b). Unfortunately, a later study showed a decline of only about 12% (Kashner et al., 1992), and suggested that the effects on utilization were likely to extinguish over about two years. Perhaps this outcome is related to another finding of the studies: the consultation-liaison program may save some money, but it does not lead to any improvement in overall outcomes such as physical or mental health, perceived health, or psychosocial adjustment. The physical complaints seen in somatization disorder may reflect one's psychosocial difficulties. And, if this is the case, individuals will continue to have these complaints, identify themselves as sick people, and seek and use medical services, so long as these psychosocial difficulties go unattended. Successful treatment may depend on finding a way to change these individuals' modes of self-identification, so that they will more readily accept the psychosocial interventions that they really need.

The Self, Self-Regulation, and Compliance

Paying attention to a person's self-concept and other psychosocial realities also may be the key to success in other interactions between consumers and providers of health-care services. Consider the problem of compliance with medical treatment regimens (Haynes, 1982; Haynes, Sackett, & Taylor, 1979). Once a disease has been diagnosed, and treatment involves a medication regimen, what can be done to encourage and promote adherence to that regimen? This is a particular cause of concern regarding individuals who suffer from chronic diseases such as asthma, depression, diabetes, and hypertension.

Many attempts have been made to promote adherence by improving communication (e.g., Ley, 1989). As one recent example, a new organizational form has emerged, the pharmaceutical benefit management (PBM) firm (see Canter Kihlstrom, 1996a, 1996b, 1997a, 1997b; Reissman, 1995), which specializes in managing prescription benefits for employers and managed care organizations. A PBM verifies clients' eligibility for benefits, processes claims for reimbursement, and handles communications with pharmacists on the retail level. However, it also engages in physician and patient education programs designed to enhance adherence to medication regimens. For example, the pharmacy staff of the firms will mail patients informational brochures pertaining to their disease and its treatment, and physicians will receive information about the drugs and their proper doses. The pharmacy staff also examines refill patterns using a computerized database as a way of monitoring adherence to the regimen.

Most recently, PBM firms have adopted an approach to care, known as disease management (DM), which carves out an entire illness for specialized management (Terry, 1995). While DM goes beyond strictly pharmaceutical concerns and focuses on the entire spectrum of care for a particular condition, including outpatient, inpatient, and ancillary services, PBM firms that develop DM programs continue to focus on pharmaceuticals.

A specialized focus on drugs, or on specific disorders, may improve the quality and outcome of care generally and adherence to therapeutic regimens in particular. However, the DM strategy, as used by PBMs, seems to be based on perhaps invalid assumptions about adherence. The focus on providing information to individuals seems to be predicated on a communication model of compliance that holds that adherence will occur if individuals receive, understand, remember, and believe the correct information about their illnesses. Unfortunately, research suggests that whereas informational and educational efforts can enhance adherence over the short run, these same efforts may not have much effect in the long run (Haynes, Wang, & Gomes, 1987). It seems that effective management of pharmacy benefits, or of whole diseases, will require a better understanding of the complex compliance process.

It is in this context that we return to the self-regulation model of compliance developed by Leventhal and his colleagues (Leventhal & Cameron, 1987; Leventhal, Nerenz, & Steele, 1984). According to this model, compliance and other adaptive illness behaviors involve a sequence of three stages: interpretation, coping, and appraisal. At the interpretation stage, a person develops a cognitive representation of his or her illness, its symptoms, etiology, course, prognosis, treatment, and prevention. Based on this representation, one then considers the available coping strategies, selects one or more for implementation, and puts it into action. Finally, one engages in an appraisal of the action plan's outcome, which then feeds back to affect both the representation of the problem and the action plan itself.

Leventhal and his colleagues have been particularly interested in the role of emotion in this process. For example, fear appeals may increase the salience or threat value associated with the cognitive representation of the disease, but may actually interfere with coping by making one afraid to find out whether he or she has a disease in the first place. However, aspects of the self clearly play an important role as well. Thus, one's autobiographical memory for previous illness episodes, his or her own and other people's, may affect the representation of the illness, the selection of coping strategies, and the appraisal of outcomes.

Other aspects of selfhood may also be critical to effective self-regulation of compliance and other illness behaviors. For example, self-regulation begins with a cognitive representation of one's current state, or a mental representation of one's current self, and a cognitive representation of the goal state. This is what Markus and Nurius (1986) might call the "possible self." Receiving a medical diagnosis, especially of a chronic condition, will likely alter one's mental representation of self, and so it is necessary to understand how such new knowledge gets incorporated into the self-concept. And, of course, there are other possible selves to consider, including the one that lies waiting in the future if a person does not effectively comply with doctor's orders.

An illness like hypertension, with no symptoms identifiable without special equipment, may be especially hard to incorporate into the self-concept. There is no pain, or lump, or gastric distress, or difficulty breathing to remind one that he or she does, in fact, have an illness. And the act of compliance itself may involve changes, such as medication routines, side effects, and activity restrictions, which have to be incorporated into the self-concept: cat lovers with cat allergies, people with diabetes who no longer can eat what they want, and asthma sufferers who can no longer jog with their friends, must alter their self-concepts if they are to get healthy and stay healthy. Further, in the case of diseases like cancer that often have chronic deteriorating courses, and for which treatment is sometimes risky and uncertain, one actually has to choose between two goal states or two possible selves. Given compliance, the treatment may work, leading to remission of the disease, but have such a profound impact on physical appearance and quality of life that individuals no longer feel like themselves; or individuals can retain their current sense of self and lifestyle through noncompliance but pay for it with a shorter life, and perhaps a more difficult end. Thus, in order to understand how one comprehends an illness, or complies with a prescription, it is necessary to understand not only how he or she represents the disease and its treatment but also how he or she represents *himself* or *herself* as concept, as memory, as story, and as image.

Acknowledgements: The point of view represented here is based on research supported by research grant #MH-35856 and training grant #MH-15783 from the National Institute of Mental Health awarded to Yale University.

Notes

1. J. Kihlstrom (1992, 1994) has argued that conversion disorder properly belongs in the category of dissociative disorders, along with psychogenic amnesia, psychogenic fugue, and multiple personality disorder, on the grounds that conversion symptoms reflect pseudoneurological disorders of consciousness affecting the special senses and voluntary motor function. These are divisions of

consciousness ultimately involving the mental representation of the self (J. Kihlstrom, 1997). By contrast, somatization disorder, body dysmorphic disorder, and hypochondriasis involve the types of symptoms that, if organically based, would be diagnosed and treated by internal medicine. This argument was considered (Martin, 1996), but ultimately rejected, in the framing of DSM-IV (American Psychiatric Association, 1994).

2. Additional examples, outside the domain of the somatoform disorders, are *anorexia nervosa* and *bulimia nervosa*, where in addition to disordered eating behavior, a person may actually perceive certain body parts (e.g., the abdomen, buttocks, thighs) as too fat. In such cases, where one's perception of his or her own body shape is so out of proportion to objective reality, we can think literally of a disturbance in self-image. *Transsexualism*, the feeling of being a woman trapped in a man's body, or vice versa, may also reflect a discrepancy between self-image and perceptual reality.

References

American Psychiatric Association. (1987). *Diagnostic and statistical manual of mental disorders*. (3rd ed., rev.). Washington, DC: American Psychiatric Association.

American Psychiatric Association. (1994). *Diagnostic and statistical manual of mental disorders* (4th ed.) Washington, DC: American Psychiatric Association.

Bandura, A. (1977). Self-efficacy: Toward a unifying theory of behavior change. *Psychological Review, 84,* 191–215.

Bandura, A. (1997). *Self-efficacy: The exercise of control.* New York: Freeman.

Becker, M. H. (Ed.). (1974). The health belief model and personal health behavior. *Health Education Monographs, 2,* 324–508.

Blackwell, B. (1967). Upper middle class adult expectations about entering the sick role for physical and psychiatric dysfunctions. *Journal of Health and Social Behavior, 8,* 83–95.

Briquet, P. (1859). *Traite clinique et therapeutique a l'hysterie.* Paris: Balliere et Fils.

Canter Kihlstrom, L. (1996a). *Managed care and mergers in the prescription drug industry.* Paper presented at the annual meeting of the Association for Health Services Research, Atlanta.

Canter Kihlstrom, L. (1996b). *Pharmaceutical benefit management firms: Their characteristics and role in managing chronic illnesses.* Paper presented at the annual meeting of the American Public Health Association, New York.

Canter Kihlstrom, L. (1997a). *The management of chronic illness by PBMs: Compliance is complex.* Paper presented at the annual meeting of the National Council on Patient Information and Education, Washington, DC.

Canter Kihlstrom, L. (1997b). *The role of Pharmaceutical Benefit Management (PBM) firms in improving medication compliance: The example of hypertension.* Paper presented at the annual meeting of the Association for Health Services Research, Chicago.

Canter Kihlstrom, L., & Marsh, K. F. (1994). *Identifying young adults with multi-*

ple unexplained symptoms. Paper presented at the annual meeting of the American Public Health Association, Washington, DC.

Cantor, N., & Kihlstrom, J. F. (1987). *Personality and social intelligence.* Englewood Cliffs, NJ: Prentice-Hall.

Carver, C. S. (1979). A cybernetic model of self-attention processes. *Journal of Personality and Social Psychology, 37,* 1251–1281.

Carver, C. S., & Scheier, M. F. (1982). Control theory: A useful conceptual framework for personality-social, clinical, and health psychology. *Psychological Bulletin, 92,* 111–135.

Carver, C. S., & Scheier, M. F. (1985). Aspects of self, and the control of behavior. In B. R. Schlenker (Ed.), *The self and social life* (pp. 146–174). New York: McGraw-Hill.

Carver, C. S., & Scheier, M. F. (1991). Self-regulation and the self. In J. Goethals & G. R. Goethals (Eds.), *The self: Interdisciplinary approaches* (pp. 168–207). New York: Springer-Verlag.

Cloninger, C. R. (1986). Somatoform and dissociative disorders. In G. Winokur & P. Clayton (Eds.), *The medical basis of psychiatry* (pp. 123–151). Philadelphia: Saunders.

Cloninger, C. R. (1987). Diagnosis of somatoform disorders: A critique of DSM-III. In G. L. Tischler (Ed.), *Diagnosis and classification in psychiatry: A critical appraisal of DSM-III* (pp. 243–259). New York: Cambridge University Press.

Cloninger, C. R. (1996). Somatization disorder. In T. A. Widiger, A. J. Frances, H. A. Pincus, R. Ross, M. B. First, & W. W. Davis (Eds.), *DSM-IV sourcebook* (Vol. 2, pp. 885–892). Washington, DC: American Psychiatric Association.

de Leon, J., Bott, A., & Simpson, G. M. (1989). Dysmorphophobia: Body dysmorphic disorder or delusional disorder, somatic subtype? *Comprehensive Psychiatry, 30,* 457–472.

Engel, G. L. (1977). The need for a new medical model: A challenge for biomedicine. *Science, 196,* 129–135.

Engel, G. L. (1980). The clinical application of the biopsychosocial model. *American Journal of Psychiatry, 137,* 535–544.

Epstein, S. (1973). The self-concept revisited: Or a theory of a theory. *American Psychologist, 28,* 404–416.

Fenigstein, A., Scheier, M. F., & Buss, A. H. (1975). Public and private self-consciousness: Assessment and theory. *Journal of Consulting and Clinical Psychology, 43,* 522–527.

Fitts, S. N., Gibson, P., Redding, C. A., & Deiter, P. J. (1989). Body dysmorphic disorder: Implications for its validity as a DSM-IIIR clinical syndrome. *Psychological Reports, 64,* 655–658.

Guze, S. B. (1967). The diagnosis of hysteria: What are we trying to do? *American Journal of Psychiatry, 124,* 491–498.

Guze, S. B., & Perley, M. J. (1983). Observations on the natural history of hysteria. *American Journal of Psychiatry, 119,* 960–965.

Haynes, R. B. (1982). Improving patient compliance: An empirical review. In R. B. Stuart (Ed.), *Adherence, compliance and generalization in behavioural medicine.* New York: Brunner/Mazel.

Haynes, R. B., Sackett, D. L., & Taylor, D. W. (Eds.). (1979). *Compliance in health care.* Baltimore: Johns Hopkins University Press.

Haynes, R. B., Wang, E., & Gomes, M. de M. (1987). A critical review of interventions to improve compliance with prescribed medications. *Patient Education and Counseling, 10,* 155–166.

Jones, E. E., Farina, A. Hastorf, A. H., Markus, H. Miller, D. T., & Scott, R. A. (1984). *Social stigma: The psychology of marked relationships.* New York: Freeman.

Kashner, T. M., Rost, K., Smith, G. R., & Lewis, S. (1992). The impact of a psychiatric consultation letter on the expenditures and outcomes of care for patients with somatization disorder. *Medical Care, 30,* 811–821.

Kellner, R. (1990). Somatization: Theories and research. *Journal of Nervous and Mental Disease, 178,* 150–160.

Kihlstrom, J. F. (1992). Dissociative and conversion disorders. In D. J. Stein & J. Young (Eds.), *Cognitive science and clinical disorders* (pp. 247–270). San Diego: Academic.

Kihlstrom, J. F. (1994). One hundred years of hysteria. In S. J. Lynn & J. W. Rhue (Eds.), *Dissociation: Theoretical, clinical, and research perspectives* (pp. 365–394). New York: Guilford.

Kihlstrom, J. F. (1997). Consciousness and me-ness. In J. Cohen & J. Schooler (Eds.), *Scientific approaches to the question of consciousness* (pp. 451–468). Mahwah, NJ: Erlbaum.

Kihlstrom, J. F., & Cantor, N. (1984). Mental representations of the self. In L. Berkowitz (Ed.), *Advances in experimental social psychology* (Vol. 17). New York: Academic Press.

Kihlstrom, J. F., Cantor, N, Albright, J. S., Chew, B. R., Klein, S. B., & Niedenthal, P. M. (1988). Information processing and the study of the self. In L. Berkowitz (Ed.), *Advances in experimental social psychology* (Vol. 21, pp. 145–177). San Diego: Academic Press.

Kihlstrom, J. F., & Klein, S. B. (1994). The self as a knowledge structure. In R. S. Wyer & T. K. Srull (Eds.), *Handbook of social cognition* (2nd ed., Vol. 1, pp. 153–208). Hillsdale, NJ: Erlbaum.

Kihlstrom, J. F., & Klein, S. B. (1997). Self-knowledge and self-awareness. In J. G. Snodgrass & R. L. Thompson (Eds.), *The self across psychology: Self-recognition, self-awareness, and the self-concept. Annals of the New York Academy of Sciences, 818,* 5–17.

Kihlstrom, J. F., Marchese-Foster, L. A., & Klein, S. B. (1997). Situating the self in interpersonal space. In U. Neisser & D. A. Jopling (Eds.), *The conceptual self in context: Culture, experience, self-understanding* (pp. 154–175). New York: Cambridge University Press.

Kirmayer, L. J. (1984). Culture, affect and somatization. I & II. *Transcultural Psychiatric Research Review, 21,* 159–188, 237–262.

Kirmayer, L. J. (1986). Somatization and the social construction of illness experience. In S. McHugh & T. M. Vallis (Eds.), *Illness behavior: A multidisciplinary model* (pp. 111–133). New York: Plenum.

Kirmayer, L. J., & Robbins, J. M. (Eds.). (1991). *Current concepts of somatization: Research and clinical perspectives.* Washington, DC: American Psychiatric Press.

Klein, S. B., & Loftus, J. (1993). The mental representation of trait and autobiographical knowledge about the self. In R. S. Wyer & T. K. Srull (Eds.), *Advances in social cognition* (Vol. 5, pp. 1–49). Hillsdale, NJ: Erlbaum.

Kleinman, A., & Kleinman, J. (1985). Somatization: The interconnections among culture, depressive experiences, and the meanings of pain. A study in Chinese society. In A. Kleinman & B. Good (Eds.), *Culture and depression* (pp. 132–167). Berkeley: University of California Press.

Leventhal, H., & Cameron, L. (1987). Behavioral theories and the problem of compliance. *Patient Education and Counseling, 10,* 117–138.

Leventhal, H., Meyer, D., & Nerenz, D. (1980). The common sense representation of illness danger. In S. Rachman (Ed.), *Medical psychology* (Vol. 2, pp. 7–30). New York: Pergamon.

Leventhal, H., & Nerenz, D. (1985). The assessment of illness cognition. In P. Karoly (Ed.), *Measurement strategies in health psychology* (pp. 517–554). New York: Wiley.

Leventhal, H., Nerenz, D. R., & Steele, D. J. (1984). Illness representations and coping with health threats. In A. Baum & J. Singer (Eds.), *Handbook of psychology and health* (pp. 219–252). Hillsdale, NJ: Erlbaum.

Ley, P. (1989). Improving patients' understanding, recall, satisfaction and compliance. In A. Broome (Ed.), *Health psychology* (pp. 74–102). London: Chapman & Hall.

Lipowski, Z. J. (1968). Review of consultation psychiatry and psychosomatic medicine: III. Theoretical issues. *Psychosomatic Medicine, 30,* 395–422.

Lipowski, Z. J. (1987). Somatization: medicine's unsolved problem. *Psychosomatics, 28,* 294–297.

Markus, H., & Nurius, P. (1986). Possible selves. *American Psychologist, 41,* 954–969.

Martin, R. L. (1996). Conversion disorder, proposed autonomic disorder, and pseudocyesis. In T. A. Widiger, A. J. Frances, H. A. Pincus, R. Ross, M. B. First, & W. W. Davis (Eds.), *DSM-IV sourcebook* (Vol. 2, pp. 983–914). Washington, DC: American Psychiatric Association.

McAdams, D. P. (1997). The case for unity in the (post) modern self: A modest proposal. In R. D. Ashmore & L. Jussim (Eds.), *Self and identity: Fundamental issues* (pp. 46–78). New York: Oxford.

McHugh, S., & Vallis, T. M. (1986). *Illness behavior: A multidisciplinary model.* New York: Plenum.

Mechanic, D. (1962). The concept of illness behavior. *Journal of Chronic Diseases, 15,* 189–194.

Morselli, E. (1891). Sulla dismorfofobia e sulla tafefobia. *Bolletinno della R accademia di Genova, 6,* 110–119.

Othmer, E., & DeSouza, C. (1985). A screening test for somatization disorder (hysteria). *American Journal of Psychiatry, 142,* 1146–1149.

Pennington, N., & Hastie, R. (1993). The story model for juror decision making. In R. Hastie (Ed.), *Inside the juror: The psychology of juror decision making* (pp. 192–221). Hillsdale, NJ: Erlbaum.

Phillips, K. A. (1991). Body dysmorphic disorder: The distress of imagined ugliness. *American Journal of Psychiatry, 148,* 1138–1149.

Phillips, K. A. (1996). *The broken mirror: Understanding and treating body dysmorphic disorder.* New York: Oxford University Press.

Phillips, K. A., & Hollander, E. (1996). Body dysmorphic disorder. In T. A. Widiger, A. J. Frances, H. A. Pincus, R. Ross, M. B. First, & W. W. Davis (Eds.), *DSM-IV sourcebook* (Vol. 2, pp. 949–960). Washington, DC: American Psychiatric Association.

Phillips, K. A., McElroy, S. L., Keck, P. E., Pope, H. G., & Hudson, J. I. (1993). Body dysmorphic disorder: 30 cases of imagined ugliness. *American Journal of Psychiatry, 150,* 302–308.

Pilowsky, I. (1967). Dimensions of hypochondriasis. *British Journal of Psychiatry, 113,* 89–93.

Pilowsky, I., & Spence, N.D. (1975). Patterns of illness behavior in patients with intractable pain. *Journal of Psychosomatic Research, 19,* 279–287.

Reissman, D. (1995, July–August). Contracted pharmacy services: The value of a carve-out PBM. *HMO Magazine, 57,* 60–61.

Robins, L. N., Helzer, J. E., Weissman, M. M., Orvaschel, H., Gruenberg, E., Burke, J. D., & Regier, D. A. (1984). Lifetime prevalence of specific psychiatric disorders in three sites. *Archives of General Psychiatry, 41,* 949–958.

Rosenstock, I. M. (1966). Why people use health services. *Millbank Memorial Fund Quarterly, 44,* 94–124.

Schank, R. C., & Abelson, R. P. (1995). Knowledge and memory: The real story. In R. S. Wyer (Ed.), *Advances in social cognition* (Vol. 8, pp. 1–85). Hillsdale, NJ: Erlbaum.

Schilder, P. (1938). *Image and appearance of the human body.* London: Kagan, Paul, Trench, Trubner.

Schwartz, G. E. (1982). Testing the biopsychosocial model: The ultimate challenge facing behavioral medicine? *Journal of Consulting and Clinical Psychology, 50,* 1040–1053.

Schwartz, G. E. (1984). Psychobiology of health: A new synthesis. In B. L. Hammonds & C. J. Scheirer (Eds.), *Psychology and health* (pp. 149–193). Washington, DC: American Psychological Association.

Shweder, R., & Bourne, E. (1982). Do conceptions of the person vary cross-culturally? In A. Marsella & G. White (Eds.), *Cultural conceptions of mental health and therapy* (pp. 97–137). Dordrecht, The Netherlands: Reidel.

Smith, G. R. (1991). *Somatization disorder in the medical setting.* Washington, DC: American Psychiatric Press.

Smith, G. R., & Brown, F. W. (1990). Screening indexes in DSM-IIIR somatization disorder. *General Hospital Psychiatry, 12,* 148–152.

Smith, G. R., Miller, L. M., & Monson, R. A. (1986). Consultation-liaison intervention in somatization disorder. *Hospital and Community Psychiatry, 37,* 1207–1210.

Smith, G. R., Monson, R. A., & Ray, D. C. (1986a). Patients with multiple unexplained symptoms. *Archives of Internal Medicine, 146,* 69–72.

Smith, G. R., Monson, R. A., & Ray, D. C. (1986b). Psychiatric consultation in somatization disorder. *New England Journal of Medicine, 314,* 1407–1413.

Swartz, M., Hughes, D., George, L., Blazer, D., Landerman, R., & Bucholz, K. (1986). Developing a screening index for community studies of somatization disorder. *Journal of Psychiatric Research, 20,* 335–343.

Taylor, S. E. (1995). *Health psychology* (3rd ed.). New York: McGraw-Hill.

Taylor, S. E., Repetti, R. L., & Seeman, T. (1997). Health psychology: What is an unhealthy environment and how does it get under the skin? *Annual Review of Psychology, 48*, 411–447.

Terry, K. (1995, April). Disease management: Continuous health-care improvement. *Business and Health*, 64–72.

Wickramasekera, I. E. (1995). Somatization: Concepts, data, and predictions from the high-risk model of threat perception. *Journal of Nervous and Mental Disease, 183*, 15–23.

The Politics of Health, Identity, and Culture

Anthropologists are trained to be inherently skeptical of generalizations; to be alert to boundaries, margins, and difference. Most, but not all of us, are "splitters" in Tambiah's idiom (1990, p. 15); that is, we seek to relativize knowledge by situating it in context. Moreover, for virtually all anthropologists, the relevant context is a culture. However, these days we must start out by specifying what we *mean* by culture; not only has this category become extremely problematic, some anthropologists wonder if it continues to be useful at all. Second, the majority of researchers insist that *all* knowledge and practices, including scientific knowledge, together with its associated ethical commentary, must in turn be contextualized, for science too is historically and culturally produced. Furthermore, accounts of actual practices and not theoretical abstractions should provide the starting point for specifying context. The goal then becomes establishing the effect of knowledge at local sites, the legitimacy of competing knowledge claims, and, above all, the impact on the lives of those people most directly affected by the resultant practices.

I commence by briefly outlining my position on the concepts of culture, self and identity, and health, all of which are complex, contested categories. I then use three specific examples to illustrate the argument that, whereas a reductionistic approach to matters relating to health and illness often provides a powerful tool for therapeutic interventions, both biomedical and psychological, at the same time illness episodes must be interpreted in the broader context of human relations, communities, and politics.[1] Only then can insights be gained into how social relations can produce illness and how the body functions, consciously and unconsciously, as a medium for the expression of distress, a subjective experience itself culturally mediated. This is by no means an original insight, but one that repeatedly gets lost in the rush by some to produce overly simple reductionistic explanations—the new molecular genetics being the latest boost for such an approach. When we relativize culture, self and identity, and health, we introduce a reflexive approach, one that ensures that we begin to understand how biomedical and psychological knowledge and practices are themselves cultural productions.

Culture: A Contested Concept

The culture concept is problematic today, particularly so for anthropologists who have over this century appropriated it as their key disciplinary category. Williams (1976) has discussed how the meanings associated with the concept have changed over the centuries. He points out that in the nineteenth century, after Darwin, three different meanings were assigned to culture: as a general process of intellectual, spiritual, and aesthetic development; as a way of life of a group of peoples, a period of time, or of humanity as a whole; and as a concept describing intellectual and artistic activity. Anthropologists have worked to refine the second usage, while carrying out fieldwork in various corners of the world.

In recent years use of the culture concept across several disciplines has proliferated—most notably in cultural studies and literary criticism. It has also been applied liberally in the politics of multiculturalism, a movement that emerged across North America during the past decade or so. Many practicing anthropologists have been troubled, and at times frankly aghast, at how the concept—its meaning honed to workable consensus—is now up for grabs, so to speak, often with crude outcomes. Of particular concern is the way in which it is frequently used as "fact," as though culture is a reality for which no further explanation is necessary.

Earlier this century, anthropologists deliberately opposed the arguments of protagonists of the theory of social evolution, who ranked societies from primitive to advanced. They argued instead that *all* human communities possess culture, meaning language use together with knowledge, values, and practices that, by definition, could not be hierarchically distinguished. Thus, culture was interpreted as a discrete, clearly bounded entity that frequently, but not always, coincided with a nation. A major difficulty arises today because a somewhat modified nineteenth-century social Darwinism persists uncontested in many quarters. This attitude is evident at times, for example, in the treatment of ethnic minorities and recent immigrants, when it is assumed that "noncompliance" with recommendations given by health-care professionals is due to "ignorance" and "superstition," when, in fact, a lack of clear provider communication and a failure to understand the economic and social situation of patients more often causes patients' noncompliance (Guarnaccia, Guevara-Ramos, Gonzales, Canino, & Bird, 1992; Jenkins, 1988; Rapp, 1988). An assumption is made that in the heartland of the so-called developed world those of us with education have in effect advanced beyond culture, except in its usage to describe aesthetic sophistication. Culture, implying a way of life of a group of peoples, remains exoticized (often unconsciously), an entity possessed by the marginalized Other, still struggling, usually not very effectively, to catch up.

In part as a response to this type of thinking, the idea of culture today is often self-consciously politicized by many groups around the world when they assert that their community exhibits a valued, inherited tradition from the past, an entity that must be put to work and fostered, deliberately set up in opposition to the "core" of normalized, Westernized society (this process is illustrated in one of the examples to come). Such a reinvented history is frequently imagined as one uncorrupted by the effects of colonization, by contemporary participation in a pluralistic society, or by the global homogenization of modernity. Thus, "mytho-history" is invoked to create an idealized past out of which culture can potentially be turned into an "exclusionary teleology" (Daniel, 1991, p. 8) in which the pivotal question becomes, who is a "true" Sri Lankan, or Québequois, or Japanese? Culture put to work in the service of nationalism cannot be understood, therefore, without reference to relationships of exclusion, power, and discrimination. Very often two types of exclusionary practices are simultaneously at work: one involves efforts to "purify" one's culture of colonizing influences perceived as corrupting, both historical and contemporary, and the other involves discriminatory practices, institutionalized within society, designed to contain groups conceptualized as outsiders. Thus, in contemporary Québec, for example, a nationalistic ideology is mobilized, designed to culminate in separation from Canada, which is understood as a colonizing force. At the same time, language laws and other measures have been institutionalized to ensure that minority groups living in Québec, including Cree, Inuit, and Anglophones born in Québec (of both Jewish and Protestant background), together with more than a hundred other ethnic groups, are culturally and politically contained. Québec is officially a unilingual province, and boasts "language police" whose task is to ensure that the language of the workforce is French, that all public signs are written in French, and, if such signs are bilingual, that the French must be in bigger letters than the second language.

However, current nationalism notwithstanding, borders and boundaries dividing the world are in a permanent state of flux and transition, adding more complexity. Appadurai argues that "the tension between cultural homogenization and cultural heterogenization" is unavoidable (1990, p. 5). For Appadurai the global economy must be interpreted as a "complex, overlapping, disjunctive order" (1990), one that cannot be understood by drawing on center-periphery or push-and-pull models or by thinking in terms simply of consumers and producers, and so on (Wallerstein, 1974). Appadurai wants emphasis to be given to "deterritorialization" and to the circulation of people, ideas, knowledge, and practices around the globe. Creating and maintaining cultural boundaries becomes, when using this approach, an exercise in artifice.

A further difficulty arises because culture is often thought of as exclusionary in an entirely different way from those previously described. Culture in EuroAmerica is conceptualized in opposition to nature, where nature is understood as another given, the "natural" order—that not created by human endeavor, but by a higher power or, alternatively, through the forces of evolution. When this particular nineteenth-century reworking of Descartesian thinking is invoked, the cultured world of the mind is set up in opposition to that of the body, a creation of nature.

Any simple equation drawn between health or illness and the domain of culture is problematic. Despite its malleability, however, something approximating the idea of a shared cultural heritage persists for many, perhaps the majority of people today (Guarnaccia & Rodriguez, 1996). Furthermore, the way in which distress and illness is subjectively experienced, together with its physical manifestations in the body, varies significantly cross-culturally (Kleinman & Good, 1985; Lock & Scheper-Hughes, 1996). This variation is produced through an exquisitely complex interaction of biological and cultural variables that must be established empirically, and not simply assumed to be at work in a stereotyped, predictable fashion in which culture is a categorical variable.

The difficulties with defining culture do not end here, however, because within any given sociocultural complex, power relationships are inevitably institutionalized. Some persons are invested with or have acquired authority one way or another over others; in Bourdieu's (1977) terms they have "symbolic capital" and usually economic advantages in addition. It is not appropriate, therefore, to focus on cultural difference at the expense of paying attention to gender, class distinctions, or other forms of hierarchy created and maintained by those in positions of power within any given cultural complex (cf. Holland, 1997).

One issue that concerns me is the relationship between individuals and the political order in contemporary society, and the effect of this relationship on subjectivity and health. With the formation of the modern state, regulatory practices were systematically enacted to monitor the health of both society and the individuals who form that society. Foucault (1979) coined the term "biopower" to express this development, and focused on the surveillance of individuals by means of the psychiatric profession, the school system, and prisons. In addition, he posited a second aspect to biopower, namely, the development of survey research in which the monitoring of the health of whole populations became prevalent, rather than simply the disciplining of individuals. Foucault has been criticized for paying little attention to just how effective such surveillance is in actual practice among ordinary people as they go about their daily lives, and feminists, among others, have noted that he leaves relatively little space for the possibility of either conscious or unconscious resistance to dominant political orders (Lock & Kaufert, 1997; Sawicki, 1991).

Above all, globalization has ensured that the majority of the world's people are aware, as never before, that other ways of being exist beyond the boundaries of their respective communities, thus heightening possibilities for reflection on and resistance to local social arrangements, or alternatively encouraging a reaffirmation of tradition, or more frequently producing an unstable mix of ongoing contestation. It is evident that the dialectics of domination and resistance take place in a cultural field that is fluid and continually open to contestation (see, for example, Nordstrom & Martin, 1992) and further that ideas about the body and health, self and identity, internalized by individuals reflect larger unstable cultural and political forces. To further this discussion, I turn briefly to the concepts of self and identity.

Selves, Subjectivities, and Health

For two decades or more, anthropologists have written about how the idea of "self" is culturally constructed. In doing so, they have added a comparative perspective to the literature produced by the philosopher Charles Taylor (1989) and others, who have argued that the idea of an individualized, interiorized, unified, psychologized self is a creation of modernity, in particular the modernity of EuroAmerica. Anthropologists have usually focused on ethnopsychologies, on the way in which the postulated location of self in the physical person varies cross-culturally, or on how the self is understood reflexively—based on the positioning of individuals in society, rather than as an internalized, autonomous entity. It is common to talk of "situated selves," "multiple selves" (Lutz, 1988) and of "dividuals" (Dumont, 1970) when discussing ethnopsychology—none of which suggests even a hint of pathology but are, on the contrary, entirely normative. Implicitly, if not explicitly, this remarkable variety of selves is usually set up as fundamentally different from that tacitly assumed to be the "true" self—the psychologized product of Western modernity, a form of self which, it is frequently believed, will eventually materialize in people everywhere as they in turn become modern. We see this tension, for example, in the practice of psychiatry in countries such as India (Kakar, 1982) and Japan (Roland, 1988). Studies such as these highlight the way in which the ideas about the self commonly presented in psychological and philosophical literature in EuroAmerica can be understood as yet another ethnopsychology (see also Baumeister, 1997).

The sociologist Rose (1996) has recently argued that it is not sufficient to assert that ideas of self vary through time and space. His position is that subjectivity and ideas about identity do not vary simply according to social and cultural context. Moreover, to assert that changes in self depend on historical and economic transformations is not adequate. Historical accounts about the rise of the autonomous individual, the product of the transformation from feudal to capitalist society, from tradition to modernity, and so on, fail to pay sufficient attention, Rose argues, to individuals as not merely reflections of history, but as active producers of meaning from events around them. Such an approach to subjectification enables us to move beyond notions of "role" and of fixed entities of "self," "individual," and so on to a conceptualization of subjectivity as "processual so that one person can simultaneously occupy many 'subject positions' (woman, female, mother, daughter, wife, reader, consumer)," the dynamics of which are "constructed within an ensemble of social relations" (Zito & Barlow, 1994, pp. 9–10).

Our very experience of selves today as certain sorts of persons, Rose suggests, as "creatures of freedom, of liberty, of personal powers, of self-realization," is not just the end result of modernization and secularization in EuroAmerica, but of the internalized effects of various institutions—legal, political, educational, medical, familial, religious, ethnic—themselves grounded in a wider moral domain (1996, p. 132). These institutions are producers and mediators of reality; they are the milieu in which we learn to interpret self, and in contemporary society the dominant ideology they reproduce is one of the self as an active agent, who seeks to exercise informed, autonomous responsibility in connection with individual destiny or self-realization. By extension, central to the moral milieu in North America produced through these various institutions is the idea that we make ourselves and that those who fail are not fully responsible citizens. The fostering of "good" health has increasingly come to be regarded as the responsibility of individuals and, further, the improvement of health is today central to the process of self-realization for many people.

A dominant assumption among governments and in the medical world is that health is simply a physical state or condition, readily subjected to biomedical measurement and management (see, for example, Frenk, Bobadilla; Stern, Frejka, & Lozano, 1991). The World Health Organization (WHO) definition of health formulated in 1981, which states that health includes not only physical but mental, social, and spiritual well-being, was designed in large part to counter the biological reductionism of the medical sciences. The position of WHO is that health-related issues should not fall primarily into the medical domain, that limited resources for health care should be better distributed, and, further, that the individual is not necessarily the basic unit around which the concept of health should be organized. The WHO recognizes that ideas about health cannot be formulated without reference to politics, but it stops at this juncture. The responses of individuals to their social milieu and their internalization of local policies and ideas about the maintenance of health and illness are not considered.

If we follow Rose's argument, then it is clear that, beyond questions of policy and of medical knowledge and practices, it is important to consider how people come actively to incorporate or resist ideas about health and how this response relates to their awareness of self in society. As noted before, in North America, and to a slightly lesser extent in Europe, a desire to be in control and maintain one's own health is frequently internalized as part of individual subjectivity (Crawford, 1994, p. 1348). However, this desire has a moral dimension built into it, and as Tesh (1988) has noted, health policies that foster such a desire and exhort individuals to change their behavior in connection with health are not only shortsighted but, more ominously, indirectly protect those institutions that threaten individual health through discrimination, exploitation, pollution, or iatrogenesis.

The "new health morality" (Becker, 1986) has, Conrad notes, transformed "health into the moral" (1994). Wellness, the avoidance of disease and illness and the "improvement of health," is widely considered as "virtue," and for some individuals takes on the aura of a secular path to salvation. Baumeister points out about contemporary America that "people feel they have a moral right and even a duty to do what is best for themselves, and people pursue self-knowledge and self-actualization with faith that what they are doing is right" (1997, p. 213). Today this duty includes the pursuit of health.

In writing about "a remarkable expansion of the health sector" over the past several decades, Crawford (1979) situates the pursuit of health in a framework of political economy. He notes that expansion of the medical sector in the 1950s and early 1960s went virtually unquestioned, the assumption being that increased medical services would lead directly to improved health across all sectors of society. This expansion was first challenged in America in terms simply of equity and access, but it was the women's movement that provided the first major critique, pointing out the role of medicine as an institution of social control as the process of medicalization reached beyond the elimination of pathology.

By the 1970s a perceived crisis created by the "aging society," as it has come to be known, contributed dramatically to an increasing sense of urgency that the climbing health-care expenditures deployed for the benefit of the elderly must be curbed. Political pressures were mobilized to cut health-care costs just at a time when citizens had come to think of health care not simply as a right but rather as an entitlement. Crawford cites Robert Whalen, the commissioner of the New York Department of Health, who asserted in the late 1970s that it was essential that people should assume "individual and moral responsibility" for their own health. John Knowles, past president of the Rockefeller Foundation went further:

> The idea of individual responsibility has been submerged in individual rights—rights or demands to be guaranteed by Big Brother and delivered by public and private institutions. The cost of sloth, gluttony, alcoholic intemperance, reckless driving, sexual frenzy and smoking have now become a national, not an individual responsibility, and all justified as individual freedom. But one man's or woman's freedom in health is now another man's shackle in taxes and insurance premiums. (1977, pp. 2–3)

Crawford argues that this victim-blaming ideology, established well before AIDS was recognized, was used to justify a retrenchment from rights and entitlements to health care. It also strongly reformulates health as an individual responsibility to which the collectivity need contribute relatively little, for to do so would constrict the interests of society. The physician Leon Kass, who has been a senior fellow at the National Institutes of Health (NIH), claimed that it is inappropriate that "excessive preoccupations" about cancer lead to government regulations that unreasonably restrict industrial activity (1975, p. 42).

Political debates such as these, designed to foster a sense of self-responsibility for the occurrence of sickness, coincided with an increased awareness among large segments of the public that individuals have very little control over the polluted environments in which they live, the quality of food they buy, and the safety of medications they are prescribed. It was in this atmosphere that the wellness-as-virtue movement exploded, a movement actively encouraged by governments, since in theory it would contribute to a decrease in health-care expenditures. The U.S. Department of Health and Human Services recently produced an elaborate position paper in which the role of individuals in maintaining their own health was once again reiterated (Rosenberg, 1997).

On the basis of empirical research, Crawford (1984) has produced a "cultural account of health" in contemporary North America. The results of open-ended interviews carried out in the Chicago area with 60 adults, women and men, from a variety of socioeconomic backgrounds, revealed two oft-repeated themes in respondents' accounts: one was self-control, together with a cluster of related concepts including self-discipline, self-denial, and willpower. A second, complementary set of themes was grouped around the idea of release and freedom. Informants repeatedly expressed the idea that working out, eating well, giving up smoking, stopping alcohol use, and so on are essential to good health; moreover, such activities were taken to be evidence of willpower and self-control. However, at times one should "let go," be free of self-imposed restraints for a while, and then return once again to a measured, controlled life. Making time to be healthy was spontaneously ranked highly by the majority of informants, who also noted that such behavior exhibited an active refusal to be coopted by the unhealthy society in which they found themselves. Crawford argues that

> [t]he practical activity of health promotion, whereby health is viewed as a goal to be achieved through instrumental behaviors aimed at maintaining or enhancing biological functioning, is integral to an encompassing symbolic order. It is an order in which the individual body, separated from mind and society, is "managed" according to criteria elaborated in the biomedical sciences. Medical knowledge, internalized and reproduced in our everyday discourse, represents a distinct, although by no means universal, way of experiencing our "selves," our bodies and our world. (1984, p. 73)

One of the master metaphors of contemporary medicine and of North American society as a whole is, of course, that of control. Crawford suggests that by taking personal responsibility for health we are displaying not only a desire for control, but demonstrating an ability to seize it and enact it—we cooperate in the creation of correct citizens, thus validating the dominant moral order. He goes on to note that in this time of severe economic cutbacks individuals refract the general mood as we attempt to control what is within our grasp. Although it is the economically deprived who are the most affected by budget constraints, Crawford argues that the middle class reaffirm their relatively protected status through personal discipline.

Thus, culture, self and identity, and health are flexible, contested categories. When producing interpretations about the causes of illness and distress experienced by individuals, illness's effects on people's lives, and the meaning it represents for both involved individuals and for society, one must not, therefore, take these concepts as self-evident givens. Rather, it is important to establish how in practice they are internalized and put to work, consciously and unconsciously, in expressing distress and creating narratives about the meanings associated with specific events. Furthermore, these same concepts are in turn used in accounts given by health-care professionals in connection with the distress and illness of individuals. Subjective and professional accounts frequently are not commensurable, and it is particularly at these sites of rupture and confusion that the political and moral aspects of health and illness are made evident (Brandt & Rozin, 1997).

For the second part of this chapter I turn to three specific, widely divergent examples to illustrate the previous arguments. The first of these is a case study about one young boy that highlights the intimate and often destructive relationship between politics, in particular the politics associated with colonialism and economic development, and individual health. The second example takes up the particular difficulties posed to concepts of self, identity, and health that arise in connection with migration and immigration and the problems of communication about bodily states between cultures. The last example focuses on medicalization of the female life cycle. The comparative perspective in this final illustration permits me to critically examine our own largely unexamined assumptions in North America about the aging body, self, and health.

Chronic Deprivation and Fractured Identities

Wilfred, I will call him, is one of over 8,000 Cree living, for the most part, in northern Québec, Canada, over two thirds of whom still practice to a large extent a subsistence economy of hunting and fishing. Wilfred, age fourteen, and his mother were flown to a Montréal teaching hospital several years ago in order to keep a psychiatric appointment, because the Cree Health Board, based in the north, was very concerned about the boy, who apparently could not speak. The psychiatrist, a young woman who specializes in the treatment of children, called in an interpreter and tried, under the usual pressure of hospital time, to recreate Wilfred's story. His mother said that he had always been very quiet, that he had never really spoken at all. A long silence ensued, and, despite further questioning, the psychiatrist could extract no further information from Wilfred's mother until she asked about the boy's father. After another long pause, the mother started to sob uncontrollably, and then gradually revealed some additional fragments of the story.

Nearly half the Cree population was relocated to sites distant from their homeland in the latter part of the 1970s in order that the massive Québec government project, the James Bay hydroelectric dam, could be completed. Wilfred's family, consisting at that time of parents and three children, were forcibly moved over 150 miles from their birthplace. They received some financial compensation from the government, but there was no work for Wilfred's father, and so he decided to continue hunting as he had always done, which now entailed traveling many miles away from their relocated home for months on end. After one or two years of this life, Wilfred's father did not return from a hunting trip. Wilfred's mother never heard from her husband again, and after waiting for over a year it appeared that she had come to terms with the idea that he had met his death. Her brother and eldest son had disappeared earlier, presumed dead in hunting accidents, or possibly they had committed suicide.

At this juncture in her life, Wilfred's mother returned to the place of her birth to which she felt an emotional attachment to the surrounding geographical terrain, characteristic of the Cree and many indigenous peoples, and where she hoped she might find some work. Wilfred's life was severely disrupted once again. He was placed in a school where the instruction was in French, whereas he had been taught in English up until that time, and his family spoke Cree at home. When questioned, his teacher reported to the Cree Health Board that he was a nice boy, very quiet indeed, and that, like most of the other boys of his age and older, he regularly drank alcohol to excess.

The story is an all too familiar one, but one that we tend to repress: forcible relocation of native populations in the name of modernization, the breakup of a community, minimal financial compensation, and a permanently marginal existence offered as the new way of life. The psychiatrist recounted that as Wilfred's mother told her story, it was as though the stored grief of years was released for the first time in an uncontrolled flood, grief not only about the losses of her husband, child, and brother, but for the ravaged land, her community, and the never-ending effects of colonialism and racism. Eventually the psychiatrist noticed some strange grunts at her side; it was Wilfred who, for the first time, gave signs of responding to the emotion-filled atmosphere in the room.

Wilfred was kept in the hospital. Given his experiences and the deep withdrawal he exhibited, he was at a 99% risk for committing suicide in the estimation of the psychiatrist. Suicide is the leading cause of death among adolescent aboriginal children, six times the rate for Canadian adolescents in general. The psychiatrist first had Wilfred checked for a physical disability and was satisfied that his muteness was indeed a potent symbol of his private suffering. The Cree, as part of their heritage as hunters, make extensive and sophisticated use of gestures and body language; Wilfred's style of resistance was a form "natural" to the Cree—a retreat to a potent silence in the face of overwhelming adversity. His plea for help was temporarily met through hospitalization, and television, but far away from his mother and sister. Despite regular therapy and some schoolwork, it was many months before Wilfred started to talk in sentences. Six months after first entering the hospital, during which time he had received only one visit from his distant family, he asked to go home. The psychiatrist reluctantly had Wilfred flown back up north, with, as she described it, a possible weapon of self-destruction in his pocket—a month's supply of antidepressant medication. Here the story trails away, because the psychiatrist has never made a follow-up phone call. She is sure in her own mind that Wilfred is dead, that he has committed suicide, and she in turn feels an overwhelming sense of helplessness.

The psychiatrist may be wrong about Wilfred. A burgeoning movement is spreading across North America in which indigenous peoples are taking the health of their communities into their own hands. Wilfred may be part of one of the many newly formed youth groups in which he is learning and gradually taking on a leadership role in connection with various traditional activities. But the task before these groups is daunting, as they put a revitalized culture of tradition to work to fill the void in the lives of countless young people who have experienced trauma and loss on a massive scale. Many of these adolescents are being taught to understand the idea of the individual as a microcosm of the larger, primary unit of the community, as was formerly the case in precolonial Cree society. The community, in turn, is understood as having a special symbolic relationship to the land from which so many Cree continue to make a livelihood. Preservation of the appropriate balance among individual, community, and the environment is regarded as a state of health for which there is a special term in Cree (Adelson, 1991). Not surprisingly, as in all societies as far as I can ascertain, with the exception only of Europe and America of the past two centuries or so, no distinction is made among the Cree between a healthy mind and body; a clear separation between the two is, in effect, not thinkable (Heelas & Lock, 1981).

Today, young Cree must find a balance between this newly politicized form of "traditional" identity and whatever they have come to understand about themselves through the formal education system in the Québec school system, much of it involving accounts of the humiliation and destruction of the lives of their grandparents and parents. Adolescent Cree, like other descendants of colonized peoples, internalize these contradictions, all the while themselves experiencing racism on an almost daily basis, not all of it self-consciously perpetrated, but nevertheless clearly discernible, enacted both by people they must engage with every day and by distant bureaucrats. These ceaseless contradictions induce a sense of vulnerability among many young Cree as they mature, which can readily lead to feelings of fracture, of not belonging to either of the worlds around them—the one perceived by many outsiders to be a dying heritage, and the second considered by many Cree to be, with justification, a rapacious powerful invader. Elders in Cree society and other indigenous societies of North America have rallied to this crisis and are currently mobilizing activities around local ideas of "being-alive-well" (Adelson, 1991) in order that their children may find the strength to cope with their being marginalized continuously in so many ways by the culture of the Canadian South.

Wilfred's story is repeated endlessly around the world, of course, variations on a theme of persecution of peoples regarded as inherently different, perhaps as old as humankind. We know from the work of numerous writers and researchers, ranging from Amartya Sen and Franz Fanon to bell hooks and others, that poverty and racism create a deadly, vicious cycle; it is a mistake to defuse the clarity of this knowledge by bringing questions of culture and ethnicity exclusively to the fore to account for illness, disease, and self-destruction. It is the violence caused by the positioning of individuals in society on which we should focus— the "structural" violence of everyday life (Bourdieu, 1977). Attention to ethnic and cultural difference highlights the Other as a distinct group; a focus on structural violence and racism, on the other hand, draws attention to what the dominant society does to others whom it defines as different and to how this negative image often becomes internalized, producing a fractured, conflicted sense of self, to the detriment of health and well-being, whether physical or mental.

Immigration, Nostalgia, and Bodily Distress

The second wave of immigrant women from Greece who arrived in the 1960s and 1970s in North America were mostly of rural origin. In Montréal, the majority of these immigrants went to work in garment factories notorious for their exploitation of the labor force. There is no security, the hours are long, termination for long periods of time is common, pay is often below the minimum wage, noise and dust levels are high and the ventilation poor. Managers still parade, as they did from the turn of the century, up and down in front of the women as they work away at their sewing machines, reprimanding them for slack and slovenly behavior. Under the circumstances, many immigrants opted to work at home, in which case they had to purchase their own machines, pick up the "pieces" to be sown, and then deliver the completed articles back to the factory door. In the 1980s there were estimated to be about 20,000 such workers in Montréal, a large number of whom were recent immigrants from Greece. Today the numbers of such workers are even larger, but the women come for the most part from the so-called developing world and not from southern Europe.

While doing research among Greek immigrants in Montréal in the late 1980s, I found that the complaint most commonly expressed by women, particularly those working in the garment industry, was of *nevra* (nerves). *Nevra* is associated with a frightening loss of control and is described as an experience of powerful feelings of "bursting out," "breaking out," or "boiling over," in other words, a sense of disruption of the normal body boundaries. Once the condition becomes more than an odd, isolated episode, then headaches, chest pain, and other pains radiating out from the back of the neck also characteristically become part of *nevra* symptomatology. This illness is so common that at least one major Montréal hospital uses *nevra* as a diagnostic category. Some women are diagnosed as clinically depressed and given antidepressants when they visit a doctor, but the majority do not meet the usual criteria for depression and there is a tendency by some physicians to dismiss the patient's complaints as being "all in her head" (Lock & Wakewich-Dunk, 1990).

The Greek concept of *nevra* is part of a larger family of similar conditions commonly experienced in the Arab world and the southern Mediterranean, and in Central and Latin America (where it appears to have been transported from Europe). The condition is also present in isolated parts of North America, including the Appalachians and Newfoundland (Low, 1985), suggesting that it was formerly widely spread throughout Europe. The term "culture-bound" or "culturally interpreted syndrome" is used to gloss the plethora of special syndromes around the world, of which the condition of *nevra* or *nervios* (in Spanish) is just one among many. Byron Good formulated the concept of a "semantic illness network" in which popular categories of illness, including the culture-bound syndromes, are understood as representing "congeries of words, metaphors, and images that condense around specific events" (1977). These conditions are usually characterized in the medical literature as "somatization" and treated as evidence of a psychological disorder that manifests itself physically (see Kihlstrom & Canter Kihlstrom, this book, chap. 2). Anthropologists, on the other hand, attempt to situate *nevra* and conditions like it in the larger cultural and political realities of the lives of sufferers.

Among Montréal immigrants it is considered normal to have *nevra* in daily life. Only when symptoms become very disabling will a woman visit her doctor. If episodes become very frequent or oscillate rapidly back and forth between *stenohoria*, in which an individual feels confined and depressed, and *agoraphobia*, in which one feels terrified at the thought of going out, even on a family expedition, then the condition is regarded as an illness. Some women are believed to be more constitutionally vulnerable to attacks than others, and men are not entirely immune. Further, *nevra* is associated by all women with the immigrant experience, and many women, when interviewed, linked it explicitly to conditions of work:

> There is more pressure in Montréal. . . . I come from a city of 40,000 in Greece but they don't have the same pressures that we have here. My aunt works in a factory there and she works hard, but not like here. Here you have someone on top of your head all the time pressuring you to work harder and harder.

Another woman expanded the difficulties to home life in addition to work: "Women are more nervous because they have many responsibilities. The house and the boss at work. At home there are the household responsibilities and the children, and the woman does everything. The Greek man doesn't wipe the dishes or do anything." This ever-present background of stress is punctuated by precipitating events ranging from crises such as being fired or laid off from work, to family quarrels, or even spousal abuse (Lock, 1990). In situations such as these the term *nevra* is used to describe the conjunction of destructive social events, uncontrolled emotional responses, and culturally characteristic disabling physical symptoms. However, in order to better appreciate the cultural significance of *nevra* and its intimate association with individual identity, I must turn very briefly and hence superficially to examine the structure of Greek family life until recently.

In common with many other societies of the world (Griaule, 1965; Hugh-Jones, 1979), Greeks relate a healthy and "correct" human body to a clean and orderly house, and this is in turn associated with moral order in society at large. The house is the focus of family life, not only because it furnishes all the physical and social needs of family members but also because it is a spiritual center, replete with icons and regular ritual activity, where family members seek to emulate the Holy Family (DuBoulay, 1986). Management of the house is the special responsibility of the woman, who is both functionally and symbolically associated with it (Dubisch, 1986). Cleanliness and order in the house are said to reflect the character of the woman, and a discussion of private, inside family matters should not cross the threshold into the threatening domain of the outside world. Ideally, a woman should never leave the house for frivolous or idle reasons or venture outside where dirt and immorality abound. A woman who spends too much of her time outside the house can be accused of damaging the all-important social reputation of her family.

Just as a distinction is made between inside and outside the house, so too is a distinction made between the inner and outer body (Dubisch, 1986). Contact between what enters the body and what leaves it must be avoided. Dirty clothes and polluting human products must be strictly segregated from food preparation. Although fulfillment of male sexual desires is considered imperative, a woman's life is hedged with taboos around menstruation, marriage, the sexual act, and childbirth, all designed to constrain any elicit desires and contain the polluting nature of her bodily products.

A woman's task is to bind the family together, to keep it ritually pure, and to protect it from the potentially destructive outside world. This task, together with the raising of children, has traditionally been the prime source of self-esteem for Greek women. While men must protect the family honor in the outside world, women have been required to exhibit modesty at all times, and their bodies were symbols of family integrity and purity as a whole. Emotional stability is valued in this situation, and any loss of control on the part of women is worrisome.

Of course, I have described the normative state, an idealized situation that in daily life is often not lived up to or may be deliberately flouted. Nevertheless, this has been the value system that has shaped the lives of Greek women until recently. As is usual among immigrant populations, such values tend to persist after migration; the uncertainties produced by a new way of life may actually promote them. For example, in Montréal, Greek immigrant women complain that they seldom have an opportunity to go out of the house unaccompanied by their husbands unless it is to go to work. A Greek-Canadian physician described many of his patients as suffering from what he called the "hostage syndrome," the results of vigilant husbands protecting their family honor in unfamiliar surroundings.

Abiding by traditional codes of conduct, once a source of pride for Greek women, can become crippling after immigration. When a harsh climate, cramped apartment life with few friends or relatives nearby, language difficulties, and debilitating working conditions are taken into account, it is hardly surprising that so many women experience acute isolation, physical suffering in the form of *nevra*, and serious doubts about the worth of their lives. The majority of the nearly 100 women whom I interviewed lived with an unresolved nostalgia for the life they had left behind long ago on Greece. Many of them had been married by their families at a very young age to Greek men paying a return visit to their native villages in search of brides. Over the years, the majority of these women had come to despair of ever having much pleasure in their own lives, and most indicated that they had transferred all their hopes for the future onto their children. As one woman said, "It's too late for me; my dreams are broken" (Lock, 1990).

One sees in this example about *nevra* the shaping by culture of subjectivity, physical and emotional, and the particular problems raised by migration to a new cultural context in which social organization, family life, and working conditions are entirely different. The second generation of Greek-Canadians are unlikely to suffer in the same way (their subjectivity is very different from that of their immigrant parents); however, similar circumstances to that of the Montréal Greek immigrants are common around the world today as the numbers of refugees and immigrants increase rapidly, together with a burgeoning rate of involuntary migration due to wars, development projects, and so on. We need to develop a sensitivity to the way in which physical dislocation can have long, profound effects on the physical body in culturally specific forms, as individuals struggle, often unsuccessfully, to find a new self, embrace a different moral order, and undertake a radically different way of life.

Taking Control of Female Aging

I turn in closing to an entirely different illustration, that of the female life cycle transition of menopause. I include this example to problematize further the relationship among biology, subjectivity, and culture. Although passage through the life cycle is simultaneously a social and a biological process, the focus of attention within medical circles in recent years, perhaps not surprisingly, has been confined with increasing intensity to changes in the physical body. The result has been that the subjective experience of maturation and associated changes in individual identity and broader human relationships have been rendered largely inconsequential in medical discourse, a situation widely reflected in turn in public discourse that also focuses intently on the pathology of aging.[2]

Of course, not all women have cooperated with the medicalization of menopause. On the contrary, the aging female body has become the site for ever more contentious debate among both medical practitioners and involved women about its representation and the medical practices performed on it. Medicalization of the female body, whether young, middle-aged, or old, is not merely the result of changing medical interests, knowledge, and practice. It is at the same time a manifestation of potent, never settled, partially disguised political contests that contribute to the way in which the female body is "seen" and interpreted by women themselves, and in the popular domain (Bordo, 1993), by policy makers and professionals working in the health-care system (Lock, 1993a), and by the pharmaceutical industry invested in the medical management of the female body (Oudshoorn, 1994).

Despite these disputes and debates, a shared assumption exists that menopause is a universal phenomenon that affects all women in essentially the same way. However, the concept of menopause was first invented early in the nineteenth-century in Europe and only gradually since that time has it become closely equated in the minds of both the public and the medical profession with the end of menstruation. In recent years another transformation has taken place, and menopause is now often classed as a disease-like state—an "estrogen deficiency" (Lock, 1993b). Moreover, dominant medical discourse is concerned with the postulated long-term effects of lowered estrogen levels on the health of women as they age. The category "postmenopausal" is applied to all women once past reproductive age who, by definition, are deemed to be at an increased risk for heart disease, osteoporosis, and other diseases associated with aging. Attention has shifted away from any short-term discomfort that may occur around the time of the end of menstruation, as was formerly the case; it is the specter of aging baby boomers and the burden they are likely to place on the health-care system in the near future that is of primary concern.

Professional literature on menopause often commences with a rhetorical flourish about the approaching excess of older women: "It is estimated that every day in North America 3,500 new women experience menopause and that by the end of this century 49 million women will be postmenopausal" (Reid, 1988, p. 25). Governments too, not surprisingly, are intently concerned about postmenopausal women and make calculations about their future medical expense. If popular literature, medication use, and the popularity of local sports complexes are any indication, a large number of women of middle age apparently live with a diffuse anxiety about aging, fueled by professional and media rhetoric; many think of themselves as being "at risk," and their internalized image is, it seems, one of living with an estrogen deficiency.[3] Despite the presence of a health-conscious population and a widely accessible health-care system, the situation is very different in contemporary Japan. A brief examination of some of these differences can permit us to re-examine certain North American assumptions about health, identity, and aging.

Aging and Japanese Society

The "graying" of Japan has taken only a quarter of a century, whereas the equivalent demographic changes occurred over the course of about a hundred years in Europe and North America. Some official estimates calculate that, if present trends continue, by the year 2025 people 65 and over will make up a remarkable 24% of the population, and among the elderly, more than 53% will be over 75 (Ogawa, 1988). Japan will be the "oldest" society in the world. It is notable that the health and aging of women in their 40s and 50s has, until very recently, received little attention in Japan; it is only as potential care givers for their elderly relatives that they appear in professional and popular literature, particularly evident compared to the number of publications on the elderly themselves.

Since the early 1970s, when the question of the elderly population first began to capture the attention of Japanese policy makers, it has been stated repeatedly, following a Confucian value system, that it is preferable for older people to be taken care of in their own homes and that family members should be the primary care givers (Kōsei Hakusho, 1989). Politicians are concerned that the government is increasingly "expected" by the public to play a larger role in the care of the aging population, and several policy changes have been implemented to reverse this trend, although some money has also been set aside to train paramedicals to assist in the home.

In contemporary Japan the "homebody" or "professional housewife" is idealized, her lifestyle and behavior are the standard by which all

Japanese women are measured (despite the fact that over 60% of women are in the labor force), but the assumption is that once she becomes middle-aged a woman is likely to become a social anomaly, no longer of obvious productive use beyond occasionally feeding her husband unless she is prevailed upon, as in times past, to carry out her lifelong duties to the extended family. Because financially secure middle-class women are assumed to represent Japanese women as a whole, the situation of the majority who must give up work to look after their relatives, often at great cost to the well-being of the entire family, is usually erased from national consciousness. Moreover, many live to be well over ninety years of age, and daughters-in-law in their seventies find themselves bound over to caring for one or more incontinent, immobile, and sometimes senile relatives. Furthermore, since stroke is the usual cause of disability among the elderly population in Japan, intensive nursing is often required, but men assist very rarely with this onerous duty. It is, therefore, the debate about home nursing and living together as a three-generation family that takes up most of the energy of activist women in Japan today, much more so than does the question of *kōnenki* (the term that glosses as menopause). Together with the politically active among the elderly people themselves, middle-aged women question the intransigence of governments, national and local, on the social implications for the family of an aging society (Lock, 1993b).

In Japan, the idea of an autonomous individual has never taken hold, despite more than a century of exposure to European and North American philosophy, and movement through the life cycle continues to be subjectively experienced for most people largely in terms of how one's relationships with other people shift through time. For women particularly, life is expected to become meaningful according to what they accomplish for others rather than for themselves (Plath, 1980, p. 139), and the expectation that middle-aged women will devote their time to care for elderly family members is deeply internalized.

It appears that the end of menstruation has never been a potent symbol for Japanese women. Although a few of them mourn for the loss of youth and sexual attractiveness, as they grow older, most emphasize the inevitable process of aging itself: graying hair, changing eyesight, faulty short-term memory, and so on (Lock, 1986).[4] Furthermore, these signs of aging, while they obviously represent irretrievable youth, are primarily signifiers for the future—for what may be in store in terms of an enfeebled body, hence dependence on others and, above all, an inability to work and to contribute to society.

This situation is reinforced by other factors. Perhaps the most important was revealed by survey research carried out in the mid-1980s, which shows that, compared with Americans and Canadians, Japanese women experience remarkably few symptoms at the end of menstruation, including those considered universally characteristic of meno-

pause, namely, hot flashes and night sweats. No word specifically signi-
fies a "hot flash" in Japanese. On the basis of this finding, I have argued
that discourses on aging are shaped not only by unexamined beliefs
about the female body and its function in society; they are also in part
the product of "local biologies" (Lock, 1993b). In other words, there is
enough variation among biological populations that the physical effects
of lowered estrogen levels on the body, characteristic of the female
midlife transition, are not exactly the same in all geographical locations.
There is evidence from other parts of the world in addition to Japan of
considerable variation in symptom reporting at menopause (Beyene,
1989; Lock, 1998b). This variation, to which genetics, diet, environment, and other cultural variables no doubt contribute, accounts for a
qualitative difference in subjective experience and associated symptom
reporting. The differences between North American and Japanese
women are sufficient to produce an effect on (but *not* determine) the
creation of knowledge, both popular and professional, about this life
cycle transition. *Kōnenki* has never been thought of as a disease-like
state, nor even equated closely with the end of menstruation, even by
Japanese medical professionals. The symptoms most closely associated
with *kōnenki* are shoulder stiffness and other similar culturally specific
sensations, including a "heavy" head.

Japanese physicians keep abreast of the medical literature published
in the West, and so one could expect them, living as they do in a country actively dedicated to preventive medicine, to have some incentive to
use hormone replacement therapy (HRT), the medication so widely
recommended by health-care professionals in Europe and North
America for lifelong use with virtually all postmenopausal women.
However, this is not the case, first because, as we have seen, symptom
reporting is different and very few women go to see physicians in connection with distressing symptoms such as hot flashes. In addition, local
biology plays a part in other ways: mortality from coronary heart disease for Japanese women is about one quarter that of American women
(WHO, 1990), and it is estimated that, although Japanese women become osteoporotic twice as often as do Japanese men, nevertheless, this
is approximately half as often as in North America (Ross et al., 1991).
These figures, combined with a mortality rate from breast cancer about
one quarter that of North America and the longest life expectancy in
the world for Japanese women, has meant that there is relatively little
pressure for Japanese gynecologists to enter into the international
arena of debate about the pros and cons of long-term use of HRT,
something about which many of them are, in any case, decidedly un-
comfortable because of a pervasive concern about iatrogenesis. The
first line of resort of Japanese doctors when dealing with healthy middle-aged women is usually to encourage good dietary practices and
plenty of exercise. For those few women with troubling symptoms,

herbal medicine is commonly prescribed, even by gynecologists (Lock, 1993b).

Certain Japanese physicians, influenced directly by trends in North America, are currently seeking to medicalize *kōnenki* and to treat it much more aggressively as a disease of aging; it will be interesting to see not only how successful they are but also whether symptom reporting by Japanese women changes as a result of this medical interest in female aging. My prediction is that this will not happen unless simultaneous widespread and massive transformations in dietary and behavioral practices change the patterning of local biology.

The politics of aging, an urgent matter in both Japan and North America, is constructed in these two cultural spaces, therefore, in very different ways. Although both discourses are in part the product of a rhetoric about biological change with its associated risk for distress and even major disease (particularly in North America), this rhetoric is shaped by local biologies, historically informed knowledge, culturally influenced medical knowledge and beliefs, government interests, and situated social exigencies. Women's experiences at the end of menstruation, including unpleasant symptoms, are also informed by this complex of situated variables and are not universal. These findings suggest that it is important to decenter assumptions about a biological universalism. The margins between nature and culture are not "natural" givens. Obviously aging cannot be avoided, but the power of both biology and culture to shape the experience of aging and the meanings—individual, social, and political—attributed to this process, demand fine-grained, contextualized interpretations.

Conclusion

All three of these examples illustrate how matters relating to the body—whether in health, illness, or as it ages—are intimately related to ideas about self and identity and, in addition, to larger social and political issues, including those related to government, community, and the health-care professions. Although clearly at times it is useful to isolate the physical body conceptually in order to carry out various medical procedures and to advance medical knowledge, if one's intent is to discuss health and illness as a lived experience, then one must inevitably contextualize the discussion in a much larger framework. I have focused on the relationships among culture, self and identity, and health and illness but must stress once again in closing that each of these concepts is unstable, subject to debate, and located in historical and geographical context. Each of the examples has used cultural difference in order to highlight the arguments. Lack of space has meant that I could not go further with these illustrations in order to show the extensive variation and debate within each of the groups discussed, including very frequently internal disputes about the political and symbolic meanings of the ideas of culture, ethnicity and identity, and even health. If I have left an impression of an exotic Other, then I have failed entirely; on the contrary, my hope has been to decenter some of the categories by which we "make up people" (Hacking, 1990) and thus subject certain of our assumptions to reflexive examination.

Notes

1. My understanding of politics is influenced by the work of Foucault (see Burchell, Gordon & Miller, 1991), and I use this term to refer to various situations wherein relationships of power and control are implicated in human relationships and in institutional settings. In this chapter, I am referring in a general way to the process whereby scientific knowledge, including medical knowledge, has come to be accepted as factual and authoritative during the course of the last two centuries, is supported by government, and drawn on to legitimize policies in connection with the health and regulation of populations (see Foucault, 1980; Hacking, 1990). I also refer to politics when discussing the transformation of life cycle events and situations of distress into medical problems—the process of "medicalization," discussed in the second and third illustrative examples used in this chapter; in addition, I use the term politics in connection with situations of colonialism, as discussed in the first illustrative example.

2. In the social and behavioral sciences, life cycle transitions are not reduced simply to biological change, but a perusal of the extensive popular literature and media coverage about menopause leaves one in no doubt that it is the medical model that has a pervasive influence among the public. Discussion of hormone replacement therapy, its risks and benefits, is a topic covered ad nauseum in popular literature today (see, for example, Kaufert & Lock, 1997; Sheehy, 1991; Utian & Jacobowitz, 1990).

3. Mary Douglas (1992) has described the idea of risk as a central cultural construct of our time. Gifford (1986) has shown how this concept is used in the management of breast cancer, and more recently, Lock (1998a) analyzes the screening and testing for genes for breast cancer, in particular for those women deemed at risk.

4. Survey research was carried out 1983 to 1984 with over 1,300 Japanese women living in three parts of Japan divided into three occupational groups: those who were doing farming, factory workers, and homemakers. Open-ended interviews were also carried out with over 100 women in their homes (see Lock, 1993b, for further details).

References

Adelson, N. (1991). 'Being alive well': The praxis of Cree health. In B. Postl et al. (Eds.), *Circumpolar health 90: The proceedings of the 8th International Congress on Circumpolar Health* (pp. 226–228). Winnipeg: University of Manitoba Press.

Appadurai, A. (1990). Disjunction and difference in the global cultural economy. *Public Culture, 2,* 1–24.

Baumeister, R. F. (1997). The self and society: Changes, problems, and opportunities. In R. D. Ashmore & L. Jussim (Eds.), *Self and identity: Fundamental issues* (pp. 191–217). New York: Oxford University Press.

Becker, M. H. (1986). The tyranny of health promotion. *Public Health Reviews, 14,* 15–25.

Beyene, Y. (1989). *From menarche to menopause: Reproductive lives of peasant women in two cultures.* Albany: State University of New York Press.

Bordo, S. (1993). *Unbearable weight: Feminism, Western culture, and the body.* Berkeley: University of California Press.

Bourdieu, P. (1977). *Outline of a theory of practice.* Cambridge: Cambridge University Press.

Brandt, A., & Rozin, P. (1997). *Morality and health.* New York: Routledge.

Burchell, G., Gordon, C., & Miller, P. (1991). *The Foucault effect: Studies in governmentality.* Chicago: University of Chicago Press.

Conrad, P. (1994). Wellness as virtue: Mortality and the pursuit of health. *Culture, Medicine and Psychiatry, 18,* 385–401.

Crawford, R. (1979). Individual responsibility and health politics in the 1970s. In S. Reverby and D. Rosner (Eds.), *Health care in America: Essays in social history* (pp. 247–268). Philadelphia: Temple University Press.

Crawford, R. (1984). A cultural account of health: Self control, release, and the social body. In J. McKinlay (Ed.), *Issues in the political economy of health care* (pp. 60–103). London: Tavistock.

Daniel, V. (1991). *Is there a counterpoint to culture: The Wertheim Lecture 1991.* Amsterdam: Center Asian Studies.

Douglas, M. (1992). *Risk and blame: Essays in cultural theory.* New York: Routledge.

Dubisch, J. (1986). Culture enters through the kitchen: Women, food, and social boundaries in rural Greece. In J. Dubisch (Ed.), *Gender and power in rural Greece* (pp. 195–214). Princeton, NJ: Princeton University Press.

DuBoulay, J. (1986). Women—Images of their nature and destiny in rural Greece. In J. Dubisch (Ed.), *Gender and power in rural Greece* (pp. 139–168). Princeton, NJ: Princeton University Press.

Dumont, L. (1970). *Homo hierarchicus: The caste system and its implications.* Chicago: University of Chicago Press.

Foucault, M. (1979). *Discipline and punish: The birth of a prison.* New York: Vintage.

Foucault, M. (1980). Body/power. In C. Gordon (Ed.), *Power/knowledge: Selected interviews and other writings 1972–1977* (pp. 55–62). New York: Pantheon.

Frenk, J., Bobadilla, J. L., Stern, C., Frejka, T., & Lozano, R. (1991). Elements for a theory of the health transition. *Health Transition Review: The Cultural, Social, and Behavioural Determinants of Health, 1(1),* 21–38.

Gifford, S. (1986). The meaning of lumps: A case study of the ambiguities of risk. In C. R. Janes, R. Stall, & S. M. Gifford (Eds.), *Anthropology and epidemiology: Interdisciplinary approaches to the study of health and disease* (pp. 213–246). Dordrecht, The Netherlands: Reidel.

Good, B. J. (1977). The heart of what's the matter: The semantics of illness in Iran. *Culture, Medicine and Psychiatry, 1*, 25–58.

Griaule, M. (1965). *Conversations with Ogotemmeli*. Oxford: Oxford University Press.

Guarnaccia, P. J., Guevara-Ramos, L. M., Gonzales, G., Canino, G. J., & Bird, H. (1992). Concepts of culture and their role in the development of culturally competent mental health services. *Hispanic Journal of Behavioral Sciences, 18*(4), 419–443.

Guarnaccia, P. J., & Rodriguez, O., (1996). Concepts of culture and their role in the development of culturally competent mental health services. *Hispanic Journal of Behavioral Sciences, 18*(4), 419–443.

Hacking, I. (1990). *The taming of chance*. Cambridge: Cambridge University Press.

Heelas, P., & Lock, A. (1981). *Indigenous psychologies: The anthropology of the self*. London: Academic Press.

Holland, D. (1997). Selves as cultured: As told by an anthropologist who lacks a soul. In R. A. Ashmore & L. Jussim (Eds.), *Self and identity: Fundamental issues* (pp. 160–190). New York: Oxford University Press.

Hugh-Jones, C. (1979). *From the milk of the river: Spacial and temporal process in North-west Amazonia*. Cambridge: Cambridge University Press.

Jenkins, J. (1988). Ethnopsychiatric interpretations of schizophrenic illness as a problem of nerves: A comparative analysis of Mexican-Americans and Anglo-Americans. *Social Science and Medicine, 26*, 1233–1243.

Kakar, S. (1982). *Shamans, mystics and doctors*. Chicago: University of Chicago Press.

Kass, L. (1975). Regarding the end of medicine and the pursuit of health. *Public Interest, 40*, 38–39.

Kaufert, P., & Lock, M. (1997). Medicalization of women's third age. *Journal of Psychosomatic Obstetrics and Gynecology, 18*, 81–86.

Kleinman, A., & Good, B. J. (1985). *Culture and depression: Studies in the anthropology and cross-cultural psychiatry of affect and disorder*. Berkeley: University of California Press.

Knowles, J. (1977). The responsibility of the individual. In J. Knowles (Ed.), *Doing better and feeling worse: Health in the United States* (p. 78). New York: Norton.

Kōsei, Hakusho (1989). *Arata na kōreishazō to katsuryoku aru chōju fukushi shakai o mezashite (Toward a new image of the aged and a vigourous long-lived society with good social welfare)*. Tokyo: Kōseishō.

Lock, M. (1986). Ambiguities of aging: Japanese experience and perceptions of menopause. *Culture, Medicine and Psychiatry, 10*, 23–46.

Lock, M. (1990). On being ethnic: The politics of identity breaking and making in Canada, or, Nevra on Sunday. *Culture, Medicine and Psychiatry, 14*, 237–254.

Lock, M. (1993a). *Encounters with aging: Mythologies of menopause in Japan and North America*. Berkeley, CA: University of California Press.

Lock, M. (1993b). The politics of mid-life and menopause: Ideologies for the second sex in North America and Japan. In S. Lindenbaum & M. Lock (Eds.), *Knowledge, power and practice: The anthropology of medicine and everyday life* (pp. 330–363). Berkeley: University of California Press.

Lock, M. (1998a). Breast cancer: Reading the omens. *Anthropology Today 14*, 7–16.

Lock, M. (1998b). Menopause: Lessons from anthropology. *Journal of Psychosomatic Medicine, 60*, 410–419.

Lock, M., & Kaufert, P. (1997). *Pragmatic women and body politics*. Cambridge: Cambridge University Press.

Lock, M., & Scheper-Hughes, N. (1996). A critical-interpretive approach in medical anthropology: Rituals and routines of discipline and dissent. In C. Sargent & C. F. Johnson (Eds.), *Medical anthropology: Contemporary theory and method* (Rev. ed.,) (pp. 41–70). Westport, CT: Praeger.

Lock, M., & Wakewich-Dunk, P. (1990). Nerves and nostalgia: The expression of distress among Greek-Canadian immigrant women. *Canadian Family Physician, 36*, 253–258.

Low, S. (1985). Culturally interpreted symptoms or culturebound syndromes. *Social Science and Medicine, 21*, 187–197.

Lutz, C. (1988). *Unnatural emotions*. Chicago: University of Chicago Press.

Nordstrom, C., & Martin, J. (1992). *The path to domination, resistance and terror*. Berkeley: University of California Press.

Ogawa, N. (1988). Population aging and medical demand: The case of Japan. Economic and social implications of population aging. *Proceedings of the International Symposium on Population Structure and Develoment, Tokyo* (pp. 254–275). New York: United Nations.

Oudshoorn, N. (1994). *Beyond the natural body: An archeology of sex hormones*. New York: Routledge.

Plath, D. (1980). *Long engagements*. Palo Alto, CA: Stanford University Press.

Rapp, R. (1988). Chromosomes and communication: The discourse of genetic counselling. *Medical Anthropology Quarterly, 2*, 143–157.

Reid, R. L. (1988). Menopause, part I: Hormonal replacement. *Bulletin: Society of Obstetricians and Gynecologists, 10*, 25–34.

Roland, A. (1988). *In search of self in India and Japan: Toward a cross-cultural psychology*. Princeton, NJ: Princeton University Press.

Rose, N. (1996). Identity, geneology, history. In S. Hall & P. duGay (Eds.), *Questions of cultural identity*. London: Sage.

Rosenberg, C. (1997). Banishing risk: Continuity and change in the moral management of disease. In A. M. Brandt & P. Rosin (Eds.), *Morality and health*. New York: Routledge.

Ross, P. D., Norimatsu, H., Davis, J. W., Yano, K., Wasnick, R. D., Fukiwara, S., Hosoda, Y., & Melton, L. J. (1991). A comparison of hip facture incidence among native Japanese, Japanese Americans, and American caucasians. *American Journal of Epidemiology, 133*, 801–809.

Sawicki, J. (1991). *Disciplining Foucault: Feminism, power and the body*. New York: Routledge.

Sheehy, G. (1991). The silent passage: Menopause. *Vanity Fair*, October, pp. 222–263.

Tambiah, S. J. (1990). *Magic, science, religion and the scope of rationality*. Cambridge: Cambridge University Press.

Taylor, C. (1989). *Sources of the self*. Cambridge, MA: Harvard University Press.

Tesh, S. N. (1988). *Hidden agreements: Political ideology and disease prevention policy*. New Brunswick, NJ: Rutgers University Press.

Utian, W. H., & Jacobowitz, R. S. (1990). *Managing your menopause*. New York: Prentice Hall.

Wallerstein, I. (1974). *The modern world system (2 vols.)*. New York: Academic Press.

World Health Organization (WHO). (1990). *World Health Statistics Annual*. Geneva: WHO.

Williams, R. (1976). *Keywords: A vocabulary of culture and society*. London: Fontana Press.

Zito, A., & Barlow, T. A. (1994). *Body subject and power in China*. Chicago: University of Chicago Press.

PART II

SELF AND SOCIAL IDENTITY IN STRESS, COPING, AND PHYSICAL DISEASE

David R. Williams
Michael S. Spencer
James S. Jackson

4

Race, Stress, and
Physical Health

The Role of Group Identity

In the United States, race has long been known to be an important predictor of variations in health (Krieger, 1987). A decade ago, a major federal report summarized the evidence that indicates that, across a broad range of indicators of health status, blacks (or African Americans) experience poorer health than whites (U.S. Department of Health and Human Services, 1985). A recent update of that report from the National Center for Health Statistics (NCHS) indicated that the health status gap between blacks and whites widened between 1980 and 1991 (National Center for Health Statistics, 1994). However, although much is known about the nature and magnitude of racial differences in health, the factors responsible for the elevated rates of morbidity and mortality for blacks, are not well understood (Kaufman & Cooper, 1995; Williams, 1997; Williams & Collins, 1995).

Increasingly, the health literature has been giving attention to the meaning and measurement of race. This body of work emphasizes that a clear understanding of race is indispensable to the development of research that would enhance our knowledge of the role of race in health (Dressler, 1993; King & Williams, 1995; Krieger, Rowley, Herman, Avery, & Phillips, 1993; LaVeist, 1996; Williams, 1997; Williams, Lavizzo-Mourey, & Warren, 1994). There is growing scientific consensus that race is a gross indicator of distinctive social and individual histories, and not a measure of biological distinctiveness (Cooper & David, 1986; Gould, 1977; Lewontin, 1972). That is, racial categories in the United States importantly capture exposure to different social

conditions. Accordingly, the challenge for health researchers is to identify how the varying social contexts of racial groups shape individual
thinking and behavior in ways that can enhance or impair health status.

More specifically, several researchers have recently emphasized the
need for enhanced understanding of how racism affects health (Cooper,
1993; Cooper, Steinhauer, Schatzkin, & Miller, 1981; Hummer, 1996;
King & Williams, 1995; Krieger et al., 1993; Williams, 1996b). The
term racism includes ideologies of superiority, negative attitudes and
beliefs about out-groups, and differential treatment of members of
those groups by individuals and societal institutions. It is a feature of
society that can lead to group differences in life chances and socioeconomic conditions, such as housing quality, employment, and education.
Racism truncates socioeconomic mobility and creates patterns of differential treatment by individuals and societal institutions that can lead
to systematic variations in the distribution of desirable societal resources. The effects of institutional discrimination are arguably the
most decisive for health, but the operation of institutionalized racism is
typically not readily visible to the individual or easy to ascertain by respondent self-report. However, there is growing recognition that subjectively experienced stress is also a salient feature of residential and occupational environments that can be shaped by racism. Stress is not
randomly distributed in society and across locations in social structure,
and occupation of particular social roles can determine both the levels
and types of stress to which an individual is exposed (Pearlin, 1989;
Williams & House, 1991). In addition to differential exposure to traditionally measured stress, racism can also lead to differential exposure to
experiences of discrimination that can adversely affect health. The
stress literature has acknowledged that unfair treatment based on race
may be an important source of stress, but stress researchers have not
typically included measures of discrimination in the standard batteries
used to assess stress (McLean & Link, 1994). However, subjective reports of bias, because they do not capture much institutional racism,
likely underestimate the full impact of racism on health (Williams,
1996b).

A small but growing body of research suggests that the psychological
and physiological correlates and consequences of discrimination are
similar to those of other psychosocial stressors (Dion, Dion, & Pak,
1992; Thompson, 1996). Several researchers have found that exposure
to racist provocation in the laboratory setting leads to increased cardiovascular and psychological reactivity (Anderson, 1989; Armstead,
Lawler, Gordon, Cross, & Gibbons, 1989; Jones, Harrell, Morris-
Prather, Thomas, & Omowale, 1996; Morris-Prather et al., 1996;
Sutherland & Harrell, 1986). These studies have tended to assess the
physiological changes and affective reactions of African Americans to
mental imagery and to videotaped vignettes of discriminatory behavior.

Epidemiologic studies, using respondent reports of experiences of racial bias, also indicate that, at least under some conditions, racial discrimination is positively related to blood pressure. For example, in a small study in rural North Carolina, James and colleagues (1984) found a positive relationship between blood pressure and discrimination for black males who scored high on John Henryism (an active predisposition to cope and overcome adversity). In a study of 101 black and white women in northern California, Krieger (1990) found that black women who responded passively to racial discrimination were four times more likely to have high blood pressure than those who responded actively to unfair treatment. More recently, Krieger and Sidney (1996) found that both reports of discrimination and a passive response to recalled bias were positively related to systolic and diastolic blood pressure in a sample of almost 2,000 black adults twenty-five to thirty-seven years old. However, findings of a positive association between discrimination and blood pressure are not uniform. In a study of 312 black adults in Detroit, Broman (1996) found that perceived racial discrimination was unrelated to reports of physician-diagnosed high blood pressure and heart disease.

Other recent studies reveal that reports of racial discrimination are related to health outcomes other than hypertension. In analyses of the National Study of Black Americans (NSBA), Williams and Chung (in press) found that a single item that measured the experience of racial discrimination in the previous month was related to higher levels of chronic health problems, disability, and psychological distress, as well as to lower levels of psychological well-being. In a related analysis, Jackson and colleagues (1996) explored the cumulative effects of exposure to discrimination in the NSBA using four waves of panel data. They found that a general measure of racial beliefs, perceiving that whites want to keep blacks down, was related to poorer physical health at wave one and predicted increased psychological distress and lower subjective well-being at wave four. Recent analyses of the third wave of data in the Americans' Changing Lives national study found that a single-item self-report measure of racial or ethnic discrimination was associated with higher levels of chronic health problems, self-reported poor health, depressive symptoms, diagnosed depression, and lower levels of life satisfaction (Jackson, Williams, & Torres, 1995). Other studies consistently indicate that racial discrimination adversely affects the psychological health of racial/ethnic minorities (Amaro, Russo, & Johnson, 1987; Dion et al., 1992; Saldana, 1995; Salgado de Snyder, 1987).

Several questions remain unanswered in the available research. It is not clear whether the association between discrimination and health is due to racial discrimination, per se, or to the more generic experience of unfair treatment. Some research suggests that the experience of unfair treatment, irrespective of race or ethnicity, may have negative consequences for health (Hannah, 1974; Harburg et al., 1973). Racial discrimination may be the most salient source of this perceived injustice for minorities, while other sources of perceived unfairness, including perceptions of reverse discrimination, may have similar adverse consequences for whites. Little attention has been given to assessing the health consequences of perceptions of unfairness for whites. In the Americans' Changing Lives Study, perceptions of racial or ethnic discrimination were associated with poorer physical and mental health for both blacks and whites (Jackson et al., in press). At the same time, Krieger (1990) found that although racial discrimination was related to hypertension for black women, gender discrimination was unrelated to high blood pressure for white women. At the present time, we know little about the racial differentials in the distribution of perceptions of inequities or about the relative health impact of different kinds of social biases.

The conceptualization and measurement of discrimination have been limited in studies to date, and most studies have assessed only major episodic experiences of discrimination. In contrast, the stress literature indicates that stressful minor recurrent experiences are more strongly linked to adverse health outcomes than major episodic experiences (Lepore, 1995). Essed (1991) has emphasized that racial discrimination consists not only of acute stressful life experiences but also of persistent and recurrent everyday experiences. Prior research has not assessed the health consequences of exposure to chronic indicators of discrimination.

Although minority racial populations are disproportionately exposed to social conditions considered to be important risk factors for poor health, they do not have the expected high rates of morbidity for all health outcomes. For example, African Americans have lower rates of psychiatric disorders than whites (Kessler et al., 1994; Robins & Regier, 1991). Similarly, risk factors such as low birth weight and stressful life events are more prevalent among blacks. However, when these risk factors occur among whites, their negative impact is larger for the health of whites than for blacks. (Kessler, 1979; Williams & Collins, 1995). This pattern of findings emphasizes the need for renewed efforts to identify the health-enhancing resources that may provide protection from at least some pathogenic risk factors. Much prior research on minority populations has focused only on pathology and deficits and has not adequately considered health-promoting resources.

All models of the stress process recognize that a variety of social and psychological moderators can affect the impact of stress on health. In the face of stress, psychosocial resources can reduce the adverse effects of stress on health. Conversely, indicators of psychosocial vulnerability can exacerbate the negative effects of stress on health. Perceptions of mastery or control and self-esteem are generally recognized as important psychological resources for coping with stress (Kessler et al., 1994). Health-enhancing factors that may be resident in minority populations, such as group identity and consciousness, may also affect the association between stress and health. That is, the strength of group identity may be an important psychosocial resource for minority group members (Phinney, 1990; Terrel & Taylor, 1980). For many whites in American society, racial and especially ethnic identification may be optional, contextual, and weak (Eschbach, 1995). In contrast, racial identity is central to the formation of identity for minority group members for whom racial identification frequently becomes incorporated into their view of the self (Omi & Winant, 1986; See & Wilson, 1988).

Recent research has emphasized that racial self-concept and identity is an often neglected resource that can buffer the relationship between stress and health. Keeping their group identity salient could protect members of stigmatized groups from the negative health effects of prejudice and discrimination because it could lead them to blame the larger society, instead of themselves, for their social situation and undesirable outcomes (Crocker & Major, 1989; Neighbors, Jackson, Broman, & Thompson, 1996). A study by Hopper (1993) found that identification with one's ethnicity promoted successful aging in older women and served as an integrating force to help them filter their personal experiences with aging and significant life changes. Dressler (1996) suggests that racism acts as an identity-relevant stressor and found that measures of stressors relevant to the definition of the self were related to blood pressure in a community sample of African Americans. At the same time, an enhanced sense of group identity could increase vulnerability to health problems by reducing motivation to cope with environmental events and conditions attributed to intransigent racist attitudes (Crocker & Major, 1989; Porter & Washington, 1993).

We used data from a major metropolitan area in the United States to examine how race-related stressors combine with traditional measures of stress to affect health status. We examined the relative contribution of acute and chronic experiences of discrimination to health. We also examined the extent to which the health consequences of racial/ethnic discrimination compare to those of bias attributed to belonging to other social categories. We also sought to understand how potential psychosocial resources that capture group identity (racial identity and racial self-concept) relate to health and can buffer or exacerbate the relationship between stress and health. Racial identity refers to the closeness or sense of belonging to one's racial/ethnic group. This closeness may be manifested in one's understanding of one's own group, behavior patterns specific to one's group, and the labels used for one's group. Racial self-concept refers to the importance of one's racial/ethnic group

to one's self-image, or self-concept, which is closely linked to one's attitudes and feelings about one's group, as well as the salience and meaning that one attributes to one's own group. We statistically controlled
the association between group identity and health for our two measures
of self-identity (self-esteem and mastery). Self-esteem refers to an aspect of self-concept that involves judgment about one's own worth and
the feelings associated with those judgments. The Rosenberg (1979)
measure of self-esteem provides a global assessment of self-respect,
self-acceptance, and feelings of worth. Mastery captures the extent to
which people view themselves as having control over the forces that impact their lives (Pearlin, Lieberman, Menaghan, & Mullan, 1981).This
allowed us to see any incremental contribution of group identity net of
these widely recognized, self-related psychosocial resources. In addition, in the absence of longitudinal data, adjustment for self-esteem and
mastery provides a more conservative estimate of the association between perceptions of discrimination and self-reported health. It is plau-
sible that one's underlying psychological state could affect perceptions
of unfair treatment and health. Given that socioeconomic status (SES)
is strongly related to health, as well as to the resources and risk factors
that affect health (Adler et al., 1994; Anderson & Armstead, 1995;
House et al., 1990; Williams, 1990), we sought to understand how
stress and resources combine to affect health net of SES.

Identity and Health in the Detroit Area Study

Methods

The data for our analyses come from the 1995 Detroit Area Study
(DAS). The DAS is a multistage area probability sample consisting of
1,139 adult respondents, eighteen years of age and older, residing in
Wayne, Oakland, and Macomb Counties in Michigan, including the
city of Detroit. Face-to-face interviews were completed between April
and October 1995 by University of Michigan graduate students in a research training practicum in survey research and by professional interviewers from the Survey Research Center. The response rate was 70%.
Race was measured by respondent self-identification. Blacks were over-
sampled, and the final sample included 520 whites, 586 blacks, and 33
Asians, American Indians, and Hispanics. All of the analyses reported in
this chapter use only the black and white respondents.

Measures

Age and gender are sociodemographic control variables used in the
analyses. Marital status was also assessed using a series of dummy varia-

bles for cohabiting (persons who were living with a partner for at least six months), widowed, divorced/separated, never married, and married. All intervally scaled variables were coded in the direction of the variable name so that high scores reflect a high value of the construct.

Two types of discrimination were assessed. First, everyday discrimination was a measure of chronic, routine, and less overt experiences of unfair treatment that was developed for this study (Williams, Yu, Jackson, & Anderson, 1997), based on the qualitative research of Essed (1991) and Feagin (1991). Our scale sums nine items that capture the frequency of the following experiences in day-to-day life: being treated with less courtesy than others, less respect than others, receiving poorer service than others in restaurants or stores; people acting as if you are not smart, they are better than you, they are afraid of you, they think you are dishonest; being called names or insulted and being threatened or harassed (Cronbach's alpha = .88). The second measure, acute experiences of discrimination, is a count of the number of major experiences of unfair treatment that the respondent had. Both blacks and whites indicated whether they had any of the following experiences: (1) "Do you think you have ever been *unfairly* fired or denied a promotion?" (2) "For *unfair* reasons, do you think you have ever not been hired for a job?" (3) "Do you think you have ever been *unfairly* stopped, searched, questioned, physically threatened or abused by the police?" Additionally, black respondents answered the following three questions: (4) "Do you think you have ever been *unfairly* discouraged by a teacher or advisor from continuing your education?" (5) "Do you think you have ever been *unfairly* prevented from moving into a neighborhood because the landlord or realtor refused to see or rent you a house or apartment?" (6) "Have you ever moved into a neighborhood where neighbors made life difficult for you or your family?" Because our pretest data revealed that these latter experiences occurred infrequently among whites, they were not asked of whites in the final questionnaire.

Preliminary analyses revealed the absence of a dose-response relationship between acute discrimination and health. The critical distinction was experiencing any major, unfair treatment versus no such discrimination. Accordingly, acute discrimination was coded as a dichotomous measure in our analyses. In addition, it was also possible to code acute experiences of discrimination in two other ways. For each measure of unfair treatment experienced, the respondent indicated whether the experience had happened in the past 12 months. Thus, we also distinguished past year (recent) experiences of discrimination from earlier lifetime episodes. An additional follow-up question to each discrimination item that was endorsed ascertained the main reason for unfair treatment. Respondents were allowed to select from a list that included ethnicity, gender, race, age, religion, physical appearance, sexual orientation, and income level/social class. We created an additional measure of discrimination by distinguishing unfair treatment attributed to race/ethnicity from discrimination attributed to other social bases.

Three general indicators of stress were utilized. Chronic role-related stress is a count of five problems respondents reported in the previous month with aging parents, children, hassles at work, balancing work and family demands, and spouse or partner. Financial stress refers to the respondent s difficulty in meeting the family s monthly payments as rated on a 5-point scale ranging from extremely difficult to not difficult at all. Life events is a count of seven possible experiences in the year prior to the interview. These include physical attack or assault, robbery or burglary, involuntary retirement, unemployment, a move to a worse residence or neighborhood, serious financial problems, and death of a loved one.

Income and education were measures of SES. Income was measured as total household income in the previous year. A logarithmic transformation of household income was computed and used in the analyses, because the variable was highly skewed. Household size is a count of the number of persons living in the household, ranging from one to six or more. It was included in all analyses that involved income because the meaning of a given level of income is related to the number of persons in the household. Education was divided into four categories that capture meaningful differences in educational credentials: 0–11 years, 12 years, 13–15 years, and 16 or more years.

Two measures were used to assess the strength of group identity. Racial/ethnic identity was a single item that captured the extent to which the respondents indicated that they felt close, in their ideas and feelings, to the group that they had earlier identified as representing their main racial/ethnic background or origin. The 4-point response scale ranged from very close to not close at all. The second item, racial/ethnic self-concept, assessed the extent to which respondents agreed (from strongly agree to strongly disagree) that their ethnic/racial group was an important part of their self-image. The correlation between racial/ethnic identity and racial/ethnic self-concept was .17 for African Americans and .24 for whites. Two measures of self-identity also were utilized. Self-esteem was measured by four items from the Rosenberg (1979) self-esteem scale, and mastery was assessed by four items from the Pearlin mastery scale (Pearlin et al., 1981). The correlation between these two measures was .41 for African Americans and .46 for whites.

Two measures of health status were used as dependent variables: self-reported health and chronic health problems. Self-reported health is a widely used general indicator of health status strongly related to mortality and other objective measures of health (Idler & Benyamini, 1997). It captures a respondent's overall assessment of health as "excellent, very good, good, fair, or poor." Respondents also indicated if a doctor or health professional had ever told them that they had any of the following 14 health problems: high blood pressure, stroke, heart attack or other heart problems, diabetes or high blood "sugar," cancer, arthritis or rheumatism, stomach ulcers, asthma, a liver problem or liver trouble, a kidney problem or kidney trouble, chronic bronchitis or emphysema, a blood circulation problem or hardening of the arteries, sickle cell anemia, or high cholesterol. These conditions represent chronic, ongoing medical problems that may lead to impairment or reduced functioning. Chronic health problems are a count of the number of health conditions reported. The correlation between self-reported health and chronic health problems was -.58 for blacks and -.48 for whites.

Data Analysis

The data were weighted to take into account differential probabilities of selection and to adjust the demographics of the sample to those of the area from which it was drawn. Simple descriptive analyses were used to present racial differences on the independent variables. Ordinary least-squares regression analyses were used to estimate the size and statistical significance of the associations between our independent variables and health status. All analyses were performed separately by race. A series of five nested models for each dependent variable was tested using hierarchical least-squares regression. The first model included the demographic covariates (gender, age, and marital status). Both measures of discrimination were added in the second model. Additional versions of the second model were estimated where alternative codings of the acute experiences of discrimination were utilized. Model three added the three measures of general stress (chronic role-related stress, financial stress, and life events), while the two indicators of SES (income and education) were included in the fourth model.

Socioeconomic status was entered after the stress variables because SES reflects, in part, the differential distribution of stress (Pearlin, 1989; Williams, 1990). Entering SES prior to stress would mask the association between stress and health. In the final model, the two indicators of self-identity (self esteem and mastery) and the two indicators of group identity (racial/ethnic self-concept and racial/ethnic identity) were included. We tested for interactions by creating cross-product terms of the relevant discrimination variable with the relevant identity variable and included the interaction term in the full model that contained all of the other variables. To facilitate the interpretation of the interactions, we standardized all of the variables without an inherently meaningful metric and "centered" each variable by adding a constant to ensure that the lowest value was zero (Cronbach, 1987).

Racial Differences in SES, Stress, and Identity   Table 4.1 presents racial differences on the measures used in the analyses. There were no racial differences for age or gender, but blacks and whites differed significantly on marital status, where blacks were over 1.5 times less likely to be married than whites and more than twice as likely to be divorced or separated. Reports of discrimination and general stress were generally higher for blacks, except for role-related stress where whites had higher levels than blacks. African Americans scored higher on chronic ongoing indicators of everyday discrimination and were significantly more likely to report the lifetime occurrence of discrimination (69.9% to 36.4%). These numbers are not directly comparable because blacks responded to six questions, whites three. If we compare responses to only the three questions asked of both racial groups, 62.3% of African Americans report discrimination compared to 36.4% of whites. Blacks are also almost three times more likely to have experienced discrimination in the last 12 months than whites, and blacks are also more likely to have attributed unfair treatment to race/ethnicity, with blacks reporting a level of racial/ethnic discrimination that is nearly 10 times higher than that reported by whites.

Whereas blacks report less chronic (role-related) stress than whites, levels of financial stress and life events were higher for blacks than for whites. The average score on the life events scale for blacks is nearly twice the average score for whites. Differences in income and educational attainment by race are observed at both ends of the distribution, where blacks were nearly four times more likely to have a total annual income of less than $10,000 and 1.4 times more likely than whites to be in the $10,000 to $29,999 range. Whites, on the other hand, were over 2.5 times more likely to have incomes of over $60,000. African Americans were 1.6 times more likely to have completed less than 12 years of education than whites, and whites were almost twice as likely as blacks to have graduated from college. The distributions for high school completion and some college are comparable for blacks and whites. Blacks had higher average scores on racial self-concept, racial/ethnic identity, and mastery, but blacks and whites did not differ on personal self-esteem. Whites had higher self-rated health than African Americans, but the races did not differ on chronic health problems.

Stress, Identity, and Self-Reported Health   Table 4.2 presents the relationship of stress, SES, and identity, with self-reported health for blacks. The first model shows the relationship between demographic characteristics (gender, age, and marital status) and self-reported health. The subsequent models add the measures of Race-Related Stress (discrimination), General Stress, SES (socioeconomic status), and Self and

TABLE 4.1. Descriptive Statistics by Race (Weighted Means and Percentages)

Variable	Blacks (N=576)	Whites (N=514)
1. Age	42.7	45.0
2. Gender (female)	56.2	52.3
3. Marital status		
a. Cohabiting	5.4	4.6
b. Widowed	10.1	7.8
c. Divorced/separated	15.6	6.7*
d. Never married	30.6	21.3*
e. Married	38.3	59.6*
4. Everyday discrimination (mean)	2.1	1.7*
5. Acute major discrimination		
a. Any lifetime (% yes)	69.9	36.4*
b. Recent versus earlier		
1. No discrimination	30.1	63.6*
2. Recent (past-year) discrimination	31.9	11.8*
3. Earlier discrimination	38.0	24.6*
c. Racial/ethnic versus other		
1. Any racial/ethnic discrimination	50.0	5.5*
2. Other discrimination	19.9	30.9*
6. Role-related stress	0.9	1.1*
7. Financial stress	2.0	1.7*
8. Major–life events stress	1.4	0.9*
9. Household income		
a. $0–9,999	21.3	5.5*
b. $10,000–29,999	32.5	23.4*
c. $30,000–59,999	30.0	29.7
d. $60,000 +	16.2	41.4*
10. Household size	3.1	2.9*
11. Education		
a. 0–11 yrs.	16.7	10.3*
b. 12 yrs.	35.2	31.9
c. 13–15 yrs.	33.1	28.4
d. 16+ yrs.	15.0	29.4*
12. Racial/ethnic self-concept	4.2	2.8*
13. Racial/ethnic identity	4.0	2.9*
14. Self-esteem	3.9	3.8
15. Mastery	3.4	3.3*
16. Self-rated health	3.4	3.7*
17. Chronic health problems	1.4	1.4

* = p < .05

TABLE 4.2. Unstandardized Regression Coefficients for the Association of
Stress, Identity, and SES with Self-Reported Health for Blacks

Independent Variables	Regression Model				
	1 Demo-graphic	2 Race-Related Stress	3 General Stress	4 SES	5 Self & Group Identity
Demographics					
1. Age	-.03***	-.03***	-.03***	-.03***	-.02***
2. Gender (female)	-.15	-.18+	-.14	-.16+	-.16+
3. Marital status					
a. Cohabitating	-.30	-.28	-.18	-.15	-.15
b. Widowed	.06	.08	.14	.17	.13
c. Divorced/separated	-.03	-.02	.03	.01	.01
d. Never married	-.07	-.06	.05	.08	.08
e. Married (omitted)					
Discrimination					
4. Chronic everyday		-.21**	-.14*	-.16*	-.12+
5. Acute major experiences					
a. One or more		.05	.13	.08	.06
b. None (omitted)					
General Stress					
6. Role-related stress			.04	.03	.04
7. Financial stress			-.12**	-.10*	-.07+
8. Major–life events stress			-.19***	-.16***	-.16***
Socioeconomic Status					
9. Household income (log)				.12	.05
10. Household size				-.02	-.02
11. Education					
a. 0–11 yrs.				.57***	-.52***
b. 12 yrs.				-.30*	-.25+
c. 13–15 yrs.				-.15	-.15
d. 16+ (omitted)					
Self and Group Identity					
12. Racial/ethnic identity					.01
13. Racial/ethnic self-concept					.07*
14. Self-esteem					.26+
15. Mastery					.19*
Constant	4.58	5.12	5.32	5.02	3.14
R^2	.13	.15	.22	.25	.27
R^2 Change		.02**	.08***	.03***	.02**

$+ = p \le .10$ $* = p \le .05$ $** = p \le .01$ $*** = p \le .001$

Group Identity. As expected, age was inversely related to self-reported health, and there was a marginally significant tendency, evident once the measures of stress were considered, for African American women to report poorer health than their male counterparts ($b = -.18$; $p < .10$). The second model shows that only one discrimination measure was associated with self-reported health. There was an inverse relationship between everyday discrimination and health. In contrast, acute experiences of discrimination, the most commonly used type of measure in prior research, was unrelated to health status. Removing everyday discrimination from the second model did not change the relationship between acute discrimination and self-reported health. Consideration of the discrimination measures made a small but significant incremental contribution to explained variance. In analyses not shown, we explored the association of self-reported health status with alternative ways of coding acute experiences of discrimination. Acute experiences of discrimination remained unrelated to health status when we (1) distinguished past year from earlier experiences of discrimination and (2) distinguished race-attributed experiences of discrimination from those not linked to race or ethnicity.

The third model shows the contribution of general measures of stress to self-reported health. The addition of these stress variables increased the explained variance by 8%. Role-related stress was unrelated to self-reported health, but both financial stress and major life events were inversely related to self-reported health status. However, the coefficient for everyday discrimination was reduced by a third, but remained significant, when adjusted for general indicators of stress, suggesting potentially substantial overlap between race-related stress and general measures of stress.

In the third model (SES), the addition of the socioeconomic variables made an incremental contribution of 3% to explained variance, but only education was related to self-reported health for blacks. Compared to college graduates, persons who had completed 12 years of education or less reported poorer health status. Consideration of SES reduced modestly the association of financial stress and life events with health but increased the relationship of everyday discrimination with health.

The final model considered the incremental contribution of the self and group identity variables to the global self-evaluation of health status. Overall consideration of self and group identity produced a small but significant 2% increase in the explained variance. For the group identity measures, racial identity was unrelated to health, but racial self-concept was positively related to self-reported health. Both of the self-identity variables were positively related to self-reported health. African Americans who reported higher levels of self-esteem (marginally significant) and higher levels of mastery also reported better health status. The self and group identity variables appear to play a small mediating role for the association of self-reported health with several other variables in the final model. The coefficients for everyday discrimination, financial stress, and SES were reduced modestly when the self and group identity variables were considered. However, the association between life events and health was unchanged when adjusted for the identity variables.

Table 4.3 shows the findings for the association between demographic variables, stress (race-related and general), SES, and identity with self-reported health for whites. Similar to the pattern observed for blacks, age was inversely related to self-reported health for whites. Unlike the pattern for African Americans, gender was unrelated to health status for whites, but marital status was associated with self-reported health. Compared to the married respondents, those who were divorced/separated and in cohabiting relationships (marginally significant) tended to report lower levels of health. These associations were reduced substantially, but remained significant, when general measures of stress were considered. However, they were reduced to nonsignificance when adjusted for SES. The coefficient for the widowed is increased in each successive model, such that there was a marginally significant tendency for widowed individuals to report better health status than the married ones in the final model when all the predictors were considered simultaneously.

Both chronic and acute discrimination were unrelated to health for whites, unlike blacks. Additionally, no relationship was found between alternative codings of acute experiences of discrimination and self-reported health for whites. However, the association of the general measures of stress to self-reported health for whites was similar to that observed for blacks. Both financial stress and life events were inversely related to self-reported health, but chronic stress was unrelated to health status. The addition of the stress variables increased the explained variance by 5%. Both income and education were positively related to self-reported health for whites, but not blacks. Although education was positively related to health for whites, the pattern of association differed somewhat to that for blacks. Among African Americans, there was a strong graded relationship, with levels of health increasing with each higher level of education and with the lowest education category markedly different than the excluded category. For whites, college graduates reported better health than those with less education, but the differences among the three lower levels of education were not marked. For both blacks and whites, consideration of SES reduced the association of health with both measures of financial stress and life events. Consideration of the SES variables made an incremental 5% contribution to explained variance.

TABLE 4.3. Unstandardized Regression Coefficients for the Association of Stress, Identity, and SES with Self-Reported Health for Whites

	Regression Model				
	1	2 Race-Related Stress	3 General Stress	4	5 Self & Group Identity
Independent Variables	Demo-graphic	Race-Related Stress	General Stress	SES	Self & Group Identity
Demographics					
1. Age	-.02***	-.02***	-.02***	-.02***	-.02***
2. Gender (female)	-.00	-.02	-.01	.06	.08
3. Marital status					
a. Cohabitating	-.39+	-.37+	-.29	-.18	-.23
b. Widowed	.02	.03	.14	.29	.30+
c. Divorced/separated	-.56***	-.54**	-.35*	-.27	-.23
d. Never married	-.11	-.11	-.03	.03	.05
e. Married (omitted)					
Discrimination					
4. Chronic everyday		-.06	-.02	-.01	.04
5. Acute major experiences					
a. One or more		-.06	.01	-.03	-.03
b. None (omitted)					
General Stress					
6. Role-related stress			.03	-.01	.01
7. Financial stress			-.15**	-.09+	-.07
8. Major–life events stress			-.16***	-.13**	-.14**
Socioeconomic Status					
9. Household income (log)				.44***	.37**
10. Household size				-.01	-.01
11. Education					
a. 0–11 yrs.				-.33*	-.30+
b. 12 yrs.				-.31**	-.28**
c. 13–15 yrs.				-.25*	-.23*
d. 16+ (omitted)					
Self and Group Identity					
12. Racial/ethnic identity					-.02
13. Racial/ethnic self-concept					.01
14. Self-esteem					.21+
15. Mastery					.25**
Constant	4.54	4.73	4.97	2.97	1.37
R^2	.12	.12	.17	.21	.24
R^2 Change		.00	.05***	.05***	.03**

+ = $p \le .10$ * = $p \le .05$ ** = $p \le .01$ *** = $p \le .001$

The final model shows that both self-esteem and mastery tended to be positively related to self-reported health for whites. However, the group identity variables were not related to health for whites. As in the pattern observed for African Americans, the self-identity variables appear to play a mediating role for the association between both chronic stress and SES with self-reported health. When adjusted for the identity variables, the coefficients for financial stress, income, and education were all modestly reduced. The variables included in the final model accounted for 24% of the variance for whites (compared to 27% for blacks) with the identity variables accounting for an incremental 3% of the variance.

Stress, Identity, and Chronic Health Problems   Table 4.4 presents the findings for the association between demographic variables, stress, SES, and identity with chronic health problems for blacks. Overall, the patterns of relationships are similar to those found for self-reported health, with a few interesting exceptions. Age is the only demographic variable that showed a clear and consistent association with health problems. Older African Americans reported more chronic health problems than their younger peers. Unlike the self-reported health pattern in Table 4.2, Table 4.4 shows that both everyday discrimination (marginally significant) and acute experiences of discrimination were significantly related to chronic health problems. The addition of discrimination made a significant incremental contribution of 2% to the model that considered only the demographic variables. However, the association between everyday discrimination was reduced to nonsignificance when adjusted for the general stress variables. In contrast, the measure of acute experiences of discrimination was reduced by about one third, but remained marginally significant, when adjusted for other types of stress.

In analyses not shown, both race-attributed and other discriminations were significantly related to chronic health problems, with the size of the coefficient being fairly similar for both (.40 for race/ethnic attributed and .44 for other discrimination compared to those who did not experience discrimination). Both coefficients were reduced somewhat when adjusted for general measures of stress but remained marginally significant in the final model when all of the variables are considered. In addition, when experiences of discrimination were categorized into past-year experiences and earlier lifetime experiences, both of them were significantly related to chronic health problems. However, adjustment for the general measures of stress reduced the association between past-year discrimination and chronic health problems to nonsignificance, whereas the association between earlier lifetime discrimination and chronic health problems was reduced some-

TABLE 4.4. Unstandardized Regression Coefficients for the Association of Stress, Identity, and SES with Chronic Health Problems for Blacks

Independent Variables	Regression Model				
	1 Demo- graphic	2 Race- Related Stress	3 General Stress	4 SES	5 Self & Group Identity
Demographics					
1. Age	.05***	.06***	.06***	.06***	.06***
2. Gender (female)	.14	.22+	.15	.10	.09
3. Marital status					
a. Cohabitating	.02	.09	-.07	-.07	-.06
b. Widowed	-.25	-.19	-.24	-.25	-.21
c. Divorced/separated	.18	.14	.06	.09	.09
d. Never married	.22	.23	.13	.12	.11
e. Married (omitted)					
Discrimination					
4. Chronic everyday		.18+	.04	.04	-.01
5. Acute major experiences					
a. One or more		.36*	.24+	.25+	.27+
b. None (omitted)					
General Stress					
6. Role-related stress			.03	.03	.02
7. Financial stress			.21***	.19**	.17**
8. Major–life events stress			.25***	.24***	.23***
Socioeconomic Status					
9. Household income (log)				-.17	-.11
10. Household size				.05	.05
11. Education					
a. 0–11 yrs.				-.01	-.05
b. 12 yrs.				-.02	-.07
c. 13–15 yrs.				-.03	-.03
d. 16+ (omitted)					
Self and Group Identity					
12. Racial/ethnic identity					.03
13. Racial/ethnic self-concept					-.02
14. Self-esteem					-.16
15. Mastery					-.24+
Constant	-1.03	-1.92	-2.28	-1.68	-.29
R^2	.23	.25	.33	.33	.34
R^2 Change		.02***	.08***	.01	.01

$+ = p \leq .10$ $* = p \leq .05$ $** = p \leq .01$ $*** = p \leq .001$

what, but remained significant, when adjusted for the general measures of stress. Given that the onset of many of the chronic conditions likely occurred years prior to the interview, this pattern of association is consistent with a causal impact for the association of discrimination with health.

Like self-reported health, chronic role-related stress was not associated with health problems for blacks. However, there was a strong positive relationship between chronic health problems and both financial stress and life events. The addition of the stress variables made an incremental 8% contribution to explained variance. The socioeconomic variables did not make an incremental contribution to explained variance, with neither income nor education related to the number of health problems for blacks. Similarly, as main effects, the self and group identity variables made little contribution to understanding variations in chronic health problems for African Americans. Neither of the group identity variables was related to chronic health problems, and for the self-identity variables, there was only a marginally significant inverse relationship between mastery and chronic health problems.

Similar models for chronic health problems are presented for whites in Table 4.5. As noted in Table 4.3 for self-reported health, age was positively related to chronic health problems and both the divorced/separated and cohabiting persons tended to experience poorer health than the married. Both measures of discrimination were unrelated to chronic health problems for whites, but financial stress and life events were both positively related to the number of chronic health problems. These general stress variables contributed an incremental 4% to explained variance. The association between SES and chronic health problems was weaker than that reported for self-reported health. Income was unrelated to health problems, and whites who had graduated from high school and had attended college (marginally significant) tended to have more chronic health problems than college graduates. Interestingly, whites who had less than 12 years of education did not differ from college graduates in the number of chronic health problems reported. However, consideration of the SES variables did not meaningfully alter the association between stress and health status, although the addition of the SES variables significantly increased the explained variance by 2%.

Self and group identity variables for whites, like blacks, manifested few associations with chronic health problems. Neither self-esteem nor mastery were significantly related to chronic health problems, and there was a marginally significant inverse relationship between racial/ethnic self-concept and chronic health problems for whites. Overall, the addition of the self and group identity variables had little impact on the stress or SES variables. One intriguing exception is that the inverse association between everyday discrimination and health problems be-

TABLE 4.5. Unstandardized Regression Coefficients for the Association of Stress, Identity, and SES with Chronic Health Problems for Whites

Independent Variables	Regression Model				
	1 Demographic	2 Race-Related Stress	3 General Stress	4 SES	5 Self & Group Identity
Demographics					
1. Age	.05***	.05***	.05***	.05***	.05***
2. Gender (female)	.19	.20	.17	.10	.09
3. Marital status					
a. Cohabitating	.67*	.64*	.51+	.41	.43
b. Widowed	-.13	-.13	-.28	-.40	-.43
c. Divorced/separated	1.07***	1.06***	.76**	.68**	.62*
d. Never married	.22	.22	.14	.10	.06
e. Married (omitted)					
Discrimination					
4. Chronic everyday		-.03	-.12	-.16	-.19+
5. Acute major experiences					
a. One or more		.15	.03	-.01	-.01
b. None (omitted)					
General Stress					
6. Role-related stress			.01	.05	.03
7. Financial stress			.22**	.24**	.23**
8. Major–life events stress			.27***	.24***	.24***
Socioeconomic Status					
9. Household income (log)				-.13	-.07
10. Household size				-.05	-.06
11. Education					
a. 0–11 yrs.				-.09	-.08
b. 12 yrs.				-.52**	.50**
c. 13–15 yrs.				.28+	.27+
d. 16+ (omitted)					
Self and Group Identity					
12. Racial/ethnic identity					.06
13. Racial/ethnic self-concept				-.07+	
14. Self-esteem					-.19
15. Mastery					-.11
Constant	-1.13	-1.15	-1.55	-.88	.21
R^2	.31	.31	.35	.37	.38
R^2 Change		.00	.04***	.02**	.01

+ = $p \leq .10$ * = $p \leq .05$ ** = $p \leq .01$ *** = $p \leq .001$

came marginally significant when adjusted for the self and group identity variables. That is, when all the variables were considered, whites with higher levels of chronic discrimination tended to have fewer health problems.

Buffering Effects of Identity   We systematically evaluated the extent to which the group identity variables might buffer or exacerbate the relationship between perceived discrimination and health. We created multiplicative interaction terms between measures of discrimination and measures of identity. These interaction terms were added to a model that included the demographic variables, discrimination, SES, and the identity variables. We first describe the findings for self-reported health for African Americans. There were no significant interaction relationships between racial/ethnic identity and the discrimination measures. The interaction between racial self-concept and everyday discrimination was not significant, but there was a marginally significant interaction between acute experiences of discrimination and racial self-concept for blacks. The pattern of the interaction was consistent with that of a classic buffering effect. At low levels of racial self-concept, persons who had experienced discrimination reported poorer health status than those with no discriminatory experiences. However, as racial self-concept increased, the negative association of discrimination on self-reported health decreased.

For chronic health problems, there were no significant interactions between racial/ethnic self-concept and the measures of discrimination for blacks. In contrast, significant interaction effects existed for both measures of discrimination and racial/ethnic identity in predicting levels of chronic health problems. The patterns of the interaction were also consistent with that of a buffering effect. At low levels of racial/ethnic identity, discrimination was positively related to chronic health problems, but as racial/ethnic identity increased, the adverse relationship between discrimination and chronic health problems decreased. Figure 4.1 depicts this relationship for the major experiences of discrimination. It clearly shows that the effect of discrimination on chronic health problems declined as racial identity increased. It indicates that when racial identity is low, black individuals who experienced discrimination were over twice as likely to have chronic health problems as individuals who reported no discrimination. This effect appears to level off as levels of racial identity increased. A similar pattern of association existed for race-attributed discrimination.

These interactions of discrimination and identity suggest that, at least for African Americans, racial identity and racial self-concept may each act independently as resources for different health outcomes. Racial/ethnic identity appears to act as a resource for chronic physical

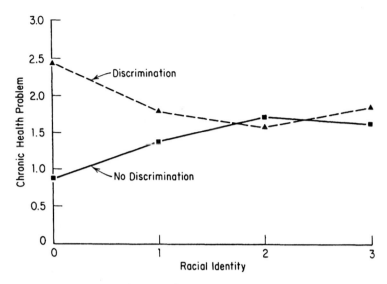

FIGURE 4.1. Interaction between discrimination and racial identity for chronic health problems among blacks.

health, while racial self-concept tends to act as a buffer for the more subjective global measure of physical health status.

For whites, there were no significant interactions between the acute discrimination measure and racial/ethnic self-concept or racial/ethnic identity in predicting self-reported health. There was one marginally significant relationship between everyday discrimination and racial self-concept in predicting self-reported health for whites, but the pattern was opposite to that observed for African Americans. At low levels of racial self-concept, everyday discrimination was positively related to health. However, this health-enhancing relationship was reduced as racial self-concept increased. Thus, racial/ethnic self-concept exacerbated the association between everyday discrimination and self-reported health. There were no significant interactive relationships between either racial/ethnic identity or racial/ethnic self-concept with measures of discrimination in predicting levels of chronic health problems for whites.

Summary and Discussion

Our findings underscore the importance of stress as a risk factor for physical health problems for both African Americans and whites. African Americans reported higher levels of financial stress and major life events than whites and also were more likely to be exposed to both acute and chronic experiences of discrimination. Financial stress and life events were more robust in predicting the health outcomes considered here than our measures of discrimination for both blacks and whites. However, discrimination was unrelated to health for whites, whereas it made an incremental contribution to variations in health status for African Americans. Our data also suggest that acute and chronic experiences of discrimination display distinctive patterns of association with different health outcomes. Whereas chronic discrimination tended to be related to global self-reports of health, acute experiences of discrimination, especially distal ones, were adversely related to chronic health conditions. Acute discrimination captures major events of discrimination that could directly affect SES (e.g., job loss) and physical health. Everyday discrimination in the form of minor recurring experiences that are similar to daily hassles was strongly related to the health status measure that had a strong evaluative component (global self-assessed health). These analyses suggest that discrimination is multifaceted rather than homogeneous, and they highlight the need to give more concerted and sustained attention to the development and empirical validation of measures that seek to capture exposure to racial bias comprehensively across a large number of domains of social interaction (McNeilly et al., 1996).

Our analyses also demonstrate that measures of both self and group identity matter in terms of understanding the distribution of physical health problems for both blacks and whites. Recent research suggests that the importance of ethnic identity is waning for whites (Alba, 1990), and our data show that whites scored lower than African Americans on both racial/ethnic identity and racial/ethnic self-concept. Moreover, these variables tended to be inconsequential in either mediating or moderating the impact of discrimination on health for whites. However, these results do not imply that it is unimportant to study the association between discrimination and health for whites. Although we found no association between discrimination and our measures of physical health, other analyses of these data indicate that these same measures of discrimination are importantly related to the mental health of whites. For example, chronic discrimination was more adversely related to the psychological well-being of whites than of blacks (Williams et al., 1997). Thus, future research needs to identify the mechanisms and processes by which perceptions of unfair treatment are differentially related to particular health outcomes for whites.

For African Americans, racial self-concept was positively related to self-reported health and tended to buffer the relationship (albeit marginally) between discrimination and the measure of physical health status that had a psychological component (self-reported health). Racial/ethnic identity, on the other hand, clearly protected African Americans from some of the adverse effects of both types of discrimination on health problems. Identity has more to do with closeness to one's racial/ethnic group, whereas racial/ethnic self-concept measures the importance of group identity to one's self-image. Racial/ethnic self-concept may differ from racial/ethnic identity in its emphasis on the salience and centrality of one's racial group to the self, which, in turn, can affect how one feels about one's health. Closeness to one's racial/ethnic group, on the other hand, appeared to reduce the likelihood of major health problems. Closeness may be more related to behaviors, norms, and social networks that promote healthy outcomes. For African Americans, a parallel pattern was evident, in terms of main effects, for the self-esteem and racial/ethnic self-concept measures. Both self-esteem and racial/ethnic self-concept tended to be related to self-reported health but not to chronic health problems.

There are several limitations to our analyses. First, our use of cross-sectional data precludes any attempt to address the causal direction of the observed associations. Second, the measures of discrimination were based on the perception of the respondent. This is a generic problem in the measurement of stress, although, in our experience, this criticism is raised more frequently regarding the assessment of discrimination than the assessment of general measures of stress. Considerable evidence suggests that experiences of bias are ubiquitous in our society and the social distribution of unfair treatment is not random (Jaynes & Williams, 1989). In addition, some limited experimental data indicate that personal reports of discrimination are consistent with objective experiences (Taylor et al., 1994; Taylor et al., 1991). At the same time, strategies that have been developed to enhance the reliability and validity of the measurement of stress (Cohen, Kessler, & Gordon, 1995) should also be utilized in future studies of discrimination. It should also be recognized that at least some victims of discrimination are unlikely to report their experiences of bias (Crosby, 1984; Krieger & Sidney, 1996). Future research should also seek to determine the extent to which denial occurs and to identify its causes and consequences.

A third limitation of our analyses is the assessment of health status. Both of our measures were based on self-report and are fairly global. The mechanisms and processes linking psychosocial factors (such as stress, discrimination, and identity) to changes in health status may vary by disease outcome. Future research must give more attention to objectively measured, specific disease entities.

A final major limitation of our analyses is the measurement of group identity. Although we utilized two indicators of group identity that were not strongly related to each other, both of our measures were based on a single item. There is growing awareness that racial identity is a complex multidimensional phenomenon (Phinney, 1990; Thompson, 1991; Sellers, Rowley, Chavous, Shelton, & Smith, 1997; Sellers, Smith, Shelton, Rowley, & Chavous, 1998).

A Research Agenda

Future research must pay more attention to how discrimination combines with other stressors in additive or interactive ways to affect health outcomes. A given stressful discriminatory experience must be understood in the light of ongoing stress, since the presence of baseline levels of stress can potentially exacerbate the health consequences of race-related stress. For example, the stress literature indicates that life events can affect health by creating new chronic strains or by changing the meaning of existing strains (Pearlin et al., 1981; Wheaton, 1990). It is currently not known whether race-related stressors affect health through a stress accumulation effect in which two types of stressors operate additively, or through a stress overload effect, in which other ongoing problems exacerbate the effect of new stressful experiences. Identifying these underlying processes may not be simple. The stress literature also recognizes that many stressors measured and summed as discrete events can be intrinsically related (Monroe & McQuaid, 1994). For example, losing one's job because of one's race can lead to financial stress and having to move to a worse neighborhood. Accordingly, the stress of racial discrimination may overlap with and trigger other stressors that at face value may not appear to be race-related. Thus, future research should collect additional information to appropriately contextualize and characterize race-related stressors so that we can understand how they relate to other kinds of stressful experiences to affect health.

Our findings suggest that group identity may be an important resource that buffers the health of African Americans from some of the negative consequences of exposure to discrimination. The literature has suggested other potential resources. African Americans are arguably the most religious population subgroup in the industrialized world, and it has been suggested that both personal religious involvement and tangible support provided by religious organizations may shield this population from some of the adverse consequences of stress (Williams, 1996a). John Henryism (a predisposition to cope actively with stress) is another psychosocial resource that deserves further study (James, 1994). It appears to be unrelated to blood pressure for whites but acts to increase blood pressure among low SES blacks and decrease blood pressure among their higher SES counterparts. Research on John Henryism highlights the importance of attending to the ways in which individual dispositions and their consequences are shaped by the larger social context. Future research must seek to identify the full range of race-related resources and risk factors and assess how they relate to each other and combine to affect health over the life course. What is needed at this time is research that seeks to identify the ways in which personal and group identity relate to each other and combine with other psychosocial risk factors and resources, including race-related ones, to affect processes of adaptation and functioning.

Our findings also highlight the need for more attention to understanding how identity affects health. There is lack of a clear conceptual framework or specification of pathways through which identity moderates the relationship between race-related stress and physical health. Crocker and Major (1989) describe how identification with a stigmatized group can lead to potential self-protective processes for psychological functioning. However, these researchers do not explicitly address how racism influences these processes. Moreover, research on identity and physical health is scarce. Research is now needed that would bridge these areas by integrating theories of stress, coping, and adaptation with those that address the role of identity in stigmatized groups.

A model for children's health, proposed recently by Williams-Morris (1996), outlines potential mechanisms by which racism and identity can affect health. In this model, racism is a social stimulus that an individual must process and interpret. Once the stimulus is processed, a response is elicited. The ability to process racism is affected by one's sense of self and acceptance of one's racial identity, which, in turn, reflects one's interpersonal and social interactions and one's physical, mental, spiritual, social, and economic resources. This interplay of person and situation shapes the response, which may be proactive, adaptive, and effective, or reactive and maladaptive. Maladaptive behavioral responses, including the internalization of hate and anger, becoming depressed, or lashing out in aggressive and violent ways, may directly affect one's physical health. Indirectly, racist assaults on one's sense of self-worth, and the values and beliefs tied to one's group membership, can increase the amount of stress one must endure, which can also affect physical health status.

To understand the extent to which identity may be a resource or a vulnerability requires the appropriate conceptualization and measurement of all the relevant dimensions of identity (Sellers et al., 1998). Some individuals could score high on some aspects of identity but low on other aspects of group identity. A recent study by Herd and Grube (1996) illustrates the importance of this approach. They found that some aspects of racial group identity led to reduced consumption of alcohol, while other aspects led to increased drinking behavior. Specifically, greater identification and involvement with blacks' social networks (in church, with friends, and in the neighborhood), and blacks' social and political involvement (importance attached to black culture in daily life, participating in organizations for black advancement, and reading black newspapers and magazines) protected individuals from heavy drinking. At the same time, African Americans who identified with and showed a stronger preference for black popular media (music, radio, and television) consumed alcohol at higher levels. This latter effect may be due to the fact that alcohol and tobacco are heavily promoted in black-oriented media and advertising. Nonetheless, it highlights the importance of the multidimensional measurement of group identity and the systematic exploration of the extent to which different components might differentially influence health behaviors and health status. Further articulation of all of identity's dimensions and its potential buffering effect on race-related stress holds great promise for research and innovative interventions that seek to promote African American health and well-being.

Acknowledgements: The research reported here was carried out with support from the University of Michigan and NIMH grant 1 RO1 MH47182. Preparation of this report was also supported by NIMH grant 1 RO1 MH57425, and the John D. and Catherine T. MacArthur Foundation Research Network on Socioeconomic Status and Health.

References

Adler, N. E., Boyce, T., Chesney, M. A., Cohen, S., Folkman, S. et al. (1994). Socioeconomic status and health: The challenge of the gradient. *American Psychologist, 49,* 15–24.

Alba, R. D. (1990). Ethnic identity: The transformation of white America. New Haven: Yale University Press.

Amaro, H., Russo, N. F., & Johnson, J. (1987). Family and work predictors of psychological well-being among Hispanic women professionals. *Psychology of Women Quarterly, 11,* 505–521.

Anderson, N. B. (1989). Racial differences in stress-induced cardiovascular reactivity and hypertension: Current status and substantive issues. *Psychological Bulletin, 105,* 89-105.

Anderson, N. B., & Armstead, C. A. (1995). Toward understanding the association of socioeconomic status and health: A new challenge for the biopsychosocial approach. *Psychosomatic Medicine, 57,* 213–225.

Armstead, C., Lawler, K., Gordon, G., Cross, J., & Gibbons, J. (1989). Relationship of racial stressors to blood pressure responses and anger expression in black college students. *Health Psychology, 8,* 541–556.

Broman, C. L. (1996). The health consequences of racial discrimination: A study of African Americans. *Ethnicity and Disease, 6*(1,2), 148–153.

Cohen, S., Kessler, R. C., & Underwood, L. G. (1995). *Measuring stress.* New York: Oxford University Press.

Cooper, R. S. (1993). Health and the social status of blacks in the United States. *Annals of Epidemiology, 3,* 137–144.

Cooper, R. S., & David, R. (1986). The biological concept of race and its application to public health and epidemiology. *Journal of Health and Politics, Policy and Law, 11,* 97–116.

Cooper, R. S., Steinhauer, M., Schatzkin, A., & Miller, W. (1981). Improved mortality among U.S. blacks, 1968–1978: The role of antiracist struggle. *International Journal of Health Services, 11,* 511–522.

Crocker, J., & Major, B. (1989). Social stigma and self–esteem: The self-protective properties of stigma. *Psychological Review, 96,* 608–630.

Cronbach, L. (1987). Statistical tests for moderator variables: Flaws in analysis recently proposed. *Psychological Bulletin, 102,* 412–417.

Crosby, F. (1984). The denial of personal discrimination. *American Behavioral Scientist, 27*(3), 371–386.

Dion, K. L., Dion, K. K., & Pak, A. W. (1992). Personality-based hardiness as a buffer for discrimination-related stress in members of Toronto's Chinese community. *Canadian Journal of Behavioral Science, 24*(4), 517–536.

Dressler, W. W. (1993). Health in the African American community: Accounting for health inequalities. *Medical Anthropology Quarterly, 7,* 325–345.

Dressler, W. W. (1996). Social identity and arterial blood pressure in the African-American community. *Ethnicity and Disease, 6,* 176–190.

Eschbach, K. (1995). The enduring and vanishing American Indian: American Indian population growth and intermarriage in 1990. *Ethnic Racial Studies, 18,* 89–108.

Essed, P. (1991). *Understanding everyday racism.* Knobbier Park, CA: Sage.

Feagin, J. R. (1991). The continuing significance of race: Antiblack discrimination in public places. *American Sociological Review, 56,* 101–116.

Gould, S. J. (1977). Why we should not name human races. A biological view. In S. J. Gould (ed.), *Ever Since Darwin,* (pp. 231–236). New York: Norton.

Hannah, T. E. (1974). The behavioral consequences of arbitrary discrimination. *Journal of Social Psychology, 93* 107–118.

Harburg, E., Erfurt, J. C., Huenstein, L. S., Chape, C., Schull, W. J., & Schork, M. A. (1973). Socio-ecological stress, suppressed hostility, skin color, and black-white male blood pressure: Detroit. *Psychosomatic Medicine, 35,* 276–296.

Herd, D., & Grube, J. (1996). Black identity and drinking in the U.S.: A national study. *Addiction, 91,* 845–857.

Hopper, S. V. (1993). The influence of ethnicity on the health of older women. *Clinical Geriatric Medicine, 9,* 231–259.

House, J. S., Kessler, R. C., Herzog, A. R., Mero, R., Kinney, A., & Breslow, M. (1990). Age, socioeconomic status, and health. *Milbank Quarterly, 68,* 383–411.

Hummer, R. A. (1996). Black-white differences in health and mortality: A review and conceptual model. *Sociological Quarterly, 37*(1), 105–125.

Idler, E. L., & Benyamini, Y. (1997). Self-rated health and mortality: A review of twenty-seven community studies. *Journal of Health and Social Behavior, 38,* 21–37.

Jackson, J. S., Brown, T. N., Williams, D. R., Torres, M., Sellers, S. L., & Brown, K. (1996). Racism and the physical and mental health status of

African Americans: A thirteen year national panel study. *Ethnicity and Disease*, *6*(1,2), 132–147.

Jackson, J. S., Williams, D. R., & Torres, M. (1995). *Perceptions of discrimination: The stress process and physical and psychological health*. Presentation at Workshop on Social Stressors, Personal and Social Resources and Their Mental Health Consequences. Office of Disease Prevention and Special Projects. Rockville, MD: NIMH, August 17–19.

James, S. A. (1994). John Henryism and the health of African Americans. *Culture of Medicine and Psychiatry*, *18*, 163–182.

James, S. A., LaCroix, A. Z., Kleinbaum, D. G., & Strogatz, D. S. (1984). John Henryism and blood pressure differences among black men, II. The role of occupational stressors. *Journal of Behavioral Medicine*, *7*, 259–275.

Jaynes, G. D., & Williams, R. M. (1989). *A common destiny: Blacks and American society*. Washington, DC: National Academy Press.

Jones, D. R., Harrell, J. P., Morris-Prather, C. E., Thomas, J., and Omowale, N. (1996). Affective and physiological responses to racism: The roles of Afrocentrism and mode of presentation. *Ethnicity and Disease*, *6*(1,2), 109–122.

Kaufman, J. S., & Cooper, R. S. (1995). In search of the hypothesis. *Public Health Reports*, *110*, 662–666.

Kessler, R. C. (1979). Stress, social status, and psychological distress. *Journal of Health and Social Behavior*, *20*, 259–273.

Kessler, R. C., McGonagle, K. A., Zhao, S., Nelson, C. B., Hughes, M., Eshleman, S., Wittchen, H., & Kendler, K. S. (1994). Lifetime and 12-month prevalence of DSM-III-R psychiatric disorders in the United States. *Archives of General Psychiatry*, *51*, 8–19.

King, G., & Williams, D. R. (1995). Race and health: A multidimensional approach to African American health. In B. C. Amick, S. Levine, D. C. Walsh, & A. R. Tarlov (Eds.), *Society and Health* (pp. 93–130). New York: Oxford University Press.

Krieger, N. (1987). Shades of difference: Theoretical underpinnings of the medical controversy on black/white differences in the United States, 1830–1870. *International Journal of Health Services*, *17*, 259–278.

Krieger, N. (1990). Racial and gender discrimination: Risk factors for high blood pressure? *Social Science and Medicine*, *30*(12), 1273–1281.

Krieger, N., Rowley, D. L., Herman, A. A., Avery, B., & Phillips, M. T. (1993). Racism, sexism, and social class: Implications for studies of health, disease, and well-being. *American Journal of Preventive Medicine*, *9*(6 suppl), 82–122.

Krieger, N., & Sidney, S. (1996). Racial discrimination and blood pressure: The CARDIA study of young black and white women and men. *American Journal of Public Health*, *86*, 1370–1378.

LaVeist, T. A. (1996). Why we should continue to study race . . . but do a better job: An essay on race, racism and health. *Ethnicity and Disease*, *6*(1,2), 21–29.

Lepore, S. J. (1995). Measurement of chronic stressors. In S. C. Cohen, R. C. Kessler, & L. U. Gordon (Eds.), *Measuring stress: A guide for health and social scientists*, (pp. 102–120). New York: Oxford University Press.

Lewontin, R. C. (1972). The apportionment of human diversity. In T.

Dobzhansky, M. K. Hecht, & W. C. Steere (Eds.), *Evolutionary biology* (Vol. 6, pp. 381–386). New York: Appleton-Century-Crofts.

McLean, D. E., & Link, B. G. (1994). Unraveling complexity: Strategies to refine concepts, measures, and research designs in the study of life events and mental health. In W. R. Avison & I. H. Gotlib (Eds.), *Stress and mental health: Contemporary issues and prospects for the future* (pp. 15–42). New York: Plenum.

McNeilly, M. D., Anderson, N. B., Armstead, C. A., Clark, R., Corbett, M., Robinson, E. L., Piper, C. F., & Lepisto, E. M. (1996). The perceived racism scale: A multidimensional assessment of the experience of white racism among African Americans. *Ethnicity and Disease, 6*(1,2), 154–166.

Monroe, S. M., & McQuaid, J. R. (1994). Measuring life stress and assessing its impact on mental health. In W. R. Avison & I. H. Gotlib (Eds.), *Stress and mental health: Contemporary issues and prospects for the future* (pp. 43–73). New York: Plenum.

Morris-Prather, C. E., Harrell, J. P., Collins, R., Leonard, K. L. J., Boss, M., & Lee, J. W. (1996). Gender differences in mood and cardiovascular responses to socially stressful stimuli. *Ethnicity and Disease, 6*(1,2), 123–131.

National Center for Health Statistics. (1994). *Health, United States 1993.* Hyattsville, MD: United States Department of Health and Human Services.

Neighbors, H. W., Jackson, J. S., Broman, C., & Thompson, E. (1996). Racism and the mental health of African-Americans: The role of self and system blame. *Ethnicity and Disease, 6*, 167–175.

Omi, M., & Winant, H. (1986). *Racial formation in the United States: From the 1960s to the 1980s.* New York: Routledge.

Pearlin, L. I. (1989). The sociological study of stress. *Journal of Health and Social Behavior, 30*, 241–256.

Pearlin, L., Lieberman, M., Menaghan, E., & Mullan, J. (1981). The stress process. *Journal of Health and Social Behavior, 22*, 337–356.

Phinney, J. S. (1990). Ethnic identity in adolescents and adults: Review of research. *Psychological Bulletin, 108*(3), 499–514.

Porter, J. R., & Washington, R. E. (1993). Minority identity and self-esteem. *Annual Review of Sociology, 19*, 139–161.

Robins, L. N., & Regier, D. A. (1991). *Psychiatric disorders in America: The epidemologic catchment area study.* New York: Free Press.

Rosenberg, M. (1979). *Conceiving the self.* New York: Basic Books.

Saldana, D. H. (1995). Acculturative stress. In D. H. Saldana (Ed.), *Hispanic psychology: Critical issues in theory* (pp. 43–56). Beverly Hills, CA: Sage.

Salgado de Snyder, V. N. (1987). Factors associated with acculturative stress and depressive symptomatology among married Mexican immigrant women. *Psychology of Women Quarterly, 11*, 475–488.

See, K. O., & Wilson, W. J. (1988). Race and ethnicity. In N. J. Smelser (Ed.), *Handbook of sociology* (pp. 233–242). Beverly Hills, CA: Sage.

Sellers, R. M., Rowley, S. A. J., Chavous, T. M., Shelton, J. N., & Smith, M. (1997). Multidimensional inventory of black identity: Preliminary investigation of reliability and construct validity. *Journal of Personality and Social Psychology, 73*, 805–815.

Sellers, R. M., Smith, M. A., Shelton, J. N., Rowley, S. A. J., & Chavous, T. M.

(1998). Multidimensional model of racial identity: A reconceptualization of African American racial identity. *Personality and Social Psychology Review, 2*(1), 18–39.

Sutherland, M. E., & Harrell, J. P. (1986). Individual differences in physiological responses to fearful, racially noxious, and neutral imagery. *Imagination, Cognition, and Personality, 6,* 133–149.

Taylor, D. M., Wright, S. C., & Porter, L. E. (1994). Dimensions of perceived discrimination: The personal/group discrimination discrepancy. In M. P. Zanna & J. M. Olson (Eds.), *The psychology of prejudice: The Ontario Symposium* (Vol. 7). Hillsdale, NJ: Erlbaum.

Taylor, D. M., Wright, S. C., & Ruggiero, K. (1991). The personal/group discrimination discrepancy: Responses to experimentally induced personal and group discrimination. *Journal of Social Psychology, 131,* 847–858.

Terrell, F. & Taylor, J. (1980). Self-concept of juveniles who commit black on black crimes. *Corrective and Social Psychiatry, 20,* 107–109.

Thompson, V. L. S. (1991). A multidimensional approach to the assessment of African American racial identification. *Western Journal of Black Studies, 15,* 154–158.

Thompson, V. L. S. (1996). Perceived experiences of racism as stressful life events. *Community Mental Health Journal, 32*(3), 223–233.

U.S. Department of Health and Human Services. (1985). *Report of the Secretary's Task Force on Black and Minority Health.* Washington, DC: United States Government Printing Office.

Wheaton, B. (1990). Life transitions, role histories, and mental health. *American Sociological Review, 55,* 209–223.

Williams, D. R. (1990). Socioeconomic differentials in health: A review and redirection. *Social Psychology Quarterly, 53*(2), 81–99.

Williams, D. R. (1996a). The health of the African American population. In S. Pedraza & R. G. Rumbaut (Eds.), *Origins and destinies: Immigration, race and ethnicity in America* (pp. 404–416). Belmont, CA: Wadsworth.

Williams, D. R. (1996b). Racism and health: A research agenda. *Ethnicity and Disease, 6*(1,2), 1–6.

Williams, D. R. (1997). Race and health: Basic questions, emerging directions. *Annals of Epidemiology, 7*(5), 322–333.

Williams, D. R., & Chung, A. (in press). Racism and health. In R. Gibson & J. S. Jackson (Eds.), *Health in black America.* Thousand Oaks, CA: Sage.

Williams, D. R., & Collins, C. (1995). U. S. socioeconomic and racial differences in health. *Annual Review of Sociology, 21,* 349–386.

Williams, D. R., & House, J. S. (1991). Stress, social support, control and coping: A social epidemiologic view. In B. Badura & I. Kickbusch (Eds.), *Health promotion research: Towards a new social epidemiology* (pp. 157–172). Copenhagen: World Health Organization.

Williams, D. R., Lavizzo-Mourey, R., & Warren, R. C. (1994). The concept of race and health status in America. *Public Health Reports, 109*(1), 26–41.

Williams, D., Yu, Y., Jackson, J., & Anderson, N. (1997). Racial differences in physical and mental health: Socioeconomic status, stress, and discrimination. *Journal of Health Psychology, 2*(3), 335–351.

Williams-Morris, R. S. (1996). Racism and children's health: Issues in development. *Ethnicity and Disease, 6,* 69–82.

James W. Pennebaker
Kelli A. Keough

5

Revealing, Organizing, and Reorganizing the Self in Response to Stress and Emotion

I love my parents. We have a perfect family life. My parents always
support me in whatever I do. . . . My father has been such a bastard.
I know that he has something going with his secretary. My mother
takes it out on me. I have to wear the clothes she wants, date the boys
she wants. I'm even at SMU because she went here, even though I
wanted to go to UT.
—20-year-old college junior, quoted in J. W. Pennebaker,
"Confession, Inhibition, and Disease" (1989)

When traumatic and stressful events occur, they touch virtually every
aspect of our lives. The loss of a spouse through death or divorce, for
example, changes our roles as wives or husbands, our social patterns, financial and living situations, daily behaviors and habits, and even sometimes our very definition of who we are. For the college junior in one of
our studies, her family life caused much stress and threatened her
ability to create and shape her own identity. The purpose of this chapter is to explore how traumas threaten people's self-definition and how
people use the act of disclosure and the most fundamental social tool,
language, to try to rebuild the self.

This chapter is divided into three sections. The first explores the
evidence that traumas—and especially those not disclosed to others—
are linked to higher rates of illness. The second section discusses our
research paradigm in which we have repeatedly found that disclosure in
the laboratory can have beneficial effects on physical health. The third
section tackles the question of how disclosure—both through writing
and talking—can help people cope with stressful and traumatic ex-
perieces. Specifically, we explore how traumas may be linked to physical
illness through their negative impact on a person's self-definition, and
how disclosure may help to assimilate the traumatic experience into a

person's self-definition and to reorganize a person's self after a traumatic experience. We look to the language people use to discuss their traumas as a marker of their self-reconstruction efforts.

Traumatic Experiences, Illness, and Disclosure

That traumatic experiences are associated with health problems is one of the best-established findings within the broad area of psychosomatics. A number of studies have shown that major life events predict higher mortality, hospitalization rates, and diagnoses of major health problems, such as heart disease, ulcers, and cancer, as well as relatively minor difficulties, such as colds and flu (e.g., Holmes & Rahe, 1967; for reviews, see Figley & McCubbin, 1984; Sowder, 1985; VandenBos & Bryant, 1987). These findings led us to ask what about these traumatic experiences makes them so harmful, and what makes some people able to better cope with these experiences than others.

Disclosure and Health

An important dimension in coping with stressors and traumatic experiences concerns the degree to which people discuss or psychologically confront these experiences after their occurrence. Jourard (1971), for example, argued that self-disclosure of upsetting experiences serves as a basic human motive. Further, when this motive is blocked, health problems could result. This argument implies that *not* talking about an upsetting experience is maladaptive because it does not satisfy this fundamental need.

In our own correlational research, we investigated the consequences of not talking with others about upsetting experiences. We have consistently found that not confiding in others about a variety of different traumatic events was associated with illness episodes and measures of subjective distress among college students and adult samples. For example, among individuals whose spouses died unexpectedly by suicide or automobile accident, the more the survivors talked with others about their spouse's death, the healthier they reported being and the less they ruminated about their spouse's death one year after the death (Pennebaker & O'Heeron, 1984). Also, individuals who had experienced a traumatic sexual experience prior to the age of seventeen were over twice as likely to have health problems once they were in college if they had not talked with others about the trauma than if they had done so. Later studies confirmed that the problem was not unique to traumatic sexual experiences. Among a sample of 200 white-collar workers in a large corporation, we found that experiencing any type of trauma in childhood that was not discussed with others was correlated with current diagnosed health problems, ranging from hypertension and cancer to bouts of influenza and diarrhea (Pennebaker & Susman, 1988).

Indeed, the inability or unwillingness to talk openly about upsetting experiences has been linked to health decrements over time in several other lines of research. Recent work by Cole, Kemeny, Taylor, and Visscher (1996a, 1996b) indicates that gay men who conceal their homosexual status are more likely to suffer from major illnesses such as cancer if they are HIV-negative and to die more quickly from AIDS if they are HIV-positive than men who are more open about their homosexuality. Convergent results have been found in studies investigating the relationship between individual differences in disclosure and increased physical illness, such as in research on repressive coping styles (e.g., Weinberger, 1990), the Type C personality and cancer (Temoshok & Dreher, 1992), and ambivalence over emotional expression (Emmons & King, 1988). The social support literature also closely parallels much of our own work in documenting the value of talking about traumatic experience. It is commonly observed, for example, that after a shared traumatic experience, such as an earthquake or the outbreak of war, people are drawn together and talk about the experience at exceptionally high rates. During this period of heightened social interaction, people's rates of illness are actually quite low (Pennebaker & Harber, 1993). This work nicely supports Jourard's (1971) argument that following virtually all upheavals—whether shared or not—people are driven to discuss the events with others and that positive consequences result when people do disclose their experiences.

Promoting Disclosure and Health Improvements

Beginning in the mid-1980s, we became convinced of the health problems associated with not talking about emotional upheavals. Rather than continue to conduct questionnaire and correlational research, we felt that it was possible to manipulate disclosure in a laboratory setting. On the untested assumption that most people would have had at least one emotional upheaval that they had not disclosed in great detail, we began a series of studies that involved people writing and, in some cases, talking about these events.

In the first study, people were asked to write about a trauma or about superficial topics on four consecutive days, 15 minutes per day. We found that confronting the emotions and thoughts surrounding deeply personal issues promoted physical health, as measured by reductions in physician visits in the months following the study, fewer reports of aspirin usage, and overall more positive long-term evaluations of the effect of the experiment (Pennebaker & Beall, 1986). The results of that initial study have led to a number of similar disclosure studies, in our laboratory and by others, with a wide array of intriguing results. Next, we briefly review the paradigm and basic findings.

The Basic Writing Paradigm   The standard laboratory writing technique has involved randomly assigning participants to one of two or more groups. All writing groups are asked to write about assigned topics for one to five consecutive days, for 15 to 30 minutes each day. Writing is generally done in the laboratory, with no feedback. Those assigned to the control conditions are typically asked to write about superficial topics, such as how they use their time. The standard instructions for those assigned to the experimental group are a variation on the following:

> For the next (three) days, I would like for you to write about your very deepest thoughts and feeling about an extremely important emotional issue that has affected you and your life. In your writing, I'd like you to really let go and explore your very deepest emotions and thoughts. You might tie your topic to your relationships with others, including parents, lovers, friends, or relatives, to your past, your present, or your future, or to who you have been, who you would like to be, or who you are now. You may write about the same general issues or experiences on all days of writing or on different topics each day. All of your writing will be completely confidential. Don't worry about spelling, sentence structure, or grammar. The only rule is that once you begin writing, continue to do so until your time is up.

The writing paradigm is exceptionally powerful. Participants—from children to the elderly, from honor students to maximum security prisoners—disclose a remarkable range and depth of traumatic experiences. Lost loves, deaths, sexual and physical abuse incidents, and tragic failures are common themes in all of our studies. If nothing else, the paradigm demonstrates that when individuals are given the opportunity to disclose deeply personal aspects of their lives, they readily do so. Even though a large number of participants report crying or being deeply upset by the experience, the overwhelming majority report that the writing experience was valuable and meaningful in their lives.

Effect of Disclosure on Outcome Measures   Researchers have relied on a variety of physical and mental health measures to evaluate the effect of writing. As summarized in Table 5.1, writing or talking about emotional experiences relative to writing about superficial control topics has been found to be associated with significant drops in physician visits after writing among relatively healthy samples. Writing or talking about emotional topics has also been found to influence immune function in beneficial ways, including t-helper cell growth (using a blastogenesis procedure with the mitogen PHA), antibody response to Epstein-Barr virus, and antibody response to hepatitis B vaccinations.

Even activity of the autonomic nervous system is influenced by the disclosure paradigm. Among those participants who disclose their thoughts and emotions to a particularly high degree, skin conductance levels (SCLs) are significantly lower during the trauma disclosures than when describing superficial topics. Systolic blood pressure and heart rate (HR) drops to levels below baseline following the disclosure of traumatic topics but not superficial ones (Pennebaker, Hughes, & O'Heeron, 1987). In short, when individuals talk or write about deeply personal topics, their immediate biological responses are congruent with those seen among people attempting to relax.

Self-reports also suggest that writing about upsetting experiences, although painful in the days of writing, produces long-term improvements in mood and indicators of well-being compared to controls. Although some studies have failed to find clear mood or self-reported distress effects, a recent meta-analysis by Smyth (1998) on written disclosure studies indicates that, in general, writing about emotional topics is associated with significant reductions in distress.

Behavioral changes have also been found. Students who write about emotional topics improve their grades in the months following the study. Senior professionals who have been laid off from their jobs get new jobs more quickly after writing. Consistent with the direct health measures, university staff members who write about emotional topics are subsequently absent from their work at lower rates than controls. Interestingly, relatively few reliable changes emerge using self-reports of health-related behaviors. That is, after writing, experimental participants do not exercise more or smoke less. The one exception is that the study with laid-off professionals found that writing reduced self-reported alcohol intake.

Procedural Differences that Affect the Disclosure Effects   Writing about emotional experiences clearly influences measures of physical and mental health. In recent years, several investigators have attempted to define the boundary conditions of the disclosure effect. Some of the most important findings follow:

(1) *Writing versus talking about traumas.* Most studies comparing writing alone to talking either into a tape recorder (Esterling, Antoni, Fletcher, Margulies, & Schneiderman, 1994) or to a therapist in a one-way interaction (Donnelly & Murray, 1991; Murray, Lamnin, & Carver, 1989) find comparable biological, mood, and cognitive effects. Talking and writing about emotional experiences are both superior to writing about superficial topics.

(2) *Topic of disclosure.* Although two studies have found that health effects occur only among individuals who write about particularly traumatic experiences (Greenberg & Stone, 1992; Lutgendorf, Antoni, Kumar, & Schneiderman, 1994) most studies have found that disclosure is more broadly beneficial. Choice of topic, however, may selectively influence outcomes. Although vir-

TABLE 5.1. Disclosure Studies Finding Beneficial Physical Effects

General Outcome Variable	Specific Outcome Variable	Studies
Physician Visits	Fewer physician visits in 2 months surrounding writing	Cameron & Nicholls (1996); Greenberg & Stone (1992); Greenberg, Wortman & Stone (1996); Krantz & Pennebaker (1996); Pennebaker & Francis (1996); Pennebaker, Kiecolt-Glaser, & Glaser (1988); Richards & Pennebaker (1996)
	Fewer physician visits in 6 months surrounding writing	Francis & Pennebaker (1992); Pennebaker & Beall (1986); Pennebaker, Colder, & Sharp (1990)
	Fewer physician visits in 16 months surrounding writing	Pennebaker, Barger, & Tiebout (1989)
Physiological markers (Long-term immune and other serum measures)	Blastogenesis (t-helper cell response to PHA)	Pennebaker et al. (1988)
	Epstein-Barr virus antibody titers	Esterling et al. (1994); Lutgendorf, Antoni, Kumar, & Schneiderman (1994)
	Hepatitis B antibody levels	Petrie et al. (1995)
	NK cell activity	Christensen & Smith (1993)
	CD-4 (t-lymphocyte) levels	Booth, Petrie, & Pennebaker (1997)
	Liver enzyme levels (SGOT)	Francis & Pennebaker (1992)
Physiological markers (Immediate changes in autonomic and muscular activity)	Skin conductance and/or heart rate	Dominguez et al. (1995); Hughes, Uhlmann, & Pennebaker (1994); Pennebaker, Hughes & O'Heeron (1987); Petrie et al. (1995)

	Corrugator activity	Pennebaker et al. (1987)
Self-reports	Physical symptoms	Greenberg & Stone (1992); Pennebaker & Beall (1986); Richards et al. (1996). Failure to find effects: Pennebaker et al. (1990); Pennebaker et al. (1988); Petrie et al. (1995)
	Distress, negative affect, or depression	Greenberg & Stone (1992); Greenberg et al (1996); Rimé (1995); Spera et al. (1994); Schoutrop et al. (1996) Failure to find effects: Pennebaker & Beall (1986); Pennebaker et al. (1988); Pennebaker & Francis (1996); Petrie et al. (1995)
Behavioral markers	Grade point average	Cameron & Nicholls (1998); Krantz & Pennebaker (1996); Pennebaker et al. (1990); Pennebaker & Francis (1996)
	Re-employment following job loss	Spera, Buhrfeind, & Pennebaker (1994)
	Absenteeism from work	Francis & Pennebaker (1992)

Only studies published or submitted for publication are included. Several studies find effects that are qualified by a second variable (e.g., stressfulness of topic). See also Smyth (1998) for a detailed account.

tually all studies find that writing about emotional topics has positive effects on physical health, only certain assigned topics appear to be related to changes in grades. For beginning college students, for example, when asked to write specifically about emotional issues related to coming to college, both health and college grades improve. However, when other students are asked to write about emotional issues related to traumatic experiences in general, only health improvements—and not academic performance—are found (Pennebaker & Beall, 1986; Pennebaker et al., 1990).

(3) *Length of writing.* Different experiments have variously asked participants to write for one to five days, ranging from consecutive days to sessions separated by a week, ranging from 15 to 30 minutes for each writing session. Smyth (1998) found a promising trend suggesting that the longer the experiment, the stronger the impact on outcomes. Although this was a weak effect, it suggests that writing once each week over a month may be more effective than writing four times within a single week. Self-reports of the value of writing do not distinguish shorter from longer writing sessions.

(4) *Actual or implied social factors.* Unlike psychotherapy and everyday discussions about traumas, the writing paradigm does not employ feedback to the participant. Rather, after individuals write about their own experiences, they place their essays into a plain box with the promise that their writing will not be linked to their name. In one study comparing the effects of having students write on either paper that would be handed in to the experimenter or on a magic pad (the writing disappears when the person lifts the plastic writing cover), no autonomic or self-report differences were found (Czajka, 1987). The benefits of writing, then, occur without explicit social feedback. Nevertheless, whether people write holding the belief that some symbolic other person may "magically" read their essays can never be easily determined.

(5) *Individual differences.* No consistent personality measures have distinguished who benefits from writing. A number of variables have been unrelated to outcomes, including age, anxiety (or negative affectivity), and inhibition or constraint. The one study that preselected participants on hostility measures found that those high in hostility benefited more from writing than those low in hostility (Christensen & Smith, 1996). Additionally, Smyth's (1998) meta-analysis revealed that men tend to benefit more from the writing paradigm than women. This sex difference is weak and may reflect methodological features specific to the

studies that Smyth examined. Our current thinking is that some individual differences are undoubtedly related to writing's effects. However, the writing paradigm itself is sufficiently powerful to statistically swamp most individual difference measures. With larger samples and more precise outcome measures, we should discover which personality factors are related to writing.

(6) *Educational, linguistic, or cultural effects.* Within the United States, the disclosure paradigm has benefited senior professionals with advanced degrees at rates comparable to those for maximum security prisoners with 6th grade educations (Richards, Pennebaker, & Beal, 1996; Spera, Buhrfeind, & Pennebaker, 1994). Among college students, we have not found differences as a function of the students' ethnicity or native language. The disclosure paradigm has produced positive results among French-speaking Belgians (Rimé, 1995), Spanish-speaking residents of Mexico City (Dominguez et al., 1995), multiple samples of adults and students in The Netherlands (Schoutrop, Lange, Brosschot, & Everaerd, 1997), and English-speaking New Zealand medical students (Petrie, Booth, Pennebaker, Davidson, & Thomas, 1995).

When individuals in the laboratory write or talk about personally upsetting experiences, consistent and significant health improvements are found. The effects include both subjective and objective markers of health and well-being. The disclosure phenomenon appears to generalize across settings, many individual difference factors, and several Western cultures and is independent of social feedback.

Why Does Disclosure of Traumatic and Stressful Events Affect Health?

There are a number of possible reasons for why disclosure affects health. In this section, we focus specifically on explanations that involve the self and the model depicted in Figure 5.1. As illustrated in this model, self-related processes and outcomes may mediate the disclosure effects in two ways. We briefly outline these possibilities here, and in the following sections, we discuss each in more detail. First, traumas may be detrimental psychologically because they threaten core aspects of the self. These threatening experiences may be either inhibited or disclosed. People may work to inhibit thinking and talking about these experiences in order to lessen the threat, but this active inhibition may be physiologically detrimental, resulting in illness (Pennebaker, Kiecolt-Glaser, & Glaser, 1988). Second, as illustrated in the lower part of Figure 5.1, disclosure may be an effective method of coping with traumas because it helps people gain meaning about their experiences, reframe these experiences as nonthreatening, assimilate them into the

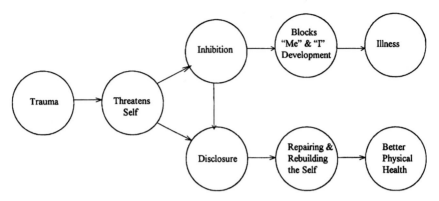

FIGURE 5.1. Disclosure and health: the self as mediator.

self, and in some cases, engage in dramatic reconstruction of the self-system (Pennebaker, 1989; Pennebaker et al., 1988; Taylor, 1991). Through disclosure, people may be able to place the experience into a meaningful framework (Pennebaker & Beall, 1986), feel greater personal coherence, enjoy heightened self-esteem, experience a heightened sense of control over the events, and experience increased optimism (Harber & Pennebaker, 1992).

These speculations have received empirical support in a variety of studies. We first focus on the evidence that traumas are indeed threats to a person's identity. We then discuss evidence that inhibiting the need to talk about the trauma is itself stressful because it serves to perpetuate the threat, resulting in further psychological and physical damage. Afterward, we discuss how the failure to translate emotional experiences into a linguistic format maintains the emotional reverberations of the trauma for an extended time. The process of disclosing the trauma helps to assimilate the threatening experience into the self so that it is no longer threatening and the physiological work that inhibition requires is no longer necessary. We will look to the process of translating the experience into language for a linguistic marker of the process of assimilating the experience into the self.

Traumas Threaten the Self   We draw on Deaux's (1992) recent conceptualization of a person's self-definition—in other words, the sense of one's identity as it is constructed and defined by an individual. The self is a reflexive project that people "work on" in everyday life, it develops over time, and the self seeks a temporal coherence reflected in the narratives people build that integrate their experiences into a meaningful life story (McAdams, 1997).

Characterizing a trauma as a threat to a person's self and identity is not new. Traumas represent significant challenges to fundamental beliefs about the world and self: that the world is basically benevolent and meaningful and that the self is effective and worthy (Epstein, 1991; Horowitz, 1986; Janoff-Bulman, 1989). Traumas destabilize or invalidate one or more of these basic beliefs and, in doing so, threaten what James (1890) termed the "I" (self as agent or process) and the "Me" (self as object or content). For example, Deaux reported:

> People who experience serious traumas earlier in their life show the impact of those events on their self-concept many years later. . . . Women who were sexually victimized, for example, show more traits related to maladaptive interpersonal behavior and fewer expectations of self-efficacy than do a comparable group of non-reported victims. Negative impact can also take the form of completely eliminating some aspect of the self-concept. Failure at school, for example, would generally eliminate a student identity and perhaps a possible self as a doctor; death of a spouse can remove (at least temporarily) one's identity as a wife or husband. (1992, p. 316)

Traumas and other significant emotional upheavals threaten the basic fabric of a person's self-definition. Following traumas, a person's assumptions about life's predictability, controllability, and meaning are shaken. With these shattered assumptions, their social identities are also fundamentally affected (cf. Janoff-Bulman, 1992). With threats to psychological coherence come threats to biological health (Booth & Ashbridge, 1993). Why is it that *not* disclosing these self-threats is so detrimental? We have investigated the possibility that inhibition may be a partial mediator between the psychological threat and illness.

Inhibition   There are a number of reasons why not talking about upsetting experiences may be a health risk. One of our original ideas was that not talking about traumas was a form of inhibition. The core idea was that actively inhibiting ongoing behaviors, thoughts, or emotions entails work—measurable physiological work. Over time, the work of inhibition serves as a stressor (cf. Selye, 1976). This active inhibition is also associated with potentially deleterious changes in information processing, so that people do not typically process these events fully. By not talking about an inhibited event, for example, people usually do not translate the experience into language that aids in the understanding and assimilation of the event (Pennebaker, 1989). Consequently, inhibited traumas likely surface in the form of ruminations, dreams, and associated cognitive symptoms (Harber & Pennebaker, 1992).

Inhibition shuts down processing so that a person cannot assimilate the trauma into the self-concept, whereas actively confronting traumas helps people to gain meaning from and ultimately assimilate the event so that it no longer violates their fundamental beliefs about the world and about the self. As the top part of Figure 5.1 illustrates, self-related processes may mediate the deleterious effects of inhibition. Inhibition is likely to have an impact on both the "Me" and the "I." Regarding the "Me," in the case of childhood sexual assault, a person who inhibits revealing this trauma cannot include in the self a coherent and understood "me as sexual being" component. Inhibition means that, because one cannot address the trauma, he or she cannot consciously think about the topic of self and sex, cannot mentally examine his or her sexuality from multiple perspectives, and cannot talk with others about self-relevant sexual issues. Inhibition of a traumatic sexual assault also harms the "I." By attempting to exclude the trauma from consciousness and discussion with others, one is left with a primitive and unexamined view in which the self is something that is affected, things are done to the self, rather than by the self. Thus, one does not learn that "I" can influence and shape the world.

One of the most striking instances of inhibition occurs when individuals have faced an emotional upheaval that they have been unable to talk about with others. Actively inhibiting thoughts and feelings surrounding these events, then, was hypothesized to cause or exacerbate a variety of mental and physical health problems. The flip side of the model was that when individuals confront these previously inhibited events by talking or writing about them, they should reduce the work of holding back, thereby improving health (for a discussion of the model, see Pennebaker, 1989, 1997).

Multiple studies have shown that when people constrain their emotions, thoughts, or behaviors, increased sympathetic nervous system (SNS) activity results. Experiments have demonstrated that instructions to suppress thoughts are associated with heightened SCLs (e.g., Wegner, Shortt, Blake, & Page, 1990); suppressed overt emotional expressions have resulted in higher SCL, HR, and lower skin temperature (Gross & Levenson, 1993); induced suppression of cold-pressor pain is linked with higher SCL (Cioffi & Holloway, 1993); and the inhibition of assorted overt behaviors has resulted in higher SCL (Fowles, 1980).

Findings to support the inhibition model in the domain of hormonal and immune function are growing as well. Young children who are considered inhibited or shy by others exhibit more health problems, such as upper respiratory infections, and have higher cortisol levels than those less inhibited (e.g., Kagan, Reznic, & Snidman, 1988). In an experimental investigation by Petrie, Booth, and Pennebaker (1998), medical students were asked to write about either upsetting emotional topics or superficial topics for 15 minutes a day for three consecutive days. After the 15-minute writing assignment, everyone was asked to stop writing. Half of the students were told to inhibit their thoughts and not think about the topic that they ahd written about. The remaining students were free to think about anything. Blood was drawn before and after the daily writing to measure circulating levels of lymphocytes (e.g., CD4, or t-helper cells; CD8, or t-suppressor cells; CD16 cells, or natural killer cells). Overall, the act of suppressing thoughts was associated with significantly reduced lymphocyte counts.

The development and growth of inhibition models to explain health problems following traumas have been quite promising. The greatest shortcoming, however, has been the failure to link inhibitory processes directly to long-term health problems. That is, no convincing studies capture the mediating effect of inhibition directly or the mediating role of self-processes in the detrimental effect of inhibition. Although the work of inhibition may well contribute to health difficulties, the failure to talk about upsetting experiences blocks a number of basic cognitive and social processes.

Disclosure and the Self Just as inhibition instructions increase SNS activity, disclosing these inhibited emotional experiences through writing or talking has been found to reduce SNS activity (Pennebaker, Barger, & Tiebout, 1989; Pennebaker, Hughes, & O'Heeron, 1987). Mendolia and Kleck (1993) found that individuals asked to express their emotions about an upsetting movie scene were less distressed and autonomically reactive to seeing the film two days later than controls who spoke factually about the film.

We earlier discussed inhibition as a partial explanation for how disclosure about traumatic and stressful experiences can promote greater physical well-being. Confronting previously inhibited experiences can reduce the amount of damaging inhibition. The self also mediates the relationship between disclosure and health. People are compelled to work toward assimilation of these threatening experiences, possibly reorganizing their self-system as a way of coping with the trauma (Epstein, 1991; Horowitz, 1986). The disclosure paradigm may promote this reorganization of the self-system, helping people achieve a sense of coherence and insight into the self-threatening experiences.

When asked to write about a personal trauma, within our experimental paradigm, a writer faces suppressed thoughts, conflicting motives and emotions, and unflattering self-perceptions. When confronted with this constellation, the writer struggles to reorder it and assimilate the information into the existing self-structure. The process of describing the trauma may help strengthen ties between it and other experiences, resulting in integration of the trauma within one's network of memories and beliefs (Harber & Pennebaker, 1992). In addition to furthering this more static assimilation process, where new interpersonal experiences are integrated into fixed and unchanging internal representations of the self, the writing paradigm may also encourage growth. The disclosure may help to update, modify, and regroup this new information about the trauma, resulting in a self-structure that may be very different from the one with which the writer started and which dynami-cally reflects current understandings of these past experiences (Ogilvie & Ashmore, 1991).

To test more directly the role of these assimilation and growth processes, we used a similar writing paradigm but specifically asked participants to focus on a theme central to their self-image as a way of potentially helping them give meaning to threatening experiences and promoting well-being. In two studies (Keough, Garcia, & Steele, 1997), participants completed writing assignments every other day for a total of 10 times. The writing assignments contained the experimen-tal manipulation, with one group randomly assigned to complete *self-integration* writing assignments. This group was asked to integrate the events and feelings they experienced during a vacation into their most important personal value in order to help them give meaning to their experiences and to help them maintain an integrated self-definition. Other participants were assigned to control groups and either wrote on neutral topics or did not write at all.

As predicted, those who integrated their experiences over vacation into their most important value were healthier at the end of vacation, as assessed by doctor visits, symptom checklists, and health-related behav-iors, and after controlling for initial levels of stress, illness, and negative affectivity. They also reported less stress than did other participants in the studies. Further analyses revealed that the self-integration interven-tion was most effective at promoting well-being in those who were most under self-threat, as measured by the number of "hassles" they re-ported experiencing that were important to their self-worth.

The findings suggest that the self-integration writing tasks pro-moted greater well-being by allowing the participants to integrate threatening experiences into a coherent narrative around their most important value and to give meaning to these experiences. The work of integrating events and giving them meaning contingent with a strongly held personal value, a core aspect of the self, may have been beneficial by helping people restore their self-image as competent and worthy in-dividuals (Markus & Nurius, 1986). These results are consistent with findings reported by Greenberg, Wortman, and Stone (1996), who ar-gued that by directly confronting stressful events through writing, their participants were reintegrating their self-concept, repairing the dam-aged domains, eliminating a chronic self-threat, and constructing more resilient possible selves.

To test some of these speculations about why and how integrating one's experiences into a central value was beneficial, we conducted a content analysis of the approximately 2,000 pages of qualitative data provided in the journals written by the participants in the Keough et al. (1997) study. Based on Taylor's (1983) work with breast cancer patients, we predicted that giving meaning to threatening experiences would serve as an adaptive coping strategy and enhance health and that the self-integration condition would facilitate this meaning-making. It was found that, in the self-integration condition, an increase over time in the use of cognitive words (e.g., *realize, see, understand*) was related to decreased illness. This finding links an attempt to understand and find causal meaning in upsetting experiences to improved health (Pennebaker & Francis, 1996). Evidently, those in the self-integration condition sought to find meaning in their experiences and this led to better health. More important, this finding was consistent with our earlier work, which had consistently shown that through language we can see these assimilation and growth processes at work.

Language as a Marker of Identity Change   In the last decade, several studies have demonstrated persuasively that writing about a trauma does more than allow for the reduction of inhibitory processes. For example, in a recent study, students were assigned randomly to a condition in which they were instructed to express a traumatic experience using bodily movement, to express an experience using movement and then to write about it, or to exercise in a prescribed manner for three days, 10 minutes per day (Krantz & Pennebaker, 1996). Although the two movement expression groups reported that they felt happier and mentally healthier in the months after the study, only the movement plus writing group evidenced significant improvements in physical health and grade point average. The mere expression of a trauma is not sufficient. Health gains appear to require translating experiences into language.

In recent years, we have begun analyzing the language that individuals use in writing about emotional topics. Of particular interest, we investigated whether we could find evidence of this self-rebuilding and reconstruction in our participants' writings. Our first strategy was to have independent raters evaluate the essays' overall content to see if we could predict who would benefit most from writing. Interestingly, judges noted that essays of people who benefit from writing appeared to be "smarter," "more thoughtful," "more emotional," and "more coherent" (Pennebaker, 1993). These early findings were consistent with McAdams' (1993) work, which suggests that through coherent narratives people make sense of their world and construct self-stories. However, the relatively poor interjudge reliability of these variables led us to develop a computerized text analysis system.

In 1991, we created a computer program called LIWC (Linguistic Inquiry and Word Count) that analyzed essays in text format and had been developed by having groups of judges evaluate the degree to which about 2,000 words or word stems were related to each of several dozen categories (for a full description, see Pennebaker & Francis, 1996). The categories included negative emotion words (*sad, angry*), positive emotion words (*happy, laugh*), causal words (*because, reason*), and insight words (*understand, realize*). For each essay that a person wrote, we were able to compute the percentage of total words that these and other linguistic categories represented.

Analyzing the experimental subjects' data from six writing studies, we found that three linguistic factors reliably predicted improved physical health. First, the more that individuals use positive emotion words, the better their subsequent health. Second, a moderate number of negative emotion words predicts health. Both very high and very low levels of negative emotion word use correlate with poorer health. Third, and most important, an increase in both causal and insight words over the course of writing is strongly associated with improved health (Pennebaker, Mayne, & Francis, 1997). Indeed, this increase in cognitive words covaries with judges' evaluations of the construction of a story or narrative. That is, people who benefit from writing begin with a poorly organized description and progress to a coherent story by the last day of writing.

The language analyses are particularly promising in that they suggest that certain features of essays predict long-term physical health. Further, these results are the first we have that can be interpreted as evidence of the rebuilding and reconstructing of the self that may occur during disclosure. These results, then, suggest that what was beneficial about the writing was the ability to construct a coherent narrative. This narrative allows people to arrive at an "enduring 'truth' about the me"—a more coherent and meaningful self-definition no longer fragmented by the self-threatening trauma or stressful event. This event is now seen within the context of the overall life narrative (McAdams, 1997, p. 68).

Further issues to be addressed concern whether and how these self-stories predict changes in real-world cognitive processes. That is, does the assimilation process produce improvements in health by reducing ruminations or flashbacks? To what degree does the rebuilding and reconstruction of the self allow one to get on with life? To what degree does the use and integration of emotional language affect a person's success at rebuilding and reconstructing the self and, ultimately, benefit health?

Language and the Self in Everyday Life   We also see evidence of the assimilation of traumatic and stressful experiences into the self in everyday disclosure. After a trauma, the shaping or rebuilding of one's identity can be accomplished in many ways. Informal talking with others is perhaps the most common method by which people think about and deal with emotional events. However, talking with others is not always possible or positive. Talking to close friends after an upheaval can place great strain on the social network. Because of this, people rely on a variety of strategies and institutions to help them deal with traumas and to rebuild their selves. Often, various institutions are available to help in this metamorphosis: religions, self-help groups such as Alcoholics Anonymous, and formal or informal groups of people who apparently possess or display the identity features to which one aspires.

In the last 50 years, a particularly powerful institution developed for changing self-definitions has been psychotherapy. Virtually all forms of talk therapy—from psychoanalysis to behavioral and cognitive therapies—have been shown to reduce distress and to promote physical and mental well-being (Mumford, Schlesinger, & Glass, 1983; Smith, Glass, & Miller, 1980). A process common to most therapies is the labeling of the problem and a discussion of its causes and consequences. Further, participating in therapy presupposes that the individaul acknowledges the existence of a problem and openly discusses it with another. The mere act of disclosure, then, can be a powerful therapeutic agent that may account for a substantial percentage of the variance in the self-repair or healing process.

Summary and Conclusions

Traumatic experiences disrupt people's beliefs about their worlds and themselves, threatening core aspects of a person's self-definition. When the self has been threatened, inhibition or not talking about upsetting experiences can increase mental and physical health problems. Undoubtedly, multiple factors contribute to the link between inhibition and illness. The physiological work and stress of inhibition, the breakdown of normal cognitive processing that does not allow the individual to resolve the experience, and the increased social isolation of not disclosing important topics to others can all contribute to stress and illness.

Rather than focus only on the correlational evidence of the dangers of not talking, our research led us to explore experimentally the physical health value of disclosing these experiences. A number of experimental studies have now demonstrated that the act of translating emotional experiences into language is a sufficient ingredient in preventing health problems following a trauma. These studies suggest to us that disclosure is beneficial because it helps people gain meaning from the experience and assimilate the threatening experience, through narrative construction, into their self-definition. This self-rebuilding and reconstruction process is only now beginning to be studied, but our early results point to the language people use in creating their narratives as a marker for the self-related processes that may be a necessary part of coping with a traumatic or stressful event.

Acknowledgments: Preparation of this paper was aided by grants from the National Science Foundation (SBR-9411674) and the National Institutes of Health (MH52391). We thank the editors for furthering our thinking about the role of the self as a mediator of the deleterious effects of inhibition.

References

Booth, R., & Ashbridge, K. (1993). A fresh look at the relationship between the psyche and the immune system: Teleological coherence and harmony of purpose. *Advances, 9,* 4–23.

Booth, R. J., Petrie, K. J., & Pennebaker, J. W. (1997). Changes in circulating lymphocyte numbers following emotional disclosure: Evidence of buffering? *Stress Medicine, 13,* 23–29.

Cameron, L. D., & Nicholls, G. (1998). Expression of stressful experiences through writing: Effects of a self-regulation manipulation for pessimists and optimists. *Health Psychology, 17,* 84–92.

Christensen, A. J., & Smith, T. W. (1993). Cynical hostility and cardiovascular reactivity during self-disclosure. *Psychosomatic Medicine, 55,* 193–202.

Cioffi, D., & Holloway, J. (1993). Delayed costs of suppressed pain. *Journal of Personality and Social Psychology, 64,* 274–282.

Cole, S. W., Kemeny, M. E., Taylor, S. E., & Visscher, B. R. (1996a). Accelerated course of human immunodeficiency virus infection in gay men who conceal their homosexual identity. *Psychosomatic Medicine, 58,* 219–231.

Cole, S. W., Kemeny, M. E., Taylor, S. E., & Visscher, B. R. (1996b). Elevated physical health risk among gay men who conceal their homosexual identity. *Health Psychology, 15,* 243–251.

Czajka, J. A. (1987). *Behavioral inhibition and short term physiological responses.* Unpublished master's thesis, Southern Methodist University.

Deaux, K. (1992). Focusing on the self: Challenges to self-definition and their consequences for mental health. In D. N. Ruble, P. R. Costanzo, & M. E. Oliveri (Eds.), *The social psychology of mental health: Basic mechanisms and applications* (pp. 301–327). New York: Guilford.

Dominguez, B., Valderrama, P., Meza, M. A., Perez, S. L., Silva, A., Martinez, G., Mendez, V. M., & Olvera, Y. (1995). The roles of emotional reversal and disclosure in clinical practice. In J. W. Pennebaker (Ed.), *Emotion, disclosure, and health.* Washington, DC: American Psychological Association.

Donnelly, D. A., & Murray, E. J. (1991). Cognitive and emotional changes in written essays and therapy interviews. *Journal of Social and Clinical Psychology, 10,* 334–350.

Emmons, R. A., & King, L. A. (1988). Conflict among personal strivings: Implications for psychological and physical well-being. *Journal of Personality and Social Psychology, 54,* 1040–1048.

Epstein, S. (1991). The self-concept, the traumatic neurosis, and the structure of personality. In D. J. Ozer, J. M. Healy, & A. J. Steward (Eds.), *Perspectives in personality, Vol. 3: Part A: Self and emotion; Part B: Approaches to understanding lives* (pp. 63–98). London: Jessica Kingsley.

Esterling, B. A., Antoni, M. H., Fletcher, M. A., Margulies, S., & Schneiderman, N. (1994). Emotional disclosure through writing or speaking modulates latent Epstein-Barr virus reactivation. *Journal of Consulting and Clinical Psychology, 62,* 130–140.

Figley, C. R., & McCubbin, H. I. (Eds.). (1984). *Stress and the family: Coping with catastrophe.* New York: Bruner/Mazel.

Fowles, D. C. (1980). The three arousal model: Implications of Gray's two-factor theory for heart rate, electrodermal activity, and psychopathy. *Psychophysiology, 17,* 87–104.

Francis, M. E., & Pennebaker, J. W. (1992). Putting stress into words: Writing about personal upheavals and health. *American Journal of Health Promotion, 6,* 280–287.

Greenberg, M. A., & Stone, A. A. (1992). Writing about disclosed versus undisclosed traumas: Immediate and long-term effects on mood and health. *Journal of Personality and Social Psychology, 63,* 75–84.

Greenberg, M. A., Wortman, C. B., & Stone, A. A. (1996). Emotional expression and physical health: Revising traumatic memories or fostering self-regulation. *Journal of Personality and Social Psychology, 71,* 588–602.

Gross, J. J., & Levenson, R. W. (1993). Emotional suppression: Physiology, self-report, and expressive behavior. *Journal of Personality and Social Psychology, 64,* 970–986.

Harber, K. D., & Pennebaker, J. W. (1992). Overcoming traumatic memories. In S. Christianson (Ed.), *The handbook of emotion and memory research and theory* (pp. 359–387). Hillsdale, NJ: Erlbaum.

Holmes, T. H., & Rahe, R. H. (1967). The social re-adjustment rating scale. *Journal of Psychosomatic Research, 11,* 213–218.

Horowitz, M. J. (1986). *Stress response syndromes* (2nd ed.). Northvale, NJ: Jason Aronson.

Hughes, C. F., Uhlmann, C., & Pennebaker, J. W. (1994). The body's response to psychological defense. *Journal of Personality, 62,* 565–585.

James, W. (1890). *Principles of psychology.* New York: Holt.

Janoff-Bulman, R. (1989). Assumptive worlds and the stress of traumatic events: Applications of the schema construct. *Social Cognition, 7,* 113–136.

Janoff-Bulman, R. (1992). *Shattered assumptions: Towards a new psychology of trauma.* New York: Free Press.

Jourard, S. M. (1971). *Self-disclosure: An experimental analysis of the transparent self.* New York: Wiley.

Kagan, J., Reznick, J. S., & Snidman, N. (1988). Biological bases of childhood shyness. *Science, 240,* 167–171.

Keough, K. A., Garcia, J., & Steele, C. M. (1997). *Reducing stress and illness by affirming the self.* Manuscript under review.

Krantz, A., & Pennebaker, J. W. (1996). Bodily versus written expression of traumatic experience. Manuscript submitted for publication.

Lutgendorf, S. K., Antoni, M. H., Kumar, M., & Schneiderman, N. (1994). Changes in cognitive coping strategies predict EBV-antibody titre change following a stressor disclosure induction. *Journal of Psychosomatic Research, 38,* 63–78.

Markus, H., & Nurius, P. (1986). Possible selves. *American Psychologist, 41,* 954–969.

McAdams, D. P. (1993). *The stories we live by.* New York: Guilford.

McAdams, D. P. (1997). The case of unity in the (post)modern self: A modest proposal. In R. D. Ashmore, & L. Jussim (Eds.), *Self and identity: Fundamental issues* (pp. 46–78). New York: Oxford University Press.

Mendolia, M., & Kleck, R. E. (1993). Effects of talking about a stressful event on arousal: Does what we talk about make a difference? *Journal of Personality and Social Psychology, 64,* 283–292.

Mumford, E., Schlesinger, H. J., & Glass, G. V. (1983). Reducing medical costs through mental health treatment: Research problems and recommendations. In A. Broskowski, E. Marks, & S. H. Budman (Eds.), *Linking health and mental health* (pp. 257–273). Beverly Hills, CA: Sage.

Murray, E. J., Lamnin, A. D., & Carver, C. S. (1989). Emotional expression in written essays and psychotherapy. *Journal of Social and Clinical Psychology, 8,* 414–429.

Ogilvie, D. M., & Ashmore, R. D. (1991). Self-with-other representation as a unit of analysis in self-concept. In R. C. Curtis (Ed.), *The relational self: Theoretical convergences in psychoanalysis and social psychology* (pp. 282–314). New York: Guilford.

Pennebaker, J. W. (1989). Confession, inhibition, and disease. In L. Berkowitz (Ed.), *Advances in experimental social psychology* (Vol. 22, pp. 211–244). New York: Academic Press.

Pennebaker, J. W. (1993). Putting stress into words: Health, linguistic, and therapeutic implications. *Behaviour Research and Therapy, 31,* 539–548.

Pennebaker, J. W. (1997). *Opening up: The healing power of expressing emotions* (2nd ed.). New York: Guilford.

Pennebaker, J. W., Barger, S. D., & Tiebout, J. (1989). Disclosure of traumas and health among Holocaust survivors. *Psychosomatic Medicine, 51,* 577–589.

Pennebaker, J. W., & Beall, S. K. (1986). Confronting a traumatic event: Toward an understanding of inhibition and disease. *Journal of Abnormal Psychology, 95,* 274–281.

Pennebaker, J. W., Colder, M., & Sharp, L. K. (1990). Accelerating the coping process. *Journal of Personality and Social Psychology, 58,* 528–537.

Pennebaker, J. W., & Francis, M. E. (1996). Cognitive, emotional, and language processes in disclosure. *Cognition and Emotion, 10,* 601–626.

Pennebaker, J. W., & Harber, K. D. (1993). A social stage model of collective coping: The Loma Prieta earthquake and the Persian Gulf War. *Journal of Social Issues, 49,* 125–145.

Pennebaker, J. W., Hughes, C. F., & O'Heeron, R. C. (1987). The psychophysiology of confession: Linking inhibitory and psychosomatic processes. *Journal of Personality and Social Psychology, 52,* 781–793.

Pennebaker, J. W., Kiecolt-Glaser, J., & Glaser, R. (1988). Disclosure of traumas and immune function: Health implications for psychotherapy. *Journal of Consulting and Clinical Psychology, 56,* 239–245.

Pennebaker, J. W., Mayne, T. J., & Francis, M. E. (1997). Linguistic predictors of adaptive bereavement. *Journal of Personality and Social Psychology, 72,* 863–871.

Pennebaker, J. W., & O'Heeron, R. (1984). Confiding in others and illness rate among spouses of suicide and accidental-death victims. *Journal of Abnormal Psychology, 93,* 473–476.

Pennebaker, J. W., & Susman, J. R. (1988). Disclosure of traumas and psychosomatic processes. *Social Science and Medicine, 26,* 327–332.

Petrie, K. J., Booth, R. J., & Pennebaker, J. W. (in press). The immunological effect of thought suppression. *Journal of Personality and Social Psychology.*

Petrie, K. J., Booth, R., Pennebaker, J. W., Davison, K. P., & Thomas, M. (1995). Disclosure of trauma and immune response to hepatitis B vaccination program. *Journal of Consulting and Clinical Psychology, 63,* 787–792.

Richards, J. M., Pennebaker, J. W., & Beal, W. E. (1996). *The effects of criminal offense and disclosure of trauma on anxiety and illness in prison inmates.* Paper presented the Midwest Psychological Association, Chicago. Manuscript submitted for publication.

Rimé, B. (1995). Mental rumination, social sharing, and the recovery from emotional exposure. In J. W. Pennebaker (Ed.), *Emotion, disclosure, and health.* Washington, DC: American Psychological Association.

Schoutrop, M. J. A., Lange, A., Brosschot, J., & Everaerd, W. (1996). Overcoming traumatic events by means of writing assignments. In A. Vingerhoets, F. van Bussel, & J. Boelhouwer (Eds.), *The (non)expression of emotions in health and disease* (pp. 279–290). Tilburg, The Netherlands: Tilburg Press.

Selye, H. (1976). *The Stress of Life.* New York: McGraw-Hill.

Smith, M. L., Glass, G. V., & Miller, R. L. (1980). *The benefits of psychotherapy.* Baltimore: Johns Hopkins University Press.

Smyth, J. M. (1998). Written emotional expression: Effect sizes, outcome types, and moderating variables. *Journal of Consulting and Clinical Psychology, 66,* 174–184.

Sowder, B. J. (Ed.). (1985). *Disasters and mental health: Selected contemporary perspectives.* Rockville, MD: National Institute of Mental Health.

Spera, S. P., Buhrfeind, E. D., & Pennebaker, J. W. (1994). Expressive writing and coping with job loss. *Academy of Management Journal, 37,* 722–733.

Taylor, S. E. (1983). Adjustment to threatening events: A theory of cognitive adaption. *American Psychologist, 38,* 1161–1173.

Taylor, S. E. (1991). *Health psychology* (2nd ed.). New York: McGraw-Hill.

Temoshok, L., & Dreher, H. (1992). *The Type C connection: The behavioral links to cancer and your health.* New York: Random House.

VandenBos, G. R., & Bryant, B. K. (Eds.). (1987). *Cataclysms, crises, and catastrophes: Psychology in action.* Washington, DC: American Psychological Association.

Wegner, D., Shortt, J. W., Blake, A. W., & Page, M. S. (1990). The suppression of exciting thoughts. *Journal of Personality and Social Psychology, 58,* 409–418.

Weinberger, D. (1990). The construct validity of the repressive coping style. In J. L. Singer (Ed.), *Repression and dissociation.* Chicago: University of Chicago Press.

SELF-RELATED PERSONALITY STRUCTURES, IDENTITY DEVELOPMENT, AND DISEASE-RELATED BEHAVIOR

The Relationship between Personality and Health

What Self and Identity Have
to Do with It

How and why might personality be linked to changes in health? The aim of this chapter is to show that compelling and useful responses to this question hinge on researchers' broad complex thinking about personality, including specifically an appreciation of personality's complicated structures and processes of self and identity. The chapter is intended as an antidote to trivial depictions of personality in discussions of health. Oversimplifications may be found in only part of the formal personality and health research literature, but they permeate the popular representations of that literature (e.g., Dreher, 1995). From these sources, readers might get the impression that researchers investigating the link between personality and health study personality only in the form of simple traits.[1] Readers might be misled to think that personality is something fixed, caught in a ready label such as a "hostile personality" or "introverted personality," and that personality consists of no more than particular isolated dimensions of behavior on which individuals are said to differ from one another, as in the view of personality in a phrase such as "those subjects who scored higher on neuroticism were twice as likely to get sick as those who scored low on neuroticism."

On the contrary, there has long been, and there still is, good reason to think that personality changes, that more than quick summary labels are required to describe it, and that it consists not of isolated dimensions of behavior but of complex psychological, social, cultural, and biological structures and processes (cf. Barresi & Juckes, 1997; Pervin, 1990; Sanford, 1982). Along with the conceptual opportunities, there are methodological tools available to investigators for such a rich view. For example, several recent commentators on the state of general personality psychology (e.g., McClelland, 1996; Westen, 1996) have highlighted particularly promising and underutilized strategies. They discuss explicitly psychodynamic processes, systems of self-regulation, scripts and schemas, and life narratives. The aim of this chapter is to highlight the approaches in which self and identity are primary concerns and to show how more inclusive ways of thinking about personality advance our understanding of the psychology of health and illness.

This is not my first plea for personality and health researchers to take better advantage of what basic personality psychology has to offer (cf. Ouellette, 1993; Ouellette Kobasa, 1985; Ouellette Kobasa, 1990). Why repeat it here? I want to broaden the view of personality beyond the currently very popular (and very particular) trait approach of the Five-Factor Model (FFM) or Big Five approach to traits (Digman, 1990; Goldberg, 1992, 1993; McCrae & Costa, 1997). In addition, personality and health researchers might use conceptual and methodological developments from a variety of social sciences in the study of self and identity.

The chapter has five parts. I first offer observations on the current state of general personality psychology and explain what is at stake, particularly for the health-and-illness researcher, in the maintenance of a broad view of the personality research enterprise. I then turn to the more specific literature on health and personality constructs to show that, despite the prevalent simple-trait or Big-Five view, research has been moving beyond simple traits and toward more complicated self and identity concepts. I use the personality constructs of sense of coherence and hardiness to illustrate both the need for and possibility of stretching beyond simple trait ideas. The third part is a critical interlude. I present scenes constructed from field notes of observations and interviews conducted with persons living with serious health concerns. In the fourth section, I use these data and a new integrative scheme of personality description to create a full view of a self and identity approach to personality in the health arena. In the fifth and final part, I consider model studies and suggestions on ways to facilitate and inspire future research in the personality-as-self/identity approach to health.

What Is in the General Personality Literature: Tensions between a Broad View of Personality and a Focus on Simple Traits

General Concerns about a Narrow Focus

Commentaries on the current state of personality psychology reveal many different ways of asking questions about persons. McAdams

(1996b), for example, recently offered an integrative framework for the study of personality that explicitly names the trait approach as only one of three possible levels of personality description. Other major indicators of the state of the art—recent symposia at the meetings of the American Psychological Association and whole issues of prominent journals such as the *Journal of Personality, Journal of Research in Personality*, and *Psychological Inquiry*—claim that the study of personality needs to recognize, to allow for, and to demand different analytical units as well as different perspectives on personality.

But why so much talk now about diversity of approaches? It is difficult not to hear in all of this a reaction against a move toward a singular way of doing personality psychology: the Big Five and related taxonomic enterprises. As Pervin puts it, many current enthusiasts are "virtually equating a particular trait model with trait theory and trait theory with the field of personality" (1994, p. 103). Proponents of the Big Five approach claim that a consensus has been reached on five basic dimensions in personality structure through which personality is described: Surgency or Extroversion, Agreeableness, Conscientiousness, Emotional Stability versus Neuroticism, and Openness to Experience (Costa & McCrae, 1992; Goldberg, 1992). Derived through factor analysis of data from research participants typically asked to fill out questionnaires by indicating the extent to which specified trait labels or brief trait statements describe them (or some designated other they are asked to describe), these dimensions are said to constitute "a universal descriptive framework . . . for the comprehensive assessment of individuals" (McCrae, 1989, p. 243). These five factors are presented as the solution to the key mystery in personality psychology, the discovery that allows and sets the agenda for the inevitable progress of personality science. Two prominent critics (Block, 1995; Pervin, 1994) of the Big Five effectively quote Big Five proponents to show their assumption of primacy. As the critics well document, it is difficult now to work as a personality psychologist and not feel the domineering presence of simple trait discourse.

My intention here is not to argue that there have been no contributions from the Big Five approach—it has been promoted by an extraordinarily productive and resourceful group of researchers. Nor is it the aim of this chapter to provide a detailed critique of this approach; two significantly better qualified critics have already been cited, and others can be added (e.g., McAdams, 1996a; Mischel & Shoda, 1995). Instead, this chapter seeks to identify the particular problems that Big Five personality psychology poses for the health researcher and to caution personality and health researchers against jumping on the Big Five bandwagon at the expense of other personality approaches to their work. Given the general concerns I have raised elsewhere about personality and health research, I would understandably be worried about any single approach securing a position of primacy in the field, but there are also concerns specific to the Big Five.

The Health Researcher's Particular Worries about a Narrow Focus

The Emphasis on Consistency in Behavior   Possibly because of the charge that personality is not stable across situations—a charge that occupied the attention of many personality psychologists after Mischel's (1968) influential ctitique—the emphasis of the Big Five approach has been on personality stability and pervasiveness across situations. This promotes a view of personality as fixed and consistent and thereby having an existence prior to and independent from life occurrences (such as stressful life events). For personality and health researchers intent on establishing the predictive or causal role of personality in the onset of illness (e.g., Booth-Kewley & Friedman, 1987; Friedman et al., 1993), the orientation of the Big Five may, indeed, be well suited. Nonetheless, for personality and health researchers interested in how personality might change as a result of serious illness (e.g., Dakof & Mendelsohn, 1986), or in how one might intervene to alter a personality orientation to minimize the risk to health posed by factors like stress (e.g., Maddi, 1990), or in the general view of personality as emergent and not fixed (Giddens, 1991), the conceptual emphasis upon stability is restrictive and possibly contradictory to their theoretical commitments.

A Decontextualized View of Behavior   The lens of the Big Five approach is so focused on the person that it offers at best only a blurred view of the situations or contexts in which that person participates. In his characterization of the Big Five approach as a psychology of the stranger, McAdams describes the current trait enterprise as "relatively nonconditional, relatively decontextualized, generally linear, and implicitly comparative" (1996b, p. 303). Given that many health and illness phenomena are influenced by a variety of specific situational as well as social, cultural, and political factors (Ware & Kleinman, 1992), an approach that captures the person in isolation from situations and contexts poses the threat of reductionism. For example, given the nature of the research enterprise over the last 25 years, the personality and health researcher is likely to be interested in an observation of personality not in isolation but alongside stressors, hassles that one encounters, stressful life events, or chronic sources of stress from the environment (cf. Contrada & Guyll, in press). Major conceptual frameworks seek to include not only interactions between persons and situations/contexts, considered independent of each other, but also transactions or dynamic constellations of all the elements (Smith, 1989; Smith & Williams, 1992).

Not Enough about Process As implied above, health researchers often pursue an understanding of personality that allows for its fluidity and emergence through situational and contextual factors. They are necessarily concerned with process. Most of the Big Five work, however, puts a premium on fixed structure; there is little room for dynamic or organismic views. The worry of the personality and health researcher is similar to that of Loevinger (1976), who 20 years ago depicted the inadequacy of trait models to represent the complexity of higher levels of ego development. From her perspective, the Big Five approach, like all applications of classical psychometric theory, assumes that observed questionnaire scores are linearly related to fundamental underlying dimensions. Loevinger found, however, that trait scores have a curvilinear relationship to, *and provide only clues of,* what she sought to understand: "Thus, the received psychometric approach to trait theory, with its General Linear hypothesis . . . and paraphernalia of linear decomposition must be discarded or modified in this field" (p. 256). Like Loevinger, personality and health researchers are seeking complexity. In their case, the search is for ways of understanding the integration of sociocultural, psychological, biological/physiological, and neurological phenomena. In health and illness, like religion, spirituality, and political convictions, the personality piece of the puzzle, as McClelland (1996) so aptly described it, involves more than what a person can say on a checklist of trait descriptors.

To these concerns, I would add others about the strictly nomothetic and quantitative nature of simple trait research. Health and illness provide phenomena to the personality investigator that call for idiographic and qualitative work, as many medical sociologists and anthropologists have well demonstrated (e.g., Charmaz, this book, chap. 9; Fox, 1979). But the simple trait researchers' emphasis on five components of personality that apply universally belie health researchers' recognition of the importance of cultural specificity to personality and health phenomena (e.g., Dressler, 1991).[2] Finally, there is the worry that has beset personality and health researchers since the early days of psychosomatic medicine: the issue of blaming the victim (cf. Sontag, 1977). With its focus on a stable, independent, decontextualized, and linear view of personality, the Big Five approach might be read to promote a discourse in which it appears that individuals are to be held accountable for negative changes in their health, absolving potential social and cultural sources of stress and distress of blame (cf. Lock, this book, chap. 3; Ouellette & DiPlacido, in press).

Underlying all the worries noted above is my basic concern that what is being captured about personality through the Big Five approach does not sufficiently supply what many personality and health researchers seek to undersand. Further, for some of what personality and health researchers are seeking to do, the Big Five approach threatens to be misleading. In other words, only some of what is being sought here is a simple combination of Big Five with other approaches (cf. Wiggins, 1996). For example, researchers can do more than just assess context alongside the administration of Costa and McCrae's Big Five NEO (McCrae & Costa, 1983) questionnaire and then enter both NEO and context scores into the regression equation that seeks to predict a health outcome. The "it" of personality that the Big Five scores are thought to capture is simply not all that some health researchers seek to understand about personality. Many of the basic conceptual assumptions of these health researchers are different from those of the Big Five approach and what they want to know about change, context, and process appears to require methodological strategies quite different from the self-report questionnaires that Big Five investigators employ.

What Is in the Literature on Personality and Health: Traits and a Movement beyond to Self and Identity Concerns

The Place of Traits—Prominent but Limited

A simple trait view seems prevalent in the literature on personality and health. It is what one hears in many depictions of the Type A individual (the one said to be at higher risk for cardiovascular disease) as hard-driving, competitive, ambitious, hostile, and impatient, in contrast to the Type B individual who is passive and relaxed (Matthews & Haynes, 1986; Robbins, Spence, & Clarke, 1991). In a summary of a wide range of personality studies, Friedman and Booth-Kewley (1987) conclude their meta-analysis by announcing a "disease-prone personality" characterized as anxious, depressed, angry, and hostile. And, indeed, a number of review articles that highlight different traits demonstrate the important connections between personality conceived of as traits and physical health (Contrada & Guyll, in press; Scheier, Carver, & Bridges, 1994; Miller, Smith, Turner, Guijarro, & Hallet, 1996).

Smith and Williams (1992), in their review of personality and health research, call all of the major constructs *traits* (they include Type A behavior, hostility, neuroticism, hardiness, optimism, inhibited power motivation, health locus of control, alexythymia, and sense of coherence) and claim that the future of health research depends on greater attention to the linkage between these constructs and the personality components of the FFM. In a similar spirit, in a recent introductory chapter for an issue of the *Journal of Personality* dedicated to new studies of personality and coping, Suls, David, and Harvey (1996) predict that, now that investigators have the Big Five in hand to settle how we need to study personality, there can be an outpouring of coping research unencumbered by debates about how to conceive of and measure personality.

Alongside the enthusiasm about the trait approach, however, one also finds recognitions of its limitations. For example, the 1992 Smith and Wiliams review, cited above for its portrayal of the Big Five as the gold standard against which all health-related personality variables might be tested, ends revealingly with a call for health researchers to stretch beyond traits to use other approaches to personality. In a "yes . . . but" style, they point out that research guided by the trait approach and its tools, such as the NEO, have filled the measurement need for easily administered personality questionnaires in health projects that are typically interdisciplinary (i.e., projects in which personality data collection has to be squeezed in along with the assessment of other variables intended to cover biomedical and demographic domains).[3] As a number of review articles make clear, this approach has generated a good deal of description of self-reported psychological correlates of health constructs. What is missing, however, not provided by the trait-oriented research, is an explanation of how the described links between personality and health are forged and how they might be changed.

Smith and Williams (1992) also describe a second limitation. The trait approach threatens to focus on the main effects of personality on health and neglect how personality combines with other factors, such as environmental stressors, to determine whether someone becomes ill or, if ill, gets sicker. And Smith is not calling for simply the observation of additive or interactive effects between trait and situational constructs, each thought to be independent of the other. Smith, a major contributor to the personality and health literature, pleads for a better recognition of the *transactions*, not just interactions, between persons and events (1989; Smith and Williams, 1992). Personality is not independent of the experience of stress. Personality determines which stressors occur and is itself shaped by past stressful events. Smith (1989) worries that traits have led psychologists to neglect the "dynamic, reciprocal relationship between persons and situations." His remedy is a personality approach that captures persons in their contexts. In their concluding remarks, Smith and Williams (1992) suggest that only by looking at persons in context, and at personality as a construction process, can researchers consider dynamic reciprocal relationships and understand basic psychological processes in health and illness.

Other revealing looks at the limitations of a simple trait approach in the health arena are presented by Contrada and his colleagues. In a recent review of the research on personality, stress, and physical illness, Contrada and Guyll (in press) describe the conceptual and empirical viability of many different approaches to the study of personality and health that do not fit within a narrowly defined taxonomic and descriptive enterprise. Also, Contrada, Leventhal, and O'Leary (1990) point specifically to the study of processes and of self and identity as key elements in the needed broader view of personality.

Critiquing much Type A research, Contrada and colleagues demonstrate that to understand how someone described as showing the Type A behavior pattern develops risk for coronary heart disease, researchers need to look beyond simple traits and at the complex processes of self-regulation situated within the broader processes of stress and coping. Contrada and his co-authors effectively bring together the work of Glass, Matthews, Price, and others, showing that each implicates particular cognitive structures or belief systems related to individuals' views of self and world. More specifically, Contrada et al. (1990) find in these many studies of personality and cardiovascular disease that what is said to predispose one to illness is a set of self-evaluative standards and associated self-appraisals. A person said to be at risk of poor health thinks that he or she must always remain in control but often sees himself or herself as out of control. He or she is also likely to have a generalized way of understanding the world as a place primarily for one's demonstration of control.

Contrada et al. (1990) elaborate their conceptual critique through an important methodological point. They demonstrate that the confrontation and behavioral sampling strategies of the Type A structured interview do a better job than the self-report Type A questionnaires at predicting who will develop heart disease, precisely because the interview allows greater access to the personality processes that matter for health and illness. The Type A questionnaires, perhaps like simple trait measures would in such a setting, provide what Loevinger calls only a clue about what needs to be considered.

Pushing beyond Traits to Self and Identity: The Constructs of Sense of Coherence and Hardiness

Summing up the contributions of Contrada, Smith, and their colleagues, one can say that the current literature on personality and health allows one to make the case that the future viability of the research enterprise depends on all of the following: (1) movement beyond description of personality to an explanation of its role in health and illness processes; (2) recognition of persons in their contexts, with contexts understood broadly to include specific situational demands, interpersonal relationships, group settings, and broader social and cultural structures; (3) a close look at processes that reveal how personality operates not only in context but also in its relationship to neurological and biological/physiological mechanisms associated with disease onset and exacerbation; (4) utilization of many different approaches to personality study, including many different units of analysis, conceptual frameworks, *and* measurement strategies; and (5) appreciation of the key roles played by notions about self such as self-regulation within these many different approaches. The case that the field requires more than a simple trait approach also applies for specific personality constructs within that field, such as the constructs of sense of coherence and hardiness.

The turn to specific constructs is important, given the tendency in the literature to label all personality constructs as traits (e.g., Smith and Williams, 1992). In so doing, commentators may have in mind a broader view of traits than the restrictive one fretted about in this chapter. Nonetheless, it seems useful in the current climate to warn against a confusion of the intentions of the originators of constructs like sense of coherence and hardiness with the goals of many Big Five researchers and to point out that sense of coherence and hardiness were conceived of as broad-based personality ideas and they need to be so pursued in empirical research. The particular point I seek to make in this section is twofold. There remains a large gap between the promise in the original conceptual frameworks and its realization through research. A recognition of the extent to which the original conceptualizations relied upon self and identity concepts may help fill the gap in the future.[4]

The Critique   Elsewhere, I have provided details on both the gains and the weaknesses of research on sense of coherence and hardiness and their connections both to stress resistance and health and health-related behaviors (Ouellette, 1993; Ouellette & DiPlacido, in press). The reader may also want to consult other reviews and critiques for a fuller picture of these constructs than can be provided in this chapter (Antonovsky, 1987, 1991; Funk, 1992; Orr & Westman, 1990; Wiebe & Williams, 1992). The critique here is focused on the limited view of measurement in the published work and its accompanying narrow methodology: on the one hand, the lack of attention to critical subjective, experiential process, and, on the other, social structures and the transactions between structures and persons.

The standard way of measuring within both sense of coherence and hardiness projects has been the administration of paper and pencil self-report questionnaires. Current hardiness research now most frequently employs the Personal Views Survey or what Maddi called the third-generation measure (Maddi, 1990), whereas most sense of coherence research relies on the Orientation to Life Questionnaire (Antonovsky, 1993; Frenz, Carey, & Jorgensen, 1993). These questionnaires present items such as the following: "I often wake up eager to take up my life where it left off the day before" (hardiness; Maddi, 1990), and "How often do you have the feeling that there is little meaning in the things you do in your daily life?" (sense of coherence; Antonovsky, 1993). A respondent is asked to read the statement and reflect on how much it describes him or her. That strategy holds for hardiness, sense of coherence, and the five-factor components assessed through the Costa and McCrae NEO. In spite of the conceptual differences between sense of coherence/hardiness and simple trait ways of thinking critiqued in this chapter, researchers operate in very much the same ways in their collection and analysis of data. For the majority of health-related personality constructs, researchers have come very close to Kuhn's notion of a paradigmatic way of operating in personality psychology: a paradigm that explicitly and implicitly requires that the work include self-report item construction, factor analysis, and increasingly the entrance of Big Five scores in equations that predict health to demonstrate that the personality construct of interest (e.g., hardiness) contributes to the focal health problem *above* and *beyond* the assumed-to-be-fundamental Big Five traits.

Missing from this way of working are at least four kinds of information. First, one learns how much research participants agree or disagree with statements that researchers think reflect the constructs, but one hears nothing about how participants themselves construe sense of coherence and hardiness in their lives. Second, one learns how participants willingly and consciously describe their behavior in particular research settings, but one hears nothing about what may be outside participants' direct awareness or what is being held back in such a situation (cf. McClelland, 1996). This is especially worrisome because many assessment settings may include pulls for a certain kind of responding; for example, given the extent of its coverage in the nursing literature, it would be difficult for a nurse not to think that hardiness is the correct response to a high-stress nursing situation. Third, one gets a quick snapshot of the other through check marks on a written form but nothing like the long view of the person so many personality psychologists have argued is essential (e.g., Sanford, 1982), a view obtained through a variety of observations and interactions with participants and a sampling of verbal as well as stylistic behaviors (e.g., Allport, 1961).

Finally, one also misses hearing about the social and cultural structures within which sense of coherence and hardiness operate. Indeed, cross-cultural studies have asked after matters like gender differences, but these have been guided primarily by attempts to demonstrate generalization. Rare has been the attempt to consider seriously how these constructs might emerge in different contexts and to clarify *why* differences matter if one is interested in issues like gender and race. For this, one requires assessment at social, cultural, and individual levels. For example, in the treatment of stress, the sense of coherence and hardiness literatures have often failed to look empirically beyond specific stressful life events or daily hassles and to assess the social, cultural, and political structural sources of stress these events and hassles reflect. By structural sources of stress, I mean the realities such as racism, sexism, and homophobia in society that investigators are now able systematically to document in empirical research (e.g., Meyer, 1995; Williams et al., this book, chap. 4). Although sense of coherence and hardiness research efforts have often been conducted with groups of people who confront serious and frequent stressors, the empirical look has not been close and broad-based enough to understand what Smith (1989) calls the dynamic and transactional relationships between persons and their contexts that shape the experience of these stressors.

Back to Basics   The measurement histories of these constructs were not doomed to turn out this way. A look at the basic conceptualizations of sense of coherence and hardiness reveals complex and dynamic ideas that suggest an approach to measurement that includes more than simple self-report questionnaires. The conceptualizations support a view of personality as that revealed through persons' subjective ways of experiencing self and world and that inexorably tied to the contexts in which people find themselves.

> The sense of coherence is a global orientation that expresses the extent to which one has a pervasive, enduring though dynamic feeling of confidence that (1) the stimuli deriving from one's internal and external environments in the course of living are structured, predictable, and explicable [comprehensibility]; (2) the resources are available to one to meet the demands posed by these stimuli [manageability]; and (3) these demands are challenges, worthy of investment and engagement [meaningfulness] (Antonovsky, 1987, p. 19).

Sense of coherence was a key piece of Antonovsky's argument for *salutogenesis*, the process through which persons remain healthy in the face of stressors. In his emphasis upon positive adaptation, Antonovsky deliberately rejected the use of the word trait for three basic reasons. First, he sought to go beyond the description provided by a simple list of attributes—he wanted to understand the processes that link self and health. Second, he feared psychological reductionism. Third, he wanted at all costs to keep researchers vigilant about both the cultural-historical context for the development of the sense of coherence orientation and the socially structured situations in which this orientation comes to be expressed in people's lives. Working as sociologist, he was interested in how institutionalized roles, cultural values, and norms influenced all of the following: which stresses occur, how people deal with them, and the resulting outcomes of that confrontation. Although he thought most people's sense of coherence would be reflected in their behavior as "a stable, enduring, and generalized orientation . . . that characterizes a person throughout adulthood, barring radical, lasting changes in one's life situation" (1987, p. 182), he saw that stability as dependent on the active and deliberate maintenance of social structures that facilitate sense of coherence.

Hardiness, as conceptualized by Kobasa, Maddi, and their colleagues (Kobasa, 1979; Kobasa, Maddi, & Kahn, 1982; Ouellette, 1993), was drawn from existential personality theory as a representation of a person's distinctive way of understanding self, world, and the interaction between self and world. Existentialism, both in its European forms and in the American version found in some of James's (1911) work, disputes a view of the person as simply a passive victim of life's stresses and requires all investigation to begin with persons' subjective experience of life's demands. The originators of the hardiness construct drew on the existential idea of *authenticity*, a way of living that expresses both a struggle after human fulfillment and a recognition of the limitations and chaos that are part and parcel of human life. They elaborated this idea with an eye toward empirical research through the psychological literature on adult development and on the construct of control (Kobasa, 1979). They located hardiness in the extent to which a person is able to express commitment, control, and challenge in his or her actions, thoughts, and feelings.

Commitment refers to a person's engagement in life and view of his or her activities and experiences as meaningful, purposeful, and interesting. Control has to do with an individual's recognition that she/he has some influence over what life brings. Challenge indicates an orientation toward change as an inevitable and even rewarding part of life matched by cognitive flexibility and tolerance of ambiguity. The dynamic interplay of all three in a person's basic stance toward life is theorized to promote stress resistance and to enhance psychological and physical health. Hardiness is said to lessen the negative effects of stress by its influence upon the perception and interpretation of stressful events and its promotion of actions that minimize the toxicity of those events. It is assumed that as one looks across most lives, one finds a characteristic level of hardiness expression, but an existential orientation requires the investigator to see that characteristic level as something the observed person constantly works on, or, in the existential terminology, repeatedly chooses for his or her life.

Even these brief characterizations of the constructs provide theoretical ground for the supplementation of the typical way of doing hardiness and sense of coherence research with other measurement strategies. For example, given the conceptual roots of sense of coherence in sociology and Antonovsky's interest in the sociocultural structural supports of salutogenesis, it is surprising that group-level or collective units of analysis have not been employed. Indeed, Antonovsky's last theoretical work suggests that he was moving in that direction (1991). Given the foundation of hardiness in existentialism, it is equally surprising that more phenomenological—that is, participant-based, qualitative, and open-ended—strategies have not been attempted (cf. Ouellette, 1993).

Sightings of Self and Identity   The available conceptualizations probably stand to be better applied in empirical research in many ways. My aim in this chapter is to illustrate the conceptual and methodological possibilities that self and identity bring to the research table. It is not difficult to understand sense of coherence and hardiness as essentially about self and identity. From those "large, amorphous, and changing phenomena that defy hard and fast definitions" (Ashmore & Jussim, 1997, p. 5) that constitute self and identity discourse, the originators of sense of coherence and hardiness have selected to focus on what James (1890) called the "I" and the "Me" of self and identity. For the "I," sense of coherence and hardiness concern processes of the self that constitute ongoing subjective experience—experiences of individual consciousness, agency, and choice, as well as limitation and constraint. For example, the commitment aspect of hardiness describes an "I" that is realized through engagement with the environment and others, while the challenge piece highlights those "I" processes that have to do with curiosity and an "I" that discovers itself both in the present and in possibilities for the future.

For the "Me," sense of coherence and hardiness depict particular kinds of objectifications of self and identity. There are explicit self-concepts or self-representations associated with each of these constructs. For example, hardiness consists of being able to conceive of oneself as a person who has commitments in life, who feels he or she influences things, and who is challenged. There are also particular representations of the world in which the hardy or coherent self operates. For example, sense of coherence involves seeing the world as a place within which one has the possibility of understanding oneself as managing things and as keeping things meaningful.

Before turning to some of the formal research on self and identity and what it has to offer to a new agenda for personality and health research, I would like to turn to the promised interlude. I was drawn to self and identity as beacons for a new way of doing health research through real life and close encounters with research participants. It seems right to share data drawn from my field notes on those encounters. These scenes display the basic human accessibility of personality and health issues and the speed and strength with which ideas and questions about self and identity come to the surface as one observes and interacts with people contending with some challenge to their health.

Four Scenes about Self, Identity, and Health

The first scene was constructed from notes on open-ended interviews conducted with executives who participated in the first hardiness, stress, and health study (Kobasa, 1979). These interviews were conducted to help interpret the large amount of questionnaire data collected from nearly 400 business executives. Mr. Jones, a white, male, middle-aged business executive, arrives more than 30 minutes late for the interview. Before greeting me, he stops at the office administrator's desk to call his office and let them know where he is. Within minutes of his perching on a chair in my office with trench coat still on and bulging briefcase in hand, the phone rings; he jumps up—he knows it is for him. He takes the call while I fiddle with my pencil. He comes back, the phone rings again, and he's off. We begin and abruptly end our interview three more times. Finally, he says, "I came here to find out what you learned about me from those questionnaires that I filled out. I mean, you might have something to say that could be helpful for all this stress I am under. But these calls are really important, I need to take 'em. Here's my tape recorder. Why don't you just talk into this and I will listen to what you have to say about me when I get a chance."

The second scene is drawn from participant observations of interactions between patients, their families, and health-care professionals at a tertiary care cancer center. It involves Mrs. Rossi, an older and seemingly traditional Italian woman who observes her husband of many years in a medical crisis. The husband is delirious and struggles with the doctors and nurses on the oncology unit who are trying to do a test. He curses them in Italian and English, using words that most New Yorkers would find surprisingly obscene. The wife is shocked by his behavior and begins moaning to her daugher and all else present, "This is who he really is. Fifty years, we've been married and I never knew the kind of person he really was but now it's all come out. What he says to people, all the hate and dirtiness. This is who he really is." She asks her daughter to take her away. She withdraws herself and her support from his room.

The third and longest scene is drawn from notes on the intake interviews I am now doing as a volunteer clinician and researcher in a community-based AIDS organization. Mr. Ortiz is a Puerto Rican man in his midthirties who has been diagnosed with AIDS. He describes his diagnosis as *the* catastrophic event that shuts down all possibilities of his ever being the kind of person he always thought he could be. As he describes with much affect a very strong and positive ideal self-image, he reminds me of Marlon Brando in the back of that taxi: "I coulda been a contender, I coulda been somebody." His self-image survived many blows in his life: alcohol use since age 9, drug use since age 14, living on the streets, being in prison. Alongside all of this, Mr. Ortiz was able to continue his education, hold jobs, maintain significant personal relationships, and hope for better things in his life. But AIDS, he fears, he and his self-image cannot withstand. "AIDS means never having children, AIDS means watching my wife die, AIDS means being very sick, AIDS means dying." I wonder what will keep Mr. Ortiz off drugs and alcohol. For the first time in his life, since he was nine, he has been clean for more than three months at a time. But the pain he describes feeling seems so strong. Who could blame Mr. Ortiz for wanting to numb this kind of pain? But if he goes back to using, his illness will get worse. Along with how alcohol and drugs will directly influence his health, I worry about how his doctor will respond. I have heard about doctors who are reluctant to put some of their patients on protease inhibitors—those seemingly magical AIDS drugs—if they fear they will not take them as they should. Drug users often get assigned the identity of poor compliers. And there does not appear to be anyone in Mr. Ortiz's life who could advocate for him if such questionable medical practice were to occur. Mr Ortiz describes poor relations with social service providers: "Because I'm a Puerto Rican with AIDS who used drugs, they think I'm just dumb and stupid. That's all I am to them."

The final story is about a 40-something-year-old woman who has a retinal detachment in her right eye and requires emergency care. The retinologist—whom she meets for the first time during the crisis situation—recommends, on the basis of a necessarily quick interaction, that he perform laser surgery on the left eye along with the more complicated and extensive surgery needed on the eye with the detachment. He explains that the former procedure could be put off for a while, until after her recovery from the operation on the detachment, but he supports the more hurried strategy involving both of her eyes because "I know you have the kind of personality that would make you not want to delay anything." She was the kind of person, he knew, who did not procrastinate and was task-oriented; she would be likely to join him as a good team player in this medical adventure. She would want to get these medical things over with quickly so she could get back to work. Unfortunately, that scene is drawn from my notes on my own medical experiences.

Beyond Simple Traits: Goals and Projects, Self and Identity

Personality emerges in these scenes in many different forms. A description and understanding of the health- and illness-related behaviors displayed requires one to work with the conceptual and methodological tools from all "three relatively independent levels on which modern persons may be described" (McAdams, 1996b, p. 295), the full complement of a new broad-based integrative framework for the study of personality. The simple trait approach, McAdams's first level, captures only some of the information one needs, and the self and identity tools that make up much of the other two levels promise to be very useful.

McAdams describes traits as providing us with a psychology of the stranger, quick capsule summaries for someone we do not need to know very well. His characterization rings true as one tries out traits in an interpretation of the scenes. One could say that the Big Five trait of openness to experience or the simple trait version of the challenge component of hardiness describes that business executive as he says he is curious to learn more about himself. Mr. Jones might indeed strongly agree with a hardiness item like: "It's exciting for me to learn something about myself." The trait label, however, reveals nothing of the important observation that Mr. Jones was content to hear what a psychologist had to say about him and his questionnaire data from a tape recording. He did not require a conversation with her. Many self and identity approaches would usefully foster this additional observation. Work by Hermans (1996), for example, demonstrates the importance, for an understanding of Mr. Jones's personality, of taking into account the differences between what emerges in a dialogue between him and another (or, in the case of Mr. Jones and openness to experience, what does not emerge), and what is revealed as he, in isolation and in an abstract and general way, thinks about who he is.

Simple traits seem to figure most prominently in these scenes in their use by the retinologist. His treatment course appears to have been shaped by his depiction of me on at least four of the Big Five: my openness to experience would make me amenable to the more expansive form of treatment, my conscientiousness would lead me to be both serious about what the doctor thought best and eager to go back to work, my agreeableness would mean I would be unlikely to protest or sue, and my assumed low neuroticism would mean I would not be too difficult a patient for him or the nurses to manage when I woke up from the operation, unable to see out of either eye. The limitation of the trait approach here was not experienced as a complete mislabeling (in fact, in many situations I would be content to be so simply labeled). The problem was my sense that the trait labels were keeping the doctor from recognizing other things about me I felt he should know, *and* that these same labels might keep me from fully experiencing certain possibilities in this situation—a situation that I felt to be a critical illness, a life crisis, and a moral situation.[5] Through his focus on simple traits, the retinologist failed to address such things as the strong feelings such as fear that I was experiencing and wanted acknowledged by this up-until-now stranger on whom I had become so dependent. The trait labels might be reassuring, but they did not represent what I found myself confronting, that is, those many concerns about what the surgical procedure would mean for the many projects I was working on and my struggles with how to include the identities of patient and possibly that of a person with limited sight in my understanding of who I am and could be.

It is on McAdams's (1996b) other two levels of personality analysis that one finds aspects of what the retinologist missed about my personality. On the second or "personal concerns" level, McAdams places all of that recent personality psychology research focused on what it is people are seeking to get done in their lives and the relationships within which such seeking is enhanced or restrained. Constructs such as personal projects (Little), personal strivings (Emmons), current concerns (Klinger), and patterns of self-with-other identities (Ogilvie & Rose) are the major conceptual tools at this level. Nancy Cantor calls these *doing* rather than *having* aspects of personality. One finds here aspects of both James's "I" and "Me." Investigators are interested both in how life tasks are enacted and experienced and what new objectifications of self are represented in the world through the pursuit of these tasks. What is being done as people undertake personal projects is not just the pursuit of goals but also the construction, maintenance, and change in how these individuals understand who they are and how they present themselves in the world through a variety of personal and social identities. These second-level elements force the researcher to look at personality as that which is being built through and in particular times, places, and social interactions or roles. These second-level elements do a better job than simple traits at capturing my personality as it emerges in my self-reflections and interaction with the physician.

Constructs like personal strivings, ideal self, and self-with-other also promise to reveal important facts about Mr. Ortiz. Mr. Ortiz is actively seeking to find ways of furthering his life goals but also confronting the possibility that his vision of his ideal self may never be realized. He struggles against those identities that others with whom he must necessarily interact in the health-care system are imposing upon him. For the man living with AIDS, it is the illness's ultimate threat to his ideal self-image that provokes a pain that may be sufficient to lead him to resume his drug use. Others who are responsible for his health care may fail to see the pain because of their focus on the stigmatized identities that they associate with him (an AIDS patient who is also a former drug user and a person of color).

Even more can be said about these scenes through McAdams (1996b) "identity as a life story" level of personality inquiry. On his third level, one finds matters of self and identity as fully definitive of what personality investigators investigate. On this level, McAdams (e.g., 1997) places his own research and gives center stage to the life stories or narratives about the self that individuals tell to unite and give coherence to their pasts, presents, and anticipated futures. He also finds on this level the research of Bruner on meaning making, Cohler on the role of personal narratives through the life course, Hermans and Kempen on the dialogical self, and Gergen on the saturated self. Take again the case of Mr. Ortiz. He is not only cognitively processing a variety of self-concepts, both undesired and positive, both real and ideal; he is also very much involved in the construction of a story about who he was, who he is now, and might or might not be in the future. In this interview with another who is responsible for helping him secure needed resources from a health-care organization, one hears him struggling with the interviewer and with himself to discover what can now be meaningful in a life dominated by AIDS. In contrast to this, there is Mr. Jones, who has clearly not chosen the interview as a setting for identity narrative work. In his plan for looking at how he deals with stress, he listens only to bits of a tape between phone calls.

In the case of Mrs. Rossi, one also observes a new narrative about self being constructed. But in this case it is one's narrative about another—Mrs. Rossi's narrative about her husband—that stands to have serious health implications. Here, we reach beyond McAdams's framework to take advantage of what feminist psychologists like Lykes (1994) observe about the social or relational nature of the self and the ways in which one's understanding of who one is in the world evolves through relationships with others, both immediate others and the larger community of which one is part. What Mrs. Rossi says about the self that she now knows her husband "really is" will likely shape the reality he will confront when he is free of his delirium. Moreover, what she says about her husband's self has itself been shaped by the social representation of a repressed person and the power of the unconscious accessible to her as one of the many identities our modern psychologically savvy collective has made available. In Craik's (1996) scheme for the analysis of life stories, Mrs. Rossi is making use of a "community-generated" story about the unconscious in her unfolding narrative for herself, her husband, and their family. Unfortunately, the new narrative with its elements of her feeling betrayed by his former self and her disgust at the current self she attributes to him leads her to withdraw support from him at a time in their lives when, according to a good deal of research, support is very important for her husband's well-being.

Three final comments about self and identity in the scenes elaborate McAdams's framework. First, the moral nature of the work of personality description, in its simple traits as well as self and identity forms, emerges here in ways the personality health researcher needs to know. As a Puerto Rican and drug user, Mr. Ortiz was already feeling marginalized by his society. As he seeks to go through life with a serious illness, he experiences even more stigma because in this society, to be healthy is to be good (cf. Lock, this book, chap. 3; Marcus, Kitayama, & Heiman, 1995). In his assignment of personality traits to me, the retinologist was not only telling me what he thought I was like but also what for him constituted the *good* medical patient and what I *should* be like. A second comment concerns the importance of the co-construction of what McAdams calls the life story (cf. Ouellette, 1996; Spence, 1987). As I review my field notes, it is clear that the story about self that Mr. Ortiz told was a narrative, like all narratives, that both persons in the dialogue constructed. For example, by the end of the interview, he was talking optimistically about volunteering at the agency where he was seeking help. It would be naive of me not to see this as somehow connected with what I have thought and written about volunteering as coping (Ouellette, Cassel, Maslanka, & Wong, 1995). In the case of Mr. Jones, the identity story, or lack of such, speaks of the failure of relationship, connection, and storytelling between two people.

Finally, these scenes reveal the importance of self and identity, as well as goals and projects, for the kind of understanding of personality that enables the participant observer to intervene meaningfully in health situations. I have no doubt that my knowing something about Mr. Ortiz's goals, projects, and self-concepts; the social identities imposed on him by others; and the story he was struggling to tell about himself enabled me, better than Big Five scores would have, to connect him with agency services. I believe that understanding the identity confusion that Mrs. Rossi felt, and her turn to an oddly distorted psychoanalytic view of people, gave me what I needed to find words to comfort her. The recognition that I was not just a collection of traits but a person still involved in the construction of her life story, even if it meant weaving in some episodes about not seeing, helped me cope with the stress of eye surgery.

Self and Identity in a Comprehensive, Integrated Approach to Personality and Health: Model Studies and Future Directions

At this point, I can almost hear the reader say, "This is interesting, but how does one actually do this kind of personality and health research?" The tone is especially poignant in the voice of a graduate student trying to get through a dissertation. To minimize worry and inspire hopefulness, I offer published exemplars of how self and identity may contribute to the broader agenda for personality and health research sought in this chapter. This is followed by a general sketch of the directions that theoretical and empirical work might take in the future.

Some Model Studies

On personality as that revealed through the projects and related life concerns that the self engages, what McAdams places on his second level of personality inquiry, one can cite the work of Rapkin and his colleagues (1994). They have developed the Idiographic Functional Status Assessment (IFSA) strategy for systematically observing others' goals. This is an interview through which each research participant describes, from his or her unique perspective, their personal goals: "Things they want to accomplish, problems they want to solve, situations they hope to avoid, roles and relationships they want to maintain, and pursuits they want to relinquish" (p. 111). In a study of 224 people living with AIDS, Rapkin and colleagues had participants rate the goals they said they were pursuing over the last month on difficulty and other performance dimensions. What persons living with AIDS said about their goals significantly correlated with their well-being and other health issues. For example, the greater the number of important goals not pursued because of health problems, the poorer the respondents' physical, role, social, and mental functioning. Also, differences were observed in the determinants of well-being among respondents with different personal goals. Rapkin and colleagues present their strategy as one that will enable researchers, as well as clinicians, to take into account when and how individuals and subsamples within samples differ and agree on what they may be seeking in life and what enhances various forms of quality of life. One wishes one had a profile from the IFSA on Mr. Ortiz to show those social workers and other health-care professionals that among his many goals were some that most would see as long-term, socially approved goals (for example, to be a good husband and father). The data would likely strongly support his claim that he is not simply a "dumb and stupid" Puerto Rican with AIDS "trying to get high."

Moving to McAdams's third level of inquiry for personality, one can cite a series of papers by Sabat and Harré (1992, 1994; Sabat, 1994) that demonstrate the effectiveness of discourse analysis in health research. Using the methods of constructionist psychology, these investigators present empirical evidence obtained from persons living with Alzheimer's disease that (a) the subjective experience of oneself as a self persists through the late and most debilitating stages of disease, and (b) the social selves that one presents to the world are constructed only by and with the cooperation of others—selves may indeed be lost through the ways that these others view and act toward the person living with the disease (see Charmaz, this book, chap. 9). These investigators' emphasis upon all of the following—the self that is experienced and the self that is attributed by others, discourse, and the construction/deconstruction of the self of the person living with illness—makes them likely clarifiers of the scenes depicted.

Sabat and Harré (1994) analyzed records of their conversations with persons living with Alzheimer's disease, both in treatment centers and at their homes; their interviews with care givers; and interviews conducted by social workers with the Alzheimer's sufferer and his or her care giver together. Their involvement with their research participants was long-term; for example, one woman was interviewed for two hours weekly for approximately two years. The interviews with persons living with Alzheimer's disease were deliberately conducted to allow the patients' voices and efforts at meaning to emerge. Interviewers' strategy involved not interrupting and allowing participants the time they needed to speak. They analyzed the plentiful empirical material they collected on the many discursive events with an intensional design, an in-depth look at a few individual cases to exemplify types in as much detail as possible. Their reports provide remarkably rich information that offers new ways of thinking about Alzheimer's disease. Their analysis of discourse reveals high levels of cognitive functioning in patients who were diagnosed through standardized psychometric measures as severely debilitated in concept formation, memory, and word finding. In addition, their data support recommendations for care givers, which, if followed, may reduce the damaged self-esteem and general loss of personhood that now accompanies Alzheimer's disease. Their methodology offers a systematic way of understanding the wife in the cancer hospital, the Puerto Rican man living with AIDS, and the middle-aged female professor as we all struggle in a kind of dance with others about what identities are to be assigned and used as the basis for decisions and actions (see Kihlstrom & Kihlstrom, this book, chap. 2)—as we construct new selves and tell narratives about selves lost.

Directions for the Future

With fuller description and understanding, and more successful intervention at stake, I suggest the following ideas for conceptual and methodological development.

Elaboration of Existing Schemes   Self and identity concerns point out new ways to stretch sense of coherence and hardiness ideas. For example, with the focus on self-experience as it unfolds in particular time and space, I have come to prefer the word *stance* to orientation when speaking of hardiness. Stance better conveys hardiness as something embodied and expressed by persons who are grounded in real physical space—in other words, hardiness is not just "something in your head." Relatedly, in my ongoing work with clients, volunteers, and staff at a community-based AIDS organization, I find essential the description and understanding of that setting as a special environmental niche for the expression and support of hardiness, what might be called a *hardiness zone*. This stretching of ideas is ironically a harkening back to some original ways of thinking about hardiness. For example, there has been a good deal of talk here about the importance of process and the dynamic nature of personality. That personality needs to be understood as both facticity and possibility and that one wishes to capture not only where the research participant is now in his or her life, but where he or she might be going are notions central to a basic existential view of personality (Gendlin, 1962, 1997; Kobasa & Maddi, 1977).

Integration of Individual and Sociocultural Levels of Analysis   Self and identity play a key role in bringing the researcher's attention simultaneously to subjective and experiential dimensions of personality and the variety of contexts through which personality is expressed. The message here is that researchers need to use not only both individual and social levels of analysis but also explanatory principles that represent the integration of the two levels. Being ill or at risk of being ill involve the self of the experiencing subject as well as the selves and identities confronted within and shaped by the society and culture in which that subject operates. For example, inspired by the self and identity discourse, the personality and health researcher who seeks to understand high-risk sexual behavior in HIV-positive gay men is drawn to ask about *how* these men seek to define who they are as they experience the limitations and possibilities that accompany a life-threatening illness, *what* identities are imposed on them as they confront the social stigma associated with HIV and homosexuality, and *what* new selves and identities are created as a result of the struggle (e.g., the activist person with AIDS, the altruistic AIDS volunteer, or the rejected victim).

Application of a Greater Variety of Methodological Strategies   The majority of studies within the personality and health arena have relied on the administration of self-report scales. Exceptions to the psychometric strategy such as the Type A structured interview, Thematic Apperception Test (TAT) assessment of motivation (e.g., McKay, 1991), and the content analysis of attributional style (e.g., Peterson, Schulman, Castellon, & Seligman, 1992) are rare. Block's (1995) commentary on the need to go beyond self-report questionnaires is especially apt within the arena of personality and health research: "Certainly, straightforward self-report or layperson-report measures can be immensely useful. . . . But often enough to pose serious theoretical and empirical problems . . . to study certain crucial phenomena lying within the domain of personality psychology, personality psychologists often will need to turn, or return, to more complicated and complex ways of studying persons" (1995, p. 209). With a focus on self and identity, one particular call in this chapter is to the greater reliance on phenomenology and qualitative research strategies. These include intensive open-ended interviewing through which the researcher gathers self and identity narratives, participant observation, intensive field notes, and a highly self-reflexive process of review of research materials. In this last step, one needs to appreciate how one's own stories about self and illness influence how one hears, records, and interprets another's story. Taking seriously the social identity piece of self and identity, phenomena of social representation, and Antonovsky's (1987) emphasis on sociocultural structural sources of stress resistance, one also wants to engage in group- or collective-level data collection and analysis. Archival materials, representations of group ideology, content analysis of news reports and popular media are all tools for the personality and health researcher.

The Importance of Collaboration   For the future, it is important to take seriously one's partners in health research. Through constructs such as the co-construction of narratives, the researcher comes to appreciate the extent to which he or she and the research participant are collaborators. The self and identity approach to personality also provides important ways for psychologists to think about what they do in relationship to work in medical anthropology and medical sociology, of which there are powerful examples in other parts of this book (Charmaz, chap. 9; Lock, chap 3).

There is also collegueship with other psychologists. With a firm conceptual and methodological grasp of personality as self and identity in hand, one may then collaborate with other personality psychologists, including trait psychologists. I intend that the breaking away from strict reliance on self-report scales will also be liberating for them. After all, the conscious self-concept triggered as people respond to items on the NEO may be less adequate as a proxy for personality for trait psychologists than it is for researchers working from a self and identity perspective (cf. Westen, 1996). But in the future, the collaborative enterprise should not be primarily about demonstrating whose personality construct is the biggest, as in pitting hardiness and neuroticism against each other in a regression analysis. Rather, the work will be about how best to recognize that hardiness and neuroticism are fundamentally different ways of thinking about personality and how best to combine the insights of each approach to understanding health. Such a collaboration might indeed bring us back to the complex promise of traits that Allport had in mind. And there is encouragement for this kind of collaboration in the literature. There is McClelland's (1996) now long-standing claim that motivation has both its explicit and implicit forms and that the possible conflicts between the two need to be taken into account in an understanding of behavior and health. There is Little's (1996) recent and, as far as I know, not yet pursued suggestion that negative changes in health may concern the disjuncture between traits understood as temperament and the projects that a self takes on later in life.

Being Aware of the Researcher's Stance   Finally, there is a need to say something about the stance of researchers in their work. The scene about Mr. Ortiz and the narratives he told would not have been in my notes if the two of us had not come to a particular way of being together in the interview. At the start of the interaction, Mr. Ortiz seemed very reluctant to say anything. His body was all turned in on itself; he looked down at his shoes. In response to questions, he mumbled replies. But I pressed on, using a style agreed upon in both meetings of the research team[6] and clinical supervision. I presented myself as intent on being very engaged in the process, intent on communicating the purpose of the interview, eager to have the client see the interview as joint work. I encouraged Mr. Ortiz to ask about unclear questions and to suggest alternative approaches to the interview to better meet the goals of registration for services and research that we shared. And then something clicked. Stories, self and identity, and hardiness and sense of coherence emerged.

Just as the Type A interviewer behaves in a somewhat hostile way in the structured interview—interrupting, pressing the interviewee to talk faster, so as to provide a setting in which Type A might emerge if it is indeed part of the interviewee's behavioral repertoire—the interviewer here seems to have been setting the stage for commitment, control, and challenge as she looked for self and identity through the qualitative research interview. But the stage director metaphor is not quite right. It does not allow room for the changes observed in both the interviewee and interviewer that are possible in this kind of research. This is not an easy or quick way to do personality and health research, but I never felt more rewarded or useful in my work. Personality and health research can indeed be the kind of action research that Nevitt Sanford described years ago, research that provokes simultaneously an increase in understanding and an intervention in which all the parties involved are changed.

Notes

1. The adjective, *simple*, is deliberately used here to indicate that it is *particular and not all uses* of the trait word that trouble this writer. When it was used by Allport (1937, 1961), a pioneer and still influential figure in the field of American personality psychology, traits were anything but simple (cf. Ouellette Kobasa, 1990; Zuroff, 1986). They had to do with the "dynamic organization within the individual of those psychophysical systems that determine his characteristic behavior and thought" (1961, p. 28). They were not static entities but represented processes. They were expected to combine with situational factors in complex ways to influence behavior. They could be characterized as common and descriptive of groups of people, but, more compellingly, Allport said traits could be unique to individuals and thereby identified only through intensive idiographic investigation of persons in the social and cultural contexts in which

they found themselves. Some contemporary researchers (e.g., Block, 1995) seek to maintain many of Allport's complex uses of the term *trait*. But, as is argued in this chapter, the usage of traits associated with the Big Five approach that dominates the current scene in personality psychology is different from much of what Allport intended. And it is beyond that particular usage that I want the gaze of the personality and health researcher to stretch. The story of how we got to the current usage, through such pathways as the turmoil in the field that followed Mischel's (1968) influential critique of personality research and the efforts by personality psychologists to distinguish their work from that of social psychologists, is important but beyond the scope of this chapter.

2. For readers who fear that my worry is exaggerated, note the following quotation: "It took personality psychologists many decades to resolve questions about the number and nature of basic trait dimensions in English-speaking populations. Fortunately, it appears that that long struggle need not be repeated in every other culture. The FFM at least provides a solid beginning for understanding personality everywhere" (McCrae & Costa, 1997, p. 515).

Having seen how much basic knowledge can be gained through ethnographic work like that by Burton and her colleagues (Burton, Obeidallah, & Allison, 1996) in inner-city African American communities—work that does not impose pre-established categories and enables a particular community to speak for itself about matters such as stress and coping—I urge caution about the easy transfer of knowledge that McCrae and Costa suggest.

3. Concerns about a trait approach that does not take the complex and important matters of context and process into account but does provide researchers with an easy to administer self-report questionnaire led Contrada et al. (1990) to use the metaphor of the "comfortable though faulty marriage with epidemiology" in their review of personality psychologists' contribution to health research.

4. Although the self and identity case is made here for the constructs of sense of coherence and hardiness, the same could be done for other health-related personality constructs. For example, many of the constructs that emphasize control or control-like ideas have at their very core a variety of self and identity ideas. These range from more individual-based concerns like self-regulation in the research on optimism (e.g., Scheier & Carver, 1987) to broader-based concerns about self and society and the identities assigned to self by society in work like that on John Henryism (e.g., James, 1994).

5. See Frank (1995) for a brilliant call for the recognition of critical illness situations as essentially moral situations.

6. This interview cited is part of an ongoing study at the Gay Men's Health Crisis (GMHC) in New York City, with the support of a PSC-CUNY Research Award.

References

Allport, G. W. (1937). *Personality: A psychological interpretation.* New York: Holt.

Allport, G. W. (1961). *Pattern and growth in personality.* New York: Holt, Rinehart, & Winston.

Antonovsky, A. (1987). *Unraveling the mystery of health.* San Francisco: Jossey-Bass.

Antonovsky, A. (1991). The structural sources of salutogenic strengths. In C. I. Cooper & R. Payne (Eds.), *Personality and stress: Individual differences in the stress process* (pp. 67–104). New York: Wiley.

Antonovsky, A. (1993). The structure and properties of the sense of coherence scale. *Social Science and Medicine, 36*, 725–733.

Ashmore, R. D., & Jussim, L. (1997). Toward a second century of the scientific analysis of self and identity. In R. D. Ashmore & L. Jussim (Eds.), *Self and identity: Fundamental issues.* (Vol.1, pp.3–19).New York: Oxford University Press.

Barresi, J., & Juckes, T. J. (1997). Personology and the narrative interpretation of lives. *Journal of Personality, 65*, 693–719.

Block, J. (1995). A contrarian view of the five-factor approach to personality description. *Psychological Bulletin, 117*, 187–215.

Booth-Kewley, S., & Friedman, H. S. (1987). Psychological predictors of heart disease: A quantitative review. *Psychological Bulletin, 101*, 343–362.

Burton, L. M., Obeidallah, D. A., & Allison, K. (1996). Ethnographic insights on social context and adolescent development among inner-city African-American teens. In R. Jessor, A. Colby, & R. A. Shweder (Eds.), *Ethnography and human development: Context and meaning in social inquiry.* Chicago: University of Chicago Press.

Contrada, R. J., & Guyll, M. (in press). On who gets sick and why: The role of personality and stress. In A. Baum, T. A. Revenson, & J. E. Singer (Eds.), *Handbook of health psychology.* Hillsdale, NJ: Lawrence Erlbaum.

Contrada, R. J., Leventhal, H., & O'Leary, A. (1990). Personality and health. In L. A. Pervin (Ed.), *Handbook of personality theory and research* (pp. 638–669). New York: Guilford.

Costa, P. T., Jr., & McCrae, R. R. (1992). The five factor model of personality and its relevance to personality disorders. *Journal of Personality Disorders, 6*, 343–359.

Craik, K. H. (1996). The objectivity of persons and their lives: A noble dream for personality psychology. *Psychological Inquiry, 7*, 326–330.

Dakof, G. A., & Mendelsohn, G. A. (1986). Parkinson's disease: The psychological aspects of a chronic illness. *Psychological Bulletin, 99*, 375–387.

Digman, J. M. (1990). Personality structure: Emergence of the five-factor model. *Annual Review of Psychology, 41*, 417–440.

Dreher, H. (1995). *The immune power personality: Seven traits you can develop to stay healthy.* New York: Dutton.

Dressler, W. W. (1991). Life style, stress, and blood pressure in a Southern Black community. *Psychosomatic Medicine, 52*, 182–198.

Fox, R. C. (1979). *Essays in medical sociology.* New York: Wiley.

Frank, A. W. (1995). *The wounded storyteller: Body, illness, and ethics.* Chicago: University of Chicago Press.

Frenz, A., Carey, M. P., & Jorgensen, R. S. (1993). Psychometric evaluation of Antonovsky's Sense of Coherence Scale. *Psychological Assessment, 5*, 145–153.

Friedman, H. S., & Booth-Kewley, S. (1987). The "Disease-Prone Personality": A meta-analytic review of the construct. *American Psychologist, 42*, 539–555.

Friedman, H. S., Tucker, J. S., Tomlinson-Keasey, C., Schwartz, J. E., Wingard, D. L., & Criqui, M. H. (1993). Does childhood personality predict longevity? *Journal of Personality and Social Psychology, 65*, 176–185.

Funk, S. C. (1992). Hardiness: A review of theory and research. *Health Psychology, 11*, 335–345.

Gendlin, E. T. (1962). *Experiencing and the creation of meaning: A philosophical and psychological approach to the subjective.* New York: Free Press of Glencoe.

Gendlin, E. T. (1997). How philosophy cannot appeal to experience, and how it can. In D. M. Levin (Ed.), *Language beyond postmodernism: Saying and thinking in Gendlin's philosophy* (pp. 3–41). Evanston, IL: Northwestern University Press.

Giddens, A. (1991). *Modernity and self-identity: Self and society in the late modern age.* Stanford, CA: Stanford University Press.

Goldberg, L. R. (1992). The development of marker variables for the Big-Five factor structure. *Psychological Assessment, 4*, 26–42.

Goldberg, L. R. (1993). The structure of phenotypic personality traits. *American Psychologist, 48*, 26–34.

Hermans, H. J. M. (1996). Bridging traits, story, and self: Prospects and problems. *Psychological Inquiry, 7*, 330–334.

James, S. A. (1994). John Henryism and the health of African-Americans. *Culture, Medicine, and Psychiatry, 18*, 163–182.

James, W. (1890). *Principles of psychology.* New York: Holt.

James, W. (1911). *Memories and studies.* New York: Longmans, Green & Co.

Kobasa, S. C. (1979). Stressful life events, personality and health: An inquiry into hardiness. *Journal of Personality and Social Psychology, 37*, 1–11.

Kobasa, S. C., & Maddi, S. R. (1977). Existential personality theory. In R. J. Corsini (Ed.), *Current personality theories* (pp. 399–446). Itasca, IL: F. E. Peacock.

Kobasa, S. C., Maddi, S. R., & Kahn, S. (1982). Hardiness and health: A prospective study. *Journal of Personality and Social Psychology, 42*, 168–177.

Little, B. (1996). Free traits, person projects, and idio-tapes: Three tiers for personality psychology. *Psychological Inquiry, 7*.

Loevinger, J. (1976). *Ego development.* San Francisco: Jossey-Bass.

Lykes, M. B. (1994). Speaking against the silence: One Maya woman's exile and return. In C. E. Franz & A. J. Stewart (Eds.), *Women creating lives: Identities, resilience & resistance,* (pp. 97–114). Boulder, CO: Westview Press.

Maddi, S. R. (1990). Issues and interventions in stress mastery. In H. S. Friedman (Ed.), *Personality and disease* (pp. 121–154). New York: Wiley.

Marcus, H. R., Kitayama, S., & Heiman, R. J. (1996). Culture and "basic" psychological principles. In E. T. Higgins & A. W. Kruglanski (Eds.), *Social psychology: Handbook of basic mechanisms and processes.* New York: Guilford.

Matthews, K., & Haynes, S. (1986). Type A behavior pattern and coronary disease risk: Update and critical evaluation. *American Journal of Epidemiology, 123*, 923–959.

McAdams, D. P. (1996a). Alternative futures for the study of human individuality. *Journal of Research in Personality, 30*, 374–388.

McAdams, D. P. (1996b). Personality, modernity, and the storied self: A contemporary framework for studying persons. *Psychological Inquiry, 7*, 295–321.

McAdams, D. P. (1997). The case for unity in the (post)modern self: A modest proposal. In R. D. Ashmore & L. Jussim (Eds.), *Self and identity: Fundamental issues* (pp. 46–78). New York: Oxford.

McClelland, D. (1996). Does the field of personality have a future? *Journal of Research in Personality, 30,* 429–434.

McCrae, R. R. (1989). Why I advocate the five-factor model: Joint factor analyses of the NEO-PI with other instruments. In D. M. Buss & N. Cantor (Eds.), *Recent trends and emerging directions* (pp. 237–245). New York: Springer-Verlag.

McCrae, R. R., & Costa, P. Y., Jr. (1983). Joint factors in self-reports and ratings: Neuroticism, extraversion, and openness to experience. *Personality and Individual Differences, 4,* 245–255.

McCrae, R. R., & Costa, P. T., Jr. (1997). Personality trait structure as a human universal. *American Psychologist, 52,* 509–516.

McKay, J. R. (1991). Assessing aspects of object relations associated with immune function: Development of the affiliative trust-mistrust coding system. *Psychological Assessment: A Journal of Consulting and Clinical Psychology, 3,* 641–647.

Meyer, I. H. (1995). Minority stress and mental health in gay men. *Journal of Health and Social Behavior, 7,* 9–25.

Miller, T. Q., Smith, T. W., Turner, C. W., Guijarro, M. L., & Hallet, A. J. (1996). Meta-analytic review of research on hostility and physical health. *Psychological Bulletin, 119,* 322–348.

Mischel, W. (1968). *Personality and assessment.* New York: Wiley.

Mischel, W., & Shoda, Y. (1995). A cognitive-affective system theory of personality: Reconceptualizing situations, dispositions, dynamics, and invariance in personality structure. *Psychological Review, 102,* 246–268.

Ogilvie, D. R., & Rose, K. M. (1995). Self-with-others representations and a taxonomy of motives: Two approaches to studying persons. *Journal of Personality, 63,* 643–679.

Orr, E., & Westman, M. (1990). Does hardiness moderate stress, and how? A review. In M. Rosenbaum (Ed.). *On coping skills, self-control, and adaptive behavior.* New York: Springer.

Ouellette, S. C. (1993). Inquiries into hardiness. In L. Goldberger & S. Breznitz (Eds.), *Handbook of stress: Theoretical and clinical aspects* (2nd ed.). New York: Free Press.

Ouellette, S. C. (1996). Building a useful personality psychology. *Psychological Inquiry, 7,* 357–360.

Ouellette, S. C., Cassel, J. B., Maslanka, H., & Wong, L. M. (1995). GMHC volunteers and the challenges and hopes for the second decade of AIDS. *AIDS Education and Prevention, 7* (suppl), 64–79.

Ouellette, S. C., & DiPlacido, J. (in press). In A. Baum, T. A. Revenson, & J. E. Singer (Eds.), *Handbook of health psychology.* Hillsdale, NJ: Erlbaum.

Ouellette Kobasa, S. C. (1985). Personality and health: Specifying and strengthening the conceptual links. *Review of Personality and Social Psychology, 6,* 291–311.

Ouellette Kobasa, S. C. (1990). Lessons from history: How to find the person in health psychology. In H. S. Friedman (Ed.), *Personality and disease* (pp. 14–37). New York: Wiley.

Pervin. L. A. (1990). A brief history of modern personality theory. In L. A. Pervin (Ed.), *Handbook of personality theory and research* (pp. 3–18). New York: Guilford.

Pervin, L. A. (1994). A critical analysis of current trait theory. *Psychological Inquiry, 5*, 103–113.

Peterson, C., Schulman, P., Castellon, C., & Seligman, M. E. P. (1992). CAVE: Content analysis of verbatim explanations. In C. P. Smith (Ed.), *Motivation and personality: Handbook of thematic content analysis* (pp. 383–392). New York: Cambridge University Press.

Rapkin, B. D., Smith, M. Y., Dumont, K., Correa, A., Palmer, S., & Cohen, S. (1994). Development of the idiographic functional status assessment: A measure of the personal goals and goal attainment activities of people with AIDS. *Psychology and Health, 9*, 111–129.

Robbins, A. S., Spence, J. T., & Clark, H. (1991). Psychological determinants of health and performance: The tangled web of desirable and undesirable characteristics. *Journal of Personality and Social Psychology, 61*, 755–765.

Sabat, S. R. (1994). Excess disability and malignant social psychology: A case study of Alzheimer's disease. *Journal of Community and Applied Social Psychology, 4*, 157–166.

Sabat, S. H., & Harré, R. (1992). The construction and deconstruction of self in Alzheimer's disease. *Aging and Society, 12*, 443–461.

Sabat, S. R., & Harré, R. (1994). the Alzheimer's disease sufferer as a semiotic subject. *Philosophy, Psychiatry, and Psychology, 1*, 145–160.

Sanford, N. (1982). What have we learned about personality? In S. Koch & D. Leary (Eds.), *A century of psychology as a science* (pp. 490–513). New York: McGraw-Hill.

Scheier, M. F., & Carver, C. S. (1987). Dispositional optimism and physical well-being: The influence of generalized outcome expectancies on health. *Journal of Personality, 55*, 169–210.

Scheier, M. F., Carver, C. S., & Bridges, M. W. (1994). Distinguishing optimism from neuroticism (and trait anxiety, self-mastery, and self-esteem): A reevaluation of the Life Orientation Test. *Journal of Personality and Social Psychology, 67*, 1063–1078.

Smith, T. W. (1989). Interactions, transactions, and the Type A pattern: Additional avenues in the search for coronary-prone behavior. In A. W. Seligman & T. M. Dembroski (Eds.), *In search of coronary-prone behavior* (pp. 91–116). Hillsdale, NJ: Erlbaum.

Smith, T. W., & Williams, R. B. (1992). Personality and health: Advantages and limitations of the five-factor model. *Journal of Personality, 60*, 395–423.

Sontag, S. (1977). *Illness as metaphor.* New York: Farrar, Straus, and Giroux.

Spence, D. (1987). Turning happenings into meanings: The central role of the self. In P. Young-Eisendrath & J. A. Hall (Eds.), *The book of the self: Person, pretext, and process* (pp. 131–150). New York: New York University Press.

Suls, J., David, J. P., & Harvey, J. H. (1996). Personality and coping: Three generations of research. *Journal of Personality, 64*, 711–736.

Ware, N. C., & Kleinman, A. (1992). Culture and somatic experience: The social course of illness in neurasthenia and chronic fatigue syndrome. *Psychosomatic Medicine, 54*, 546–560.

Westen, D. (1996). A model and a method for uncovering the nomothetic from the idiographic: An alternative to the Five-Factor Model? *Journal of Research in Personality, 30*, 400–413.

Wiebe, D. J., & Williams, P. G. (1992). Hardiness and health: A social psychophysiological perspective on stress and adaptation. *Journal of Social and Clinical Psychology, 11,* 238–262.

Wiggins, J. S. (Ed.) (1996). *The five factor model of personality.* New York: Guilford.

Zuroff, D. C. (1986). Was Gordon Allport a trait theorist? *Journal of Personality and Social Psychology, 51,* 993–1000.

Jeanne Brooks-Gunn
Julia A. Graber

What's Sex Got to Do with It?

The Development of Sexual Identities during Adolescence

I was mad at my mom or my sister or my dad. So I wanted to release the anger in some way. . . . . It's [sex] an escape from what you were thinking about.

As far as just sex for sex's sake . . . guys, young guys are just walking hormones really. You know, that's completely hormonal thing, they might not have anything to do with it, brainwise.

If you're like really down and you know the person, it's just when they say things to you like made you feel good or you know 'I like being with you.' It just makes you feel like you're ten times bigger than everything else in life.

—quoted in S. Turner and S. Feldman,
"The Functions of Sex in Everyday Life"
(1994)

The time between childhood and adulthood is often characterized as a period of consolidation, refinement, and acquisition of multiple identities. We use the term "identities" rather than "identity" to highlight the fact that individuals have multiple selves (Harter, 1997; Rosenberg, 1997). While other epochs of the life course also require that identities be revised or acquired, adolescence is sometimes considered unique in part because of the multiple arenas in which change is occurring, the press for more adult-like behavior, the rapid growth of cognitive skills, the more sustained interactions with same-age peers, and the physical growth (Feldman & Elliott, 1990; Graber, Brooks-Gunn, & Petersen, 1996; Gunnar & Collins, 1988). Although it is clear that identities during the adolescent years are preceded by childhood identities, the questions "Who am I?" and "What are the attributes of me that are most salient in different contexts?" seem to be asked more frequently in the teenage years (Damon & Hart, 1982; Harter, 1990, 1997). At the same time, youth begin a search for more balance between needs for autonomy and connectedness (Cooper, Grotevant, & Condon, 1983; Erikson, 1968), which is often played out in relationships with parents and peers (Conger & Ge, in press; Graber & Brooks-Gunn, in press; Holmbeck, Paikoff, & Brooks-Gunn, 1995; Powers & Welsh, in press).

Interwoven with all of these challenges, and competing demands and desires, is the development of a reproductively mature body (Brooks-Gunn & Reiter, 1990). This set of physical changes heralds increases in sexual desire; heightened concern about one's own body shape, size, and attractiveness; increased interaction with opposite-sex peers; more sexual exploration; and, in the majority of youth in Western countries today, the onset of sexual intercourse. Additionally, the biology of re-productive maturity is gender-specific. Consequently, the associated psychological changes also may be considered gendered. They may also become part of one's gender identity or gender identities (Ashmore, 1990; Huston, 1983; Maccoby, 1990, 1995).

Adolescent sexuality has many implications for physical health and well-being. The increased risk of HIV and other sexually transmitted infections is, of course, a major direct consequence of unsafe sexual practices, especially when those practices involve multiple partners falling into high-risk categories. But sexuality may affect physical health in other, less direct ways, both in the short- and long-term. Sexual activity can form part of a pattern of high-risk behaviors, includ-ing abuse of alcohol and other substances, that exact a major mental and physical toll in adolescents and young adults. Out-of-wedlock childbirth has social and economic consequences that limit life chances for both mother and child. And psychological problems connected to sexuality in adolescence may have a lasting impact on a person's oppor-tunity and ability to form the types of social relationships that have been associated with stress-buffering and other health-protective ef-fects. Thus, sexual development can be seen as playing a crucial role in a number of behaviorally and psychosocially induced physical health problems.

This chapter is entitled "What's Sex Got to Do with It?" because, in general, the emergence of an adult male or female body, although a hallmark of adolescence, is not always addressed in discussions of ado-lescent identities. At the same time, identity has been left out of discus-sions of adolescent sexuality. Our position is that the physical changes of the teenage years, in conjunction with their meaning to individual adolescents, their girlfriends and boyfriends, their parents, their teach-ers, and society in general, become incorporated into their identities. Another way of thinking about this process is to postulate that sexual identities are formed during the adolescent years and that these identi-ties influence adolescent health behavior and attitudes, as well as the formation and refinement of other identities (e.g., gender, ethnic, aca-demic identities).

We chose the quotations that open this chapter to highlight the ways in which identity and sexual feelings and behavior might influence one another. Each of these adolescents, who live in northern California (Turner & Feldman, 1994), is discussing a sexual experience. A boy describes the sexual experiences he has had thus far as pure sexual release, without other feelings or thoughts. A girl interprets her sexual experiences as reactions to her anger toward others (not the person with whom she had sex). Yet another girl perceives sex in terms of being valued (or liked); the experience makes her feel bigger than life. Thus, adolescents are able to see sexuality as part of their biological and social selves and as an important source of positive self-regard. And their identities also likely influence their sexual feelings and behaviors.

Why have sexual feelings and behavior been left out of discussions of adolescents' self-identities? One reason is the pervasive squeamishness about sex in our country, especially when adolescents are involved, making studying feelings about sex difficult (Brooks-Gunn, 1990; Brooks-Gunn & Reiter, 1990; Smith, 1994). Studying sexual feelings may be especially problematic in research programs that rely on school-based samples (which is the norm for work on adolescent identities). We have found that most school districts are reluctant to allow us to ask about sex, even in studies where we are talking with youth about pubertal processes (e.g., breast development, pubic hair, menarche; Brooks-Gunn, Newman, Holderness, & Warren, 1994). Consequently, most of our information about sexual feelings comes from national studies of somewhat older adolescents (and young adults). These studies tend to focus on the onset of sexual intercourse, the use of contraceptives, and (sometimes) the frequency of sexual activity (Brooks-Gunn & Furstenberg, 1989; Brooks-Gunn & Paikoff, 1997; Hofferth & Hayes, 1987). Even the work of Rosenthal (in press), from which we draw later in this chapter, is based on interviews with adolescents in their late teenage years, because of school district and parental concerns.

Our goal is to consider sexual identities broadly, unconstrained by societal interests in the regulation of intercourse. Thus, the first three sections of the chapter focus on three different frameworks for studying adolescent sexuality: studying adolescent sexuality as behaviors, studying sexuality as transitions, and studying sexuality as identities. Then, we briefly address the gendered contexts in which sexual identities develop and the personal factors that likely influence the development of these identities. All of these issues are considered as they relate to adolescence, the period defined as "betwixt and between" (Graber & Brooks-Gunn, 1996). This terminology is appropriate for the study of sexual identities, given the inherent focus on the developing body as part of the development of identities; in this sense, the adolescent is betwixt and between a child-like and adult physical form.

This chapter attempts to bring sexual identity (or identities) into the discussion of adolescent identities because sexuality has been left out of discussions of adolescent identity, just as identity has been omitted from discussions of adolescent sexuality. However, we are undertaking this discussion with some trepidation, as most of the work on adolescent sexuality, with a few notable exceptions (to be discussed), has not been framed in identity terms, just as sexuality is not often an explicit topic of inquiry in the identity literature. Instead, adolescent sexuality has been studied vis-à-vis the components of sexual well-being, the salience of sexual desire and arousal, the risk and protective factors associated with either early intercourse or unsafe sex, the co-occurrence of early sexual behavior with other health-related behaviors (i.e., tobacco, alcohol, and illegal drug use and other risk-taking behaviors), and gender and ethnic differences in sexual behaviors and attitudes (Graber, Brooks-Gunn, & Galen, in press). We use this range of frameworks because adolescent sexuality is studied by demographers, psychologists, sociologists, economists, and pediatricians, as well as public health and policy scholars. Each discipline has a somewhat different "take" on the salient issues and on the antecedents and consequences of adolescent sexual behavior.

As we have noted previously, the process of mastering emerging sexual feelings and forming a sense of oneself as a sexual being involves a multifaceted set of tasks (Brooks-Gunn & Paikoff, 1993, 1997; Graber et al., in press). For example, this process may include learning to manage sexual feelings such as arousal and attraction, developing new forms of physical and emotional intimacy, increasing autonomy in the regulation of one's behavior, developing interpersonal relationships that may involve varying levels of physical and emotional intimacy, and acquiring the skills to regulate sexual behavior to avoid undesirable consequences of that behavior. In addition, forming sexual identities involves not only sexual behavior but also the integration of behaviors and feelings into the construction of other developing identities. And sexual identities are often forged within relationships. Furthermore, sexual identities are developed within a societal context, and most societies have attempted to impose limits on the sexual behavior of youth. Thus, sexual identities are involved in intrapersonal, interpersonal, and societal phenomena.

Historically, societies have placed strictures on the sexual behavior of youth to regulate the timing of childbearing (e.g., preferably during adulthood) and context of childbearing (e.g., preferably confined to married couples; Paige & Paige, 1985). Today, the ensurance of physical health, specifically the absence of sexually transmitted disease, would also be a reason for regulating or intervening in adolescent sexuality or at least in the practice of safer sex. On a more emotional than physical level, concern is also raised about the ability of adolescents, and perhaps adults as well, to engage in sexual intercourse in a way that respects both individuals, so that neither is manipulated or coerced. Adults' desire to regulate adolescent sexual behavior co-exists with adolescents' experience of sexual desire that is part and parcel of becoming a man or woman. No matter how much adults might like to ignore it, the multiple facets of sex have great meaning in the lives of youth, whether they have had any sexual experience or not.

Regardless of concerns, sexual identities will, and perhaps must, be formed as adolescents seek to create an integrated sense of themselves as sexual beings. For most individuals, sexual exploration (kissing, intercourse, or just dreaming) occurs during the adolescent years. In addition, the negotiation of intimate relations occurs within sexual situations that are increasingly autonomous from parent or other adult control. On perhaps a more cautionary note, youth will also have to recognize situations in which sexual behavior is more difficult to control, in which others may use coercion or pressure to obtain sex, in which partners may have differing expectations for intimacy versus sex, and in which their choices (either to engage or not engage in a sexual behavior or experience) may not be accepted by their peer group. And, even though parents, teachers, or members of society overall would like it to be otherwise, sexuality is, in many ways, still gender-specific, reflecting imbalances between dominance and status (Brooks-Gunn & Paikoff, 1997; Orenstein, 1994).

Thus, adolescent sexuality can be viewed in three major senses in which psychologists have used the concept of self (Baumeister, 1998). It is an important aspect of reflexive consciousness, or knowledge and awareness of self; it enters into the interpersonal self, or perceptions, interactions, and relationships involving others; and it is the target of executive function, or the regulation of internal urges and desires vis-à-vis the affordances and constraints of the social environment.

Studying Adolescent Sexuality as Behaviors

Typically, articles on adolescent sexuality (including those that we have written; e.g., Brooks-Gunn & Furstenberg, 1989; Brooks-Gunn & Paikoff, 1993; Graber et al., in press; Paikoff & Brooks-Gunn, 1994) use frameworks that document all possible influences on sexual behavior. These include contexts such as family, peer, school, neighborhood, and work settings, as well as individual biological, emotional, cognitive, and physical characteristics. The developmental challenges and potential pitfalls of adolescence are also charted. Factors associated with risk-taking behavior and conditions that connote resilience to risky situations are often used as organizing frames for examining sexual behavior (Brooks-Gunn & Paikoff, 1997).

Much of this work focuses on the onset of sexual intercourse. On average, most adolescent boys (75%) and girls (60%) have had intercourse by the time they are 17 or 18 years of age (Alan Guttmacher Institute [AGI], 1994). This represents a dramatic increase over the past 30–40 years in the percentage of youth who have had intercourse (Hopkins, 1977; Zelnik & Kantner, 1980). However, onset of sexual intercourse varies by gender, ethnicity, family structure, family income, and academic engagement (Brooks-Gunn & Paikoff, 1993; Moore, Miller, Glei, & Morrison, 1995; Paikoff & Brooks-Gunn, 1994; Zabin & Hayward, 1993). Despite variability, the overall percentages of youth who have intercourse during adolescence exemplify the salience of sexual behaviors, experiences, and feelings to adolescent development.

From a behavioral perspective, variability in sexual experiences has been charted in several dimensions. For example, more individuals who engage in intercourse during adolescence are having first intercourse at earlier ages than in prior decades (AGI, 1994). Because "normative" ages, or at least the average age for first intercourse, vary by context, it is difficult to demarcate ages that differentiate early or late engagement in sexual behaviors. We define early as the onset of sexual intercourse in the junior high or middle school years (i.e., sixth through ninth grades), when adolescents are sixteen or younger. Often, late engagement or onset is defined as having intercourse for the first time at nineteen or older. An argument could be made for differentiating those youth who have sex at ages nineteen or twenty from those who wait until 21 or older, given that the latter event is much rarer for today's youth. From a developmental perspective, those who are early may be less prepared psychologically for the challenges of managing sexual behavior and may not yet have adequately formed a sexual identity or integrated it coherently with other identities. Earlier onset of intercourse has been associated with risks to sexual well-being such as increased risk for sexually transmitted diseases (STDs) or early pregnancy (Zabin & Hayward, 1993).

The meaning of other sexual behaviors has also been considered in efforts to study adolescent sexuality, although information on intercourse is by far the most abundant. Commensurate with pubertal changes, adolescents experience increased sexual arousal (Katchadourian, 1990). Even though prepubertal sexual experiences, including intercourse, have been documented (Paikoff, 1995), rates of these behaviors are relatively low, vary by context, and are not necessarily directly associated with arousal or sexual feelings. For most adolescents, sexual feelings increase dramatically with pubertal development, and subsequently exploration of sexual behaviors also ensues or increases.

Most boys (about 60%) and many girls (about 33%) will have masturbated by the midadolescent years in response to increased arousal (Chilman, 1983; Coles & Stokes, 1985). These likely are underestimates of this sexual behavior, as adolescents report that acknowledgment of engagement in this behavior carries some stigma (Coles & Stokes, 1985). Along with increased arousal and possibly masturbation, most adolescents begin kissing and noncoital and coital touching in early or midadolescence. (See Katchadourian, 1990, and Westney, Jenkins, & Benjamin, 1983, for reviews of these behavioral progressions.) The progression through each of these activities leading to intercourse is most common for white adolescents, with African-American youth demonstrating greater variability in the order of engagement in these behaviors; for example, African-American adolescents are more likely to progress from experimenting with kissing directly to first intercourse (Udry, 1988).

As the preceding discussion indicates, much of the research on adolescent sexual behaviors has focused almost exclusively on the onset of first intercourse. While the extensive literature in this area has charted individual differences, historical trends globally and by subgroups, and the factors that may account for different experiences, the adolescent sexuality as behavior approach has two significant and intertwined shortcomings. First, studying adolescent sexuality as behavior is an "outsider" perspective and does not address the important question of how teenagers give meaning to sexual behaviors. This issue of giving meaning has two subquestions. How exactly do adolescents define various sexuality-related actions? How do teenagers personalize sexual behaviors? Regarding the first, how do teens define kissing, petting, intercourse? Are there individual adolescent and subgroup differences in how these interactions are viewed? For example, do adolescents view the interactions as "play," "us-against-you games," "contests to demonstrate to my same-sex peers that I can do something the group defines as important," or "building a relationship?" All of these questions take on an added importance when the referent is one's own sexual behaviors—what do *my* kissing, petting, and intercourse mean? And this involves not just giving meaning to my actions themselves but additionally identifying the ways in which the actions affect *my* relations with other people and *my* thoughts about *my* body, and the like.

Second, the adolescent sexuality as behavior approach does not address how these issues of meaning occur in multiple overlapping contexts. How teens "define" and personalize sexual actions depends on their social context, which is multifaceted and multilayered (Bronfenbrenner & Morris, 1998). Social context can be seen as a set of concentric and partially ovelapping rings around the teenager—from the immediate family, to friends and peers, to the school and the social crowds of the school and neighborhood, to the larger sociological aggregates such as the neighborhood and ethnic group, the region, and ultimately society itself and its institutions. It is difficult to account for the interplay between meaning and context within a sexuality as behavior approach.

Studying Adolescent Sexuality as Transitions

Along with studying behavioral aspects of adolescent sexual experience, one can also study transitions, another framework for understanding the role sexuality plays in adolescent development. Transitional periods focus on roles, expectations, and choices as determinants of behavior. That is, physical, social, and psychological changes converging at a particular time of development create a period when one's roles and identities are in the process of being re-defined. As we and others have noted, research on adolescent development has often focused on the transitions that define and shape the experiences of adolescents (Graber et al., 1996; Lerner et al., 1996; Rutter, 1994). In fact, historically, adolescence was considered "the transition from childhood to adulthood, suggesting the experience of a single (albeit potentially lengthy) transition period" (Graber & Brooks-Gunn, 1996, p. 768). Alternatively, current approaches have focused more intensely on two primary transitional periods, the entry into adolescence and the exit from adolescence or entry into adulthood.

We have noted that "[t]he importance of transitional periods (e.g., entry into adulthood) or processes (e.g., puberty) as defining features of adolescent development has led to the testing of developmental models in relation to concepts involving transitions (e.g., Brooks-Gunn, Graber, & Paikoff, 1994; Elder, 1998; Lerner et al., 1996; Pickles & Rutter, 1991). Transition periods or processes have been distinguished from life events in that transitions require reorganization at either the structural or functional level (Kagan, 1984; Rutter, 1994). Clearly, pubertal events at the entry to adolescence and role changes at the entry to adulthood fit the criteria for a reorganization of function or behavior" (Graber et al., in press). In one sense almost all of adolescent research is concerned with adolescent transitions. Yet very little directly addresses transitions in the sense of examining "turning points," as described by Pickles and Rutter (1991), or in the sense of delineating how a specific transition, event, or ecological niche influences adolescent behavior. In transition, these experiences result in changes in roles and expectations for behavior (Bronfenbrenner, 1979; Lewin, 1939). As adolescents make transitions and take on new roles, they choose actively to enter certain peer groups, engage in particular health-compromising behaviors, and focus on specific activities—all of these choices are linked to how youth perceive themselves in different contexts.

As indicated, the entry into adolescence is shaped by pubertal development, school changes (usually from elementary to a middle or junior high school structure), changing peer relationships that include new-found interests in sexual interactions, and changing relationships with parents through redefining of roles and increased adolescent autonomy. Thus, the transformation of one individual teenager into a reproductive being occurs simultaneously with a great many other transitions. In contrast with the entry into adolescence, with its clear physical indicator (i.e., puberty), the exit from adolescence is influenced by the economy and the societal structure of each era (Modell & Goodman, 1990; Paige, 1983). That is, the exit from adolescence is determined by one's ability to take on adult roles such as supporting oneself, living independently, and potentially starting a family of one's own. Such behaviors are dictated by economic opportunities available and societal expectations for self-sufficiency.

These synergistic transitions merit attention in these two periods of adolescence. Less frequently studied, but perhaps just as salient, are transitions such as the onset of sexual behavior (i.e., intercourse) that may occur during adolescence rather than as a part of the entry or exit from it. Thus, most research on sexual behavior examines the middle or late adolescent years, focusing on sexual intercourse as a singular event or transition rather than as embedded within a sequence of transitional experiences.

For example, the pubertal transition results in a reproductively mature individual and necessitates relational changes between the adolescent and parents and peers (Paikoff & Brooks-Gunn, 1991). Pubertal and school transitions may open up a wide range of behavioral options to the young adolescent, via dating and unsupervised peer time (Stattin & Magnusson, 1990), resulting in a series of new social and sexual events to be mastered. Pubertal changes herald the intensification of sexual desire, as well as changes in others' responses to the young adolescent. At the same time, cognitive and social-cognitive changes allow the individual to reflect upon and organize thoughts about the self and relationships with others in more systematic and integrated ways (Keating, 1990). Enhanced social-cognitive abilities permit the mastery of these relational and situational changes (Smetana, 1988, 1991). However, how these changes are mastered may vary, depending on sexual content, opportunity, desire, or a combination of these factors.

Pubertal maturity may trigger interest in sexual intimacy and increase sexual arousal (either directly via pubertal hormones or indirectly via secondary sex characteristics; see Udry, 1988; Udry & Campbell, 1994). Relational changes that result in more unsupervised time and more time in dating situations may enable sexual activity; conversely, increased parental restrictiveness may limit such opportunities (Hill & Lynch, 1983). In either case, multiple factors related with pubertal transitions alter the social situations where sexual behavior is possible, and influence motivation and desire. When social events arise that may potentiate sexual activity, responses to these events are likely to vary as a function of biological, social-cognitive, and motivational characteristics. In addition, the occurrence of these events, as well as the relational changes of adolescence, may alter sexual identities, which, in turn, may influence behavioral choices.

Limitations of the transitions approach are similar to those of the behavioral approach to studying sexuality. Specifically, although researchers are considering how turning points, roles, and transitions related to sexuality contribute to adolescents' identities, few have focused on the meaning of roles and turning points to youth. If the experience of first intercourse is a (potential) turning point, what does the event mean to adolescents—do youth perceive the event as a turning point or not? How do adolescents personalize such turning points? What conditions surrounding the event color adolescents' perspectives? For example, first intercourse may occur within a dating relationship, with a friend, or with a stranger. The experience may be based on a mutual decision to have sex, on coercion, or on direct force. The construction of meaning may vary as a function of contextual factors, such as family mores, peer influences, or features of the larger culture.

Studying Adolescent Sexuality as Identities

Defining Sexual Identities

Personal identities are considered "affective, cognitive, and behavioral links between [aspects of an] individual's self and biological/physical/ material factors, interests and abilities, relationships with specific other people, social categories and dimensions of affect and personality, and styles of behaving" (Ashmore, 1990, p. 514). These links, perceived or unperceived, serve to answer the implicit question, "Who am I?" The answer is that "I am many things." Thus, personal identity is multifaceted (Harter, 1997; Rosenberg, 1997). For example, one adolescent may define himself or herself, in part, as follows: "I am growing fast" (biological/physical/material self-definition); "I am a freak: I don't like parties" (interests); "I can't dance" (abilities); "I am a Japanese-American (social category); "I often feel sad; I am a loner" (dimensions of affect and personality); and "I walk like a klutz" (styles of behaving). Each individual, beginning especially in adolescence, tries to organize these, and many other, specific self-construal elements into an organized personal identity structure (McAdams, 1997).

It is important to note that the foregoing definition delineates aspects of gender identity. However, we maintain that such structured sets of links are necessary for most (if not all) personal identities. Additionally, the sets of factors presented above, set out specifically in describing gender identity (Ashmore, 1990), seem equally appropriate for sexual identity. Thus, just as "gender identity is an individual's structured set of gendered personal identities," (Ashmore, 1990, p. 514), so is sexual identity an individual's structured set of sexual personal identities. These include personal beliefs and attitudes as well as shared beliefs and attitudes. This distinction is important in that individuals have differing particular identities (e.g., "I do not wish to have sexual intercourse until I am older;" "I do not believe that girls should have intercourse until they are in their twenties"), even though they may have similar, contextually based beliefs (e.g., "Most of the girls in my high school have had intercourse;" "Most girls believe that they should have intercourse during the high school years or they will lose their boyfriends or not be popular").

Contents of Sexual Identities

The work on gender identities by Ashmore (1990), Huston (1983), and Ruble and Martin (1998) has proposed several domains for sexual identities: physical and biological factors, social relationships, perceptions of others, interests and abilities, and stylistic behaviors (Ashmore, 1990, p. 515). The first three have been studied most extensively (although typically not under the rubric of sexual identities). In contrast, interests and abilities and styles of behavior have only recently been studied as aspects of sexual identities and are discussed separately under current research.

Biological and Physical Factors   Biological and physical factors cover a wide terrain. Included here are all aspects of the pubertal process, which result in a particular body size and shape, as well as attractiveness. Hamburg (1980) has described the physical changes of early adolescence as an involuntary "lottery," since young people enter the process not really knowing what the eventual outcome will be for their own bodies. That is, they realize that what emerges is an adult body, but they are unclear as to what the exact proportions will be. Consequently, it is not surprising that both boys and girls portray their responses to pubertal changes as exciting but slightly anxiety-provoking (Gaddis & Brooks-Gunn, 1985; Ruble & Brooks-Gunn, 1982).

Specific changes are described as more desirable than others, as we illustrate from our work on pubertal changes in girls. For example, girls anticipate breast development more favorably than pubic hair development (Brooks-Gunn, Newman, Holderness, & Warren, 1994). Similarly, certain aspects of puberty are discussed with close friends while others are not (Brooks-Gunn & Ruble, 1982). In one of the few studies on this topic, breast development was linked to positive body image and perceived popularity in fifth and sixth grade girls (Brooks-Gunn & Warren, 1988). By middle school, however, more advanced breast development is not always positively associated with body image, in large part because of the co-occurring (normal) increases in body fat (Dornbusch et al., 1981; Garguilo, Attie, Brooks-Gunn, & Warren, 1987; Tobin-Richards, Boxer, & Petersen, 1983).

Weight plays the most significant role of all physical characteristics in the development of a positive body image for girls (Attie & Brooks-Gunn, 1989, 1995; Tyrka, Graber, & Brooks-Gunn, in press). Body images, at some point during adolescence, become incorporated into one's identity in terms of whether one has a body that is attractive to others. At the same time, the importance of weight to adolescent girls' body images varies with respect to ethnicity and social class (Striegel-Moore & Smolak, 1996). The slender ideal has been most pronounced in white, middle- and upper middle-class girls, although recent trends suggest that the reification of thinness is becoming more common across groups (Hoek, 1993). Spending more time with boys (via dating or attending coeducation schools) decreases the link of body image to weight in white girls, to an extent (Garguilo et al., 1987; Swarr & Richards, 1996). Perhaps being seen as desirable by boys reduces the salience of weight. At the same time, girls may be more critical of weight gains than are boys. Physical attractiveness (facial features, hair), over and above body shape and size, also may be a factor in the construction of sexual identities. We know little about the emergence of perceptions of attractiveness in young adolescents, although much work has been done on physical attractiveness and sexual desirability in older adolescents and young adults (Berscheid, 1994).

Physical concerns are not only the province of girls. Boys, too, wish to be perceived as attractive and spend increased time on physical exercise and grooming during the pubertal years and are particularly cognizant of their growth in height and weight (i.e., muscle mass) in comparison to other boys (Duncan, Ritter, Dornbusch, Gross, & Carlsmith, 1985). The point has been made, however, that the definitions of attractiveness are much less restrictive for boys than for girls, leading to speculations that body images may be less tightly linked with sexual identities or affective responses to shape and size.

Social Relationships   Social relationships have explicit links to sexual identities. Sexuality most often occurs within a relationship with another person. Links between relationships and sexual identities may change throughout the adolescent years. For example, sexual encounters in the late elementary school years have been described in the context of running and chasing games (Paikoff, 1995; Westney et al., 1983). Maccoby (1990, 1995) has described the ways in which the childhood years are most often spent in sex-segregated groups. Forays into opposite-sex interactions often take the form of teasing and games between groups of boys and girls. Later on, more sustained interchanges between dyads begin to develop. Indeed, in a small sample of elementary school children who engaged in sexual play and intercourse, girls and boys spent much more time in play not supervised by adults than is typical for children this age. Initiation of sexual activity may be more playful than emotional for prepubertal or early pubertal youth (Paikoff, 1995). Later in adolescence, presumably, sexual relationships are more intimate. Older youth talk about the importance of sex with intimacy, although great variation exists across individuals, in the perceived salience of closeness in sexual relationship (Feldman & Araujo, 1996).

Do these early experiences and identities have any influence on later behavior? For example, do youth who first experience sex as a game develop different identities than those who have intercourse within an intimate relationship? Or are the effects more transient? The vignettes offered at the beginning of this chapter provide some grounds for speculation. For some boys, at least, early experimentation and sexual release are less linked to emotional experience or to relationships. This might be akin to the game playing described by Paikoff and by Westney. By the end of adolescence, a number of male respondents began discussing sexual identity in terms of relationships, intimacy, and feelings. Whether a similar progression is experienced by some girls is not known. For example, do the girls who begin sexual behavior in a game-playing context become increasingly concerned with relationships over time?

Brown, Dolcini, and Leventhal's (1997) discussion of peer crowds is helpful. In high school and college, adolescents come in contact with peer crowds that are often defined in terms of both sexuality and other health-related behaviors. In crowds, adolescents may experiment with possible identities. This type of exploration may have implications for sexuality and for the acquisition of health-damaging behaviors, even if the identities are not swallowed whole. Some of these implications may result from direct contact with members of peer crowds. Some may reflect the operation of peer crowd membership as social identity. For example, others may see the experimenting adolescent in terms of a peer crowd membership regardless of the adolescent's initial level of identification with the peer crowd. That is, the adolescent must confront the discovery that he or she is being socially categorized as "slut," "cheerleader-type," "druggie," or, simply, "bad kid."

Generally, the nature of experiences of social comparison and evaluation may exert an impact on perceived control and on behavioral choices or decision-making processes. Such experiences may alter an individual's confidence in decision making, although research in this area is limited (see work by Brooks-Gunn & Paikoff, 1992, and Steinberg & Cauffman, 1996, for research in this area).

Perception of Others   Another potential factor in the formation of sexual identities concerns perceptions of others. With regard to sexual identities, again, perceptions, like biological and physical factors, are often gendered. That is, the perceptions of the opposite sex are likely linked to sexual identities. Perceptions have been studied in relation to men's reports of what is sexually desirable in women. In work primarily with young adults (in contrast to research on adolescents), men rate low waist-to-hip ratios (around 0.7) as desirable (Singh, 1994, 1995).

Men also connote being overweight with being sexually unappealing, although they may be less likely than women to rate being very thin as attractive (Fallon & Rozin, 1985). Such perceptions, certainly represented in the media images of women and girls (Attie & Brooks-Gunn, 1987; Faust, 1983; Garner, Garfinkel, Schwartz, & Thompson, 1980; Wolf, 1991), are believed to affect girls' and women's body images, which in turn could be incorporated into sexual identities.

Summary   Thus, the contents of sexual identities are varied as they are constructed from a range of intra- and interpersonal experiences. Whereas behavioral approaches to sexuality and health focus on charting responses to behaviors or predictors of behaviors, and transition-based approaches more fully embed the behaviors into a developmental context, the construction of sexual identities focuses on more internal processes. For example, when biological changes occur (e.g., puberty), they are unpredictable and uncontrollable. Much (e.g., self-esteem, self-efficacy) rides on how the changes turn out, as a consequence of normative beliefs about biology and appearance that are internalized as evaluative standards, meaning-making personalization, and socially available identities. The specific links of these processes to health-related behaviors are not well defined and have received very little attention.

Current Research on Sexual Identities

Developmentalists focusing on adolescence have most often conceptualized identity in Eriksonian terms. Since Erikson's (1968) original theory of identity development during adolescence, subsequent work has expanded and refined the concept of identity to include multiple domains (Grotevant, Thorbecke, & Meyer, 1982; Waterman, 1982). In this same way, researchers interested in understanding identities constructed around the sense of self as a sexual being have moved from initial constructions of sexual identity as no more than indications of preference or orientation (e.g., homosexual, heterosexual) to encompass activities, interests, and styles of behavior that might be tied to the gender of one's partner. Sexual identities experience significant development during adolescence (Brooks-Gunn & Matthews, 1979; Gagnon & Simon, 1987; Money & Ehrhardt, 1972).

Notably, Rosenthal and her colleagues (Buzwell & Rosenthal, 1996; Moore & Rosenthal, 1993) began with a multifaceted conceptualization of sexual identity and explored aspects of sexual expectancies, behaviors, and feelings in defining different sexual identities of adolescents. Thus, a sexual self or identity is multidimensional. Specifically, their model for sexual selves includes sexual self-esteem (e.g., feelings of self-worth in sexual situations), sexual self-efficacy (e.g., feelings of competency in not only using contraception but discussing and negotiating sexual situations with partners), and sexual self beliefs (e.g., attitudes and beliefs about commitment and sexual behavior, interest in sex, and comfort levels in sexual situations). In a study of 470 high school age adolescents in Melbourne, Australia, Buzwell and Rosenthal identified five distinct sexual styles or "identities" based on cluster analysis of items tapping these constructs. They have labeled these styles as "sexually naive," "sexually unassured," "sexually competent," "sexually adventurous," and "sexually driven." Of particular interest was the finding that all groups were comprised of both boys and girls (although gender distributions were not always equal), as well as virgins and nonvirgins. Thus, these identities seemed to reflect evolving constructions of sexual identity that did not require having experienced intercourse, although those who had had intercourse were more likely to fall into certain groups rather than others.

(1) Sexually naive youth, as the name implies, were more often virgins and also more often girls (76%) than boys (24%). They tended to report low rates of confidence or efficacy in sexual situations and lower rates of exploration or desire. They also were likely to consider emotional intimacy and some type of commitment as necessary for intercourse to occur in a relationship.

(2) The sexually unassured youth were also more often virgins, but this group was comprised of more boys (84%) than girls. The unassured demonstrated some interest (e.g., desire) in sexual interactions but had little confidence in their sexual abilities (i.e., sexual self-esteem) and reported high levels of anxiety around sexual situations. Thus, the naive and unassured shared some characteristics, especially in demographic terms as both groups were more often virgins and younger (i.e., sophomores and juniors). However, the two groups were unique in their sexual identities on some dimensions. Presumably, issues around gendered behavior are relevant for the divergence in self-constructions between the two groups, given that one contained more girls and the other more boys.

(3) The sexually competent group was comprised of about equal numbers of boys and girls with more older than younger

adolescents (i.e., seniors), and more than half (around 60%) had had intercourse. They reported high levels of efficacy in their regulation of their behaviors and comfort with their sexuality and, like the unassured, valued commitment as a component of sexual relationships.

(4) The sexually adventurous shared many characteristics with the competent group in that these youth also reported high levels of efficacy and comfort in sexual situations. However, these youth reported very high levels of desire and interest in sexual exploration, with less focus on commitment as a component of a sexual interaction or relationship. This group was as likely as the competent youth to be virgins (again, about 40% were virgins), but the adventurous group was comprised mostly of boys (85%) rather than girls (15%). Interestingly, although none of these youth defined themselves as homosexual, they reported the highest rates of engagement in homosexual experiences of any of the groups.

(5) In contrast, the sexually driven group was comprised almost exclusively of boys (97%) and had the highest representation of nonvirgins (71%). Sexually driven youth were characterized by very high sexual self-esteem (more than just comfort), relatively low beliefs in commitment as necessary for sex, and moderate to low levels of efficacy. Overall, these youth seemed to have great interest in sexual interactions and their own desirability but felt less skilled at "saying no" or negotiating precautions in sexual situations.

Buzwell and Rosenthal (1996) further reported that the interplay of beliefs about efficacy and attitudes toward commitment did translate into behavioral differences among the five groups for behaviors often associated with potential health risks for adolescents (and adults). The behaviors examined included contraceptive use with casual and regular partners, the number of partners in the past 6 months, and the number of one-night stands. As expected, the unassured and naive have fewer of all of these experiences than other youth by definition as more are virgins and have experienced fewer sexual situations. Also as might be expected from the defining characteristics of the groups, the sexually driven engaged in more risk taking with either casual or regular partners, had more partners than other groups, and had more one-night stands. In many respects, the sexually competent and sexually adventurous had similar behavioral patterns. Of note is that the two groups differed in their risk-taking behaviors with regular partners. For this behavior, the sexually competent were somewhat more likely than the adventurous (but less than the driven) to engage in higher-risk behaviors with regular partners. For the sexually competent, risk behavior was lower when they were with casual partners than when they were with regular partners.

These findings correspond with those of older studies that have focused on a single style or identity type. For example, Chilman (1983) also identified adventurous youth who were likely to have multiple partners and lower rates of contraceptive usage. "Adventurous" may not fit the two studies though, as Chilman's adventurous youth appear to be more similar to the sexually driven in the Australian study. Rosenthal's work, in both the study discussed and prior studies, is unique again in its simultaneous examination of multiple dimensions that may comprise a sexual identity and the clustering of these dimensions to examine multiple types at the same time. From a developmental perspective, it would be interesting to consider whether these identities form any type of developmental progression or indicate a developmental process for sexual identity. Buzwell and Rosenthal (1996) reported preliminary findings from a follow-up assessment of their sample, finding that youth move into other groups as they age and engage in more sexual experiences. As would be expected, most movement is seen from the naive and unassured groups into the sexually competent group. Further exploration of the correlates and predictors of these progressions will be informative for understanding sexual identity from a developmental perspective.

Another innovative look at sexual identities has been undertaken by Andersen and Cyranowski (1994), who have developed a sexual self-schema scale in a series of studies of college-age women. The scale measures how descriptive each statement is of one's identity as a sexual woman. Both positive and negative self-schemas can be identified. Positive schemas were defined by perception of oneself as very passionate and romantic with little embarrassment or self-consciousness around one's sexuality. Such characterization of self was associated with sexual behaviors—more sexual behavior, more partners, more sexual arousal (Andersen & Cyranowski, 1994, 1995). Compared to the conceptualization of sexual identities by Rosenthal and her colleagues, this work focuses on sexual identity more globally. It provides a look at the emotional valence of sexual identity. Whether this conceptualization is appropriate for adolescents or for men is unknown.

Links between sexual self-schemas and biological/physical factors have also been examined. In one study, several hundred college women provided information on sexual schemas, body image, weight, and perceived and actual attractiveness (Wiederman & Hurst, 1997). Interestingly, in this sample actual weight was not associated with sexual schemas; one might have predicted that heavier young women would have less positive sexual schemas (and, in this sample, one fifth of the women were classified as obese according to a body mass index). Additionally, body dissatisfaction also was unrelated to emotional valence in sexual schema. Of course, in this study and others, very positive body images were not common; as Rodin and her colleagues have pointed out, body dissatisfaction has become a "normative discontent" in many groups of women in our society (especially white, well-educated women; Attie & Brooks-Gunn, 1987; Rodin, Silberstein, & Striegel-Moore, 1984).

Gendered Nature of Sexual Identities

Fine (1988) has written eloquently on the discourse of sexual desire, making the important point that sexual relationships are often not egalitarian, given differential dominance of boys and girls. Thus, boys are more likely to be the pursuers and girls the pursued. And girls may find it difficult to refuse sexual overtures made by particular boys, because of their status, their persistence, or their physical power.

Contrary to what is often believed, sexual encounters as a match between boys as persuaders and girls as reluctant participants are not a vestige of the past. Some (but not all) adolescents still describe interchanges in these terms. Presumably, gender power divergences are much greater when men have high sexual arousal levels, high levels of sexual self-efficacy, low interest in commitment, and high interest in exploration, and females do not. We would venture that the sexually adventurous and sexually driven males described by Rosenthal and colleagues would be most likely to exhibit dominance behaviors in sexual interchanges. Of interest but unstudied is the reaction of different girls to boys with high arousal and low commitment. Also unknown is how many boys described as sexually competent use overt persuasion to initiate a sexual relationship and whether the use of overt pursuit or dominance is tempered by the status of the girl, the relationship with the girl, or the age of the girl. This last point is very important given that young adolescent girls are likely to have intercourse with older boys (Zabin & Hayward 1993).

One of the themes emerging from the interviews in northern California, with which we began this chapter, is how adolescents balance their own needs and those of others in the negotiations over sexual exchanges, as well as the definition of boundaries between self and other, between boys and girls (Turner & Feldman, 1994). These themes may be paradigmatic of the sexual self as "I" versus "Me." Unlike the preceding section, the *self as executive function*, rather than the *self as content and structure*, is of concern.

The struggle between intimacy and autonomy, which reoccurs throughout development, is played out on the sexual stage as well as in relationships with parents, same-sex peers, and siblings. The theme of

being manipulated or used by the other person exemplifies this struggle. One eighteen-year-old boy talked about the pain of having his former girlfriend dating his best friend while still visiting him for the sole
purpose of sex (Turner & Feldman, 1994). The physical pleasure was finally not worth the pain of feeling manipulated. This young man
yearned for intimacy with his former girlfriend; sex without intimacy
was too painful, so it became necessary to reestablish sexual boundaries
between them.

In another interview, a young woman in her twenties recounted one
sexual relationship in which she felt used. She would visit the person's
room for several weeks and

> Then, when he was through with me, he just like stopped calling, or I
> went over there once and he just didn't have anything to say to me and
> I felt, like, embarrassed and humiliated about having gone over there and
> I remember moaning that even though I was not into having a relation-
> ship any more than he was, I still felt like he had sort of called the shots,
> you know, he had used me, maybe because he finished with me first. . . .
> I remember that having something to do with my sort of starting to re-
> think this whole casual sex thing, that maybe I didn't want to be a part of
> that.

This young woman was speaking of the meaning of sex in relation to
experimenting with what it meant to be a sexual person. Indeed, she
refers to the differences "between being myself having sex and just sort
of playing a game and acting how I think somebody who is having sex
should be acting" (Turner & Feldman, 1994). Such a statement is remi-
niscent of the ways in which young adolescents try on different identities (Harter, 1990, 1997) and may reflect the *self as process*. At the same
time, this young woman acknowledged that she felt trashy, and she
liked feeling that way for a bit.

These vignettes are particularly interesting in light of the narratives
supplied by Rosenthal's Australian youths, who were all still in high
school (in contrast, most of Feldman's respondents were out of high
school and reflecting on adolescent experiences). No data exist on the
developmental trajectories of the high school students in the five sexual
style groups characterizing the Australian sample. That is, do many of
the sexual adventurers find commitment more important as they age?
And, if so, what are the reasons for such changes? A glimmer of such
change is seen in this interview with a twenty-two-year-old man, talking about the decision to have sex with someone now, as opposed to
when he was in high school:

> When I have sex, I consider whether this is something she really wants,
> and I consider if it's something I really want because after sex often it will
> lead to more—at least when I have sex I want it to lead to more. I want to

know if she wants it to lead to more. I want to know where I stand. I don't just want to have sex. I kind of got that over with in high school, that kind of thing. (Turner & Feldman, 1994)

Has behavior changed, from an experimentation with a sexual identity that manifested itself in terms of exploration of sex for sex's sake, toward more intimacy and commitment? Such progressions, if they occur, need to be documented, as well as the various paths that individuals take as sexual selves. An account of temporal and between-person variation in sexual identities may shed light on unresolved questions regarding adolescent sexuality.

Conclusion

Developmental changes in self-feelings, social cognition, puberty, and relationships all contribute to the development of personal identities related to sexuality. Descriptions of the normative developmental changes of adolescence have often relegated sexual behavior and feelings to footnotes or brief comments just as studies of sexual behaviors have disembedded sexuality from development (Graber et al., in press). It is unfortunate that examination of the development of sexual identity from the perspective of sexuality as a part of healthy or normative development has been limited by societal biases against discussing sexuality with youth. Aspects of sexuality or the development of sexual identities likely are more interconnected with other aspects of adolescent development than has previously been suggested. For example, discussions of sexual behaviors note the importance of parental supervision for limiting behaviors. In contrast, discussions of changes in parent-adolescent relationships at puberty and continuing throughout adolescence identify increased autonomy as the result of the resolution of conflicts surrounding the desire of adolescents to have less supervision. To what extent are adolescent strivings for less supervision and greater independence driven by increased sexual arousal and desire? Are the unspoken goals in parent-adolescent discussions more often about sexual intercourse rather than curfews per se? Thus, as with peer interactions among adolescents, parent-adolescent relationships may be viewed as reflecting the adolescent's developing propensity to regulate his or her own sexuality and to enact a preferred sexual identity.

Furthermore, development of identity or different selves may have also been disconnected from sexual identity. In as much as identity development has been viewed as occurring via interactions with the social world and those most close to the individual (e.g., Erikson, 1968; Sullivan, 1947), we have indicated ways in which sexual identity would seem inherently to play a part in the construction of an "interpersonal self" (Markus & Cross, 1990). The experience of the construction of the self in connection to or in relationships with others, as demonstrated in other domains, clearly has implications for how adolescents construct their sexual identities—whether they feel unassured or competent may be based in part on whether they have incorporated aspects of interactions based only on friendship or parental acceptance or rejection. At the same time, forming intimate relationships with others and successfully managing sexual dimensions of those relationships undoubtedly crosses over to other aspects of identity. Certainly, the connection of the sexual self to other selves is also underexplored at least for adolescents.

The identification of multiple sexual identity styles, each with differing types of behavioral experiences, may be informative for planning programs that help youth make decisions about sexual behaviors. No doubt, the nature of what might be termed "health-related" experiences (e.g., contracting an STD) will lead to different constructions of sexual identities. Understanding the meaning of these experiences to adolescents and the bidirectionality of the constructs involved is the next step for improving the health of adolescents and helping them form identities that effectively navigate a complex sexual world.

The use of standard curricula for all youth has been cited as a problem with many prevention and intervention programs targeting sexual behavior among adolescents (Brooks-Gunn & Furstenberg, 1990; Brooks-Gunn & Paikoff, 1993). In at least one study that utilized the naturally occurring intervention of increased national attention to the HIV epidemic, it was clear that condom use among boys, in general, was influenced by the increased publicity (Sonenstein, Pleck, & Ku, 1989). However, boys who were at greater risk for contracting HIV (i.e., boys who had tried intravenous drugs or had homosexual experiences) were still the least likely youth to use condoms on a regular basis. Further investigation of the development of different sexual identities and the role that different behaviors play for youth with different identities would potentially lead to more effective programming with those youth engaging in the most health-compromising behaviors.

Acknowledgments: The writing of this chapter was supported by funding from the National Institute of Child Health and Human Development (NICHD), the NICHD Research Network on Child and Family Well-being, and the National Institute of Mental Health (NIMH). We wish to thank our colleagues Doreen Rosenthal and Shirley Feldman for sharing their vignettes with us; Sally Narain, Andrea Bastiani, Veronica Holly, and Britt Galen for their editorial help; and Richard Jessor for his theoretical contributions. We also appreciate the guidance and comments of Richard Contrada and Richard Ashmore. The section "Gendered Nature of Sexual Identities" is taken from Brooks-Gunn and Paikoff (1997), pp. 206–209.

References

Alan Guttmacher Institute. (1994). *Sex and America's teenagers*. New York: Author.

Andersen, B. L., & Cyranowski, J. M. (1994). Women's sexual self-schema. *Journal of Personality and Social Psychology, 67,* 1079–1100.

Andersen, B. L., & Cyranowski, J. M. (1995). Women's sexuality: Behaviors, responses, and individual differences. *Journal of Consulting and Clinical Psychology, 63,* 891–906.

Ashmore, R. D. (1990). Sex, gender, and the individual. In L. A. Pervin (Ed.), *Handbook of personality: Theory and research* (pp. 486–526). New York: Guilford Press.

Attie, I., & Brooks-Gunn, J. (1987). Weight concerns as chronic stressors in women. In R. C. Barnett, L. Biener, & G. K. Baruch (Eds.), *Gender and stress* (pp. 218–254). New York: Free Press.

Attie, I., & Brooks-Gunn, J. (1989). The development of eating problems in adolescent girls: A longitudinal study. *Developmental Psychology, 25*(1), 70–79.

Attie, I., & Brooks-Gunn, J. (1995). The development of eating regulation across the lifespan. In D. Cicchetti & D. J. Cohen (Eds.), *Developmental psychopathology,* (Vol. 2, pp. 332–368). New York: Wiley.

Baumeister, R. F. (1998). The self. In D. Gilber, S. Fiske, & G. Linzey (Eds.), *Handbook of social psychology* (4th ed., pp. 680–740). New York: McGraw-Hill.

Berscheid, E. (1994). Interpersonal relationships. *Annual Review of Psychology, 45,* 79–129.

Bronfenbrenner, U. (1979). *The ecology of human development*. Cambridge, MA: Harvard University Press.

Bronfenbrenner, U., & Morris, P. A. (1998). The ecology of developmental processes. In W. Damon (Ed. in Chief) & R. Lerner (Vol. Ed.), *Handbook of child psychology* (5th ed., pp. 993–1028). New York: Wiley.

Brooks-Gunn, J. (1990). Overcoming barriers to adolescent research on pubertal and reproductive development. *Journal of Youth and Adolescence, 19*(5), 425–440.

Brooks-Gunn, J., & Furstenberg, F. F. (1989). Adolescent sexual behavior. *American Psychologist, 44*(2), 249–257.

Brooks-Gunn, J., & Furstenberg, F. F. (1990). Coming of age in the era of AIDS: Sexual and contraceptive decisions. *Millbank Quarterly, 68,* 59–84.

Brooks-Gunn, J., Graber, J. A., & Paikoff, R. L. (1994). Studying links between hormones and negative affect: Models and measures. *Journal of Research on Adolescence, 4*(4), 469–486.

Brooks-Gunn, J. & Mathews, W. (1979). *He and she: How children develop their sex-role identity*. Englewood Cliffs, NJ: Prentice Hall.

Brooks-Gunn, J., Newman, D., Holderness, C., & Warren, M. P. (1994). The experience of breast development and girls: Stories about the purchase of a bra. *Journal of Youth and Adolescence, 23,* 539–565.

Brooks-Gunn, J., & Paikoff, R. L. (1992). Changes in self feelings during the transition towards adolescence. In H. McGurk (Ed.), *Childhood social development: Contemporary perspectives* (pp. 63–97). East Sussex, UK: Erlbaum.

Brooks-Gunn, J., & Paikoff, R L. (1993). "Sex is a gamble, kissing is a game":

Adolescent sexuality and health promotion. In S. G. Millstein, A. C. Petersen, & E. O. Nightingale (Eds.), *Promoting the health of adolescents: New directions for the twenty-first century* (pp. 180–208). New York: Oxford University Press.

Brooks-Gunn, J., & Paikoff, R. (1997). Sexuality and developmental transitions during adolescence. In J. Schulenberg, J. Maggs, & K. Hurrelmann (Eds.). *Health risks and developmental transitions during adolescence* (pp.190–219). New York: Cambridge University Press.

Brooks-Gunn, J., & Reiter, E. O. (1990). The role of pubertal processes. In S. Feldman & G. Elliot (Eds.), *At the threshold: The developing adolescent* (pp. 16–53). Cambridge, MA: Harvard University Press.

Brooks-Gunn, J., & Ruble, D. N. (1982). Developmental processes in the experience of menarche. In A. Baum & J. E. Singer (Eds.), *Handbook of psychology and health* (Vol. 2, pp. 117–147). Hillsdale, NJ: Erlbaum.

Brooks-Gunn, J., & Warren, M. P. (1988). The psychological significance of secondary sexual characteristics in 9- to 11-year-old girls. *Child Development, 59*, 1061–1069.

Brown, B. B., Dolcini, M. M., & Leventhal, A. (1997). Transformations in peer relationships at adolescence: Implication for health-related behavior. In J. Schulenberg, J. L. Maggs, & K. Hurrelmann (Eds.), *Health risks and developmental transitions during adolescence* (pp. 161–189). Cambridge: Cambridge University Press.

Buzwell, S., & Rosenthal, D. (1996). Constructing a sexual self: Adolescents' sexual self-perceptions and sexual risk-taking. *Journal of Research on Adolescence, 6*(4), 489–513.

Chilman, C. S. (1983). *Adolescent sexuality in a changing American society: Social and psychological perspectives for the human service professions* (2nd ed.). New York: Wiley.

Coles, R., & Stokes, G. (1985). *Sex and the American teenager*. New York: Harper & Row.

Conger, R., & Ge, X. (in press). Conflict and cohesion in parent-adolescent relations: Changes in emotional expression from early to mid-adolescence. In M. Cox & J. Brooks-Gunn (Eds.), *Conflict and closeness: The formation, functioning, and stability of families*. Mahwah, NJ: Erlbaum.

Cooper, C. R., Grotevant, H. D., & Condon, S. M. (1983). Individuality and connectedness in the family as a context for adolescent identity formation and role taking skill. In H. D. Grotevant & C. R. Cooper (Eds.), *Adolescent development in the family: New directions for child development* (pp. 43–59). San Francisco: Jossey-Bass.

Damon, W., & Hart, D. (1982). The development of self-understanding from infancy through adolescence. *Child Development, 53*, 841–864.

Dornbusch, S. M., Carlsmith, J. M., Gross, R. T., Martin, J. A., Jennings, D., Rosenberg, A., & Duke, P. (1981). Sexual development, age, and dating: A comparison of biological and social influences upon one set of behaviors. *Child Development, 52*, 179–185.

Duncan, P. D., Ritter, P. L., Dornbusch, S. M., Gross, R. T., & Carlsmith, J. M. (1985). The effects of pubertal timing on body image, school behavior, and deviance. *Journal of Youth and Adolescence, 14*, 227–235.

Elder, G. H., Jr. (1998). The life course and development. In W. Damon (Ed. in Chief) & R. Lerner (Vol. Ed.), *Handbook of child psychology* (5th ed., pp. 939–991). New York: Wiley.

Erickson, E. H. (1968). *Identity: Youth and crisis.* New York: Norton.

Fallon, A. E., & Rozin, P. (1985). Sex differences in perceptions of body shape. *Journal of Abnormal Psychology, 94,* 102–105.

Faust, M. S. (1983). Alternative constructions of adolescent growth. In J. Brooks-Gunn & A. C. Petersen (Eds.), *Girls at puberty: Biological and psychosocial perspectives* (pp. 105–125). New York: Plenum Press.

Feldman, S. S., & Araujo, K. B. (1996, August). *Sexual betrayal in the relationships of youths aged 18–24.* Paper presented at the meeting of the International Society for the Study of Behavioral Development, Quebec City, Quebec.

Feldman, S., & Elliott, G. (Eds.). (1990). *At the threshold: The developing adolescent.* Cambridge, MA: Harvard University Press.

Fine, M. (1988). Sexuality, schooling, and adolescent females: The missing discourse of desire. *Harvard Educational Review, 58,* 29–53.

Gaddis, A., & Brooks-Gunn, J. (1985). The male experience of pubertal change. *Journal of Youth and Adolescence, 14*(1), 61–69.

Gagnon, J., & Simon, W. (1987). The sexual scripting of oral genital contacts. *Archives of Sexual Behavior, 16(1),* 1–25.

Gargiulo, J., Attie, I., Brooks-Gunn, J., & Warren, M. P. (1987). Girls' dating behavior as a function of social context and maturation. *Developmental Psychology, 23*(5), 730–737.

Garner, D. M., Garfinkel, P. E., Schwartz, D., & Thompson, M. (1980). Cultural expectations of thinness in women. *Psychological Reports, 47,* 483–491.

Graber, J. A., & Brooks-Gunn, J. (1996). Transitions and turning points: Navigating the passage from childhood through adolescence. *Developmental Psychology, 32*(4), 768–776.

Graber, J. A., & Brooks-Gunn, J. (in press). "Sometimes I think that you don't like me": How mothers and daughters negotiate the transition into adolescence. In M. Cox & J. Brooks-Gunn (Eds.), *Conflict and closeness in families: Consequences for children and youth development.* Mahwah, NJ: Erlbaum.

Graber, J. A., Brooks-Gunn, J., & Galen, B. R. (in press). Betwixt and between: Sexuality in the context of adolescent transitions. In R. Jessor (Ed.), *New perspectives on adolescent risk behavior.* New York: Cambridge University Press.

Graber, J. A., Brooks-Gunn, J., & Petersen, A. C. (1996). Adolescent transitions in context. In J. A. Graber, J. Brooks-Gunn, & A. C. Petersen (Eds.), *Transitions through adolescence: Interpersonal domains and context* (pp. 369–383). Mahwah, NJ: Erlbaum.

Grotevant, H. D. Thorbecke, W. L., & Meyer, M. L. (1982). An extension of Marcia's identity status interview into the interpersonal domain. *Journal of Youth and Adolescence, 11,* 33–47.

Gunnar, M., & Collins, W. A. (Eds.). (1988). *Development during transition to adolescence: Minnesota symposia on child psychology* (Vol. 21). Hillsdale, NJ: Erlbaum.

Hamburg, B. A. (1980). Early adolescence as a life stress. In S. Levine & H. Ursin (Eds.), *Coping and health* (pp. 121–143). New York: Plenum Press.

Harter, S. (1990). Self and identity development. In S. Feldman & G. R. Elliott (Eds.), *At the threshold: The developing adolescent* (pp. 352–387). Cambridge, MA: Harvard University Press.

Harter, S. (1997). The personal self in social context: Barriers to authenticity. In R. D. Ashmore & L. Jussim (Eds.), *Self and identity: Fundamental issues* (pp. 81–105). New York: Oxford University Press.

Hill, J. P., & Lynch, M. E. (1983). The intensification of gender-related role expectations during early adolescence. In J. Brooks-Gunn & A. C. Petersen (Eds.), *Girls at puberty: Biological and psychosocial perspectives* (pp. 201–228). New York: Plenum.

Hoek, H. W. (1993). Review of the epidemiological studies of eating disorders. *International Review of Psychiatry, 5,* 61–74.

Hofferth, S. L., & Hayes, C. D. (1987) *Risking the future: Adolescent sexuality, pregnancy, and childbearing.* Washington, DC: National Academy Press.

Holmbeck, G. N., Paikoff, R. L., & Brooks-Gunn, J. (1995). Parenting of adolescents. In M. Bornstein (Ed.), *Handbook of parenting: Vol. 1. Children and parenting* (pp. 91–118). Mahwah, NJ: Erlbaum.

Hopkins, J. R. (1977). Sexual behavior in adolescence. *Journal of Social Issues, 33*(2), 67–85.

Huston, A. C. (1983). Sex-typing. In E. M. Hetherington (Ed.), *Socialization, personality, and social development* (4th ed.). New York: Wiley.

Kagan, J. (1984). *The nature of the child.* New York: Basic Books.

Katchadourian, H. (1990). Sexuality. In S. Feldman & G. Elliot (Eds.), *At the threshold: The developing adolescent* (pp. 330–351). Cambridge, MA: Harvard University Press.

Keating, D. P. (1990). Adolescent thinking. In S. Feldman & G. R. Elliott (Eds.), *At the threshold: The developing adolescent* (pp. 54–89). Cambridge, MA: Harvard University Press.

Lerner, R. M., Lerner, J. V., von Eye, A., Ostrum, C. W., Nitz, K., Talwar-Soni, R., & Tubman, J. (1996). Continuity and discontinuity across the transition of early adolescence: A developmental contextual perspective. In J. A. Graber, J. Brooks-Gunn, & A. C. Petersen (Eds.), *Transitions through adolescence: Interpersonal domains and context.* Mahwah, NJ: Erlbaum.

Lewin, K. (1939). The field theory approach to adolescence. *American Journal of Sociology, 44,* 868–897.

Maccoby, E. E. (1990). Gender and relationships: A developmental account. *American Psychologist, 45*(4), 513–520.

Maccoby, E. E. (1995). The two sexes and their social systems. In P. Moen, G. H. Elder, & K. Luscher (Eds.), *Examining lives in context: Perspectives on the ecology of human development* (pp. 347–364). Washington, DC: American Psychological Association.

Markus, H., & Cross, S. (1990). The interpersonal self. In L. A. Pervin (Ed.), *Handbook of personality: Theory and research* (pp. 576–608). New York: Guilford Press.

McAdams, D. P. (1997). The case for unity in the (post)modern self: A modest proposal. In R. D. Ashmore & L. Jussim (Eds.), *Self and identity: Fundamental issues* (pp. 46–78). New York: Oxford University Press.

Miller, B., Card, J., Paikoff, R., & Peterson, J. L. (1992). *Preventing adolescent pregnancy.* Newbury Park, CA: Sage.

Modell, J., & Goodman, M. (1990). Historical perspectives. In S. Feldman & G. Elliott (Eds.), *At the threshold: The developing adolescent* (pp. 93–122). Cambridge, MA: Harvard University Press.

Money, J., & Ehrhardt, A. (1972). *Man and woman, boy and girl: The differentiation and dimorphism of gender identity from conception to maturity.* Baltimore, MD: Johns Hopkins University Press.

Moore, K., Miller, B., Glei, D., & Morrison, D. (1995). *Adolescent sex, contraception, and childbearing: A review of recent research.* Washington, DC: Child Trends.

Moore, S. M., & Rosenthal, D. A. (1993). *Sexuality in adolescence.* New York: Routledge.

Orenstein, P. (1994). *School girls: Young women, self-esteem, and the confidence gap.* New York: Doubleday.

Paige, K .E. (1983). A bargaining theory of menarcheal responses in preindustrial cultures. In J. Brooks-Gunn & A. C. Petersen (Eds.), *Girls at puberty: Biological and psychosocial perspectives* (pp. 301–322.) New York: Plenum.

Paige, K. E., & Paige, J. M. (1985). *Politics and reproductive rituals.* Berkeley: University of California Press.

Paikoff, R. L. (1995). Early heterosexual debut: Situations of sexual possibility during the transition to adolescence. *American Journal of Orthopsychiatry, 65*(3), 389–401.

Paikoff, R. L., & Brooks-Gunn, J. (1991). Do parent-child relationships change during puberty? *Psychological Bulletin, 110,* 47–66.

Paikoff, R. L., & Brooks-Gunn, J. (1994). Psychosexual development across the lifespan. In M. Rutter & D. Hay (Eds.), *Development through life: A handbook for clinicians* (pp. 558–582). Oxford: Blackwell Scientific.

Pickles, A., & Rutter, M. (1991). Statistical and conceptual models of 'turning points' in developmental processes. In D. Magnusson, L. R. Bergman, G. Rudinger, & B. Torestad (Eds.), *Problems and methods in longitudinal research: Stability and change.* Cambridge: Cambridge University Press.

Powers, S. I., & Welsh, D. P. (in press). Mother-daughter interactions and adolescent girls' depression. In M. Cox & J. Brooks-Gunn (Eds.), *Conflict and closeness: The formation, functioning, and stability of families.* Mahwah, NJ: Erlbaum.

Rodin, J., Silberstein, L. R., & Striegel-Moore, R. H. (1984). Women and weight: A normative discontent. In T. B. Sonderegger (Ed.), *Nebraska symposium on motivation: No. 32. Psychology and gender* (pp. 267–307). Lincoln: University of Nebraska Press.

Rosenberg, S. (1997). Multiplicity of selves. In R. D. Ashmore & L. Jussim (Eds.), *Self and identity: Fundamental issues* (pp. 23–45). New York: Oxford University Press.

Rosenthal, D. (in press). Understanding sexual coercion among adolescents: Communicative clarity, pressure and consent. *Archives of Sexual Behavior.*

Ruble, D. N., & Brooks-Gunn, J. (1982). Expectations regarding menstrual symptoms: Effects on evaluations and behavior of women. In A. Voda & M. Dinnerstein (Eds.), *Changing perspectives on menopause* (pp. 209–219). Austin: University of Texas Press.

Ruble, D. N., & Martin, C. L. (1998). Gender development. In W. Damon

(Ed. in Chief) & N. Eisenberg (Vol. Ed.), *Handbook of child psychology* (5th ed., pp. 933–1016). New York: John Wiley.

Rutter, M. (1994). Continuities, transitions and turning points in development. In M. Rutter & D. F. Hay (Eds.), *Development through life: A handbook for clinicians* (pp. 1–25). London: Blackwell Scientific.

Singh, D. (1994). Is thin really beautiful and good? Relationship between waist-to-hip ratio and female attractiveness. *Personality and Individual Differences, 16*, 123–132.

Singh, D. (1995). Female health, attractiveness, and desirability for relationships: Role of breast asymmetry and waist-to-hip ratio. *Ethology and Sociobiology, 16*, 465–481.

Smetana, J. G. (1988). Concepts and social convention: Adolescents' and parents' reasoning about hypothetical and actual family conflicts. In M. R. Gunnar & W. A. Collins (Eds.), *Twenty-first Minnesota symposium on child psychology: Development during the transition to adolescence* (pp. 79-122). Hillsdale, NJ: Erlbaum.

Smetana, J. G. (1991). Adolescents' and mothers' evaluations of justifications for conflicts. In R. L. Paikoff (Ed.), *Shared views in the family during adolescence: New directions for child development* (Vol. 5, pp. 71–86). San Francisco: Jossey-Bass.

Smith, T. W. (1994). Attitudes toward sexual permissiveness: Trends, correlates, and behavioral connections. In A. S. Rossi (Ed.), *Sexuality across the life course* (pp. 63–97). Chicago: University of Chicago Press.

Sonenstein, F. L., Pleck, J. H., & Ku, L. C. (1989). Sexual activity, condom use and AIDS awareness among adolescent males. *Family Planning Perspectives, 21*(4), 152–158.

Stattin, H., & Magnusson, D. (1990). *Paths through life: Volume 2. Pubertal maturation in female development.* Hillsdale, NJ: Erlbaum.

Steinberg, S., & Cauffman, E. (1996). Maturity of judgment in adolescence: Psychosocial factors in adolescent decision making. *Law and Human Behavior, 20*(3), 244–272.

Striegel-Moore, R. H., & Smolak, L. (1996). The role of race in the development of eating disorders. In L. Smolak, M. P. Levine, & R. Striegel-Moore (Eds.), *The developmental psychopathology of eating disorders: Implications for research, prevention, and treatment* (pp. 259–284). Mahwah, NJ: Erlbaum.

Sullivan, H. S. (1947). *Conceptions of modern psychiatry.* New York: Norton.

Swarr, A. E., & Richards, M. H. (1996). Longitudinal effects of adolescent girls' pubertal development, perceptions of pubertal timing, parental relations and eating problems. *Developmental Psychology, 32*(4), 636–646.

Tobin-Richards, M., Boxer, A., & Petersen, A. C. (1983). Early adolescents' perception of their physical development. In J. Brooks-Gunn & A. C. Petersen (Eds.), *Girls at puberty: Biological and psychosocial perspectives* (pp. 127–154). New York: Plenum.

Turner, S., & Feldman, S. (1994). The functions of sex in everyday life. Unpublished manuscript, Stanford University.

Tyrka, A., Graber, J. A., & Brooks-Gunn, J. (in press). A developmental perspective on disordered eating. In M. Lewis & A. J. Sameroff (Eds.), *Handbook of developmental psychopathology* (2nd ed.). New York: Plenum.

Udry, J. R. (1988). Biological predispositions and social control in adolescent sexual behavior. *American Sociological Review, 53*, 709–722.

Udry, J. R., & Campbell, B. C. (1994). Getting started on sexual behavior. In A. S. Rossi (Ed.), *Sexuality across the life course* (pp. 187–207). Chicago: University of Chicago Press.

Waterman, A. S. (1982). Identity development from adolescence to adulthood: An extension of theory to a review of research, *Developmental Psychology, 18*, 341–358.

Westney, O. E., Jenkins, R. R., & Benjamin, C. A. (1983). Sociosexual development of preadolescents. In J. Brooks-Gunn & A. C. Petersen (Eds.), *Girls at puberty: Biological and psychosocial perspectives* (pp. 273–300). New York: Plenum.

Wiederman, M. W., & Hurst, S. R. (1997). Physical attractiveness, body image, and women's self-schema. *Psychology of Women Quarterly, 21*, 567–580.

Wolf, N. (1991). *The beauty myth: How images of beauty are used against women.* New York: William Morrow.

Zabin, L. S., & Hayward, S. C. (1993). *Adolescent sexual behavior and childbearing.* Newbury Park, CA: Sage.

Zelnik, M., & Kanter, J. F. (1980). Sexual activity, contraceptive use and pregnancy among metropolitan teenagers: 1971–1979. *Family Planning Perspectives, 12*(5), 230–237.

PART IV

INFLUENCES OF ILLNESS
ON SELF AND IDENTITY

Howard Leventhal

Ellen L. Idler

Elaine A. Leventhal

8

The Impact of Chronic Illness on the Self System

In this chapter we integrate a model of illness cognition with self and identity concepts to develop hypotheses about the interactions between the self and chronic illness. By chronic illness, we refer to conditions that typically are multiply determined, slowly developing, incurable, and degenerative, such as cardiovascular disorders, many cancers, and diabetes. We begin by describing the central features of our model of illness cognition, the common-sense model of illness representation. Our discussion of the common-sense model characterizes the content of people's mental representations of acute and chronic illness and presents hypotheses and data describing how these representations are constructed. The common-sense model is also used to show how representations of illness and its treatment interact with representations of personal and social resources for combating illness threats. These include the individual's evaluation of his or her own skills and knowledge and of the tangible, emotional, and other supports available from friends, family, community, and systems for health care. In sum, the common-sense model provides a framework for understanding how representations of illness threat, treatment options, and coping resources are integrated to define goals and to generate coping procedures for managing and living with chronic illness.

After describing the common-sense model, we focus on the pro cesses involved when a person confronts a severe chronic illness that impinges upon self and identity. Our view of self and identity parallels in many ways our perspective on illness cognition. Just like the latter, which includes a representational component (i.e., the individual's lay model of illness), as well as a process component (i.e., generation of procedures for managing illness), the self (or identity)—we believe, following James (1890)—contains both knowledge structures (e.g., self-concept, self-narrative) and processes (e.g., self-evaluation, self-enhancement) (see Ashmore & Jussim, 1997, for a discussion of this distinction). We also assume that self-referent knowledge structures, like common-sense models of illness, are complex, multifaceted, and structured. We distinguish between aspects of self that are central or important, well-elaborated, or salient in many situations and those that are peripheral and less important, less well-elaborated, or enacted less often (Rosenberg, 1997).

Our interest in adaptation to chronic illness leads to additional assumptions about self-illness interactions. For example, because perception of physical status plays an important role in the present analysis, a major theme is that chronic illness often creates barriers to physical performance and turns the spotlight of attention on social and behavioral capacities that are lost or threatened (H. Leventhal, 1975). One consequence of this change in awareness can be the redefinition of self and identity (i.e., an alteration in how the self is perceived and evaluated), a process in which coping procedures used to adapt to the ill physical self play a key role. In addition to shifting attention to one's representation of his or her physical being, chronic illnesses also change the way others view and treat a chronically ill person. Thus, the impact of illness on self involves social inputs, as well as personal and physical ones. Moreover, an individual's representation of his or her illness, and the perception of this illness by others, are, in turn, influenced by the pathophysiology of the disease, the disease's cultural stereotype, the prior history of the individual with it and related diseases, and a set of psychological factors that includes the individual's pre-illness beliefs about both physical and nonphysical aspects of self.

As each chronic disease has a specific biological, psychological, and social imprint, both theory and empirical research on adaptation to illness tend to be disease-specific. However, we will attempt to identify effects common to all or most chronic diseases, as well as those particular to cardiovascular disease and cancers, which we use here for clinical examples and research results. Age-related changes will also be part of the picture, as the chronic illnesses appear primarily in the later years (Dingle, 1973), and the psychological and social resources available for coping with disease vary with age.

The Common-Sense Model of Illness Representation

People facing illness threats (e.g., a college student dealing with flu prior to a midterm exam, patients with hypertension or cancer), are active problem solvers or common-sense scientists (e.g., Kelly, 1955; Lewin, 1935), constructing and testing the validity of their understanding of the threat by selecting, performing, and evaluating the efficacy of specific procedures for threat management and for regulating their emotional reactions (H. Leventhal, Diefenbach, & E. Leventhal, 1991; H. Leventhal, E. Leventhal, & Contrada, in press; H. Leventhal, Meyer, & Nerenz, 1980). The perceived severity of an illness threat and the specific coping procedures for managing it reflect the individual's mental representation of features of the threat, evaluation of his or her ability to perform procedures for threat management, and expectations regarding consequences of the performed procedures.

Five Facets of Illness Representations

Multiple studies have uncovered five substantive attributes of the representations of illnesses ranging from the common cold to cancer (e.g., Lau & Hartman, 1983; Petrie & Weinman, 1997; Skelton & Croyle, 1991): the *identity* of the disease (i.e., its symptoms and label); its *timeline* (e.g., onset, duration, and recovery time); perceived *cause(s)* (e.g., germs, genetic mutation); *consequences* (e.g., death, disability, pain, social and economic loss); and *controllability* (e.g., intractable versus susceptible to self-treatment, medication, surgery). The content and organization of these attributes may vary across individuals, and within individuals over time, as a function, in part, of underlying beliefs about diseases in general and about the specific disease at issue. For example, most individuals in industrialized nations carry a more or less well-formed model of everyday, acute illnesses, one in which illness symptoms reflect physical disease, diseases are caused by external pathogens, have relatively well-defined and brief timelines (time from exposure to the pathogen to the appearance of symptoms, as well as the duration of symptoms), have symptoms that are controllable by one or another form of medication, and the consequences of these illness episodes are limited. The availability of this acute illness model in the individual's repertoire of illness representations may reflect personal experiences with the many acute diseases of early childhood. Its ready accessibility and application in shaping the construal of physical symptoms, including those that do not, in fact, indicate acute illness, may reflect self-related motivation stemming from the threat value of alternative disease models, such as those involving more serious, longer-lasting, and less controllable chronic conditions.

Depending on the nature of the symptoms, the acute illness model may subdivide into more specific model classes, for example, those for upper-respiratory illnesses, such as the common cold, and those for gastric illnesses, such as stomach flu. Both classes will contain the general features of the acute model described before, as well as features that distinguish between classes (e.g., the location and particular sen-

sory attributes of symptoms). The feature of acute disease most ger-
mane to the purposes of this chapter is that the illness is not chronic.
Common-sense models for acute and chronic diseases can differ on
multiple attributes, but most important is the timeline. For chronic illnesses, the timeline is unlimited; that is, the symptoms are with the person permanently, and their likely trajectory is to worsen. The shift in
timeline and trajectory also is associated with perceptions of limited
controllability, either by one's own efforts or those of experts, and the
lack of control and temporal trajectory hold the threat of potentially
more serious consequences. Causal perceptions also may differ from
those for acute illnesses, as the occurrence of chronic illness is more
likely to be perceived as reflecting internal weakness, for example, a familial or genetic factor, rather than an exogenous pathogen, such as a
virus. In addition, the models for specific chronic diseases, such as hypertension and breast cancer, will differ on their attributes (e.g., type
and severity of symptoms, susceptibility to partial control through
change in lifestyle), forming clusters of chronic disease models with
similar representations in a multi-attribute space. Available data suggest
that these common-sense models reflect both generalizations from specific illness experiences and cultural information that helps organize
such experience (Bishop, 1991, in press; Lock, this book, chap. 3;
Schober & Lacroix, 1991). It also appears that illness-specific chronic
disease models (e.g., the representation of breast cancer as chronic or
acute, or of hypertension as symptomatic or asymptomatic) can vary
over time within the person as a consequence of experience with illness
and its treatment, and as a result of the point in the life span at which a
chronic illness is experienced (H. Leventhal, Easterling, Coons,
Luchterhand, & Love, 1986).

Illness Representations Are Multilevel

Data from many laboratories also show that the attributes of illness
representations are experienced in abstract form (i.e., as declarative
knowledge such as disease labels) and in concrete, episodic form (i.e., as
somatic sensations or symptoms, as images of a parent who died of cancer). Both the abstract and concrete components of a disease representation define or set goals and motivate behavior. Abstract and concrete
representations may be inconsistent with one another. In these cases,
the compelling perceptual quality of somatic symptoms often appears
to have a preemptory character that enables them to override abstract
attributes of illness representations in generating behavior. For example, patients are told by doctors that hypertension is a chronic, asymptomatic condition and that regular and constant use of medication can
keep it under control and allow one to avoid serious consequences such
as stroke and heart attack. Patients claim to agree with these truisms

when asked how hypertension is experienced by, and should be treated in, *other* people. Their beliefs and behavior differ, however, for *themselves*. Their own adherence to treatment is heavily influenced by their somatic experience. Adherence is good if they perceive their medication as having a favorable impact on the concrete sensations that they attribute (incorrectly) to their elevated blood pressure (Meyer, Leventhal, & Gutmann, 1985). If the symptoms are unaffected by medication, they are likely to be nonadherent and to drop out of treatment. These effects occur even though the symptom indicators are unrelated to resting levels of blood pressure, the levels that define hypertension. Concrete feedback from medical adherence and other coping procedures, in the form of changes in symptom experience, constitutes one of the critical, active ingredients in the modification and ongoing construction of illness representations.

Parallel Processing of Phenomenal Reality and Subjective Affect

Illness threats generate two separate, interactive streams of information processing. One involves the generation of abstract and concrete mental representations of illness threats and the procedures to manage them, and the other involves the generation and regulation of emotional reactions that accompany exposure and responses to such threats (see Figure 8.1). In the first form of information processing, originally called "danger control," and later, "objective" processing, one's beliefs about the realities of the illness threat instigate procedures to further clarify its nature and severity (e.g., measure one's blood pressure at the mall; get a chest X ray) or to eliminate or to minimize its impact (e.g., eat less salt; quit smoking). In the second form of information processing, originally called "fear control," and later, "subjective processing," emotional reactions, such as anger, fear, and depression, elicit their own control procedures (e.g., seek emotional reassurance from one's spouse; have a drink "to calm the nerves"). These two forms of information processing, though separable, can interact with one another. A low blood pressure reading or a negative X ray not only alters the cognitive representation of one's physical health status; it also reduces fear and anxiety. Efforts to manage fear may interfere with actions to detect threat by inhibiting the taking of blood pressure measurements or chest X rays, or they may motivate behaviors to avoid threat by generating short-term reductions in salt intake or cigarette smoking. Although the most obvious effects of emotions such as fear are usually short-lived and locked to a particular time, success or failure in the regulation of concrete emotional experiences can play a critical role in the formation of illness representations (H. Leventhal & Watts, 1966; H. Leventhal, Watts, & Pagano, 1967; also see Millar & Millar, 1995, 1996).

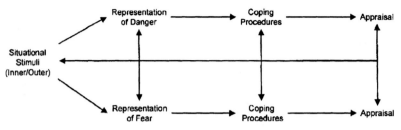

FIGURE 8.1. The parallel response model: a descriptive model for classifying and identifying variables. Situational stimuli, both internal and external, generate both cognitive and emotional representations in response to possible danger. Each form of representation elicits coping procedures that lead to outcome appraisals that, in turn, can result in revised outcome criteria, the selection of new procedures, change in representation, and change in eliciting stimuli.

Enter the Self (through the Back Door)

Our early studies (e.g., H. Leventhal, Singer, & Jones, 1965; H. Leventhal et al., 1967) focused on the way people represent health threats and the procedures they adopt to manage them and ignored the self as either a category of mental representations or a dynamic factor in adaptation to threat. When the self was included, it was in the form of a variable such as self-esteem that statistically moderated the way people responded to health warnings. For example, we found that messages arousing high levels of fear inhibited (for 24 hours) the self-protective action of getting a tetanus inoculation for subjects who were low in self-esteem but did not inhibit an immediate inoculation for subjects who were high in self-esteem (H. Leventhal, 1970). In retrospect, however, the self may have played a more pivotal role in both these studies. Specifically, there is reason to infer that because the health communications generated images of physical harm to the self, they elicited expressions of fear, desires to be inoculated to avoid the danger of tetanus (H. Leventhal et al., 1965), and intentions to quit smoking to avoid death from lung cancer (H. Leventhal et al., 1967). And apparently the changes in the physical self—that is, the experience of bodily symptoms such as headaches, flushed face, and bodily tension—were the salient factors in guiding hypertensive individuals' evaluations of the effectiveness of treatment and their continued use of medication (Baumann, Cameron, Zimmerman, & H. Leventhal, 1989; Baumann & H. Leventhal, 1985).

Concepts having to do with self and identity became somewhat more explicit when we attempted to understand how individuals falling into different age groups responded to symptoms signifying potential health threats. Had we treated age (or cohort) in the same way as we did self-esteem, that is, as merely a statistical moderating variable, we may not have been led to consider the processes whereby it affects responses to symptoms and decisions to use health care. Instead, we decided to incorporate age explicitly into our illness cognition model (see Figure 8.2) and, when we did so, we were surprised by the wide range of questions it raised (E. Leventhal & Crouch, 1997; H. Leventhal, E. Leventhal, & Schaefer, 1991). We saw that we needed to ask whether age affected the way specific diseases were experienced (i.e., did age affect the body's response to pathogens?), the way symptoms were interpreted (i.e., are symptoms perceived as signs of aging or signs of illness?), the emotional reactions elicited by the symptom experience (i.e., do older persons react with less intense feelings?), and the strategies and specific procedures used to cope with health dangers (i.e., do older persons adopt risk averse strategies to deal with health threats?). In asking these questions about the effects of age on illness cognition, we saw the need to distinguish among effects attributable to biological

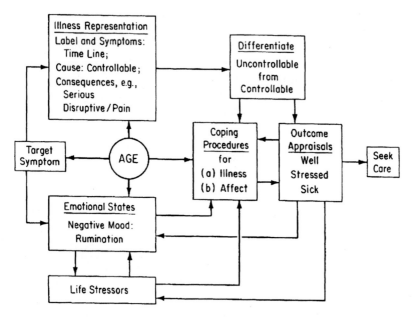

FIGURE 8.2. Age and illness representation model. Age can affect the target symptoms, the ways symptoms are represented, emotional responses, coping procedures, and appraisals. Age (or cohort) effects may reflect biological age; age-related changes in beliefs about self, aging, and illness; coping; and age-related changes in work roles and social relationships and the personal meaning and importance the individual assigns to these roles.

aging; to age-related changes in beliefs about self, aging, and illness; and to age-related changes in work roles and social relationships and the personal meaning and importance the individual assigns to these roles. We also saw that self-related beliefs concerning age, and age-related procedures for managing illness threats, are but a subset of self-related psychological structures and processes that might interact in informative ways with the components of our common-sense model. In the sections that follow, we begin to outline some of those interactions.

Self and Identity in the Representation and Management of Chronic Illness

To begin our sketch of the self into our common-sense model of illness, we highlight the impact of disease on the physical self, on one's perception and interpretation of symptoms and changes in functional capabilities. This emphasis, in turn, suggests a distinction between "bottom-up" and "top-down" processes. Through bottom-up processes, bodily changes pose a threat by potentially challenging central beliefs and feelings about the physical self, with implications that may spread from health-related domains of self-knowledge to the nonphysical self. Through top-down processes, abstract conceptions about disease, treatment, and their social and physical consequences, similarly create a challenge to the pre-illness self. By adding a temporal dimension to this analysis, we can distinguish early phases in the process, such as that involving an individual's initial perception that he or she faces chronic, rather than acute illness, from later phases, as when a "diseased self" assumes a prominent location in one's overall conception of self. An individual's behavioral responses to the threat to self presented by chronic illness involve both personal (intrapsychic) and social (interpersonal) actions aimed at preserving or restoring the pre-illness self and at warding off possible future selves that are feared or depressogenic.

The Physical Self

Though exceptions exist (e.g., Epstein, 1973; H. Leventhal, 1991), contemporary social and personality psychology often fails to emphasize that human selves are *embodied active performers,* just as surely as they are *socially defined cognitive categories.* And what is true for the psychological theorist is true for many, if not most, of his or her research participants. Though our sense of ourselves as physical beings is always available to consciousness, it is typically in the background. Most people pay little attention to their bodies and to the physical functions that they perform daily during their waking lives. The surprise one expresses at the misfit of last year's clothes attests to people's ability to ignore the physical self and the lag this creates in updating changes in physical self representations. The physical embodiment of the self means that self-referent cognition is a collaborative activity involving both bottom-up and top-down information processing. Our examination of the impact of illness on the self emphasizes the importance of this bottom-up perspective.

Illness: A Question about and a Possible Challenge to the Self

Illness, whether acute, cyclic, or chronic, generates changes in bodily sensations and function. Running noses, headaches, fatigue, stomach cramps, and sore muscles are the signs and symptoms of everyday afflictions. Chest pain, lumps, blood in urine, and severe, unremitting pain are the palpable, bottom-up signals that can be interpreted as signs that cardiac disease, cancer, ulcers, and other serious maladies are making dangerous and possibly permanent assaults upon our physical structures and functions. Processing these events involves an altered focus of attention, linking the somatic event with the model of one or another disease, appraising its implications for the self, and evaluating one's physical strength and resources for defeating the disease.

Is It Acute (Not Me)? Is it Chronic (Me)?   The typical first stage of processing problematic somatic information is usually focused on identifying the nature of one of many possible, temporary, acute conditions, or "not-me" episodes, from more stable, self-involving, chronic threats. The perceived severity of an illness will also reflect that aspect of the pre-illness self affected by its symptoms and consequences. Here, bottom-up and top-down processes interact. For example, a medical condition affecting the leg will have vastly different implications and lead to different treatment options for an athlete who earns a living in sports and perceives his or her occupation and physical prowess as central aspects of self, than for a computer programmer with a sedentary lifestyle and rich inner life, whose occupational self-construal does not rely so heavily on having healthy legs (cf. Levine & Reicher, 1996). The physical disruption caused by the injury is interpreted in the light of common-sense models of the health problem and abstract notions about the condition and its treatment as they relate (or do not relate) to central aspects of self.

Encounters with a chronic illness can begin in multiple ways. They can be asymptomatic, (e.g., an elevated blood pressure reading, suspicious mammogram, or a high prostate-specific antigen level leading to a biopsy that confirms the presence of cancer), can start with catastrophic symptoms (e.g., a disabling stroke or a heart attack), or can begin in response to suspicions about relatively mild symptoms whose physical appearance (bleeding, changes in bowel and urinary function), or timeline (e.g., rate of change) exceeds the limits of changes previously observed with acute conditions. Events such as these can stimulate a variety of coping procedures, including self-treatment (rest, over-the-counter [OTC] medications) and social comparisons (questioning others about their similar symptoms), followed by the seeking of medical care (H. Leventhal, Hudson, & Robitaille, 1997; Suls, Martin, & H. Leventhal, 1997). These sequences often precede the diagnosis of life-threatening, chronic conditions, cancers, and cardiovascular diseases. The procedures are designed to answer questions ("Is it a cold?" "Is it pneumonia?" "Is it a heart attack?" "Is it a cancer?") generated by the various illness models evoked by the presenting symptoms and the individual's beliefs about his or her susceptibilities to specific diseases.

Not all symptoms will stimulate self-evaluative procedures and self-treatments in the early stages of an illness episode. Data suggest that many older persons (that is, those over 65 years of age), adopt a generalized strategy of rapid use of health care in response to any symptom they regard as moderately serious (E. Leventhal & Crouch, 1997; E. Leventhal, H. Leventhal, Schaefer, & Easterling, 1993). In using expert services for the evaluation and control of a symptom episode, this strategy minimizes the risk of ignoring a potentially dangerous and life-threatening disease, maximizes the possibility of effective care, and minimizes the need to expend one's own energy on worry and excessive efforts on symptom control. It is likely that these strategies reflect one's growing sense of the vulnerability of the physical self with increasing age, in addition to a history of satisfaction with the medical care system.

Initial encounters vary, therefore, on "stimulus" attributes such as presence or absence of symptoms, speed of onset, symptom severity, and disruption of function. The ambiguity of the initial contact, the procedures adopted for its removal (e.g., self-care, social comparison, seeking medical care), and the speed with which this ambiguity is removed will vary with these stimulus attributes. In addition, what one brings to this encounter with physical symptoms will be significant. Of central importance here are self and identity. These include current self-definitions (e.g., "I am a mother," "I am a husband and have a wife and child to support") and desired future selves (e.g., "I want to be a grandmother"), as well as self-motives (e.g., "I can overcome any problem with hard work"). These too influence initial steps in interpreting and acting on symptom perception.

Once diagnosed with colon or breast cancer, or with congestive heart failure or some other type of cardiac disease, typical individuals enter an unknown realm of treatment and adaptation to disease for an extended period of time, often lifelong. Abundant information must be assimilated to manage intrusive treatments, lengthy recoveries, and alterations in lifestyle, ranging from changing diet to adhering to complex medical regimens and managing prosthetic devices. These tasks are a challenge to one's ability to sustain physical, mental, and social functions in the face of illness and treatments that may be severely disabling, long-lasting, and potentially life-threatening. The challenge is greater if functions are linked to important identities and if top-down processes involving the projected impact of the disease on those identities lead to pessimistic expectations.

In summary, operating like the immune system, the mental system must distinguish the temporary from the permanent, the "not me" from the "me." Symptoms of acute illness are in the temporary, "not-me" category and do not threaten or require reconsideration of self. Episodes of upper-respiratory congestion, gastrointestinal upset, and the like are intrusions into daily life, labeled as colds, stomach flu, and so forth, assigned transient timelines, presumed to have mild consequences, assigned realistic or unrealistic causes ("A sick person sneezed on me," versus "I got chilled when I went out"), and they generate expectations about control and cure. That is, they are represented in terms of the five major attributes of common-sense models of illness. The actions motivated by these representations—for example, OTC medication use, dietary changes, extra rest—are relevant for the management of acute conditions, and the diagnostic aspects of these procedures and the questions they address reflect underlying beliefs about specific diseases. Whether these processes lead to benign disease interpretations, or threatening interpretations with strong self-relevance, depends on the symptoms, one's repertoire of common-sense illness models, and one's beliefs about the self and its vulnerability. People may be predisposed to form an acute illness representation both for cognitive reasons (early learning about infectious diseases) and affective reasons (chronic illness threatens central self-motives, self-esteem, and self-control). Once a chronic illness enters the self, its attributes—that is, its symptoms, timeline (time until death), consequences (functional change and life change), and procedures for control—contrast with and force change in these attributes of the self.

Reformulating the Self: Pressure for Change from the Bottom Up   A striking aspect of disabling chronic illness is its ability to focus attention on physical activities and bodily functions previously taken for granted. Disruption of automatic performances previously not central to one's conception of self, such as walking, dressing, talking, now creates a threat to the physical self, possibly a mortal threat. Conscious awareness of previously automatically regulated physical and biological functions presents one with novel information and the task of learning how to place these activities under voluntary control. Diabetes provides excellent examples. Changes in blood sugar, usually experienced as hunger, now cause blurred vision, dizziness, and blackouts that reflect the hypo- and hyperglycemic states generated by abnormalities of insulin function (Gonder-Frederick & Cox, 1991). A diabetic person must learn to attend to early versions of these signals and to use them to regulate insulin levels. Diseases that can disable functioning permanently, for example, prostate and colon cancer, whose treatment can result in an unrecoverable loss of control of basic eliminatory functions, require one to learn alternative modes for regulating these bodily functions. Disruption of functions that are automatic or taken for granted, raises core questions: "Who am I?" "What am I becoming?" "Can I function as a human being?" "Am I to be permanently damaged and useless?" "Am I skilled in learning how to manage a damaged somatic system?" The questions raised by the symptoms and functional declines create pressure from the bottom up to rethink and to restructure a physically evolving self.

Reconstruction from the Top Down   Pressure to reformulate the self also emerges from the top down, from anticipations and beliefs about the consequences of disease (e.g., anticipated loss of function, income, social relationships and death). The specter of death raised by life-threatening chronic illnesses invokes questions about the meaning and value of life. Answers depend, in part, on predisease self-concept. Individuals who have succeeded in raising a healthy and happy family and have achieved career goals may be expected to react differently than those who have not. Anticipation of future physical and psychological decline and the need for noxious treatment creates questions such as, "Is it is worth going forward?" Answers, again, depend on how the self is construed. For example, the impact of hair loss resulting from chemotherapy may be different depending on the importance cancer patients attach to physical attractiveness. Thoughts of the nonexistence of the self appear to bolster the value we place on it (Greenberg, Pyzynski, & Solomon, 1986), but how this process influences adaption to chronic disease has not been fully explored.

An individual's model of a disease, based upon prior experience (e.g., death of a friend or relative from cancer) and social information (e.g., a doctor's warnings of what is to be anticipated), will affect how he or she represents the cardiovascular disease or the cancer that is looming. This representation will set the time frame and the context for imagining what one is likely to experience physically, mentally, and emotionally, and the procedures available for controlling these consequences and their likely efficacy, and will set up a framework for imagining a revised self. These representations may be particularly vivid and carry a heavy component of fear if the images they are based on were formed at an earlier time in life (e.g., a child's observations of a dying relative), and they may include an "understanding" of the disease based on outdated styles of medical management and their less auspicious outcomes. Reformulations of self influenced by previously acquired images of this type would fit Markus and Nurius's (1986) model in which current identity is reshaped by an imagined "possible self." Chronic illness also generates an influx of new information. Contacts with family members and friends (and the implications of noticeable absences), interactions with medical practitioners, and exposure to media messages create a complex informational mix. This affects the ill person's representation of the disease, perceptions of the procedures available for disease management including their efficacy, other consequences (so-called "side effects"), timelines, and other costs. The information can provide direct assistance and reassurance in working through illness and treatment episodes and can suggest higher-order themes for sustaining and relabeling the self. Thus, the self as "Who I am, and who I am becoming" is constructed through top-down effects that interact with common-sense illness models developed during the ongoing illness experience.

Reformulating the Self: An Illustrative Example   Both bottom-up and top-down processes will be involved in the reconstruction of the self as one attempts to enact the various roles and other identities defining the pre-illness self and to perform non-self-defining behaviors. Reynolds Price's (1982) description of his fight with a slow-growing tumor of the spinal column provides insight into the nature of this process. As his tumor spread, the pain and physical disability accompanying it (inability to walk, or to write) altered his feelings of vulnerability and disrupted his identities as professor of English and successful novelist (i.e., conducting seminars and writing). Activities that were not self-defining also were disrupted. Price could no longer perform manual tasks, such as walking, driving, and lifting, all needed for daily housekeeping and shopping. Price's self-definitions (scholar, teacher, novelist), and non-self-defining capabilities were built upon an extremely high level of personal autonomy, and the pain flooding his mind and the disruption of basic physical functions destroyed his ability to perform the most basic tasks that sustained his activity and autonomy. The destruction of somatic functions common to all of us, actions previously irrelevant to defining Reynolds Price, the scholar and novelist, became a salient threat to self.

Price used a wide range of procedures to maintain his most important role identities and non-self-defining functions. These included seeking advice from family and friends in the search for expert medical care and creating a mutually satisfactory arrangement with a former student who assisted Price with household chores in return for a place to live and work. In short, Price devised coping procedures, some of which attacked and eventually brought the tumor under control, others substituting for basic functions he was no longer able to perform (e.g., cooking, food shopping, driving), and others allowing him to sustain his central identity as professor of English. The coping procedures called on in response to the massive life changes introduced by cancer are critical for managing specific life problems and for building new ways for the self to work and new concepts and labels for valued identities. These procedures helped Price create and validate these revised self-definitions, though there were many false paths, as not every procedure worked. Persistent trial and error, social support, and more than a little luck (the advent of laser surgery) allowed Price to reconstruct his physical self, sustaining and elaborating his overall personal identity structure, creating new identities (e.g., self-managing patient), while maintaining existing ones (professor; novelist).

The immediate determinants of Price's successful adaptation were the development of valid representations of his disease and treatment procedures (i.e., they generated care-seeking procedures appropriate for disease control) that sustained motivation for action. The procedures generated by these representations provided critical feedback reshaping Price's view of his disease and his understanding of how he could maintain himself so as to sustain his most valued identities. Patients' efforts to form valid representations of threatening medical environments have long been known to facilitate adaptation in those environments, ensuring, one would hope, improved match between the representations and external reality. This improved fit will often, though by no means always, promote effective coping, enhance one's sense of control, and reduce emotional distress (e.g., Johnson, 1975; E. Leventhal, H. Leventhal, Shacham, & Easterling, 1989). Careful observation of feedback from active coping can allow one to identify and to differentiate aspects of disease susceptible to influence (e.g., symptomatology) from those that are not (e.g., the underlying disorder). Making this differentiation decreases distress by providing suitable targets for coping (Mullen & Suls, 1982; Suls & Fletcher, 1985); inability to make the differentiations can result in failure, loss of control, and increased emotional distress caused by efforts to change the unchangeable.

Frank (1995), who has dealt with chronic disease burdens similar to those faced by Price, argues that the disease must be viewed as a communication from the body and understood in the patient's terms, in the patient's narrative, rather than as a biological, medical, or externally defined entity. While Frank's words caution us about our efforts to couch the experience of illness in conceptual tags such as representations with identity, timelines, and procedures for managing illness threats, we believe that formulating the patient's narrative in these terms will enhance the scientist's and physician's understanding of the narrative itself, thus allowing these interested outsiders to make predictions regarding future adaptation and cover all relevant bases when communicating with the chronically ill and assisting them in reconstructing their self systems. We believe that narration (e.g., Pennebaker and Keough, this book, chap. 5), and other mental operations such as daydreams allow one to imagine and to test how the self can be preserved and changed. Thus, they permit the individual to devise new abstract tags, or self-representations, and to connect these tags with both existing and emerging representations that control performance of the self in illness, in treatment, in remission, and in living with disease and facing death.

Determinants of the Reconstruction of the Self   As Price's experience suggests, his story might have unfolded in many ways, and its particular structure and ending reflect the context in which he lived and the way he approached the task of self-regulation and management of his cancer. Price's success was partly determined by chance, that is, the timely discovery of laser surgery effective in treating the tumor. Were the disease different and procedures for management unavailable, Price's reformulations of his self may have gone in a different direction. Price used the laser surgery because his coping procedures were guided both by generalized strategies that lead him to search for solutions in the biomedical domain and by his representation of cancer.

What sustained Price in moving from an identity as a disabled, dying self to that of a functional, living self, in the face of severe pain and physical dysfunction? Current psychological approaches tend to focus on interpersonal resources, such as support from spouse, family, and friends (Buunk & Gibbons, 1997; Cohen & Syme, 1985; Wood & VanderZee, 1997), and to underestimate the importance of personal, spiritual resources and institutional, contextual resources. Price's views of the potential for curing cancer and the procedures for its treatment were clearly conditioned by his immersion in Western culture with its biomedical emphasis (cf. Lock, this book, chap. 3). His view of diseases, for example, that cancer did not belong in the category with infectious diseases and other similar acute episodes that belong in the "not-me" category, reflected his confidence in the "magic bullets" that biomedicine has created for the control of acute conditions. We dread the cancers both because medicine has failed to conquer them and because their treatments often appear as disfiguring and painful as the disease itself (Patterson, 1987).

In addition to shaping our views of disease and treatment, our relationships with these health-care institutions reflect generalized rules (compare the concepts of affordances and constraints as discussed by Greeno, 1998), which define how one ought to behave in relation to medical experts. The formal and informal rules governing the patient role give permission for specific actions and limit and constrain others. Price's dealings with the medical system benefited from his position as a university professor. His professorial role at Duke University endowed him with medical insurance and access to an elite medical institution.

Price's informal, social networks, and their overlap with that of the medical care system, provided assistance unavailable to the average person. Price's brother, his physician brother-in-law, and close friends (one the chief of surgery at the university hospital) gave him accurate and valuable advice about his disease and treatment and imbued him with an added level of perceived importance in the eyes of the medical and nursing staff. A sharp contrast is provided by the treatment of a Puerto Rican AIDS patient described by Ouellette (this book, chap. 6). Thus, a person's social identities (the social categories others place one in) influence treatment in the health-care system.

These supports did not breed dependency. Price used them to guide and to strengthen his own coping procedures in this extraordinarily difficult situation. Indeed, a striking feature of Price's story is his systematic calling on others to provide needed assistance when his cancer restrained his physical competencies. The result was that he controlled support provision and was ready to resume tasks when physical decline was halted or reversed.

Other top-down factors facilitating Price in recreating his identity were the cognitive and emotional skills needed to identify when assistance was needed, the desire to overcome his disease and live, to return to writing and teaching. Central to his identity, Price's religious commitments, his sense of belonging to a spiritual universe unlimited by time and place, created a base from which he could use his talents, maintain awareness of his interpersonal and personal resources, and function with severe pain and lost motion, while acting to create a new self-concept. He wrote:

> In my case, life has meant steady work, work sent by God but borne on my own back and on the wide shoulders of friends who want me to go on living and have helped me with a minimum of tears and no sign of pity. My work admittedly has been of the sort that, when it's available, permits deep absorption. (1982, p. 186)

This commitment created a sense of personal value and granted him permission to ask for assistance and to accept temporary dependencies on valued others. He was also sensitive enough to others' needs to judge whom to ask, and how and when to do so. Indeed, one could argue that Price's unusual cognitive skills, and his commitment to an intellectual life, allowed him to separate physical and psychosocial selves, including spiritual, role-related, and social components, and to focus on retaining as much of the latter as possible. These resources allowed the multifaceted psychosocial self to transcend the physical self and to accept the need for dependence and expert help to sustain the activities of the professor-novelist.

The importance of occupation/profession/vocation and associated role identities that facilitate adaptation to even the most severe of chronic illnesses is illustrated further by Kleinman's (1988) report of Paddy, an Irish-Italian American male, who adapted to serious myocarditis, a progressive inflammatory disease of the heart. Paddy worked as a bereavement counselor in a New England hospital. Paddy, who described himself as having "a way with words," was always short of breath and seriously incapacitated yet worked until his early death counseling the families of the dying. Kleinman recounts Paddy's self-described transformation from a restless, ambitious, egotistical law school student to a counselor for people in desperate situations. After Paddy's diagnosis, he spent three years in India and Southeast Asia; when he returned "his health was much worse but, in his felicitous words, 'I was so much better'" (Kleinman, 1988, p. 141). Kleinman describes him as "a natural therapist," who freely quoted Shakespeare and Joseph Conrad and whose presence made people feel "a deep sense of calm (1988, p. 140). Paddy's predisease personal identity structure was transformed by illness into a new self-configuration, and this new self system gave him self-esteem, personal efficacy, and a sense of meaning and purpose.

Success in mustering support by the Prices and Paddys of the world also reflects the models of their diseases held by other persons. These models shape expectations as to how a disease will unfold, its impact on one's physical and mental constitutions, and provide a framework for viewing the characterological and emotional strength of the ill person. If the stereotype of Price's cancer differed—for example, if it was similar to that for an illness such as chronic fatigue syndrome, where the support system views the disorder as only mildly disabling and possibly due to self-generated psychological stress—Price's supporters may have been less willing to assist over the long term. Because their view of cancer was of a deadly, disabling disease, in some ways more deadly than Price's view, they were willing to provide the instrumental and emotional support needed to allow Price to function in the more limited, yet central identities critical for redefining his self. Some diseases prevalent in today's world, most notably AIDS, elicit a substantial moral judgment that creates a tarnished social identity for the patient to cope with, and this stigmatizing disease label may interfere with both social support and medical treatment.

In short, the social environment can provide the acceptance and understanding of a patient's functional and emotional state to sustain hope, self-esteem, and efforts at control. By doing so, it provides the context for reshaping identity from the top down as well as the working environment for the instrumental behaviors needed to live, so a patient can explore his or her internal resources and skills and create new skills when the old are insufficient. In Price's case, the social context, family, students, friends, and medical practitioners, provided a context for self-evaluation and change, rather than one of loss of hope and inefficacy in the face of illness. However, not all social networks provide support; some collapse under the burden. We suspect that a patient's self-concept and how others view him or her influence the operation of social networks in chronic disease, but this hunch awaits empirical test. Findings in available studies are promising (e.g., Andreasen & Norris, 1972; Schulz & Decker, 1985) but require more direct examination of self and of psychological process.

Varieties of "Disease Selves"

Vastly different adaptations and self-constructions have been described in response to specific chronic illnesses such as cardiovascular diseases and cancers. These differences reflect the biological properties of these diseases; that is, their impact on function exerts bottom-up effects on self-perception. They also reflect social and personally held stereotypes of the diseases and other social and personal factors that exert a top-down influence on self-construal.

Selves Emerging from Confrontation with Cardiovascular Disease The symptoms of heart attack are well known (e.g., crushing pain, breathlessness, racing and irregular pulse) and warn us that the pump that sustains us is failing. These signals show "how quickly life can go out of a body" (Frank, 1991, p. 2). They evoke images of sudden death, a timeline that requires immediate action and leaves no room for equivocation. As the symptoms are often generated by one's own activity, and terminated by inactivity, each stab of angina says, "Take it easy, relax. If you push too hard, you'll explode." Death can be avoided by physical inaction. It is not surprising that recovering coronary patients worry about excessive exertion and frequently ask about acceptable limits for a variety of activities: "Is it safe to have sex?" "How far can I walk?"

If these internal communications calling for restraint and inactivity are not successfully countered by other voices calling for active procedures to restore the self, the reconstructed personal identity will be that of the "incapacitated self." This identity is at work when the individual is sitting on the couch, watching television, avoiding stress, and giving maximal attention to the conservation of energy by leading a passive life. Other voices can result in a quite opposite outcome: the "rehabilitated cardiac self" or, in extreme cases, the "cardiac athlete." Physicians and family can provide encouragement for cardiac rehabilitation after bypass surgery, and the ex-patient can be engaged in a systematic program of physical and cardiac strengthening. As postsurgical pain and distress wane and are differentiated from the presurgical pain of angina, one's body communicates that he or she is recovering from the insults of surgery and is no longer under threat of imminent cardiac collapse. Engaging in carefully monitored, increasingly vigorous exercise can be seen as "expanding the limits" and enhancing daily functioning. As one gradually "pushes the system," the feel of its successful, energetic response creates a sense of vigor and soundness. The absence of danger signals during newly achieved high levels of exertion can convey a sense of safety throughout the remainder of one's waking hours lived at a far lower level of experienced demand.

What factors determine which self will emerge after a coronary attack? The pre-illness self—for example, a history of athletic performance—will obviously play a part, as will one's social network and medical care providers. The disease itself, its treatment, and commonsense representations will also contribute. One way that the disease may influence this movement is through the presence or absence of symptoms. Not all coronary patients have symptoms. A subset that have silent cardiac attacks may learn of their illness on routine examination. As they have not experienced angina in the period before hospitalization and treatment, their diagnosis comes as a suprise and their treatment may be the sole source of their somatic distress. As far as their bodies are concerned, *treatment* has caused injury and pain; cured them of an impalpable, nonexistent, crisis; and left them posttreatment exactly as they were in pretreatment. Not having recovered from a palpable event, their bodies do not encourage them to engage in self-strengthening. They feel, and felt, nothing, and doubt they will feel any better if they engage in rehabilitative exercise. Paradoxically, then, because of lack of bottom-up signals, silent heart disease patients may be more likely to adopt the incapacitated self identity.

Cancer: The Victim, the Spirited Fighter, and the Compartmentalizer   In contrast to cardiovascular disease, which is typically experienced as a failure of the body's own machinery, cancer is often viewed and felt as an invader, "an alien and living invader that gave little or no warning before 'eating' into people" (Patterson, 1987, p. 30). The nineteenth century model of cancer, a "'lurking' . . . evil and surreptitious monster on the prowl" (Patterson, 1987, p. 31), was described as a "disease which has carried off its victims with . . . unerring certainty. . . . For centuries it has been the dread of the human race. . . . Its distinctive character has rendered its very name significant of malignancy; . . . leprosy could scarcely have been regarded with more terror" (Shimkin, 1853, in Patterson, 1987, p. 31).

In the absence of strong beliefs in positive outcomes and powerful commitments to living bolstered by communications supporting the possibility of cure, cancer, the dreaded, incurable disease (control), that abbreviates one's lifetime (timeline; Heidrich, Forsthoff, & Ward, 1994) and fills this brief time frame with pain and treatment–related mutilation (consequences), can readily create a sense of self as victim. Victimization is likely to be strengthened by attributions stressing uncontrollable causes (e.g., injuries, heredity) and by perceived negative consequences of a cancer diagnosis.

Feelings of victimization are likely to be sustained if the disease is metastatic and incurable. Other resolutions appear more likely when cancer is treatable—for example, a tumor is removed by surgery and chemotherapy is presumed to have killed cells escaping from the tumor. Some women mentally *compartmentalize* the disease and treat it as a temporary medical condition (Shapiro, Angus, & Davis, 1997). Two sets of factors appear to contribute to such a resolution: a supportive environment and personal commitment to traditional values that encourage and sustain efforts to maintain an unchanged, precancer self (Shapiro et al., 1997).

Compartmentalization, along with an optimistic outlook, at times creates the conditions for conceiving the disease as a foreign entity and adopting a "fighting spirit" to combat it while maintaining contact with a social environment that encourages sustained performances of usual identities. By sustaining pre-illness identities, the individual keeps the cancer in a "box," a noncentral aspect of self, where it is denied access to one's cherished identities. Participants in our studies of adaptation to chemotherapy (e.g., H. Leventhal et al., 1986) regularly reported, "I'm a cancer patient when I'm at the hospital. When I'm home, I'm me." Their highly instrumental outlook neither denied nor ignored the presence of cancer or progress and setbacks in treatment. Powerful commitments to current interpersonal and professional identities appeared to determine this resolution.

When conditions do not support maintenance of pre-illness identities, changes in self-construal can result. The intensive interviews conducted by Shapiro et al. (1997) point to two such changes: *rebirth*, the adoption of a new self, and *turning point*, in which previously unexpressed facets of the self come to the fore. Both revisions reflect awareness of the dynamic nature of the self. Rebirth appears to be the product of turning away from existing social roles and networks and searching for and finding new ones, while the turning point experience reflects the expression of beliefs and values suppressed due to concerns or anxiety about making them public. The contrast of these anxieties with those associated with cancer, that is, the "worst possible" threat, trivializes the concerns associated with the expression of these values.

Concluding Comments

The analysis presented in this chapter is based upon five broad themes: (1) representations of the self and disease threats are actively generated products of the interaction among cognitive and affective processes; (2) cognitive processes are complex and differentiated in that both representations of diseases and the self are multifaceted and multilevel (abstract and concrete); (3) procedures, both overt and covert, actively test the implications of illness and self-representations and are the primary ingredients of the constructive process, confirming and disconfirming hypotheses, creating certainty and uncertainty while modifying old hypotheses and constructing new ones; (4) representations of disease and self are constructed from biological realities and personal experience, shaped by the biological system, the pre-illness self, and the surrounding culture, institutions, and social networks; (5) chronic illnesses can introduce new somatic experiences and major functional disruptions that focus attention on both central aspects of self and taken-for-granted, non-self-defining functions and capacities; (6) the self-reconstructive process is affected by the biology and representation of the disease and the social and institutional context for action.

These themes establish a preliminary framework for building theory. The movement from framework to theory requires more detailed specification of key variables. Identities of diseases and self vary on labels and symptom and functional properties, timelines vary in duration and number, and so on. These constructs may differentiate further, some into subcategories and others into dimensions. It will be necessary to examine further the similarities and differences among models of the process of reconstruction of the self with varieties of cancer (e.g., colon, breast, lung), cardiovascular disease (e.g., heart attack, stroke, hear failure), arthritis (e.g., rheumatoid, osteoarthritis), diabetes, and other diseases. Questions must be addressed regarding the organization of representations. For example, what are the central and peripheral elements of the representation of cancer or heart disease, and how do they relate to the central and peripheral elements of the physical and nonphysical self? How does the individual's identity structure influence the type of procedures employed to manage disease impact, and how does feedback from these procedures influence self-concept? The contrast between the very brief list of psychosocial constructs presented in this chapter with those used to describe the sequencing of nucleotides making up the double helix that generates the human genome, and the array of proteins involved forming the cascades for cell growth and apoptosis, demonstrates that we have merely crossed the threshold for making science.

Acknowledgments: We thank Richard Ashmore and Richard Contrada for their patience throughout the time in which this chapter was written and for their invaluable comments on earlier drafts.

References

Andreasen, N. J., & Norris, A. S. (1972). Long-term adjustment and adaptation mechanisms in seriously burned adults. *Journal of Nervous and Mental Disease, 154,* 352–362.

Ashmore, R. D., & Jussim, L. (1997). Toward a second century of the scientific analysis of self and identity. In R. D. Ashmore & L. Jussim (Eds.), *Self and identity: Fundamental issues* (Vol. 1, pp. 3–19). New York: Oxford.

Baumann, L. J., Cameron, L. D., Zimmerman, R. S., & Leventhal, H. (1989). Illness representations and matching labels with symptoms. *Health Psychology, 8*(4), 449–469.

Baumann, L. J., & Leventhal, H. (1985). "I can tell when my blood pressure is up, can't I?" *Health Psychology, 4,* 203–218.

Bishop, G. D. (1991). Understanding the understanding of illness: Lay disease representations. In J. A. Skelton & R. T. Croyle (Eds.), *Mental representation in health and illness* (pp. 32–59). New York: Springer-Verlag.

Bishop, G. D. (in press). East meets West: Illness cognition and behaviour in Singapore. *Applied Psychology: An International Review.*

Buunk, B, & Gibbons, F. X. (1997). *Social comparisons, health, and coping.* Hillsdale, NJ: Lawrence Erlbaum.

Cohen, S., & Syme, S. L. (1985). Social support and health. Orlando, FL: Academic Press.

Dingle, J. H. (1973). The ills of man. *Scientific American, 229,* 77–84.

Epstein, S. (1973). The self concept revisited: Or a theory of a theory. *American Psychologist, 28,* 404–416.

Frank, A. W. (1991). *At the will of the body.* Boston: Houghton Mifflin.

Frank, A. W. (1995). *The wounded storyteller: Body, illness and ethics.* Chicago: University of Chicago Press.

Gonder-Frederick, L. A., & Cox, D. J. (1991). Symptom perception, symptom beliefs, and blood glucose discrimination in the self-treatment of insulin-dependent diabetes. In J. A. Skelton & R. T. Croyle (Eds.), *Mental representation in health and illness* (pp. 220–246). New York: Springer-Verlag.

Greenberg, J., Pyzynski, T., & Solomon, S. (1986). The causes and consequences of a need for self esteem: A terror management theory. In R. F. Baumeister (Ed.), *Public self and private self* (pp. 189–212). New York: Springer-Verlag.

Greeno, J. G. (1998). The situativity of knowing, learning, and research. *American Psychologist, 53,* 5–26.

Heidrich, S. M., Forsthoff, C. A., & Ward, S. E. (1994). Psychological adjustment in adults with cancer: The self as mediator. *Health Psychology, 13,* 346–353.

James, W. (1890). *The principles of psychology.* New York: Holt.

Johnson, J. E. (1975). Stress reduction through sensation information. In I. G. Sarason & C. D. Speilberger (Eds.), *Stress and anxiety* (Vol. 2, pp. 361–373). Washington, DC: Hemisphere.

Kelly, G. (1955). *The psychology of personal constructs.* (2 vols.). New York: Norton.

Kleinman, A. (1988). *The illness narratives: Suffering, healing, and the human condition.* New York: Basic Books.

Lau, R. R., & Hartman, K. A. (1983) Common sense representations of common illnesses. *Health Psychology, 2,* 167–185.

Leventhal, E. A., & Crouch, M. (1997). Are there differences in perceptions of illness across the lifespan? In K. J. Petrie & J. A. Weinman, *Perceptions of health and illness: Current research and applications.* (pp. 77–102). Amsterdam, The Netherlands: Harwood.

Leventhal, E. A., Leventhal, H., Schaefer, P., & Easterling, D. (1993). Conservation of energy, uncertainty reduction, and swift utilization of medical care among the elderly. *Journals of Gerontology, 48,* 78–86.

Leventhal, E. A., Leventhal, H., Shacham, S., & Easterling, D. V. (1989). Active coping reduces reports of pain from childbirth. *Journal of Consulting and Clinical Psychology, 57,* 365–371.

Leventhal, H. (1970). Findings and theory in the study of fear communications. *Advances in Experimental Social Psychology, 5,* 119–186.

Leventhal, H. (1975). The consequences of depersonalization during illness and treatment: An information-processing model. In J. Howard & A. Strauss (Eds.), *Humanizing health care* (pp. 119–161). New York: Wiley.

Leventhal, H. (1991). Emotion: Prospects for conceptual and empirical development. In R. J. Lister & H. J. Weingartner (Eds.), *Perspectives on cognitive neuroscience* (pp. 325–348). New York: Oxford University Press.

Leventhal, H., Diefenbach, M., & Leventhal, E. A. (1991). Illness cognition: Using common sense to understand treatment adherence and affect-cognition interactions. *Cognitive Therapy and Research, 16,* 143–163.

Leventhal, H., Easterling, D. V., Coons, H., Luchterhand, C, & Love, R. R. (1986). Adaptation to chemotherapy treatments. In B. Andersen (Ed.), *Women with cancer* (pp. 172–203). New York: Springer-Verlag.

Leventhal, H., Hudson, S., Robitaille, C. (1997). Social comparison and health: A process model. In B. Buunk & F. X. Gibbons, (Eds.), *Social comparisons, health, and coping* (pp. 411–432). Hillsdale, NJ: Erlbaum.

Leventhal, H., Leventhal, E. A., & Contrada, R. J. (in press). Self regulation, health, and behavior: A perceptual-cognitive approach. *Psychology and Health.*

Leventhal, H., Leventhal, E. A., & Schaefer, P. (1991). Vigilant coping and health behavior: A life span problem. In M. Ory & R. Abeles (Eds.), *Aging, health, and behavior* (pp. 109–140). Baltimore: Johns Hopkins.

Leventhal, H., Meyer, D., & Nerenz, D. (1980). The common sense representation of illness danger. In S. Rachman (Ed.), *Contributions to medical psychology* (Vol. 2, pp. 7–30). New York: Pergamon.

Leventhal, H., Singer, R., & Jones, S. (1965). Effects of fear and specificity of recommendations upon attitudes and behavior. *Journal of Personality and Social Psychology, 2,* 20–29.

Leventhal, H., & Watts, J. C. (1966). Sources of resistance to fear-arousing communications on smoking and lung cancer. *Journal of Personality, 34,* 155–175.

Leventhal, H., Watts, J. C., & Pagano, F. (1967). Effects of fear and instructions on how to cope with danger. *Journal of Personality and Social Psychology, 6,* 313–321.

Levine, R. M., & Reicher, S. D. (1996). Making sense of symptoms: Self-categorization and the meaning of illness and injury. *British Journal of Social Psychology, 35,* 245–256.

Lewin, K. (1935). *A dynamic theory of personality.* New York: McGraw-Hill.

Markus, H., & Nurius, P. (1986). Possible selves. *American Psychologist, 41,* 954–969.

Meyer, D., Leventhal, H., & Gutmann, M. (1985). Common-sense models of illness: The example of hypertension. *Health Psychology, 4,* 115–135.

Millar, M. G., & Millar, K. (1995). Negative affective consequences of thinking about disease detection behaviors. *Health Psychology, 14*(2), 1141–146.

Millar, M. G., & Millar, K. (1996). The effects of anxiety on response times to disease detection and health promotion behaviors. *Journal of Behavioral Medicine, 19,* 401–413

Mullen, B., & Suls, J. (1982). Know thyself: Stressful life events and the ameliorative effects of private self-consciousness. *Journal of Experimental Social Psychology, 18,* 43–55.

Patterson, J. T. (1987). *The dread disease: Cancer and modern American culture.* Cambridge, MA: Harvard University Press.

Petrie, K. J., & Weinman, J. A. (1997). *Perceptions of health and illness: Current research and applications.* Amsterdam, The Netherlands: Harwood.

Price, R. (1982). *A whole new life: An illness and a healing.* New York: Penguin.

Rosenberg, S. (1997). Multiplicity of selves. In R. D. Ashmore & L. Jussim (Eds.), *Self and identity: Fundamental issues* (Vol. 1, pp. 23–45). New York: Oxford.

Schober, R., & Lacroix, J. M. (1991). Lay illness models in the enlightenment and the 20th century: Some historical lessons. In J. A. Skelton & R. T. Croyle (Eds.), *Mental representation in health.* New York: Springer-Verlag.

Schulz, R., & Decker, S. (1985). Long-term adjustment to physical disability: The role of social support, perceived control, and self-blame. *Journal of Personality and Social Psychology, 48,* 1162–1172.

Shapiro, S., Angus, L., & Davis, C. (1997). Identity and meaning in the experience of cancer: Three narrative themes. *Journal of Health Psychology, 2,* 539–544.

Skelton, J. A., & Croyle, R. T. (1991). *Mental representation in health and illness.* New York: Springer-Verlag.

Suls, J., & Fletcher, B. (1985). Self-attention, life stress, and illness: A prospective study. *Psychosomatic Medicine, 47,* 469–481.

Suls, J., Martin, R., & Leventhal, H. (1997). Social comparison, lay referral, and the decision to seek medical care. In B. Buunk & F. X. Gibbons, (Eds.), *Social comparisons, health, and coping* (pp. 195–226). Hillsdale, NJ: Erlbaum.

Wood, J. V., & VanderZee, K. (1997). Social comparisons among cancer patients: Under what conditions are comparisons upward and downward? In B. Buunk & F. X. Gibbons, (Eds.), *Social comparisons, health, and coping* (pp. 299–328). Hillsdale, NJ: Erlbaum.

From the "Sick Role" to Stories of Self

Understanding the Self in Illness

Social scientific understanding of the self in illness has grown over the past forty-six years since Talcott Parsons (1951) first wrote about the "sick role." He outlined institutional expectations and role obligations of both physicians and patients and provided a theoretical analysis of the role of the patient in sickness and care and of the reciprocal relationship between physician and patient. In brief, the sick role temporarily exempts patients from their usual duties and obligates them to seek help, to accept medical advice, and to work for recovery. From a sociological view, the self refers to all those qualities, attributes, values, and sentiments, including feelings of moral worth, that a person assumes to be his or her own. This approach to studying the self acknowledges that selves possess consistent qualities yet can change as experience unfolds. The shift from sick role to self in medical sociology reflects a growing emphasis on studying patients' experience from their perspective.

The purpose of this chapter is threefold: (1) to revisit the concept of the sick role, (2) to trace its relationship to contemporary analyses of the self in illness, and (3) to offer an analysis of the self in illness that is grounded in the metaphor of the self as story. A story integrates past, present, and future and makes them understandable (McAdams, 1997). The self as story makes disparate images of self coherent and gives purpose to the self. Sociological views of self were submerged in early works in medical sociology but began to emerge as researchers studied how people responded to sickness. The concept of the sick role spawned sociological discussion in two ways: a developing literature directly examined, extended, and critiqued the concept, and ethnographic challenges emerged within varied settings. These discussions also reflected and developed their respective traditions in sociological thought: structural-functionalism, with its focus on the maintenance and functioning of social institutions including subsequent behavioral prescriptions, and Chicago School sociology, with its emphasis on inductive, ethnographic studies of what people in natural settings think, feel, and do. Many of these studies built upon symbolic interactionism, which addresses how language and meaning shape action, interaction, and self and looks at interaction processes rather than institutional structures.

Parsons's (1951) sick role gave rise to sociological analyses of the patient's place and part in the institutional arrangements in medical care. Parsons never intended to address the self in illness; it was not part of his structural-functional paradigm. Yet his analysis spurred debates that led to sociological portrayals of the self in illness several decades later. In the interim, other significant trends appeared in the literature on the social psychology of health and illness that I can only mention here: illness behavior (Mechanic, 1978; Mechanic & Volkart, 1961), the health belief model (Becker, 1974; Rosenstock, 1966), and stress and coping (Aseltine & Kessler, 1993; House, Stretcher, Metzner, & Robbins, 1986; Pearlin, 1989; Pearlin & Schooler, 1978).

Both structural-functionalists and early ethnographers in medical sociology began to discern limits of Parsons's concept of the sick role as they studied it empirically. These ethnographers challenged the overriding presence of this concept as they made alternative reality claims about life with chronic illness. Chronic illness persists. Varied chronic illnesses pose similar problems. When serious, they force changes in occupation, daily routines, social interactions, and views of self. People often live with intrusive symptoms, arduous regimens, and uncertainty. Among the many chronic illnesses are rheumatic diseases (e.g., arthritis, lupus erythmatosus, fibromyalgia), neurological diseases (e.g., multiple sclerosis, myasthenia gravis), circulatory diseases (e.g., heart conditions, cerebrovascular accidents), metabolic diseases (e.g., diabetes), and certain metastatic diseases.

The early ethnographers studied how people with chronic conditions managed their daily lives, social stigma, and public and private identities (Davis, 1963; Goffman, 1961; Roth, 1963; Scott, 1968). Identities simultaneously locate an individual within groups and distinguish him or her from other people.[1] As early ethnographers looked at identity, portrayals of the self surfaced in their accounts. Recent researchers have built upon these ethnographies by listening to chronically ill people's stories about themselves and their conditions.[2] In this chapter, after describing earlier studies, I develop a theoretical analysis of such stories and illustrate it with data from my research. In contrast to the sick role, the narrative turn toward storytelling shifts attention from objectivity to subjectivity, from acts and facts to thoughts and feelings, and from portrayals of prescribed roles to images of past, present, and future selves (see, for example, Shotter & Gergen, 1989; Smith, 1994). Despite its promise, this narrative turn holds both potentials and pitfalls for understanding subjects' and social scientists' stories of self in illness. Thus, my chapter starts with the sick role, looks at early studies, then moves toward an analysis, follows with a theoretical perspective, and ends with a note of caution.

Revisiting the Sick Role

The Concept of the Sick Role

Talcott Parsons (1951) developed the concept of the sick role to explain how deviance from institutionalized norms affected the larger theoretical problem of maintaining social order. As a *legitimate* form of deviance, illness poses intriguing theoretical issues. People enter the sick role involuntarily and cannot exit it by whim or will. Parsons presented this role as an abstract construct based on what he saw as its major characteristics, rather than on empirical research. Thus, the concept of the sick role provides a *theoretical* typology to build theory and facilitates comparative empirical analyses, rather than replicating the real world.[3]

The concept of the sick role assumes healthy, fully functioning adults as the norm. Parsons argued that the social system has to account for and manage deviance resulting from illness. The concept of the sick role then emphasizes institutionalized social control over patients and institutionalized practices that keep deviance and disruption contained. Hypothetically, the way the sick role is played controls deviance. Parsons saw the sick role as a "safety valve" in an institutional system, such as the family, to reduce periodic strains. Doctors then control the safety valve. Waitzkin's (1971) research within the justice system affirms that repressive organizations such as prisons curtail potential disruptions by expanding access to the sick role.

Parsons's great insight was to portray the part patients, as well as physicians, played within the system. A *patient* also has expectations and obligations to fulfill and receives certain privileges by virtue of adopting the sick role. A sick person's rights and duties include:

- Temporary exemption from ordinary adult functions without punishment,
- Lack of responsibility for being ill or for getting well by an act of will,

- A desire to recover; an obligation to try to get well,
- Relinquishment of usual responsibilities, procurement of appropriate (i.e., medical) help, and concentration on getting well (i.e., compliance with medical advice).

Entering the sick role means becoming a patient. To obtain the legitimacy of the sick role, sufferers must play by its rules. They must avail themselves of medical care. Physicians' special expertise allows them to define illness and prescribe appropriate treatment, and patients are expected to relinquish control and to accept and follow prescriptions. Physicians' rights include free access to taboo areas of a patient's body, exclusive claims to a patient's trust, and exclusive control over treatment (Gerhardt, 1989). Physicians are expected and obligated to take control, make decisions, and direct a course of action.

According to Parsons, a physician's expertise lies beyond patients—not simply because of specialized medical training but also because of a patient's presumed emotional and physical state. Consistent with his Freudian leanings, Parsons argued that sickness makes patients vulnerable and less than rational (Gerhardt, 1989). Being relieved of usual adult responsibilities results in being absolved of decisions, including fateful medical decisions about life and death. The paternalism within the medical care system remains unexamined and is built into the concept of the sick role.

Although Parsons did not identify contradictions within the sick role, entering it raises a two-edged sword. It grants legitimacy for leaving responsibilities but revokes rights by imposing dependency and usurping decision making. The culmination of loss of rights can be seen in the hospital patient of the 1950s from whom crucial information was routinely withheld, whose movement was externally controlled, and who held low status in the hospital hierarchy.

Not everyone gains access to the sick role; not everyone's complaints are deemed legitimate. A physician permits a bona fide patient to enter into treatment and to receive medical intervention. The sick role is predicated upon unquestioned professional authority, rapid professional intervention, patient compliance, and a timely recovery (Charmaz & Olesen, 1997). For Parsons, the doctor-patient relationship was based on an active but dispassionate expert, who made rational decisions and ordered scientific treatments, and a passive patient, who relinquished adult responsibilities and concentrated on getting well. His depiction of the sick role assumes scientific medicine, rather than medicine as an art, or as an emergent product of interaction. Recovery is assumed and depends on patient compliance with medical orders.

The sick role is built on assumptions of acute illness and on the acute care model that still dominates our health-care system. People get sick—suddenly—seek help, become legitimate patients, relinquish usual responsibilities, follow medical advice, and then, *voilà*, recover. Physicians solve medical problems and dispense care, while remaining dispassionate, unbiased scientists. According to Parsons (1951), strain in the doctor-patient relationship derives from frequent clinical uncertainty about diagnosis, treatment, and outcome.

Uncertainty is temporary—largely fleeting—in the acute care model, which is set up for resolution, action. The model of acute care assumes episodic patient contact with physicians, an active physician and passive patient, a rigid social hierarchy, immediate medical intervention and amelioration, and full recovery. This model also assumes that all modes of care require the quasi-military social structure of emergency care.

The concept of sick role spawned a number of theoretical and empirical works (Bloom, 1963; Cole & Lejune, 1972; Erikson, 1957; Gallagher, 1976; Gordon, 1966; Kassebaum & Baumann, 1965; Mechanic & Volkart, 1961; Segal, 1976; Siegler & Osmond, 1979; Twaddle, 1969). The concept became known for what it overlooked in addition to what it addressed. Freidson (1961) argued that the sick role fit almost no empirical observations. He showed that patients in a New York health plan negotiated with physicians extensively about their status and treatment.

Despite Freidson's astute observations, the sick role still holds under specific conditions: sudden illness, a desire to survive, defined need for rapid intervention, and trust in practitioners. The sick role is enforced during crises. Patient and family may try to enforce it as vigorously as practitioners. The sick role holds when central participants agree about a patient's situation and the course to take about it (Stewart & Sullivan, 1982; Twaddle, 1969). The concept also holds when patients expect hierarchical relationships with physicians, share medical goals, and have faith in their regimens (see Becker, 1974).

Challenges to the Sick Role

The concept of the sick role fails to account for much of what happens when people suffer from chronic illness or disability (Freidson, 1970; Mechanic, 1959). Illness itself is not a given. Rather, it is socially constructed and may be contested (Mishler, 1981). Care and symptom control instead of cure becomes the goal, at least of some central participants. Miraculous reversals of recalcitrant chronic conditions seldom occur. Active medical intervention may stall further deterioration rather than hasten recovery. And if reversals occur, a specialist, rather than the primary care physician, likely effects them.

A physician's role changes dramatically when cure is unlikely. Instead of instituting a definitive course of treatment, physicians experiment with medications, regimens, and, perhaps, alternative modes of healing such as biofeedback for blood pressure. Should a physician remain the authoritarian expert, he or she still has to rely on patients and caregivers to evaluate symptoms, medications, and treatment effectiveness. The physician's control over treatment plan, regimen maintenance, and outcome shrinks. Managing illness occurs at home, not in a doctor's office or hospital. The hierarchical doctor-patient relationship inherent in the sick role becomes more of a partnership. Then decisions are negotiated and often made by patient and family. Patients gain empowerment but also must take, or are left with, responsibility for their health and illness.

Patienthood can confer a master status, which means that it overshadows all one's other statuses, identities, and characteristics. However, people who have chronic illnesses are neither patients, nor occupants of the sick role, much of the time. They are also workers, spouses, parents, community members. These involvements may supersede their sporadic patient status and sick role occupancy for years. Unless illness consumes their lives, they likely identify themselves more with their ordinary roles than with the sick role.

Nonetheless, chronically ill people do move in and out of the sick role, as Parsons (1975) himself later noted. Still, chronic illness is not a temporary aberration; chronically ill people do not enter the sick role at unambiguous points. Rather, entry into the sick role is problematic. Even those in the midst of heart attacks normalize their symptoms (Cowie, 1976; Radley, 1988; Speedling, 1982). Ambiguous symptoms delay entry into the sick role. Stewart and Sullivan (1982) found, for example, that the diagnosis of multiple sclerosis took $5\frac{1}{2}$ years on average to make (this was before use of Magnetic Resonance Imaging [MRI]). The sick role concept assumes patients trust physicians. However, trust erodes when repeated visits to doctors do not result in finding a cause for distressing symptoms.

Doubt spawns noncompliance, rather than cooperation, and spurs further attempts to establish legitimate claims to sickness. Assumptions that helpseekers are isolated and atomized and that the medical model is the only possibility may be called into question. Rebuffed helpseekers may not be isolated or remain in the system. Kotarba (1983) finds that people with chronic pain developed referral networks outside the medical care system. These people get acquainted while making the rounds of practitioners in search of relief. When they exhaust their list of traditional practitioners, they seek alternative healers (Kotarba, 1983).

Chronic pain sufferers pose an interesting case. Their patient careers may begin with legitimacy due to their physical status, but their moral status rapidly deteriorates (Jackson, 1992; Kotarba, 1983). When recast as malingerers, they may also find that professionals revoke *all* their claims to legitimate symptoms and medical help. Their respective meanings come into sharp conflict (Hilbert, 1984). A similar process occurs when chronic illness proves difficult to treat, although this process may not proceed so quickly or so completely.

A legitimate diagnosis of a serious chronic illness, however, may not mean a desire to be in the sick role. Instead, people with chronic illnesses often avoid acting or being "sick" and may talk of being "well" (Radley & Billig, 1996). Speedling (1982) and Locker (1983) observe that chronically ill men and women resist "giving in" to their illness and may forego seeking further care. Social and economic resources affect how, when, and for how long chronically ill people enter the sick role (Charmaz, 1991; Radley & Green, 1987). When they can enlist the assistance of others, maintain economic independence, and control their environments, they can forestall entering the sick role and leave it more easily than less fortunate counterparts. Stigma-potential alters and overrides this equation (see Mitteness, 1987; Murphy, 1987; Schneider & Conrad, 1983). Visible impairment usually confers a master status. Stigmatizing intermittent visibility, such as loss of bodily control in public, prompts retreating to home and, likely, to the sick role.

A hallmark of the sick role is lack of culpability for occupying it. Siegler and Osmond (1979) point out that professionals, family, and friends blame ill people if they refuse to enter or remain in the sick role when all others deem that they should. Legitimacy of the sick role varies under different conditions. For example, handling an acute flare-up contrasts with managing a daily cycle of chronic symptoms. Certainly the cardiac patient who leaves the hospital against medical advice is blamed for not remaining in the sick role. However, unless chronically ill people can reaffirm their rights to the sick role, they also may experience blame for trying to be partly or completely within it.

Blame for being in the sick role commonly follows lack of recovery. As Zola (1972/1996, p. 406) contends, blame is but a pinprick away in medical care, despite patients' supposed blamelessness in causing their illnesses. How a person responds to an evident illness and a legitimate diagnosis may also elicit a litany of moral judgments. Lifestyle choices cause or contribute to certain chronic conditions. Behavioral causes and psychological predispositions are imputed to a host of others. If the individual is held accountable for his or her illness, stigma and punitive attitudes prevail. As time elapses, other people forget or never knew that a person with chronic illness entered the sick role involuntarily. Davis (1963) found that months later people blamed children who had poliomyelitis for their disabilities, despite the nature of the virus and its transmission. Thus, disability becomes separated from disease and pinned to the person.

Entry into the sick role presumably exempts a person from ordinary duties. However, a shrinking social contract (i.e., the agreement of society to provide its citizens with basic care) makes sick role exemption as remote for many people with chronic conditions as it is for temporary hourly workers with acute illnesses. Nonetheless, the sick role still reflects how many Americans view and act toward illness, at least for others, if not also for self. We seem slow to understand chronic illness—we still expect recovery and may wait for it (Charmaz, 1991).

As a *concept* that stimulated comparison and critique, the sick role worked admirably. As an *empirical description* and *explanation* of the full range of actual circumstances in illness, it performed abysmally. The concept of the sick role led to asking what people do—and what the observable properties of the role should be, not what sick people think and feel about it. Although role and self impinge upon each other, examining the sick role poses different kinds of questions than a foray into the effects of sickness on the self. To understand what ill people think and feel about their role and how they construct and enact it, we need to look elsewhere.

From Role to Self in Understanding the Experience of Chronic Illness

The Nascent Self and Identity Development

Early ethnographic and qualitative studies on chronic illness, disability, and dying brought researcher and reader nearer to studying the self by observing how people influenced and played their roles (Davis, 1963; Glaser & Strauss, 1965, 1968; Goffman, 1961, 1963; Roth, 1963; Scott, 1968). Unlike logical deductive structural-functional research on social roles, these inductive studies started with actual experience and aimed to discover what it meant. Symbolic interactionists viewed action and meaning as emergent and open-ended rather than preconceived and determined by larger social forces, as in structural-functional theory. Patients' efforts to manage information, negotiate treatment, and control their lives brought images of self closer to the foreground. A nascent self in illness began to emerge in the research.

As the self emerged, ethnographic research challenged assumptions in the sick role about recovery, roles, and rationality (Charmaz & Olesen, 1997). Davis (1963, 1956/1972) challenged its assumptions about recovery. He observed that treatment for children with poliomyelitis resulted in a somewhat improved permanent disability, not regained function. Lack of recovery had profound consequences for both professionals' treatment management and patients' identities and lives. Parsons's notion of clinical uncertainty disappeared in real situations. Yet physicians acted as if real uncertainty prevailed. Patients and families still hoped for full, or at least partial, recovery long after physicians knew such hopes were futile. Patients and families struggled to reclaim a past self while physicians left them in limbo about their present and future selves. In essence, physicians contrived a rhetoric of uncertainty to manage patients and families (Davis, 1956/1972). Meanwhile, parents naively expected a short-term full recovery requiring few intermediate steps between acute care and discharge. Davis also showed that children were not immune from sharing devalued views of people with disabilities. Hence, they struggled with identity maintenance and did so by "passing" (disguising disability), normalizing (claiming to be essentially indistinguishable from unimpaired persons) and dissociating (relinquishing parts of the normal standard). Despite these children's efforts, their strategies did not work. The disparity grew between their definitions of self and social validation of them.

Invoking such strategies means more than minimizing disability; it means bargaining for the ruling definition of social and, by extension, personal identities. According to Hewitt (1992), social identities derive from cultural meanings and community memberships conferred upon the person, whereas personal identities define a sense of location, differentiation, continuity, and direction by and in relation to self (see also, Charmaz, 1994b; Goffman, 1963). Repeated affirmation of negative social identities erodes personal identity and self-worth (Goffman, 1963). When patients bargain for rights, for treatment, for discharge, they also bargain for rights and claims to be who they want to be. Roth's (1963) tuberculosis patients bargained long and hard over their treatment timetables. Freidson's (1961) health plan patients bargained for the kinds of medications they wanted. In each situation, patients played active roles and, from their viewpoint, used rational tactics to assess their bodies, to obtain their goals, and to realize their identities. Given the information they had, albeit typically nonmedical and limited, their actions made sense. Then the onus lay on the physician to teach patients why their actions did not make sense from a medical perspective. Roth describes the classic scenario:

> When patient Jones argues, "Smith got such-and-such, why shouldn't I?", the physician is faced with the prospect of trying to convince Jones that he is making an incorrect comparison. In effect, the physician tries to get Jones to change his criteria for grouping patients so that his categories will be closer to those of the physician. His best chance of convincing Jones is to provide him with specific details about the case of patient Smith to show that Jones and Smith belong in different treatment categories, as well as to relate specific details about cases much more similar to Jones's to which he may more appropriately compare himself in determining how often he should have a pass (or whatever the issue may be). However, it is generally regarded as unethical to give one patient details about another patient's condition. (1963, p. 39)

Thus, physicians could not reveal their most powerful arguments during negotiations with patients. Roth frames his book around negotiations and conflict over treatment timetables. His example above can be read as negotiating identities as well as concrete privileges and a way to play "a," rather than "the," sick role. Classic sick role behavior à la Parsons breaks down at this point. Patients, as well as professionals, have careers and negotiate their roles. Their identities emerge. As tuberculosis patients, mental patients, and blind individuals sought professional care, these patients and clients found themselves in moral careers with stages, markers, and passages (see Goffman, 1961; Roth, 1963; Scott, 1968). Qualitative studies moved toward looking at identity directly and, thus, became more theoretical (Charmaz, 1987; Glaser & Strauss, 1965, 1968; Goffman, 1963).

Identities are inherently comparative; people locate themselves with others and differentiate themselves from others through these comparisons. Roth's example shows how patients in the same institution or program compare themselves with other patients. They locate themselves and assess their direction and progress through these comparisons— even if they make the wrong comparisons. Gold (1983) found stroke patients comparing themselves to paraplegics. A woman in my study who had had angioplasty was the youngest person in a cardiac rehabilitation program. She felt that she outstripped all other participants because they were old and had had heart attacks—until she learned that having angioplasty was considered as serious as a heart attack. Incongruent personal and social identities are also evident in these examples. A patient observes peers, compares himself or herself with them, and constructs a sense of personal identity, accordingly. Subsequently, the practitioner's stance refutes those comparisons and assumes an altered social identity based on the patient's medical status.

Sociologists find the concept of identity compelling because it links a person with society. It places people within their social worlds and, in turn, reveals the effects of society on these individuals without viewing them as socially determined beings. Identity then allows for fluidity and agency. As Davis points out, this concept "neither imprisons (as does much in sociology) nor detaches (as does much in philosophy and psychology) persons from their social and symbolic universes" (1991, p. 105). Serious illness can accelerate and magnify socialization to new identities in adult life. Studying stories about these identities offers us a window into the self.

Meanings of Loss and Stigma for Identity

Chronically ill people often define themselves as having grown psychologically despite having had harrowing experiences. They reconstruct their views of self-development through reflection after the original events (Charmaz, 1994a). Just as people respond to positive and negative events in other areas of adult life (Harkness, Super, & Keefer,

1992), ill people attend less to positive events than to negative ones. For many chronically ill people, negative events and difficult times occur sporadically and may be separated by long periods of quiescence or manageable plateaus. The following analysis distills their experience to pivotal points in which taken-for-granted views of self become challenged or entirely contested. Other ill people, however, have long histories of disputed identities and contested selves. Age of onset, severity, legitimacy of symptoms and diagnosis, degree of attributed blame, extent and visibility of disability all shape such histories.

Most identity troubles in chronic illness revolve around loss—loss of valued attributes, physical functions, social roles, and personal pursuits (Charmaz, 1991, 1994b, 1995). All amount to loss of corresponding valued identities (i.e., positive definitions of self, including both socially conferred and personally defined positive identities [Charmaz, 1983, 1987]). Jarring losses consume thoughts and feelings. Dilemmas arise as people face knotty problems, acknowledge incapacities, and make hard decisions that result from identity losses (e.g., Pinder, 1988; Reif, 1975; Wiener, 1975). Dilemmas also arise when different participants disagree on whether or which losses occurred, when they occurred, the extent to which they occurred, and what, if anything, should be done about them. A fragile balance exists between suffering losses, claiming them, receiving concurrence about them, and, simultaneously, preserving past valued identities.

Losses in chronic illness differentially affect men's and women's identity resources. These include all the physical, social, psychological, and economic attributes, props, people, and assets that support identity claims and entitlements. Women fear loss of attractiveness and relationships (Charmaz, 1995). They often see their future identities as partners as at stake, particularly when they are not in long-term relationships. Women without financial protection plummet into poverty. Middle- and upper-class men typically possess more social and economic resources than women, such as assistance, sustained emotional support, financial stability, competent medical care, and early retirement options. These resources help stave off spiraling consequences of chronic illness: poverty, social isolation, poor care, and complications. As implied earlier, resources also affect whether, when, how, and for how long an individual enters the sick role. Such resources can mean the difference between having illness flood social and personal identity and separating it from identity and, therefore, from self. For example, a secretary who screens callers and staggers visitors affords her employer short rest periods. A wife who cooks, cleans, and chauffeurs frees her sick husband to concentrate on work and regimen. Money can buy care and, perhaps, companionship. When social and economic resources continue, valued identities are preserved. If men's daily pursuits ensure getting these resources, their key sources of identity are maintained.

For example, Murphy, whose benign tumor left him quadriplegic and in a wheelchair, writes:

> As I have stepped back from household activity, I have felt at times as if I had been put on a shelf, sidelined. In light of this position of passivity and dependency, my role as chief financial support of the family has acquired greater symbolic importance in my mind; it became a mainstay of my ego. (1987, p. 212)

Women in my study experienced loss of economic resources, partners, and therefore their identities as partners, more frequently than men but showed greater emotional resilience in the face of loss. When men lack or lose their social advantages, chronic illness can wreak havoc on their identities (Charmaz, 1994b). If serious illness comes early in life, it can disrupt or destroy roles and relationships. Chronic illness can undermine, alter, or end men's involvement in work, sports, leisure, and sex and thus affect how men identify themselves as men. Serious illness can reduce a man's status in masculine hierarchies, shift his power relations with women, and raise his self-doubts about masculinity. Consequently, chronic illness can relegate a man to a position of "marginalized" masculinity (Connell, 1987; Sabo & Gordon, 1992). Murphy states:

> Paralytic disability constitutes emasculation of a . . . direct and total nature. For the male, the weakening and atrophy of body threaten all the cultural values of masculinity: strength, speed, virility, stamina, and fortitude. . . . Afflictions of the spinal cord have a further devastating effect upon masculinity, aside from paralysis, for they commonly produce some degree of impotence or sexual malfunction. . . . Being a man does not mean just having a penis—it means having a sexually useful one. Anything less than that is indeed a kind of castration, although I am using this lurid Freudian term primarily as a metaphor for loss of both sexual and social power. (1987, pp. 95–96)

Identity issues are further confounded when a person suffers visible losses of function. Murphy's disability made him rely on his wife for every small request. His stature quite literally shrunk to 3½ feet. Most interaction occurred two feet above him and sped right over him. Thus, colleagues at social gatherings either isolated him or engulfed him with unwanted attentions. Murphy felt the full measure of his disabled status and loss of identity.

Visible disability marks a person as flawed (Jones et al., 1984). People who view their disability as a stigmatizing mark and have that view affirmed suffer identity losses. A stigmatizing mark can spread across multiple identities. Davis (1963) found that efforts toward prior identity preservation fail in direct proportion to the degree and extent of visible disability. In contrast, invisible disability allows the person to conceal the potentially stigmatizing mark of difference and to preserve prior identities—for a time and under certain conditions. Many disabilities do not remain completely invisible. Some may surface in the eye of a discerning observer. Fatigue, flare-ups, or distressed feelings may render symptoms visible. Disabling illnesses such as arthritis or multiple sclerosis grow in severity and, thus, visibility. In the interim, if the person exerts substantial effort to keep it secret, it then takes on enlarged meaning for personal identity and self-concept. As Jones et al. (1984) contend, the person cannot put this aspect of self into perspective because normal social comparisons have been precluded.

Visible and invisible disabilities lead to different kinds of interactional problems. Visible disability elicits rude intrusions and judgments of difference. For example, a middle-aged woman in my study used an electric wheelchair because multiple sclerosis had left her quadriplegic. She recounted going down a busy street when "some guy stopped his car and got out and put his hand on my shoulder and wanted to pray for me. Yeah, it's a weird world. And they look at me as though *I'm* weird. They really do." People who have invisible illnesses can find themselves at odds with what other people assume and expect. Allowances for illness remain limited. Another of my interviewees, a school nurse, suffered extreme fatigue and confusion from respiratory conditions and a rare adrenal disease. She said:

> We want to be treated more like handicapped people in that we don't want to be pitied and we don't want a bunch of sympathy, but we want to have a certain amount of understanding—like, "well, this is the way it is." Like a person would feel toward a wheelchair patient, you'd treat them independently as a person and not just out of sympathy but sort of understand the fact that they do have the problem.

The sick role assumes that people recover from illness. This assumption affects social identities conferred upon chronically ill people and may be played out within a social context with its own consequences for social identity. For example, the nurse's co-workers and supervisors knew she had several illnesses. But they treated them as discrete events delimited in time. She received their sympathy when hospitalized for pneumonia. Their concern ceased at discharge when her return to work coincided with downsizing staff and an increased workload. Like many other relatives and associates of chronically ill people, this woman's co-workers interpreted her discharge and return to work as recovery. Her physical problems became translated in the workplace into problems of character and competence, of will and worth. Margins of sympathy seldom stretch beyond assumptions and expectations (Clark, 1987). Like many other chronically ill people, this woman vacillated between hiding her symptoms and seeking co-workers' concurrence that they were real and legitimate (Bury, 1988). Silent messages and overt accusations of malingering, shirking, and incompetence take their toll. For several years, only the nurse's teen-age daughter viewed her symptoms as real. Until a sympathetic doctor validated her complaints, the woman sometimes berated herself for her sporadic absences from work and for not getting more done.

Chronically ill people may lose a clear sense of inner and outer boundaries. What emanates from self blends with what emerges from other sources. What is self and what is social grows ambiguous. At this point, social identities these people had resisted become part of self. They often lack clear measures of who they now are and how their bodies have shaped their present and future identities. Their waning physical and psychological health may be pushed to the limits, although unrecognized by those around them. One of Plough's respondents said of his dialysis staff:

> I don't think they know what it means to the patient to have to dialyze every other day. I mean once upon a time, we had several days in between dialysis and there was this feeling of *being yourself*, of having control of your own life. But every-other-day dialysis really takes that away—and now I will find guys taking "mental health days" [unauthorized days off dialysis]—You have to. . . . Doctors have never come to ask us how do we feel about three days on dialysis. (1986, p. 66)

Failing health and demanding regimens immerse chronically ill people in an ambiguous state in a separate world. Their earlier worlds shrink and they lose sight of whether social expectations are realistic and legitimate, especially in relation to their diminished capacities. Thus, they lose markers and measures that ordinary adults invoke. Sacks (1984) traces an insidious flow of events. He observes that ill people's worlds can shrink without their slightest awareness. In turn, as their worlds shrink, their selves also shrink because their frame of reference has shrunk.

Whatever these people's worlds are, chronic illness occurs within a life—with all its parameters, pleasures, and pain. The school nurse lived in a closed world on the grounds of the private school where she worked. She lacked adult companionship because the job exhausted her, co-workers shunned her, her parents lived two thousand miles away, and her closest friend was across the mountain and her fatigue prohibited driving there. When troubles multiply, support diminishes, isolation increases, and former valued identities dwindle, ill people wonder whether and how they themselves might have contributed to these troubles. Like the nurse, other chronically ill people ask themselves, "Am I exaggerating the pain and fatigue because the situation is so unpleasant? Am I trying to escape? Might I be sabotaging myself?"

Being singled out and stigmatized dramatizes difference and magnifies loss. Discovering how one looks and seems to other people can be devastating (Charmaz, 1994a). Like relationships, not all events have the same value and meaning. Marker events are points of reference from which individuals can distinguish changes or measure periods of time. The chronology of illness may be replete with such markers. Some are significant events that reverberate in consciousness and are long replayed in memory (Charmaz, 1991). These events have boundaries, intensity, and emotional force. In a single event, an ill person may reverse assumptions about self, situation, and other. Negative significant events take on increased force when someone has already sensed, defined, or raised nagging identity questions. The more shame the person feels during the event, the more difficult to disentangle self from it.

A person who previously felt understood and accepted reels in shock. Feelings of betrayal, loss, and shame follow. A college professor had heart disease and emphysema. He felt mortified when he realized that his dean wanted him to retire because colleagues and students had called his competence into question. The professor felt betrayed and abandoned. In such situations, taken-for-granted assumptions about self, relationships, and social location are undermined. Self-esteem plummets, and as it does, the likelihood for redefining self negatively increases. One may search the past to see if cues were missed, if identifying moments had been discounted. Stigma no longer is an abstract category to apply to less fortunate others. It has become a category to apply to self and often one shared *by* self. In this case, one has entered the world of other—outsider—however unwillingly cast out (see Goffman, 1963; Murphy, 1987).

Murphy (1987) observes that before becoming paralyzed, disability had no relevance to him—it was something that happened to other people. As he lived with increasing disability, he felt stigmatized by other people and viewed himself as a damaged human being, which reduced his self-esteem, increased his feelings of shame, and diminished his sense of self. He writes:

> A wheelchair cannot be hidden; it is brutally visible. And to the extent that the wheelchair's occupant is treated with aversion, even disdain, his sense of worth suffers. Damage to the body, then, causes diminution of the self, which is further magnified by debasement by others.
>
> Shame and guilt are one in that both lower self-esteem and undercut the facade of dignity we present to the world. Moreover, in our culture they tend to stimulate each other. The usual formula is that a wrongful act leads to a guilty conscience; if the guilt becomes publicly known, then shame must be added to the sequence, followed by punishment. A fascinating aspect of disability is that it diametrically and completely reverses this progression, while preserving every step. The sequence of the person goes from punishment (the impairment) to shame to guilt and, finally, to the crime. This is not a real crime but a self-delusion that lurks in our fears and fantasies, in the haunting, never articulated question: What did I do to deserve this? (Murphy, 1987, p. 93)

Sorrow results when people see themselves being torn away from the social fabric. Like old age for some Americans, serious chronic illness disconnects people—sporadic episodes at first, then later, as months and years elapse, a permanent state. The radical individualism in our culture leaves individuals to handle disconnection privately; that can amount to independently and alone. But such disconnection also reveals that the foundation of the self lies in a web of relations and actions with other people (Lofland, 1982; Marris, 1974). Part of the sorrow, if not also the shame, is losing those relations and shared actions. This shame and sorrow derives from accepting social meanings imposed in demeaning events and experiences. Moreover, chronically ill people mourn the lost self that those meanings imply.

Stories of Self in Chronic Illness: A Theoretical Analysis

Transforming Loss and Identity through Stories

How, then, do people handle marker events in illness? Whatever becomes part of an assembled story, a statement about self, and recounted to an audience, gains credence as reality. These stories contain a narrative tone, moral stance, marker events, and idealized personifications of self and reflect the storyteller's commitments and felt entitlements (see also McAdams, 1997). Patients and families may not disclose a shocking diagnosis until assured of its accuracy. To tell this story may seem to award it an obdurate and irreversible meaning (Charmaz, 1994a). Someone may avoid dwelling on a shocking event and evade recounting it to try to keep it less pinned to self—at least in the present. Silence may allow adapting to bad news on one's own terms in one's own time. Remaining silent about a poor prognosis, for example, allows an ill person to maintain prior identity without having to deal with other people's feelings and judgments. The meaning of the event can shift without an audience. If no one of significance witnesses the event, or, should someone witness it and discount its significance, an ill person can more easily detach the event from enduring images of self.

Drawing upon Lewis (1971), Scheff (1990) argues that pride and shame are core sentiments for the shaping of self. To Lewis and Scheff, shame signals a threatened bond. For chronically ill people, this bond may consist of views attached to self, as well as attachments to other people. Acknowledged shame elicits the kind of questions that Murphy (1987) thought remained unstated (but see Blaxter, 1983, 1993; Charmaz, 1980; Crawford, 1984; Herzlich & Pierret, 1987). Chronically ill people do voice these questions, though perhaps to select audiences: "What did I do to deserve this?" "Why me?" "What kind of person am I?"

Stories of illness become one way of recasting reality and of resolving shocking images of self. Through telling and retelling the event to self and, often, to others, the tale simultaneously becomes tied to self and separate from self (Charmaz 1991, 1994a). Repeated retelling makes the event real, commits the teller to a point of view on it, and strengthens that view through audience affirmation. The logic of the story provides the basis for understanding, justifying, and managing the emotions experienced within the event (cf. Hochschild, 1990; Sarbin, 1986). Paradoxically, telling the story allows the teller to see and to evaluate self and others from a slightly or decidedly different position, with stakes different from those inherent in the experience.

The more shrouded in shame a negative significant event, the more effort it takes to transform it into a positive turning point. Shame becomes tied to the *self*, not merely to an embarrassing *event*, soon to be forgotten or retold with humor (Charmaz, 1994a). Under this condition, rebuilding a valued self takes time, effort, and, typically, repeated success. Thus, many indications of positive value are needed to repair a shamed self.

An earlier devastating turning point can later become redefined as the significant event that spurred reconstruction of a stronger, better self (Charmaz, 1991). Struggle and hardship can give rise to a more resilient self (see also, Sandstrom, 1990; Weitz, 1991). For one woman whose cancer threatened to become terminal, her question changed from "Why me?" to "Why not me?" But after years of wondering, she now raised the question without blaming herself for having the disease. Bowe quotes his interviewee, Susan Daniel, a rehabilitation counselor with disabilities:

> My question is not "Why me?" but "What next?" There is no answer to the first question. Nobody knows why certain people are born disabled. But "What next?" asks the question, "What are you going to do with the rest of your life?" And that is something I can do something about. (1981, p. 52)

Taking an active stance can provide new images of self even if that stance resulted from external pressures. A single mother with myasthenia gravis knew she would have to find less physically demanding work. She returned to school part-time to prepare herself. Never having enjoyed school before, she found to her amazement that she excelled in her classes and new worlds opened to her. Another young woman had spent her youth in despair, not wanting to live. When she realized that she could still act in her own behalf, she began to change. Her tales of loss became stories of successes. She learned to acknowledge and value her efforts and to take pleasure in tiny gains. She said:

> The only thing that is important to me is that I try. It's like when I feel I've really tried at something, even if its something real small, I feel like

I've done as much as I can, I feel real good about it. So I don't know if I am going to try and that just makes me feel fantastic. I feel real good about that. . . . I do have limits so I do what I can. If I'm not feeling good one month, that is as much as I can do. I don't blame myself anymore if I'm not capable of doing as much as I really want to do.

Moments of insight can also transform despair and become turning points. For one young woman, separating her self from her body allowed her to have a painful body without having a sick self. Previously, she had accepted messages heaped on her that her illness was all in her head. Several people felt too sick to do anything—not even watching television or reading—yet they still remained sentient. This time of prolonged quiet provided the opportunity for a transforming life review and reappraisal of self. Their thoughts led back into the past as they tried to understand the present. They found events and meanings they had previously overlooked or minimized that spawned new insights about themselves and their lives.

Many chronically ill adults find themselves cut off from the ebb and flow of conventional life. As the outer world slips away from them, they may arrive at new realizations. Frank (1991) says that illness presents an opportunity for change, but a dangerous one. Through being ill, people may experience gains as well as losses. One man said he had learned how to put things into perspective without creating a melodrama. Another said he had learned of patience. A third said he could face the future without having to control it. They transform their stories of loss into tales of transcendence. These people believed they had learned to live with illness with new clarity and dignity. They may lose battles against illness but regain themselves.

Self-Construction and Stories

How might stories of the self contribute to the maintenance and change of self? Distinguishing between self and self-concept and delineating where and how these concepts contrast and coincide allow us to reconcile the nature of selfhood *both* as process and structure and as subject and object. A Gecas (1982) observes, the self is an ongoing process; it is continually unfolding, becoming. It is emergent, made from the material of the past, yes, but slightly different because of the newness of the present (Mead, 1932).

A story of self is a rendering of a reality. That rendering changes as facts and fictions of the present inform the past. The newness of the present makes for different intentions and different audiences. A story about receiving a dreadful diagnosis changes as experience changes— whether that diagnosis is shocking or vague. The self known in the story differs as experienced thoughts, feelings, and actions give rise to new meanings and new images of self. For example, Deanne, a young mother with multiple sclerosis, initially viewed herself as unchanged by her diagnosis and disease until she learned what the diagnosis portended and as symptoms and regimen interfered with her life. She said, "I was diagnosed with MS without having any symptoms. None that I knew, whatever was there went away quickly, like within weeks. . . . I didn't know what MS was. [Six months later,] I think I had an exacerbation because that's what people expected." Prior to her exacerbation, Deanne defined a smooth flow of self and, thus, saw herself as the same single mom she had been in the past. Despite the positive results on the MRI, her neurologist had declared that he could not confirm her diagnosis for five or six years and had told her to call her primary care physician for any advice about what to do in the interim.

This process of the self unfolding reflects the emergent nature of experience. The self in process emerges continually in response to events and experiences, other people, social roles, cultural constraints and imperatives, and subjective appraisals of them. By two years after diagnosis, Deanne had remarried and had another child. She also had had several episodes of MS and saw herself differently. Her poor balance meant she sometimes used a cane, and she now had considerable fatigue, weakness, some vision loss, and sporadic urinary incontinence. She and her husband disagreed on the meanings of those episodes and on who she was becoming through them. She said:

> It's kind of hard, he sees me as normal with these problems. I see myself as sick with these problems. . . . I see things the worst that they can possibly be and then I accept what's good. So if it works out OK, that's fine. And he sees everything in a positive light and then deals with the negative as it comes. Me, I see the worst of everything with my MS—I'm more optimistic about other things and plan for things being bad. . . . Like when we moved . . . we thought about we might have to end up moving into a condo, just because we couldn't find a house we could afford. And I said, "We have to get a condo because they don't have two stories. I can't climb stairs and if it gets bad, climbing up and down stairs is difficult." And—all of a sudden [he blurts out], "Why can't you climb stairs?" He knows why I can't climb stairs up and down. That's when it hits him that I have a disease and it's very easy to forget about this disease because it doesn't affect us.

Stories of illness place it in the temporal frame of one's life (Robinson, 1990) and may, in fact, give rise to a temporal frame (Charmaz, 1991). Deanne's story derived from a different temporal frame than that indicated by her husband's response. Hers took illness as a continued intrusion, an ever present threat. His viewed it as an occasional, and relatively inconsequential, disruption. Although Deanne agreed with her husband that MS did not affect them, she also enlisted his help and orchestrated her day, household, and childcare. That way she could usually manage despite her tendency to fall and difficulty in lifting the baby. By telling the story of how she managed, she created a frame for understanding illness and self. Stories of illness reflect the way things seem and feel to the ill person, despite their possible incongruence with practitioners and family. Stories may change as the self felt and claimed changes. While Deanne strove to have her husband view her as changed—different, she strove to teach friends and acquaintances that her self had not changed, though her body now had some limitations. The stories of self created are also ones that arise for the occasion and audience.

The self as process, or perhaps the self *in* process, is grounded in sentiment and feeling (Cooley, 1902). Deanne's feelings about self reflected whether her husband validated her sense of vulnerability and whether her friends validated her assertions of continued capability. In turn, she could and did evaluate her feelings. Though annoyed with her husband's seeming dismissal of her condition, Deanne drew upon the context to make it understandable and acceptable. The subjective part of self feels and experiences. The objective part defines, weighs, and reflects on those feelings.

Thus, the self is both subjective and objective. It is objective in the sense that people can draw on, interpret, or apply the language, culture, standards, and meanings of their respective groups (Charmaz, 1994a). As socialized beings, we already have the cultural and symbolic tools with which to make "objective" appraisals, that is, invoke or interpret the standards of our group. We make objective appraisals of ourselves and our actions and responses in the same way we appraise and judge any other object (Mead, 1934). Hence, estimations of self-worth affect the unfolding self. These estimations come from without and within. During telling moments, chronically ill people receive images of self laden with judgments of their worth. After a nasty holiday visit, Deanne stopped seeing her mother-in-law, who had disapproved of her son marrying someone with MS and of their having a baby. She felt her mother-in-law saw her only as a liability and failed to see the love she and her husband shared.

Deanne viewed her stance toward her mother-in-law as an assertive response to a negative situation. She decided her in-laws were the ones who missed out for they had hurt their son, alienated her, and lost their grandchild. Yet their rejection did raise nagging questions about whether and how long she could care for small children and manage a household. Emotions underlie assessments of self-worth, and both emotions and assessments may be revised.

Under which conditions might Deanne change her feelings about her relationship with her mother-in-law? Might she come to accept, even share, her mother-in law's view of her? I found that chronically ill people became more open to redefinition of self, whether positive or negative, when their worlds shrunk, support dwindled, and their health deteriorated. Many chronically ill adults find themselves cut off from the ebb and flow of conventional life. As the outer world slides into the distance, their previous taken-for-granted beliefs about self slip away. Without firm anchors, the boundaries of the self become permeable. Under these conditions, people become open to ongoing definition and redefinition. With neither resources nor with strong ties to stable personal relationships and groups, people are systematically disadvantaged in the face of devastating loss. If so, the self may become shaped by the experienced process rather than exerting control over the shape of the process. Choices diminish and external control increases. Yet the person still makes continual interpretations of self as he or she interacts with others and mentally converses with self. However, those interpretations more likely concur than conflict with those who have greater power to make their identifications stick.

At this point, the self as process leads to a revised self-concept. What is the self-concept? If people are buffeted about by events, why do they still remain the same? Understanding the nature of self-concept helps here. We can view the self-concept as a product of accumulated processes. Yet the self-concept is much more than a stack of experiences; it is an organized entity. According to Rosenberg (1979) and Turner (1976), the self-concept is a relatively stable *organization* of attributes, feelings, and identifications that a person takes as defining himself or herself. The self-concept then has form—it has boundaries, parts, and elements integrated through memory and habit (Charmaz, 1994a). In this sense, the self-concept is built upon the past and how the person thought, felt, and acted. Because the self-concept is an organized entity, a person does not assume that all of his or her behavior, moods, actions, or experiences reflect his or her self-concept. Rather, one takes certain behaviors, moods, actions, and experiences as reflecting his or her "real" self (Turner, 1976).

Because the self-concept is organized and stable, it resists change. Furthermore, experience may seem to speed ahead; it typically unfolds and changes more rapidly than the self-concept (Charmaz, 1991, 1994a). Thus, the self-concept lags behind experience and the possible images of self given in it. For example, Deanne sought and received information about MS from the local MS society soon after her diagnosis, but she did not realize what MS might mean for her life until she had intrusive symptoms and disabilities. Only then did the diagnosis of MS begin to be part of her self-concept. When social identities are internalized, they become part of the self-concept. Until then they remain apart; a person may neither wholly accept them nor be aware of them.

Self-concepts particularly lag behind experience when that experience overwhelms a person and occurs within an alien setting, when subsequent events differ from what a person views as ordinary life, *and* when a person defines that experience as apart from, unrelated to, his or her "real" self. Such scenarios take place when sudden, catastrophic illness causes immediate hospitalization with drastic treatment procedures. Then the experience seems disconnected from real life and, likely, from one's real self. Therefore, devastating changes can occur to ill people's bodies without their immediate realization and without integration within their self-concepts. A reorganized self-concept has not yet caught up to the experiencing self as process.

Serious illness forces reevaluation and, often, redefinition of self. The lessons come in daily measures of chronicity. Function, speed, endurance, efficiency, and effectiveness all become sources of measuring a changed body and contribute to an altered view of self. A changed body and decreased functioning means relationships and roles must be renegotiated. An ill housewife cannot keep a spotless house. An attorney cannot remember the details of his cases. A secretary lags behind in getting her correspondence out. Speed slows—sometimes to a halt. Once a brisk three-mile walk beckoned, but now getting to the mailbox becomes impossible. But when markers of illness occur slowly and the person adapts to them, demarcations fade and remain unnoted. Then not merely bodies, but selves may change without awareness, without resistance.

Conclusions and Caveats

Moving from stories about the sick role to stories of self shows how several traditions intersect in the social psychology of health and illness. I have outlined why the concept of the sick role has only limited application for understanding the self in chronic illness. It assumes recovery that is not forthcoming, lack of culpability for illness (yet stigma and blame are common), exemption from usual roles although chronically ill people try to preserve them, and a hierarchical patient-physician relationship when care occurs at home and information and decisions are shared. An abstract role analysis fails to account for subjective experience and its meaning to patients. Meaning is revealed in stories chronically ill people tell of illness and of self. These stories are filled with loss. Many of them are tragic tales. Yet these sad stories also become reconstructed as tales of transformation and redemption when people define themselves as changed in positive ways.

Stories are a powerful way of responding to loss and redefining oneself. But what might be the potentials and pitfalls of stories of self? The current interest in seeking stories as a way of knowing has some notable strengths; it also has potential pitfalls. Stories bring chronically ill people's voices into the research narrative. Their stories of sickness resonate with self. These stories of self in illness are much more than "illness *as* narrative, narrative *about* illness, and narrative *as* illness" (Hyden, 1997, p. 49). Insiders' stories have a different texture than those observed from the outside (Maines, 1993). These storytellers offer a sense of their experience and a glimpse of their world. Suffering, ambiguity, troubles, and triumphs may all be revealed. These storytellers bring writer and reader closer to their experience and their ways of knowing it. Their stories reveal the logic of their experience, a logic that might seem bizarre or irrational from ordinary vantage points. Storytellers infuse their tales with reason, as well as feeling. Their choices and actions are rational, given the logic of their experience within the worlds they live. Taking their stories seriously can give rise to policy implications that differ from those advocated by both sympathetic professionals and budget-chopping politicians (Strauss & Corbin, 1988).

The story and the storyteller take center stage. However, stories do not emanate entirely from the self. They arise in *social*, as well as experiential, context, although they easily become separated from it. A powerful story may beguile storyteller and social scientist, both of whom may then ignore or gloss over the social conditions that gave birth to this story. It is our task to bring the social back into the story, to place a person within his or her social and symbolic universes, as Davis (1991) puts it, even if the storyteller is unaware of them.

Stories of self ripple through time and through the experience of illness. People with chronic illness develop their stories in different ways at different points in their illness. Early in the course of the illness, stories provide a way of putting the incomprehensible into words. The story becomes a device for trying to catch up to overwhelming events and to remake them into something comprehensible. Illness makes disease real and stories make illness real (Charmaz, 1991; Charmaz & Olesen, 1997).

Tales of loss are transformed into tales of learning—of learning what illness means to the teller and of making it meaningful to the listener. Then too, the tale provides a way of knowing and locating self as well as illness. Thus, stories of self provide ways of disclosing self to self through telling the tale to others. These storytellers are trying to grasp and understand the self unfolding before them. They seek some certainty when everything has become uncertain (Weitz, 1989). The story symbolically slows the flow of time sweeping over the storyteller—it separates the past, defines a turning a point, and foretells the future.

Initial stories can serve as a way to cope with difference, with being separate or cast out. These stories aim to create some coherence in the face of disruption (Bury, 1982; Charmaz, 1991; Frank, 1995; Karp, 1996; Kleinman, 1988). Such stories often reflect a quest for new meaning when old meanings no longer suffice. Experience seems amorphous, ambiguous, uncertain to the storyteller and likely to the audience as well (Kotarba, 1980). Later, however, storytellers may use their stories to teach others of their sameness, their common humanity, not of their differences. The story then becomes a tale of shared feelings and mutual fates. It celebrates connections with, rather than differences from, other people.

Stories of self are crafted—more or less. They may spill out or pop up. They can be considered accounts and they might be dramas; they may be identity celebrations, carefully staged and played for full effect. And they may serve as identity claims to separate self from illness. Whether understated or embellished, discrete events or lifelong odysseys, stories are crafted, but experience is lived (see also Mathieson & Stam, 1995). A story never wholly replicates experential reality. To an extent, the researcher and researched mutually produce the story (Smith, 1994). It is a social product whether previously constructed or barely articulated. In either case, a story of a contested self may arise only when the teller feels safe to tell it. The researcher's concerns and questions offer a frame for eliciting and developing the story. The subject's experiences and reflections reshape and fill this frame.

Constructing a story connects disjointed events, makes sense of the unexpected, and lends meaning to the whole. These stories provide selective, purposeful, and active sources of self construction (Richardson, 1990; Riessman, 1990; Robinson, 1990). Through constructing their tales, storytellers shape themselves and make their experience meaningful. Stories of illness shift and change over time. Memory, metaphor, and meaning shift as the present informs the past and foretells a future. How ill people construct their stories at any given time not only suggests the "implicit schism" (Mathieseon & Stam, 1995) between lived and narrated experience but also schisms between past, present, and future selves. Stories of the present may foretell a desired or dreaded future. Stories of the past may symbolize attempts to find closure, to keep self alive in memory, if not in present acts, and to create a frame through which other people may view self. Narrative here is proactive rather than reactive. Stories of illness are often tales of loss and transcendence, of challenge and heroism. Still, not all stories may be told. Not all receptive listeners are accepted to hear the story. Not all ill persons can find words to frame their inchoate experiences. Not all who have a story to tell can bear to tell it. Untold narratives may be as significant as those paraded for public consumption (see Pennebaker & Keough, this book, chap. 5).

Stories of self in illness are more of a saga than a single, significant narrative. One pitfall is to take a narrative of the present and offer it as enduring fact, a template of the inner person. We freeze the narrative in time in our writing. Yet life goes on. Yes, the portrayal in the story might fit this person today. But not tomorrow. Stories of self may not be enduring. They must be grounded in time. Like our subjects' views of the past changing as their experience changes, our renderings of them change accordingly. We too reinterpret the past through the present.

Beyond the danger of failing to situate experiential meaning within its social fabric and temporal order, stories pose three other potential pitfalls to researchers. First, we may get lost in the structure of the story instead of the action in the scene. When we do, we may look for meaning primarily in this structure and not in the story and storyteller. Second, we may grant our stories greater significance than they merit. The current enthusiasm for reducing reality to texts oversimplifies social and psychological existence. All the world is *not* a text. All social science is *not* a story. Stories dramatize some events and meanings and obscure others. Stories may reveal sides of the self in slices of time but not all of the self. Stories may provide a useful tool to see certain views of reality, but they are not reality itself.

Third, just as all the world is not a text, not all of our work is a story. Some of our narratives are more than a story, some are less. Yes, we use rhetorical devices to tell stories to shape our arguments, but we need not all aim for stories. Varied ways of knowing and writing are needed—research analyses, personal essays, policy arguments can all contribute to understanding the self in illness. We need to be reflexive about our methods, whatever they might be, including storytelling. Storytelling appeals to most middle-class professionals, but as a research approach, it favors higher social classes and may slight ethnic groups whose stories emerge through indirectness, nonverbal nuance, and sustained intimacy.

Neither our subjects' stories nor our social scientific tales reflect some ultimate truth. Rather, they are interpretations, sometimes artfully created and dramatically told. Yet to the extent that they speak to the human condition, we have made our contribution. After revisiting the sick role and reflecting on the story, I call for liberation. Liberation from the sick role. Freedom from the story. The sick role is not all of the self. The story does not tell all of the scene. Let us borrow the words of Heidegger and instead return *to the things themselves*.

Acknowledgments: I thank Richard D. Ashmore, Richard J. Contrada, Virginia Olesen, Leonard I. Pearlin, and Jonathan A. Smith for their careful reviews of an earlier draft. I also appreciate comments from members of one of my writing groups at Sonoma State University, Michael Baldigo, Noel Byrne, Paula Hammett, and Linda Lopez.

Notes

1. Ashmore and Jussim (1997) point out that identities are both social and personal. Thus, they are conferred and created. The self as story gives coherence to identities and the social roles associated with them (see also Thoits & Virshup, 1997).

2. This interest in storytelling derives from Meadian (1932) concepts of time and individual meanings (Bury, 1982; Charmaz, 1991, Corbin & Strauss, 1988, Maines, 1991; Strauss et al., 1984) and the resurgence of phenomenology in narrative analysis (Brody, 1987; Gubrium, 1993; Hyden, 1997; Riessman, 1990, 1993; Robinson, 1988, 1990). Nonetheless, phenomenology has long influenced sociology and psychology (Gerhardt & Brieskorn-Zinke, 1986; Kestenbaum, 1982; Williams, 1984). As Gubrium (1993) notes, the narrative turn has redirected ethnographic work from social organization to storytelling for both ethnographers and subjects.

3. Weber (1949) articulated a methodology for developing theoretical constructs somewhat confusingly known as the "ideal type." He intended for ideal types to synthesize the most frequently occurring social actions that constituted a particular social structure or values that characterized a phenomenon. In this sense, the ideal type would take into account empirical observations and represent the modal, or general, norm, rather than the ideal. Yet ideal types can slip into becoming idealized types and therefore become prescriptive, not descriptive. To form an ideal type, Weber synthesized many discrete, diffuse, and usually present, but occasionally absent, phenomena into an abstraction. Weber saw ideal types as tools for creating unified analytical constructs for theory development, not as absolute replications of reality. He pointed out that ideal types accentuated certain values, viewpoints, and actions and recognized that they may be one-sided. However, he argued that ideal types could provide tools for social scientists to apprehend both overt action and individual intention and, thus, make developing interpretive and causal explanations possible. Despite Sica's pronouncement of the ideal type as having a "hopeless career" (1988, p. 96) as a methodological concept, Weber's method of constructing ideal types has guided social research and theory for decades.

References

Aseltine, R. H., Jr., & Kessler, R. C. (1993). Marital disruption and depression in a community sample. *Journal of Health and Social Behavior, 34*, 237–251.

Ashmore, R. D., & Jussim, L. (1997). Introduction: Toward a second century of the scientific analysis of self and identity. In R. D. Ashmore & L. Jussim (Eds.), *Self and identity: Fundamental issues* (pp. 3–19). New York: Oxford University Press.

Becker, M. H. (Ed.) (1974). *The Health belief model and personal health behavior*. San Francisco: Society for Public Health Education, Inc.

Blaxter, M. (1983). The causes of disease: Women talking. *Social Science and Medicine, 17*, 59–69.

Blaxter, M. (1993). Why do the victims blame themselves? In A. Radley (Ed.), *Worlds of illness* (pp. 124–142). New York: Routledge.

Bloom. S. W. (1963). *The doctor and his patient.* New York: Sage.

Bowe, F. (1981). *Comeback: Six remarkable people who triumphed over disability.* New York: Harper & Row.

Brody, H. (1987). *Stories of sickness.* New Haven, CT: Yale University Press.

Bury, M. R. (1982). Chronic illness as disruption. *Sociology of Health and Illness, 4,* 167–182.

Bury, M. R. (1988). Meanings at risk: The experience of arthritis. In R. Anderson & M. Bury (Eds.), *Living with chronic illness* (pp. 89–116). London: Unwin Hyman.

Charmaz, K. (1980). The social construction of self-pity in the chronically ill. In N. K. Denzin (Ed.), *Studies in symbolic interaction* (Vol. 3, pp. 123–146). Greenwich, CT: JAI Press.

Charmaz, K. (1983). Loss of self: A fundamental form of suffering in the chronically ill. *Sociology of Health and Illness, 5,* 168–195.

Charmaz, K. (1987). Struggling for a self: Identity levels of the chronically ill. In P. Conrad & J. A. Roth. (Eds.), *Research in the sociology of health care: The experience and management of chronic illness* (Vol. 6, pp. 283–321). Greenwich, CT: JAI Press.

Charmaz, K. (1991). *Good days, bad days: The self in chronic illness and time.* New Brunswick, NJ: Rutgers University Press.

Charmaz, K. (1994a). Discoveries of self in illness. In M. L. Dietz, R. Prus, & W. Shaffir (Eds.), *Doing everyday life: Ethnography as human lived experience* (pp. 226–242). Mississauga, Ontario: Copp Clark, Longman.

Charmaz, K. (1994b). Identity dilemmas of chronically ill men. *Sociological Quarterly, 35,* 269–288.

Charmaz, K. (1995). The body, identity, and self: Adapting to impairment. *Sociological Quarterly, 36,* 657–680.

Charmaz, K., & Olesen, V. (1997). Ethnographic research in medical sociology: Its foci and distinctive contributions. *Sociological Methods and Research, 25,* 452–494.

Clark, C. (1987). Sympathy biography and sympathy margin. *American Journal of Sociology, 93,* 290–291.

Cole, S., & Lejune, R. (1972). Illness and the legitimation of failure. *American Sociological Review, 37,* 347–356.

Connell, R. W. (1987). *Gender and power: Society, the person, and sexual politics.* Stanford, CA: Stanford University Press.

Cooley, C. H. (1902). *Human nature and the social order.* New York: Scribner's.

Corbin, J. M., & Strauss, A. (1988). *Unending work and care: Managing chronic illness at home.* San Francisco: Jossey-Bass.

Cowie, B. (1976). The cardiac patient's perception of his heart attack. *Social Science and Medicine, 10,* 87–96.

Crawford, R. (1984). A cultural account of "health": Control, release, and the social body. In J. B. McKinlay (Ed.), *Issues in the political economy of health care.* New York: Tavistock.

Davis, F. (1963). *Passage through crisis: Polio victims and their families.* Indianapolis: Bobbs-Merrill.

Davis, F. (1956/1972). Definitions of time and recovery in paralytic polio convalescence. In F. Davis (ed.), *Illness, interaction and the self* (pp. 83–91). Belmont, CA: Wadsworth.

Davis, F. (1991). Identity ambivalence in clothing: The dialectic of the erotic and the chaste. In D. R. Maines (Ed.), *Social organization and social process: Essays in honor of Anselm Strauss* (pp. 105–116). New York: Aldine de Gruyter.

Erikson, K. T. (1957). Patient role and social uncertainty—a dilemma of the mentally ill. *Psychiatry, 20,* 263–274.

Frank, A. (1991). *At the will of the body: Reflections on illness.* Boston: Houghton Mifflin.

Frank, A. (1993). The rhetoric of self-change: Illness experience as narrative. *Sociological Quarterly, 34,* 39–52.

Frank, A. (1995). *The wounded storyteller: body, illness and ethics.* Chicago: University of Chicago Press.

Freidson, E. (1961). *Patients' views of medical practice.* New York: Sage.

Freidson, E. (1970). *The profession of medicine: A study of the sociology of applied knowledge.* New York: Dodd, Mead.

Gallagher, E. B. (1976). Lines of reconstruction and extension in the Parsonian sociology of illness. *Social Science and Medicine, 10,* 207–218.

Gecas, V. (1982). The self-concept. *Annual Review of Sociology, 8,* 1–33.

Gerhardt, U. (1989). *Ideas about illness: An intellectual and political history of medical sociology.* New York: New York University Press.

Gerhardt, U., & Brieskorn-Zinke, M. (1986). The normalization of hemodialysis at home. In J. A. Roth & S. B. Ruzek (Eds.), *Research in the sociology of health care: The adoption and social consequences of medical technologies* (Vol. 4, pp. 271–317). Greenwich, CT: JAI Press.

Glaser, B. G., & Strauss, A. L. (1965). *Awareness of dying.* Chicago: Aldine.

Glaser, B. G., & Strauss, A. L. (1968). *Time for dying.* Chicago: Aldine.

Goffman, Erving. (1961). *Asylums.* New York: Doubleday.

Goffman, Erving. (1963). *Stigma: Notes on the management of spoiled identity.* Englewood Cliffs, NJ: Prentice-Hall.

Gold, S. J. (1983). Getting well: Impression management as stroke rehabilitation. *Qualitative Sociology, 6,* 238–254.

Gordon, G. (1966). *Role theory and illness: A sociological perspective.* New Haven, CT: College and University Press.

Gubrium, J. F. (1993). *Speaking of life: Horizons of meaning for nursing home residents.* New York: Aldine de Gruyter.

Harkness, S., Super, C. M., & Keefer, C. (1992). Learning to be an American parent: How cultural models gain directive force. In R. D'Andrade & C. Strauss (Eds.), *Human motives and cultural models* (pp. 163–178). New York: Cambridge University Press.

Herzlich, C., & Pierret, J. (1987). *Illness and self in society.* Baltimore: Johns Hopkins University Press.

Hewitt, J. P. (1992). *Self and society.* New York: Simon and Schuster.

Hilbert, R. A. (1984). The acultural dimensions of chronic pain: Flawed reality construction and the problem of meaning. *Social Problems, 31,* 365–378.

Hochschild, A. (1990). Ideology and emotion management: A perspective and path for future research. In T. D. Kemper (Ed.), *Research agendas in the sociology of emotions* (pp. 117–144). Albany: State University of New York Press.

House, J. S., Stretcher, V., Metzner, H. L., & Robbins, C. A. (1986). Occupational stress and health among men and women in the Tecumseh Community Health Study. *Journal of Health and Social Behavior, 27*, 62–77.

Hyden, L. (1997). Illness and narrative. *Sociology of Health and Illness, 19*, 48–69.

Jackson, J. E. (1992). "After a while no one believes you": Real and unreal pain. In M. D. Good, P. E. Brodwin, B. J. Good, & A. Kleinman (Eds.), *Pain as human experience: An anthropological perspective* (pp. 138–168). Berkeley: University of California Press.

Jones, E. E., Farina, A., Hastrof, A., Markus, H., Miller, D. T., & Scott, R. A. (1984). *Social stigma: The psychology of marked relationships.* New York: W. H. Freeman.

Karp, D. A. (1996). *Speaking of sadness: Depression, disconnection and the meanings of illness.* New York: Oxford University Press.

Kassebaum, G. G., & Baumann, B. O. (1965). Dimensions of the sick role in chronic illness. *Journal of Health and Social Behavior, 6*, 16–27.

Kestenbaum, V. (1982). The humanity of the ill. In V. Kestenbaum (Ed.), *The humanity of the ill* (pp. 3–38). Knoxville: University of Tennessee Press.

Kleinman, A. (1988). *The illness narratives.* New York: Basic Books.

Kotarba, J. A. (1980). Discovering amorphous social experience: The case of chronic pain. In W. B. Shaffir, R. A. Stebbins, & A. Turowetz (Eds.), *Fieldwork experience: Qualitative approaches to social research* (pp. 57–67). New York: St. Martin's.

Kotarba, J. A. (1983). *Chronic pain: Its social dimensions.* Beverly Hills, CA: Sage.

Lewis, H. B. (1971). *Shame and guilt in neurosis.* New York: International Press.

Locker, D. (1983). *Disability and disadvantage: The consequences of chronic illness.* London: Tavistock.

Lofland, L. H. (1982). Loss and human connection: An exploration into the nature of the social bond. In W. Ickes & E. S. Knowles (Eds.), *Personality, roles and social behavior* (pp. 219–242). New York: Springer-Verlag.

Maines, D. M. (1991). The storied nature of health and diabetic self-help groups. In G. Albrecht & J. Levy (Eds.), *Advances in medical sociology* (Vol. 5, pp. 35–45). Greenwich, CT: JAI Press.

Maines, D. M. (1993). Narrative's moment and sociology's phenomena: Toward a narrative sociology. *Sociological Quarterly, 34*, 17–38.

Marris, P. (1974). *Loss and change.* New York: Pantheon.

Mathieson, C. M. & Stam, H. J. (1995). Renegotiating identity: Cancer narratives. *Sociology of Health and Illness, 17*, 283–306.

McAdams, D. P. (1997). The case for unity in the (post)modern self: A modest proposal. In R. D. Ashmore & L. Jussim (Eds.), *Self and identity: Fundamental issues* (pp. 46–78). New York: Oxford University Press.

Mead, G. H. (1932). *The philosophy of the present.* La Salle, IL: Open Court.

Mead, G. H. (1934). *Mind, self and society.* Chicago: University of Chicago Press.

Mechanic, D. (1959). Illness and social disability: Some problems in analysis. *Pacific Sociological Review, 2*, 37–41.

Mechanic, D. (1978). *Medical sociology.* New York: Free Press.

Mechanic, D., & Volkart, E. H. (1961). Stress, illness behavior and the sick role. *American Sociological Review, 26*, 51–58.

Mishler, E. G. (1981). The social construction of illness. In E. G. Mishler, L. R.

AmaraSingham, S. T. Hauser, R. Liem, S. D. Osherson, & N. Waxler, *Social contexts of health, illness and patient care* (pp. 141–168). New York: Cambridge University Press.

Mitteness, L. S. (1987). The management of urinary incontinence by community-living elderly. *The Gerontologist, 27,* 185–197.

Murphy, R. F. (1987). *The body silent.* New York: Henry Holt.

Parsons, T. (1951). *The social system.* Glencoe, IL: Free Press.

Parsons. T. (1975). The sick role and the role of the physician reconsidered. *Millbank Memorial Fund Quarterly, 53,* 257–278.

Pearlin, L. I. (1989). The sociological study of stress. *Journal of Health and Social Behavior, 30,* 241–356.

Pearlin, L. I., & Schooler, C. (1978). The structure of coping. *Journal of Health and Social Behavior, 23,* 2–17.

Pinder, R. (1988). Striking balances: Living with Parkinson's disease. In R. Anderson & M. Bury (Eds.), *Living with chronic illness* (pp. 67–88). London: Unwin Hyman.

Plough, A. L. (1986). *Borrowed time: Artificial organs and the politics of extending lives.* Philadelphia: Temple University Press.

Radley, A. (1988). *Prospects of heart surgery: Psychological adjustment to coronary bypass grafting.* New York: Springer-Verlag.

Radley, A., & Billig, M. (1996). Accounts of health and illness: Dilemmas and representations. *Sociology of Health and Illness, 18,* 220–240.

Radley, A., & Green. R. (1987). Illness as adjustment: A methodology and conceptual framework. *Sociology of Health and Illness, 9,* 179–207.

Reif, L. (1975). Ulcerative colitis: Strategies for managing life. In A. L. Strauss (Ed.), *Chronic illness and the quality of life* (pp. 81–88). St. Louis: Mosby.

Richardson, L. (1990). Narrative and sociology. *Journal of Contemporary Ethnography, 19,* 116–135.

Riessman, C. (1990). Strategic uses of narrative in the presentation of self and illness: A research note. *Social Science and Medicine, 30,* 1195–1200.

Riessman, C. (1993). *Narrative analysis.* Thousand Oaks, CA: Sage.

Robinson, I. (1988). *Multiple sclerosis.* London: Tavistock.

Robinson, I. (1990). Personal narratives, social careers and medical courses: Analysing life trajectories in autobiographies of people with multiple sclerosis. *Social Science and Medicine, 30,* 1173–1186.

Rosenberg, M. (1979). *Conceiving the self.* New York: Krieger.

Rosenstock, I. (1966). Why people use health services. *Millbank Memorial Fund Quarterly, 44,* 94–127.

Roth, Julius A. (1963). *Timetables.* New York: Bobbs-Merrill.

Sabo, D., & Gordon, D. F. (1995). Rethinking men's health and illness. In D. Sabo & D. F. Gordon (Eds.), *Men's health and illness: Gender, power, and the body* (pp. 1–21). Thousand Oaks, CA: Sage.

Sacks, O. (1984). *A leg to stand on.* New York: Summit Books.

Sandstrom, K. L. (1990). Confronting deadly disease: The drama of identity construction among gay men with AIDS. *Journal of Contemporary Ethnography, 19,* 271–294.

Sarbin, T. R. (1986). Emotion and act: Roles and rhetoric. In R. Harré (Ed.), *The social construction of emotion* (pp. 83–97). London: Basil Blackwell.

Scheff, T. J. (1990). *Microsociology: Discourse, emotion and social structure.* Chicago: University of Chicago Press.

Schneider, J. W., & Conrad, P. (1983). *Having epilepsy.* Philadelphia: Temple University Press.

Scott, R. A. (1968). *The making of blind men.* New York: Russell Sage.

Segal, A. (1976). Sociocultural variation in sick role behavioural expectations. *Social Science and Medicine, 10,* 47–54.

Sica, A. (1988). *Weber, irrationality, and social order.* Berkeley: University of California Press.

Siegler, M., & Osmond, H. (1979). The "sick role" revisited. In G. L. Albrecht & P. C. Higgins (Eds.) *Health, illness, and medicine* (pp. 146–166). Chicago: Rand McNally.

Smith, J. A. (1994). Towards reflexive practice: Engaging participants as co-researchers or co-analysts in psychological inquiry. *Journal of Community and Applied Social Psychology, 4,* 253–260.

Speedling, E. J. (1982). *Heart attack: The family response at home and in the hospital.* New York: Tavistock.

Stewart, D. C., & Sullivan, T. J. (1982). Illness behavior and the sick role in chronic disease: The case of multiple sclerosis. *Social Science and Medicine, 16,* 1397–1404.

Strauss, A., & Corbin, J. M. (1988). *Shaping a new health care system.* San Francisco: Jossey-Bass.

Strauss, A. L., Corbin, J., Fagerhaugh, S., Glaser, B. G., Maines, D., Suczek, B., & Wiener, C. L. (1984). *Chronic illness and the quality of life* (2nd ed.). St. Louis: Mosby.

Thoits, P., & Virshup, L. K. (1997). Me's and we's: Forms and functions of social identities. In R. D. Ashmore & L. Jussim (Eds.), *Self and identity: Fundamental issues* (pp. 106–133). New York: Oxford University Press.

Turner, R. (1976). The real self: From institution to impulse. *American Journal of Sociology, 81,* 989–1016.

Twaddle, A. C. (1969). Health decisions and sick role variations: An exploration. *Journal of Health and Social Behavior, 10,* 105–115.

Waitzkin, H. (1971). Latent functions of the sick role in various institutional settings. *Social Science and Medicine, 5,* 45–75.

Weber, M. (1949) *The methodology of the social sciences.* Trans. and ed. E. Shils & H. Finch. Glencoe, IL: Free Press.

Weitz, R. (1989). Uncertainty in the lives of persons with AIDS. *Journal of Health and Social Behavior, 30,* 270–281.

Weitz, R. (1991). *Life with AIDS.* New Brunswick, NJ: Rutgers University Press.

Wiener, C. L. (1975). The burden of rheumatoid arthritis. In A. L. Strauss (Ed.), *Chronic illness and the quality of life* (pp. 71–80). St. Louis: Mosby.

Williams, G. (1984). The genesis of chronic illness: Narrative reconstruction. *Sociology of Health and Illness, 6,* 175–200.

Zola, I. K. (1972/1997). Medicine as an institution of social control. In P. Conrad (Ed.), *The sociology of health and illness* (5th ed., pp. 404–414). New York: St. Martin's.

Richard D. Ashmore
Richard J. Contrada

Conclusion

*Self, Social Identity,
and the Analysis of Social
and Behavioral Aspects of
Physical Health and Disease*

Our goal in devising the present volume was to delineate the use of self and identity as major elements in the social and behavioral analysis of health and illness. To achieve this goal, we asked a set of talented scholars from diverse academic disciplines to identify some of the important issues, concepts, and findings involved in conceiving of physical well-being in terms of self and social identity. In this concluding chapter, we first review the major results of the contributors' analyses. The remainder of the chapter is devoted to outlining the next generation of issues to be addressed if self and identity are to serve as a useful lens for social and behavioral scientists in analyzing physical health.

Where We Started and Where We Are Now

Three major themes were used to organize this volume: (1) systems involved in the self and health interface, (2) paths from self and identity to sickness, (3) how sickness influences self and social identity.

Systems Involved in the Self and Health Interface

Two chapters, by Kihlstrom and Canter Kihlstrom and by Lock, addressed the topic of self, systems, and sickness. Kihlstrom and Canter Kihlstrom concentrated on the social psychological level of analysis, describing individuals in face-to-face social interaction. They identified two facets of the doctor-patient relationship in which self and identity take center stage: diagnosis and treatment. They noted that patient compliance with prescribed regimens is a crucial yet problematic aspect of medical treatment. To better understand when patients do and do not comply, they suggested explicitly adding self and identity to the self-regulation model developed by Leventhal, Meyer, and Nerenz (1980). They noted the likely utility of the concept "possible selves" (Markus & Nurius, 1986). Concerning the issue of diagnosis, Kihlstrom and Canter Kihlstrom highlighted somatoform disorders, one crucial feature of which is a sharp patient-physician difference in defining the patient: body dysmorphic disorder—"I am ugly" versus "You look just fine"; somatization disorder—"I am physically sick" versus "No, you are not; you may be mentally/emotionally sick."

The patient and doctor constitute a central system in understanding the self-health interconnection: here consumer and provider come into direct contact, and the success of that interaction depends, in part, on how the doctor and patient define themselves and the other. Further, the patient-physician system is embedded in larger systems, perhaps the most important of which is the health-care system. As Kihlstrom and Canter Kihlstrom pointed out, the organization of health delivery in the United States is undergoing major transformations, with new services being added (e.g., pharmaceutical benefit management [PBM] firms). Likely, emerging forms of health care will have profound implications for the personal and social identities of providers (e.g., physicians, nurses) and consumers, and self/identity constructs will contribute to our understanding of changes in health care.

Lock described societal-level systems important to understanding how self and social identity are linked to health and disease. She first established that "culture" is not a simple and monolithic concept (cf. Holland, 1997). An important corollary of this point is that large nation states such as the United States and Canada contain multiple cultures, based on ethnicity and other factors, and that these differ in terms of societal power and prestige. Lock described how such power differentials can, in part, determine the types of selves available to people and, in turn, influence their susceptibility to physical and mental health problems. She illustrated this point by describing the case of Wilfred, a young Cree adolescent, who could not speak. Lock sought to understand this case, not in terms of the young boy's personal qualities or even of his immediate social environment, but instead she traced Wilfred's condition to the treatment of the Cree and other indigenous people by Canadian society—pejorative depictions of these groups in schools and mass media (undermining the groups' and individuals' social identity), daily experiences of discrimination (threatening self-efficacy and self-esteem), and forced relocation of large numbers of the Cree (taking them away from the physical environment that provided an important part of the group's self-definition). These social system variables set the stage for Wilfred's muteness and also for the other mental and physical health problems experienced by his people.

Lock also explained how cultural and subcultural meaning systems provide ways for individuals and groups to interpret psychological distress and bodily sensations. She illustrated this point by describing "nevra" among Greek immigrant women in Canada and the differences in how Japanese and North American women experience menopause. Lock described how in traditional Greek culture women defined themselves in terms of maintaining a clean and harmonious home. As immigrants in Montreal, however, the women not only were responsible for the home but also for contributing to the family's earnings by sewing for garment producers. Further, to "protect" them from the new society, the women were seldom allowed to leave their houses. The distress they experienced, in part because they could not live up to traditional expectations for self-definition, could be expressed via the culturally accepted syndrome termed nevra (or nerves).

Paths from Self to Sickness

Four chapters—by Williams, Spencer, and Jackson; Pennebaker and Keough; Ouellette; and Brooks-Gunn and Graber—analyzed pathways from self and social identity to physical illness and disease. Williams and his colleagues picked up on the theme introduced by Lock that societal systems are hierarchically arranged, some groups having less power and prestige than others, with important implications for the social identities of individuals. Members of groups at the bottom of a society's status hierarchy are often the targets of discriminatory behavior. As Williams and his colleagues pointed out, discrimination can take the form of major acute events (e.g., being turned down for a job) and minor everyday insults and slights (e.g., being asked to sign one's name twice to a credit card receipt). Certainly both types of discrimination are stressors, and there is considerable evidence that stress sets the stage for illness (Lin & Ensel, 1989). Williams et al. added a crucial self/identity element to this discrimination stress-to-illness pathway by demonstrating that one's ethnic identity can buffer the illness-inducing effects of racial discrimination against African Americans. More specifically, racial self-concept (basically, *how important* one's ethnic group is to personal self-definition) buffered the link between discrimination and self-assessed health; racial/ethnic identity (*perceived closeness* to one's ethnic or racial group) buffered the effect of discrimination on both self-perceived health and chronic health problems (whether one had been advised by a health-care professional that he or she had a health problem). In sum, Williams and his colleagues demonstrated that ethnic identity can moderate the stress-sickness path and that this effect may depend on both the facet of ethnic identity and the measure of physical well-being being considered.

Pennebaker and Keough concentrated not on what people bring to threatening situations (as, for example, ethnic identity in the Williams et al. research) but, instead, on what people do after a stressful experience. Pennebaker and Keough described the results of an impressive research program demonstrating that having people write about their traumatic experiences (e.g., childhood abuse, losing a job) has a positive effect on health. They then offered a "self-repair and self-rebuilding" model to account for why communicating about trauma might serve to defend against illness. The core of this model is the idea that trauma involves a threat to self and identity; that how individuals cope with this, via inhibition or disclosure, involves self-related processes and contents; and that these mediate the paths of inhibition to illness and disclosure to better physical health. If one does not reveal self-threatening traumas, development of self-motives, such as self-esteem maintenance and self-efficacy, and self-definitions (e.g., "me as a productive worker") are blocked. Disclosure, on the other hand, facilitates rebuilding and repairing the self. More specifically, people bring order and meaning to their experiences and self-concept by revising their self story (cf. McAdams, 1997). By communicating about trauma, people can confront the threatening event and make the past experience a part of an integrated and purposeful self-narrative, rather than an event that must be repressed. Thus, self-disclosure versus inhibition regarding stressful events can mediate the link between trauma and physical well-being.

Ouellette returned to the same basic issue addressed by Williams et al.—do people have personal resources that they "carry around with them" that buffer the health effects of stress? Ouellette focused not on group identity but rather on personality variables such as hardiness and sense of coherence that have been shown to have health-promoting qualities. She argued that these health-related personality variables should not be assimilated to the currently dominant Big Five position in which personality is equated with traits, with traits narrowly conceived as static individual propensities easily captured by direct self-report measures. Instead, Ouellette proposed that personality "ideas" such as hardiness and sense of coherence are most productively viewed as dynamic configurations of self and environment. Ouellette used McAdams's (1996) proposed three levels of personality variables to illustrate this more comprehensive view. Level 1 descriptions of persons are in terms of traits, and this is the terrain of the Big Five researchers. But it is not just Big Five psychologists who use traits to describe people; rather, in everyday interactions, we all mentally encode others, and, in Western societies, this often is in terms of their perceived traits. McAdams terms the Level 1 trait approach the "psychology of the stranger," and Ouellette used this concept quite literally in her chapter by describing her own encounter with a retinologist whose proposed medical treatment of her detached retina was apparently based on his encoding of her in terms of traits.

Level 2 of person description is in terms of "personal concerns," or what the individual is working on or trying to do; Level 3 of personality variables is in terms of self-narrative. As Ouellette noted, at these levels self and identity concepts are necessary to understand the dynamic interplay between the person and environment. She provided specific vignettes to illustrate these two levels and also described exemplar research programs for each. An important theme of these two self-relevant levels of personality is that they not only provide a way to link the individual to the social context in a dynamic fashion; they also require that investigators listen very carefully to the participant and not simply ask whether he or she agrees or disagrees with a set of items that the researcher has developed. Instead, a self and identity approach to the personality-health intersection requires open-ended and idiographic procedures. In both of the exemplar research programs that Ouellette described, she demonstrated that such procedures need not be isolated case studies; instead, listening to individuals yields data that can test between-person nomothetic generalizations (cf. Rosenberg, 1997).

Brooks-Gunn and Graber added an important developmental perspective to the current volume by analyzing sexual identity during adolescence. This topic is particularly important for understanding the self-health interface, because it is during the teenage years that most of America's young confront both the issue of self-definition and a set of health-related behaviors, including sexual intercourse and the issue of protected sex. Brooks-Gunn and Graber described three frameworks for studying adolescent sexuality. The first two of these—studying adolescent sexuality in terms of behaviors and transitions, while offering important insights—were criticized as not providing sufficient attention to (1) the *meanings* that adolescents attach to their sexual actions; (2) the ways in which teens *personalize* their sexual thoughts, feelings, and behaviors; (3) the *contexts* that influence the process of giving meaning to and personalizing sexuality. The third framework covered by Brooks-Gunn and Graber focuses on adolescent sexuality in terms of sexual identities. The authors defined sexual identities, identified the contents of such self-definitions, and described the multidimensional nature of sexual self-construals. Brooks-Gunn and Graer concluded by describing the intersection of gender and sexuality identities.

How Sickness Influences Self and Social Identity

The final two chapters focused on how being sick influences one's personal and social identity. H. Leventhal, Idler, and E. A. Leventhal integrated a model of illness cognition (thoughts and feelings about disease) with self and identity (thoughts and feelings about self). They began by describing the common-sense model of disease representation. The central aspects of this model are (1) that internal representations of disease involve five components; (2) that mental encoding of illness involves both abstract elements (e.g., linguistic labels such as "lung cancer") and episodic elements (e.g., physical symptoms such as shortness of breath, a mental image of one's parent in the hospital after an operation to remove a cancerous lung); and (3) that health threats are subject to parallel processing, or the generation of both cognitions and affect. In linking self and identity to this common-sense model of illness cognition, Leventhal et al. first noted the central position of the physical self, a part of self often ignored by mainstream self and identity researchers. These authors then noted the role that self-definitions and self-motives play in a person's initial encounters with an ailment that may turn out to be chronic. Following this, Leventhal and his coauthors described how a chronic illness creates both "bottom-up" and "top-down" pressures for self-change. These were illustrated by a case study of Reynolds Price, a professor/novelist, confronted by a malignant tumor. Both Price's personal identities (as author) and social identities (a professor) influenced how he coped with his condition. Leventhal et al. concluded by describing how cardiovascular and cancer patients make their illnesses part of their overall personal identity structures.

In the next chapter, Charmaz described how sociologists have altered their view of how best to conceive of the individual and illness. As she noted, Parsons (1951), working within a structural/functional framework, originally proposed the notion of "sick role" as an "answer" to the quandary that physical illness posed to smooth societal functioning and orderly social interactions. The sick role denotes the rights and responsibilities of the sick person and, as with all role concepts, the sick role is defined in relation to the rights and responsibilities of a complementary role, that of the physician. Charmaz next highlighted two major problems with this conceptualization. First, the structuralist/functionalist paradigm in general and the role concept in particular are top-down, stressing society and ignoring individuals. Second, Parsons's sick role presumed an acute medical condition that could be resolved through treatment, yet many contemporary medical conditions are chronic, not submitting to a simple and finite line of biomedical attack. As a consequence, Charmaz devoted the bulk of her chapter to reviewing work in which the focus is on the stories that people with chronic illness and disability tell about themselves and their illness.

Charmaz's discussion of stories of sickness continued the self-as-narrative analyses by Pennebaker and Keough and Ouellette. Her chapter complements and considerably extends the earlier contributions. It complements the Pennebaker and Keough treatment of the health-promoting qualities of disclosure of trauma by describing how "[s]to-ries of sickness can be transformed from stories of loss to stories of learning, how coping with long-term physical illness or limitation can provide an opportunity to learn about self and self in the world." One challenge for those who follow up on Pennebaker and Keough and Charmaz will be to identify the conditions under which stories about illness and trauma do and do not yield both physical and mental health benefits. Charmaz extends the earlier discussions of the self-as-narra-tive metaphor by stressing that stories of sickness are for both self *and others* and that getting others to understand and appreciate one's narra-tive is not a simple or one-time issue.

Where We Hope to Be in the Future

Self and Identity as Major Elements in the Social and Behavioral Analysis of Health and Illness

Our primary hope is that this volume will serve as a starting point for increased systematic use of self and identity in the social and behavioral analysis of health and illness (within the more inclusive biopsychosocial model). Movement in this direction will require addressing the follow-ing questions: (1) Why is such a new approach necessary and desirable? (2) What are self and identity? (3) What is health and illness? (4) How are self and health connected?

Why Is Such a New Perspective Necessary and Desirable?   In the study of psychosocial factors involved in health and illness, considerable insight has been provided by analyses in terms of either personal factors, such as personality (e.g., hostility and coronary heart disease [Clark, 1994, pp. 266–267]) that lie within a person, and social factors, such as a sup-portive social network (e.g., Ritter, 1988) that reside outside the indi-vidual. Establishing an explicit self and social identity perspective would help bring the personal and social together. Self and identity are inherently both personal and social (cf. Ashmore & Jussim, 1997; Markus & Cross, 1990). That is, self definition involves both personal identity elements (those selves that define one as a unique individual [e.g., "I am energetic"]) and social identity elements (those selves that link the individual to others in social groups [e.g., "I am an Ameri-can"]). Further, self conception involves both the individual choosing self-definitions (e.g., "I am a psychology major") and the social con-text—from family, to ethnic group, to society as a whole—providing, and in some cases dictating, identity elements (e.g., in the United States today a person having dark skin and Negroid facial features must ad-dress the issue of ethnic identity). The central role that social identities play in the self-health interface was illustrated in several of the preceding chapters. For example, Williams et al. described ethnic identity as a moderator of the association between discrimination and physical illness, and Lock discussed how challenges to the identities of minority populations can set the stage for mental and physical problems.

The development of a self and identity approach to well-being has another major attraction. It would bring the "me" into the psychosocial equation for health and disease. At present, beliefs and attitudes about health, health-related practices (e.g., use of a condom in sex), and symptoms are major areas of investigation (Clark, 1994). There is, however, little focused concern with beliefs and feelings about self and how they might influence the development and course of physical disease. (The literatures on self-esteem, self-efficacy, and perceived vulnerability are clear exceptions.) Thus, development of a self and identity perspective would involve consideration of not just "my illness" and "my symptoms" but also thoughts and feelings about me.

To illustrate the possible benefits of adding self-beliefs to the social and behavioral analysis of health, we follow up on a point made by Kihlstrom and Canter Kihlstrom. They described somatoform disorders as involving a sharp patient-physician discrepancy in defining the patient and suggested that the only apparent options for health workers were to "challenge" or to "accept" the patient's view. We believe that a self and identity perspective offers a third approach. Kihlstrom and Canter Kihlstrom used "I am ugly" and "I am sick" as provocative shorthand for the patient's self-definitions in body dysmorphic and somatization disorders, respectively. However, a more detailed and idiographic analysis would provide the patient's own definition of self in relation to the physical conditions in question and show how this self-definition or set of self-definitions fits within his or her overall personal identity structure (e.g., "I have a great body," "I dress well," "My nose is ugly," "People can't see the real me . . . because of my ugly nose"). Rosenberg and his associates (Gara et al., 1993; Rosenberg & Gara, 1995) have done just this with psychological disorders and have demonstrated how such personalized and detailed self-structures predict depressive episodes. A detailed idiographic analysis of the somatoform disorder patient may provide the first step in providing the person insight into his or her self-structure, including self-defeating implicit links among specific self-definitions as well as self-construals that could provide sources of self-esteem and self-efficacy (see Ogilvie [1994] for an example of how this might be done).

What Are Self and Identity?   In organizing this volume, we did not impose a single set of definitions of self and identity on the contributors. We felt that that would be premature. At the same time, if self and identity are to become a major element of the social and behavioral analysis of health and illness, it will be necessary to establish at least some working definitions of key terms. As a step in this direction we offer the following suggestions made by Ashmore and Jussim (1997; pp. 5–8). First, they differentiated self and identity as societal- versus individual-level phenomena. At the societal level, each culture specifies permissible forms of self (e.g., in Western society, self is viewed as separate and autonomous, whereas in many non-Western cultures self is defined in terms of a network of social relations [cf. Markus & Kitayama, 1991; see, however, Spiro, 1993]). In the present volume, Lock described how cultural parameters for self-definition influence the life transition of menopause, and it is likely that similar culturally specified constraints for self-conception shape other important life transitions and related health phenomena (e.g., identity development in adolescence and acquisition of health damaging behaviors such as smoking).

At the individual level, Ashmore and Jussim (1997) follow James (1890) in distinguishing "I" and "Me." "I" is self/identity as "knower/ subject/process" (p. 6) and includes both temporary processes such as objective self-awareness (Duvall & Wicklund, 1972) and enduring self-motives such as impression management (Schlenker & Weigold, 1992), self-evaluation maintenance (Tesser, 1988), and the like. The "I" can be seen in several of the foregoing chapters. Williams and his colleagues noted that minority group members often do not "see" discrimination directed against them personally because to do so would challenge the self-motive of perceived personal control. Pennebaker and Keough, Ouellette, and Charmaz all emphasized the importance of the life story construct for understanding health and disease, and, in so doing, they highlight the role of the self-consistency motive underlying this concept.

Another crucial aspect of the "I" is McAdams's (1996) "personal concerns" level of person description. As explained by Ouellette, this involves the person's trying to achieve some goal, accomplish a task, or get from here to there. In understanding health and illness, personal concerns variables are likely to be quite useful. With regard to health behaviors, different individuals may have widely differing stances regarding health-damaging behaviors such as smoking, drinking, and unprotected sex—"trying to have fun/be grown up/stop feeling so sad/enjoy myself but be careful too." Once illness has struck, personal projects and related constructs can influence how patients respond to treatment regimens and the like (e.g., the prescription to lose weight can become "I want to fit into the dress I wore at my tenth wedding anniversary party").

Probably the most important aspect of the "I" for understanding health and illness is the concept of self-regulation. An important next step is a detailed analysis of self-regulation in terms of self and identity. This volume provides some important starting points. Kihlstrom and

Canter Kihlstrom described a treatment program for somatoform disorders based on the premise that the medical encounter must provide feedback that satisfies the patient's search for information that confirms a self-definition as "sick" or "ugly." Similarly, several of the authors in this volume underline the importance of two self-motives in understanding well-being: self-esteem maintenance and self-efficacy. For example, Brooks-Gunn and Graber describe Rosenthal's model of sexual identity in which two of the three dimensions are sexual self-esteem and sexual self-efficacy. Thus, in regulating thoughts, feelings, and behaviors concerning self as a sexual being, self-evaluation and self-control seem central.

One major criticism of some existing formulations of the self-regulation construct is that it overemphasizes the individual and neglects the social context. As noted before, self and identity are inherently personal and social. Thus, consideration of self and identity can help flesh out the social side of the self-regulation principle. An example is Deaux's (1992) model of self and mental health. In this framework, challenges to emotional well-being can set in motion two types of self-change: modifying one's internal view of self (intrapersonal) and altering how one is perceived by others (interpersonal). Charmaz illustrated this regulation of both personal and social self when she described chronically ill people's difficult balancing act in trying to determine exactly what they want others to know about their condition: "I don't want my office mates to think I am totally useless; but I do want them to realize that there are times that I simply cannot contribute my share, and I can't predict when those times are." Further, Lock's chapter makes it clear that cultural models of self and illness influence self-regulation. Thus, for example, for the Cree, mental and physical health are not divisible, and both are seen as determined not only by individual qualities but also the relation of the individual to the community and of the community to the physical environment. Self-regulation, then, is not simply monitoring one's physical self, checking it against internal standards, and taking action when discrepancies are noted.

"Me" refers to the "self as known/object/structure" (Ashmore & Jussim, 1997, p. 6). "Me" includes both discrete self-definitions such as "I . . . am tall, the daughter of Dan Jones, like to fish, have no skill at cooking" and affective/cognitive structures that organize these individual self-construals. At the individual element level, the present volume suggests the importance of the following: *self-definitions*, especially concerning looks and health (Kihlstrom and Canter Kihlstrom; Leventhal et al.; Lock), sexuality (Brooks-Gunn and Graber), and physical capabilities and limitations (Charmaz; Leventhal et al.); *self-standards* such as ideal (Ouellette) and "ought" selves (Higgins, Vookles, & Tykocinski, 1992); and *summary self-judgments* including self-esteem (Brooks-Gunn and Graber; Charmaz; Williams et al.).

Self and identity structures can be studied productively as both a "snapshot frozen in time" and as a "through-time motion picture." As noted, Rosenberg and his colleagues (e.g., Rosenberg & Gara, 1985) have developed procedures for assessing people's complex and personalized identity structures at any one point in time and have demonstrated the important role these play in mental health (e.g., Gara et al., 1993). We urge an extension of this approach to understanding self and identity in relation to physical well-being. Concerning self-structures as through-time motion pictures, McAdams and others (cf. Gergen & Gergen, 1988; McAdams, 1997) have used the story metaphor to analyze people's narratives about self. This idea has appeared at several points in the preceding chapters, especially those by Pennebaker and Keough, Ouellette, and Charmaz. We agree that self as story is a fruitful direction for future research on self and health. At the same time, we feel that this work will be most productive if the story metaphor is more fully explored. For example, much self-as-narrative research simply collects the person's narrative on the apparent assumption that people's life stories are narratives for self (and the researcher). In everyday life, however, stories are told to others, and often different stories are told to different audiences. Likely, patients often provide varying narratives to self, family, employer, and physician. Examination of such variation and its relation to coping with stress, patient compliance, and disease progression would be an important contribution to the self and identity perspective that we are suggesting. Charmaz points in this direction in her emphasis that patients often work very hard to get important others to understand their account of their illness and themselves.

What Is Health and Illness?   We began by asking our authors to focus on physical health, but they resisted. And we are glad that they did. Although it is desirable to distinguish physical and mental health and illness. it is not desirable to leave out psychological well-being when considering physical health and illness. Subjective, "quality of life" measures have become important yardsticks for evaluating medical interventions. Further, there is considerable evidence of bidirectional links between physical and psychological health. Thus, a self and identity approach to social and behavioral aspects of well-being will not be able to treat self and physical health separately from self and mental health. Chapters in this volume suggest some ideas in this regard and also raise some questions. Kihlstrom and Canter Kihlstrom and Lock both discussed somatoform disorder. These analyses demonstrate why such disorders are so intractable: patient-physician conflict is not simply a disagreement about a diagnosis but instead a fundamental dispute about identity, with the patient defining self as physically sick and the doctor, seeing himself or herself as the expert on physical disease, viewing the patient as not physically ill but perhaps mentally sick. Williams and his colleagues noted that the link of unfair treatment to well-being varied for white versus black Americans. For the former, unfair treatment was associated with mental health but not physical well-being, whereas just the reverse pattern was true for blacks. Ethnic identity buffered the effect of discrimination on health for African Americans. The possible role of self and identity in whites' reactions to unfair treatment is a fruitful topic for future research.

Well-being is not static and immutable across space and time. Lock described "local biologies" and varying responses in Japanese and North American culture to the life-course condition termed "menopause" in English. How do different cultures construe health? Are physical and mental health seen as separate (as in the United States and Canada) or as inextricably linked (as in Japan and among the Cree)? In cultural belief systems, how is the health of an individual conceptually linked to views of the home and family, to the wider community, and to the physical environment?

Regarding health variations across time, over the past century in Western industrialized nations, the leading causes of death have changed from acute, infectious diseases to chronic disorders and conditions associated with lifestyle. As Charmaz noted, the sick role was predicated on the acute medical problem as the norm. In today's world, however, chronic illness and disability have taken center stage. She correctly noted that this has major implications for the personal and social identities of those afflicted with chronic conditions. We would add that self-definition is closely linked to lifestyle, and thus much is to be learned about lifestyle-related health problems by considering self and identity. For example, there is considerable evidence that adolescents associate smoking with a grown-up and independent social image and that taking up smoking is related to the fit between a teen's personal self-concept and the smoker's social image (Chassin, Presson, & Sherman, 1990). We believe that other health-damaging actions can profitably be studied in terms of personal and social identities.

How Are Self and Health Connected?   As the foregoing chapters attest, there are multiple links between self and health, including bidirectional causality and self as a moderator and mediator in pathways leading to illness. The path from self to illness was illustrated in several chapters. Both Kihlstrom and Canter Kihlstrom and Lock underscored how self and social identity factors are implicated in an individual's coming to express distress in terms of bodily complaints in the absence of doctor-detected physical causes. Whether it is the individual's personal identity "I am sick" or the person's experiencing distress because of inability to achieve culturally mandated ideals for self, somatoform disorder implicates self and identity. Brooks-Gunn and Graber described how the various health problems associated with teenage sexual behavior can profitably be studied in terms of multidimensional sexual identities.

Self and identity can also mediate links between stress and illness. Pennebaker and Keough described how lack of disclosure disrupts self processes and contents that imperil well-being and that disclosure and self-reorganization reduce the deleterious effect of stress on health.

Self and identity as moderators of paths to illness are evident in several of the foregoing chapters. Lock described how cultures and subcultures provide different meaning systems within which distress and physical symptoms are interpeted. Williams and his collaborators examined how, for African Americans, ethnic identity buffers the path from the stress of discrimination to illness. Ouellette discussed how identity-related traits such as hardiness can moderate the illness-inducing effects of stress.

The link of illness to self was demonstrated in the contributions of Leventhal et al., Charmaz, and Ouellette. The former described how the initial confrontation with a disabling condition challenges an individual's taken-for-granted notions about everyday living—walking, taking care of one's self, and the like—and how this, in turn, can convert these activities into important personal projects. Leventhal and his collaborators also described the various ways in which people adapted self to cardiovascular disease and cancer (ranging from such passive stances as victim to active fighter self-construals). Charmaz detailed the many ways in which chronic illness and disability undermine patients' personal and social identities. In terms of the latter, she stressed that those with chronic illness often face others who code them as morally lacking rather than as simply having disabilities that limit them. Ouellette noted that major illness diagnoses such as AIDS and cancer not only imperil our social faces but also threaten cherished personal ideal selves.

Self and identity are also important to understanding responses to treatment. Kihlstrom and Canter Kihlstrom proposed that "possible selves" may help elucidate patient compliance with physician-prescribed regimens. Ouellette noted several ways in which the social identities of patients influenced how they were treated by the medical system. Charmaz discussed how some treatments have major impacts on self-definition (e.g., hair loss in chemotherapy).

Consideration of Health and Disease Will Yield a Better Understanding of Self and Identity

How does consideration of health and illness alter our conceptualizations of, and methods for studying, self and identity? Again, this volume provides several important starting observations. Most obviously, consideration of health and illness brings the physical self into the spotlight. Most analyses by self and social identity researchers do not center on the physical self. (There are, of course, clear exceptions [e.g., Cash and Pruzinsky [1990] on body image, and Radley [1991] on the body and social psychology.) This is somewhat of a surprise since James gave it (termed the "material self") equal billing in his seminal chapter with the "social self" and "spiritual self." The great bulk of self and identity research has concentrated on interpersonal and intrapersonal facets of self-definition, with sociologists focusing on the former, in terms of roles, and psychologists emphasizing the latter, generally in terms of personality traits. As the Leventhal et al. chapter attests, examination of the self-health interface instructs identity researchers that traits and roles are always embodied, that individuals vary considerably in how they attend to and evaluate their material self, and that physical self-perception influences other facets of a person's overall self-concept. Health psychologists' models of and methods for studying symptom perception might serve as a guide to self scientists concerned with the physical self (Clark, 1994).

Charmaz noted that sickness can serve as a "window on the self." We concur and raise the following three questions for future work: (1) How do changes in the body accompanying disease or treatment (e.g., loss of hair as a result of chemotherapy) influence self-conception? (2) How do interpersonal conflicts over self-definition play out in medical settings, (e.g., the doctor-patient conflicts discussed by Kihlstrom and Canter Kihlstrom regarding somatoform disorder)? Such interpersonal disagreements provide a unique and powerful setting for exploring motives such as self-verification studied by self psychologists primarily in laboratory experiments (e.g., Swann, 1983). (3) How do changes in medical systems pose challenges to the self-images of patients and health-care providers (e.g., HMOs and doctors' self-definition as "independent provider" versus "employee").

Summary and Suggestions

We close by briefly summarizing multiplicity, a major theme to emerge from this volume, and offering some suggested next steps in exploring the intersections between self and health.

Our major goal in this volume was to bring self and identity constructs into greater contact with the issues of health and disease. In so doing, the issue of multiplicity/multidimensionality was highlighted in numerous ways throughout the volume. First, each side of the self-health intersection is multifaceted. Although people have a clear sense of oneness and most postadolescents seek to develop a unified self-concept (McAdams, 1997), self and identity are multifaceted—process ("I") and content ("Me"); personal and social—and both personal and social identities themselves are multiple. Similarly, health and illness are best viewed as multiplicities: self-assessed and doctor-diagnosed (Williams et al.); acute and chronic (Charmaz; Leventhal et al.); mental and physical (there are a wide variety of illnesses and multiple ways to partition them). Second, the links of self to health are many and diverse: identity influences disease; self moderates paths to illness; self and identity mediate causal progression to sickness; health influences self-conception.

Our major advice is for researchers to explore the multiple facets and links explicitly and systematically. And we urge that they do so taking into consideration the major advantages of the self and identity lens. Personal and social (look to both the individual and the surrounding context). Listen to the person (health-care providers as well as patients) and study individuals (adopt idiographic procedures where possible). Yet do nomothetic research (test across person generalizations). If this book has helped begin such a concerted analysis of the health-self interface, it will have served its twin purposes of advancing both the study of social and behavioral aspects of health and disease and of increasing understanding of self and identity.

References

Ashmore, R. D., & Jussim L. (1997). Toward a second century of the scientific analysis of self and identity. In R. D. Ashmore & L. Jussim (Eds.), *Self and identity: Fundamental issues* (pp. 3–22). New York: Oxford University Press.

Cash, T. F., & Pruzinsky, T. (1990). *Body images: Development, deviance, and change.* New York: Guilford Press.

Chassin, L., Presson, C. C., & Sherman, S. J. (1990). Social psychological contributions to the understanding and prevention of adolescent cigarette smoking. *Personality and Social Psychology Bulletin, 16,* 133–151.

Clark, L. F. (1994). Social cognition and health psychology. In R. S. Wyer, Jr. & T. K. Srull (Eds.), *Handbook of social cognition* (pp. 239–288). Hillsdale, NJ: Erlbaum.

Deaux, K. (1992). Focusing on the self: Challenges to self-definition and their consequences for mental health. In D. N. Ruble, P. R. Costanzo, & M. E. Oliveri (Eds.), *The social psychology of mental health: Basic mechanisms and applications* (pp. 301–327). New York: Guilford.

Duval, S., & Wicklund, R. A. (1972). *A theory of objective self-awareness.* New York: Academic Press.

Gara, M. A., Woolfolk, R. L., Cohen, B. D., Goldston, R. B., Allen, L. A., & Novalany, J. (1993). Perception of self and other in major depression. *Journal of Abnormal Psychology, 102,* 93–100.

Gergen, K. J., & Gergen, M. M. (1988). Narrative and the self as relationship. In L. Berkowitz (Ed.), *Advances in experimental social psychology* (Vol. 21, pp. 17–56). New York: Academic Press.

Higgins, E. T., Vookles, J., & Tykocinski, O. (1992). Self and health: How "patterns" of self-beliefs predict types of emotional and physical problems. *Social Cognition, 10,* 125–150.

Holland, D. (1997). Selves as cultured: As told by an anthropologist who lacks a soul. In R. D. Ashmore & L. Jussim (Eds.), *Self and identity: Fundamental issues* (pp. 160–190). New York: Oxford University Press.

James, W. (1890). *Principles of psychology.* New York: Holt.

Leventhal, H., Meyer, D., & Nerenz, D. (1980). The common sense representation of illness danger. In S. Rachman (Ed.), *Medical psychology* (Vol. 13, pp. 7–30), New York: Pergamon.

Lin, N., & Ensel, W. (1989). Life stress and health: Stressors and resources. *American Sociological Review, 54,* 383–399.

Markus H., & Cross, S. (1990). The interpersonal self. In L. A. Pervin (Ed.), *Handbook of personality: Theory and Research* (pp. 576–608). New York: Guilford.

Markus, H., & Kitayama, S. (1991). Culture and the self: Implications for cognition, emotion, and motivation. *Psychological Review, 98,* 224–253.

Markus, H., & Nurius, P. (1986). Possible selves. *American Psychologist, 41,* 954–969.

McAdams, D. P. (1996). Personality, modernity, and the storied self: A contemporary framework for studying persons. *Psychological Inquiry, 7,* 295–321.

McAdams, D. P. (1997). The case for unity in the (post)modern self: A modest proposal. In R. D. Ashmore & L. Jussim (Eds.), *Self and identity: Fundamental issues* (pp. 46–80). New York: Oxford University Press.

Ogilvie, D. M. (1994). The use of graphic representations of self-dynamisms in clinical treatment. *Crisis Intervention and Time-limited Treatment, 1,* 125–140.

Parsons, T. (1951). *The social system.* New York: Free Press.

Radley, A. (1991). *The body and social psychology.* New York: Springer-Verlag.

Ritter, C. (1988). Social supports, social networks, and health behaviors. In D. S. Gochman (Ed.), *Health behavior: Emerging research perspectives* (pp. 149–162). New York: Plenum.

Rosenberg, S. (1997). Multiplicity of selves. In R. D. Ashmore & L. Jussim (Eds.), *Self and identity: Fundamental issues* (pp. 23–45). New York: Oxford University Press.

Rosenberg, S., & Gara, M. A. (1985). The multiplicity of personal identity. In P. Shaver (Ed.), *Review of personality and social psychology* (Vol. 6, pp. 87–113). Newbury Park, CA: Sage.

Schlenker, B. R., & Weigold, M. F. (1992). Interpersonal processes involving impression regulation and management. *Annual Review of Psychology, 43,* 133–168.

Spiro, M. E. (1993). Is the Western conception of the self "peculiar" within the context of the world cultures? *Ethos, 21,* 107–153.

Swann, W. B., Jr. (1983). Self-verification: Bringing social reality into harmony with the self. In J. Suls & A. G. Greenwald (Eds.), *Psychological perspectives on the self* (Vol. 2, pp. 33–66). Hillsdale, NJ: Erlbaum.

Tesser, A. (1988). Toward a self-evaluation maintenance model of social behavior. In L. Berkowitz (Ed.), *Advances in experimental social psychology* (Vol. 21, pp. 181–227). New York: Academic Press.

Index

Abnormal illness behavior, 26
  See also Somatoform disorders
Acute illness
  death from chronic illness *versus*, 251
  impact of on self, 187–88, 193, 194, 195
  sick role and, 212–13
Adherence
  changes in physical self and, 190
  somatic experience affecting, 188–89
  See also Compliance
Adolescence
  attractiveness in, 165–66, 168, 171–72
  body dysmorphic disorder and, 28
  cigarette smoking in, 251
  decision making in, 167
  health in indigenous communities and, 52–55
  health-related behavior patterns in, 9
  identity in, 155–56, 164–65 (*see also* Sexual identity in adolescence)
  somatization disorder beginning in, 30–33
  somatization disorder in young adults and, 30–33

African Americans
  adolescent sexuality in, 161
  stress and health in, 71–100
  unfair treatment and well-being and, 251
  See also Ethnicity
Age and aging
  culture and, 59–63, 64n. 2
  illness cognition and, 186, 191–92, 194
  individual responsibility for health and, 50
Agreeableness, in Big Five approach, 127
AIDS, 138–39, 141–42, 144, 146
  adolescence and, 175
  goals and, 144
  impact of on self, 201
  nondisclosure of and death, 103
Alcohol consumption, self and identity and, 9
Alcoholics Anonymous, traumas dealt with in, 117
Alzheimer's disease, discourse analysis and, 144–45
America
  female aging in, 59–63, 64n. 2

America (*continued*)
  individual's responsibility for
    health and, 48–52
Americans' Changing Lives Study,
  73, 74
Anorexia nervosa, 37n. 2
Anthropology, self and identity in, 4
Appraisal, in self-regulation model of
  compliance, 35
Asthma, compliance and, 34, 36
Attractiveness in adolescence,
  165–66, 168
  sexual identity and, 171
Authenticity, hardiness construct and,
  136
Autonomic nervous system, disclosure of traumatic experiences
  and, 104–5, 106

Back pain, in somatization disorder,
  31
Behavioral changes, disclosure of
  traumatic experiences and, 105,
  107
Behavioral health, 5
Behavioral mechanisms, 7
  in health research, vii, viii, x, xi
  of physical health and illness, 5
  self and identity and, 9
Behavioral medicine, 5
  biopsychosocial model and, 5–7
  mechanisms forming causal links
    between biological and
    psychosocial elements of, 7–10
  research in, 7
  systems view of, 10–11
Behavioral patterning. *See* Personality, health and; Sexual identity, in
  adolescence
Behavioral sciences, self and identity
  in, 4–5
Big Five approach, to personality,
  126–32, 133, 139–44, 148n. 1,
  149nn. 2, 3
Biofeedback, for somatization disorder, 33
Biological processes, self and social
  identity and illness and, v, vi
Biomedical model, 5–6

impact of chronic illness on self
  and, 199
Biopower, 47
Biopsychosocial model, 24
  behavioral medicine and, 5–7
  identity in, 5–7
  self and identity in social and
    behavioral analysis of health and
    illness and, 246–52
  self in, 5–7
Body dysmorphic disorder, 27–28,
  36n. 1
Body image, in adolescence, 165–66,
  168, 171–72
Bottom-up processes, representation
  and management of chronic
  illness and, 192, 193–96, 197–98,
  202–3
Breast cancer
  common-sense models of, 188
  risk and, 64n. 3
  See also Cancer
Breast development, in girls, 165–
  66
Briquet's syndrome, 28
  See also Somatization disorder
Bulimia nervosa, 37n. 2

Canada
  female aging in, 59–63, 69n. 2
  Greek immigrants to Montréal
    and, 55–58
  health and dislocation of Cree
    Indians in, 52–58
  nationalism in Québec and, 45
Cancer
  compartmentalization and, 204
  fighting spirit and, 204
  impact of on self, 194–95, 196,
    197–98, 199–200, 201, 203–4
    (*see also* Chronic illness, impact
    of on self)
  inhibition of traumatic experience
    and, 103
  representations of, 187
  self and, 225
  self-concept and, 36
  traumatic experiences and, 102
  Type C personality and, 103

victimization and, 203–4
  See also Breast cancer
Cannon, Walter B., 13
Cardiovascular symptoms, in somatization disorder, 31
  See also Heart disease
Cellular level, in health research, vii, viii, x, xi
Challenge, personality and, 136
Childhood
  health problems and inhibition of traumas in, 102–3
  inhibition of sexual assault in, 112
  recovery from chronic illness in, 216–17
  somatization disorder beginning in, 30–33
Chronic illness
  death from *versus* death from acute illness, 251
  disconnection and, 224
  invisible disability and, 220–21
  loss and, 218–24
  loss of economic resources and, 219–20
  marker events in, 223
  occurring within a life, 222
  recovery of children and, 216–17
  stigma attached to, 222–23
  visible disability and, 220, 221
Chronic illness, impact of on self, 185–208
  abstract and concrete representations of illness and, 188–89
  acute illness model and, 187–88, 193, 194, 195
  adherence and, 188–89
  age-related changes and, 186, 191–92
  biomedical model and, 199
  bottom-up processes and, 192, 193–96, 197–98, 202–3
  cancer and, 194–95, 196, 197–98, 199–200, 201, 203–4
  challenge to self and, 193–202
  common-self model of, 185, 186–92, 193, 195
  coping procedures and, 186, 187, 194, 197–200, 199

diabetes and, 195–96
heart disease and, 194–95, 196, 201, 202–3
illness-specific models and, 188
initial encounter with illness and, 193–94
interpersonal resources and, 199, 201–2
multilevel representations, 188–89
occupation and, 200–201
parallel response model and, 189–90
physical self and, 190, 192–93, 194
prior experience and, 196–97
race, stress, identity, and, 79, 80, 86–90
reformulating self and, 197–202
relationship with health-care institution and, 199–200
religion and, 200
role identities and, 200–201
self and identity and, 216–24
self-concept and, 229–30
shame and, 224–25
social and behavioral capacities and, 186
social information and, 196–97
stories of self and, 198–99, 209, 210–11, 224–33, 234nn. 1, 2
top-down processes and, 192, 193, 195, 196–98, 200, 202
view of other and, 186
  See also Sick role
Cigarette smoking
  in adolescence, 251
  convergent and reciprocal causation and, xi
  self and identity and, 9
Cognitive appraisal, of stress, 8
Cognitive representation, self-regulation of compliance and, 35–36
Coherence and hardiness constructs, in personality-as-self/identity approach to health, 132–37, 145–46, 149n. 4
Cold, common, representations of, 187
Collaboration, in personality-as-self/-identity approach to health, 147

Colonialism
    culture and, 45
    health and, 52–55
    politics and, 64n. 1
Commitment, personality and, 136
Common-sense model, of illness
    cognition, 185, 186–92, 193, 195
Communication
    about bodily states between cul-
        tures, 52–55
    compliance promoted by improv-
        ing, 34–35
Compartmentalization, cancer and, 204
Compliance
    communication improved for,
        34–35
    culture and, 45
    self and self-regulation and, 34–37
    self-regulation model of, 35
    sick role and, 214
Conscientiousness, in Big Five
    approach, 127, 140
Consultation-liaison procedure, for
    somatization disorder, 33–34
Content analysis, in personality-
    as-self/identity approach to
    health, 146, 147
Control
    in adolescence, 167
    of female aging in North America
        and Japan, 59–63, 64n. 2
    individual's responsibility for
        health and, 48–52
    personality and, 132, 136
Convergent causation, in multilevel
    health research, ix, x, xi
Conversion disorder, 27, 36n. 1
Coping
    with chronic illness, 186, 187, 194,
        197–200
    disclosure of traumatic experience
        and, 109–10
    in self-regulation model of compli-
        ance, 35
    with stress, 8
Coronary heart disease (CHD). See
    Heart disease
Cortisol levels, shyness in children
    and, 112

Cree Indians (Québec), health and
    dislocation of, 52–55
Cue competition theory, somatization
    disorder and, 29–30
Culturally interpreted syndrome, 56
Culture
    concept of, 44–47
    female aging process and, 59–63,
        64n. 2
    personality and health and, 126,
        129, 132, 146, 149n. 2
    politics and health and identity
        and, 43–68, 64n. 1
    power and, 45–47, 64n. 1
    risk and, 60, 64n. 3
    self and, 47–52
    self-regulation and, 249
    well-being and, 251
Culture-bound syndromes, 56
Cybernetic self–regulation theories,
    somatization disorder and,
    29–30

Decision making, in adolescence, 167
Delusional disorder, somatic type, 28
Depression, compliance and, 34
Deprivation, fractured identities and,
    52–55
Detroit Area Study (DAS), identity
    and health in, 76–91
Diabetes
    compliance and, 34, 36
    impact of on self, 195–96 (see also
        Chronic illness, impact of on self)
Diarrhea, inhibition of traumatic ex-
    perience and, 103
Disabilities, visible and invisible,
    220–21
Disclosure of traumatic events, self
    and health and, 101–21
Discourse analysis, personality and
    health and, 144–45
    See also Narrative
Discrimination, stress and health and,
    71–100
Disease management (DM), 35
Disease-prone personality, 130
Dislocation, health, self and identity
    and, 52–58

Dissociative disorders, 36n. 1
Dysmorphobia. *See* Body dysmorphic disorder

Eating
disorders, 37n. 2
self and identity and, 9
Economics, individual responsibility for health and, 50
Emotion
in self-regulation model of compliance, 35
stress and, 12–13
Emotional distress, somatization disorder and, 30
Emotional experiences, regulation of and illness representations, 189–90
Emotional expression, illness and ambivalence over, 103
Emotional Stability *versus* Neuroticism, in Big Five approach, 127
Emotional upheavals, health and disclosure of, 101–21
Emphysema, identity and, 223
Epstein-Barr virus, disclosure of traumatic experiences and, 104, 106
Ethnicity
health, self and identity and, 52–58
noncompliance and, 45
stress and health in minorities and, 71–100
unfair treatment and well-being and, 251
See also African Americans
Ethnography, sick role and, 210, 216–17
Ethnopsychology, self and, 47–48
Evaluative self, 11
Existentialism
hardiness construct and, 136, 137
personality and, 146
External locus of control, stress and, 8

Feminist psychology
Foucault and, 47
self and, 142
See also Women's movement

Five-Factor model (FFM), of personality, 126, 130
Foucault, M., 47, 64n. 1
Freud, Sigmund, 13

Galen, 12
Gastrointestinal symptoms, in somatization disorder, 31
Gay men, inhibition of homosexuality and illness in, 103
Gender differences
in losses in chronic illness, 219–20
in somatization disorder, 31
Gender identity, 164–65
in adolescence, 156, 159, 168, 172–74 (*see also* Sexual identity, in adolescence)
Global economy, culture and, 46, 47
Goals, personality and health and, 143–44
Greek women, identity crisis in due to migration, 55–58
Group identity, race, stress and health and, 71–100
Growth, disclosure of traumatic experiences and, 113–14

Hardiness and coherence constructs, in personality-as-self/identity approach to health, 132–37, 140, 145–46, 149n. 4
Health
adolescent sexuality and, 156, 160, 175
definitions of, 250–51
in holistic model, 6
identity, culture and politics and, 43–68, 64n. 1
individual's responsibility for, 48–52
politics and colonialism and, 52–55
psychological well-being and, 250–51
race and stress and, 71–100
self and identity in social and behavioral analysis of, 246–52
self connected to, 251–52
social and behavioral aspects of, 5
socioeconomic status and stress and, 76–91, 92
subjective experience of, 6–7

Health (*continued*)
    traumatic experiences and, 101–21
    World Health Organization defini-
        tion, 49
    See also Illness; Mental health; Per-
        sonality, health and
Health behavior models, self/identity
    constructs in, 9
Health belief model, 24
Health-care delivery, self and identity
    in, 6–7
Health-care system
    relationship with and impact of
        chronic illness on self, 199–200
    somatization disorder and, 30
Health plan patients, negotiations of
    over medications, 217
Health psychology, 5, 7
    biopsychosocial model of, 24
    scope of, 23–24
Health research
    integrated approach to, v, vi
    interdisciplinary, v–vi
    See also Multilevel approach, to
        health research
Heart disease
    identity of patients with, 218, 223
    impact of on self, 194–95, 196,
        201, 202–3 (*see also* Chronic ill-
        ness, impact of on self)
    parallel causation and, ix
    racial discrimination and, 72, 73
    risk factors in, ix
    traumatic experiences and, 102
    Type A individual and, 130, 132
Heart rate, disclosure of traumatic
    experiences and, 105, 106
Hepatitis B vaccinations, disclosure
    of traumatic experiences and,
    104, 106
Hippocrates, 12
Holistic model, health defined in, 6
Homosexuality, illness and inhibition
    of, 103
Hormonal function, inhibition of
    traumatic experiences and, 112
Hormone replacement therapy
    (HRT), American *versus* Japa-
    nese use of, 62, 64n. 2

Hospitalization rates, traumatic
    experiences and, 102
Hypertension
    adherence to treatment for, 188–89
    common-sense models of, 188
    compliance and, 34, 36
    inhibition of traumatic experience
        and, 102
    racial discrimination and, 73, 74,
        75
Hypochondriasis, 27, 36n. 1

"I," in health and illness, 248–49, 253
"I" and "Me" (James), 4, 6, 9, 111,
    112, 137, 141, 248
Ideal type, 234n. 3, 249
Identity
    in accounts of psychophysiological,
        behavioral, and illness-initiated
        mechanisms, 7–10
    in adolescence, 155–56, 164–65 (*see
        also* Sexual identity, in adoles-
        cence)
    within biopsychosocial model, 5–7
    chronic illness and, 216–24
    culture, politics and health and,
        43–68, 64n. 1
    definitions of, 247–50
    disclosure of traumatic experiences
        and, 115–17
    dislocation and, 52–58
    ethnic (*see* Ethnicity)
    in health-care delivery, 6–7
    health connected to, 251–52
    illness affecting (*see* Chronic illness,
        impact of on self; Sick role)
    personality and health and,
        125–26, 132–47, 149n. 4
    race, stress and health and, 71–100
    self-regulation and, 248–49
    sexual, 249 (*see also* Sexual identity,
        in adolescence)
    in social and behavioral analysis of
        health and illness, v, vi, 9–10,
        246–52
    in social and behavioral sciences,
        4–5
    as societal-versus individual-level
        phenomenon, 248

somatization disorder as problem
    of, 32–33
stress and, 8–9
systems view and, 10–11
through-time motion pictures and,
    250
understanding of from considera-
    tion of health and disease,
    252–53
    See also Gender identity; Self
Idiographic analysis, 254
    of somatoform disorder patient,
    247
Idiographic Functional Status Assess-
    ment (IFSA), 144
Illness
    definitions of, 250–51
    impact of on self (see Chronic illness,
        impact of on self; Sick role)
    inhibition of traumatic events and,
        102–3, 109, 110, 111–13
    patient's experience of and patient
        care, 6
    psychological well-being and,
        250–51
    reactions to, 7
    self and identity in social and
        behavioral analysis of, v, vi, 9–10,
        246–52
    social and behavioral aspects of, 5
    subjective experience of, 6
    See also Acute illness; Chronic illness;
        Health; specific illnesses
Illness behavior, abnormal, 26
    See also Somatoform disorders
Illness Behavior Questionnaire (IBQ),
    for somatization disorder, 32
Immigrants
    health, self and identity and, 52–58
    noncompliance and, 45
Immune function
    disclosure of traumatic experiences
        and, 104, 106
    inhibition of traumatic experiences
        and, 112–13
Indigenous people, responsibility of
    for health, 52–55
Influenza, inhibition of traumatic
    experience and, 103

Information processing, inhibition
    of traumatic experiences as,
    111–12
Inhibition, as response to traumatic
    events, 102–3, 109, 110, 111–13
Integrated approach, to health
    research, v, vi
Interdisciplinary approach, to health
    research, v–vi
Interpersonal resources, impact of
    chronic illness on self and, 199,
    201–2
Interpretation, in self-regulation
    model of compliance, 35

James, William, 4, 6, 9, 111, 112,
    136, 137, 141, 186, 248, 253
Japan, female aging in, 59–63
John Henryism, 94

Kass, Leon, 50
Kissing, in adolescence, 161
Knowles, John, 50

Language, disclosure of traumatic
    experience with, 101–21
Levels of analysis, in health research.
    See Multilevel approach, to
    health research
Life story construct. See Narrative
Lifestyle, illness related to, 251
LIWC (Linguistic Inquiry and Word
    Count), 115–16
Lymphocyte counts, inhibition of
    traumatic events and, 112–13

Masturbation, in adolescence, 161
"Me," 253
    self-definitions and, 249
    See also "I" and "Me"
Medical care, initial encounter with
    chronic illness and, 194
Medicalization, 64n. 1
    of menopause, 59–63, 64n. 2
Medical problems and complaints
    (MPC) questionnaire, for soma-
    tization disorder, 31–32
Menopause, view of in North
    America and Japan, 59–63, 64n. 2

Menstrual symptoms, in somatization disorder, 31
Mental health
physical health and, 250–51
self and, 249
See also Somatoform disorder
Migration. *See* Immigrants
Minorities, stress and health in, 71–100
See also Ethnicity
Molecular level, in health research, vii, viii, x, xi
Montréal, Greek immigrants to, 55–58
Mortality, traumatic experiences and, 102
Motivation, collaboration in health research and, 147
Multilevel approach, to health research, vi–xii, 253–54
chronic illness and, 188–89
sexual identity in adolescence and, 169–71, 175
Multiple sclerosis
self and, 226–28, 229
as visible disability, 221
Myasthenia gravis, self and, 225

Narrative, 248
discourse analysis and, 144–45
impact of chronic illness on self and, 198–99
life story construct and, 248
self as, 250
of self in illness, 209, 210–11, 224–33, 234nn. 1, 2
through-time motion pictures and, 250
National Center for Health Statistics (NCHS), 71
National Institute of Mental Health (NIMH) Epidemiologic Catchment Area (ECA), somatoform disorder and, 32
National Institutes of Health (NIH), v
Nationalism, culture and, 45–46
National Study of Black Americans (NSBA), 73
Native Canadians, health and dislocation of, 52–55

Neuroscience research, levels of analysis in, vi–vii
Neuroticism Extraversion Openness Personality Inventory (NEO), 130, 131, 134, 147
Nevra, among Greek immigrants, 55–58
Nomothetic research, 254
Noncompliance. *See* Compliance
North America. *See* America; Canada

Occupation, relationship with and impact of chronic illness on self, 200–201
Office of Behavioral and Social Sciences Research (OBSSR), goals of, v–vi
Openness to Experience, in Big Five approach, 127, 140
Organ systems level, in health research, vii, viii, x, xi
Orientation to Life Questionnaire, coherence and, 133–34
Ought selves, 249

Pain disorder, 27
sick role and, 214–15
Parallel causation, in multilevel health research, ix, x
Parallel response model, 189–90
Paralysis, identity and, 223
Parsons, Talcott, 209, 210, 211, 214, 216, 218
Patient, sick role and, 211–12, 217–18
Patient care, patient's experience of illness and, 6
Peer crowds, adolescent sexual identity and, 167
Perception of others, adolescent sexual identity and, 168
Persecution, of peoples regarded as inherently different, 52–55
Personal concerns level, of person description, 248
Personal factors, health and illness and, 246
Personality, health and, 125–54, 246
Big Five approach (simple traits)

and, 126–32, 133, 139–44, 148n.
    1, 149nn. 2, 3
challenge and, 136, 140
coherence and hardiness con-
    structs and, 132–37, 140,
    145–46, 149n. 4
commitment and, 136
control and, 132, 136
culture and society, 129, 132, 146,
    149n. 2
discourse analysis and, 144–45
disease-prone personality and,
    130
Five-Factor Model and, 126, 130
future research on, 145–47
goals and, 143–44
instability of personality and, 128
methodological strategies for
    studying, 146–47
model studies on self and identity
    and, 143–45
onset of illness and, 128
process and, 129, 132
researcher's stance and, 148
scenes about, 138–39
self and identity and, 125–26,
    132–47, 149n. 4
self-regulation and, 133
situations and contexts and,
    128–29, 131, 132, 135
stress and, 128, 129, 131, 132,
    134–35, 136
transactions and, 131, 135
Type A individual and, 130, 132
Type B individual and, 130
Personal Views Survey, hardiness
    research and, 133–34
Pessimistic attributional style, stress
    and, 8
Pharmaceutical benefit management
    (PBM) firm, 34–35
Phenomenology, in personality-
    as-self/identity approach to
    health, 146–47
Physical health. See Health
Physical self, 252–53
    changes in and treatment, 190
    impact of chronic illness on, 190,
    192–93, 194

Physician
    disclosure of traumatic experiences
        and visits to, 104, 106
    sick role and, 212–14, 217–18
    view of patient and patient's self-
        concept and, 33–36
Physiological changes, discriminatory
    behavior and, 72–73
Physiological markers, disclosure of
    traumatic experiences and, 104,
    106
Planned behavior, theory of, 9
Poliomyelitis, recovery of children
    with, 216–17
Politics
    health and, 52–55
    identity, culture, and, 43–68,
        64n. 1
Possible self, 11
    self-regulation of compliance and,
        36, 252
Power, culture and, 45–47, 64n. 1
Price, Reynolds, 197–98, 199–200
Prior experience, individual's model
    of a disease and, 196–97
Profession, relationship with and
    impact of chronic illness on self,
    200–201
Protection motivation theory, 9
Proximity corollary, in multilevel
    health research, xi–xii
Psychiatrist, referral to for somatiza-
    tion disorder, 33
Psychoanalysis, stress reduction and,
    117
Psychological health. See Mental
    health
Psychologization, somatization
    versus, 29, 30
Psychophysiological mechanisms, 7
    self and identity and, 8–9
Psychosocial stress moderators, 8–9
Psychosocial vulnerability, stress and
    health and, 74–76
    See also Group identity; Self-con-
        cept
Psychosomatic hypothesis, 13
Psychosomatics, traumatic experi-
    ences and health and, 101–21

Psychotherapy, stress reduction and, 117

Pubertal changes, 165–66
  See also Sexual identity, in adolescence

Qualitative research strategies, in personality-as-self/identity approach to health, 146–47
Quality of life, biomedical interventions considering, 6
Québec
  health and dislocation of Cree Indians in, 52–55
  nationalism in, 45

Race, stress and health and, 71–100
  See also Ethnicity
Racism, health, self and identity and, 52–58
Reactions to illness, 7
Reasoned action, theory of, 9
Reciprocal causation, in multilevel health research, ix, xi
Recovery, sick role and, 221–22
Religion, relationship with and impact of chronic illness on self, 200
Responsibility, of individual for health, 48–52
Risk, as cultural construct, 60, 64n. 3
Role identities, relationship with and impact of chronic illness on self, 200–201

Salutogenesis, 135–36, 147
Self
  abnormal illness behavior and, 266 (*see also* Somatoform disorders)
  in accounts of psychophysiological, behavioral, and illness–initiated mechanisms, 7–10
  adolescent sexuality and, 159
  biological processes and illness and, v, vi
  within biopsychosocial model, 5–7, 24
  chronic illness and (*see* Chronic illness, impact of on self)
  culture and, 47–52

definitions of, 247–50
evaluative, 11
feminist psychologists and, 142
in health-care delivery, 6–7
health connected to, 251–52
illness affecting (*see* Chronic illness, impact of on self; Sick role)
as knowledge structure, 24–26
mental health and, 249
personality and health and, 125–26, 132–47, 149n. 4
self-definitions and, 249
self-motives and, 11
self-regulation and, 248–49
self-regulation and compliance and, 34–37
as sick person, 28
in social and behavioral analysis of health and illness, v, vi, 9–10, 246–52
in social and behavioral sciences, 4–5
as societal–versus–individual-level phenomenon, 248
somatoform disorder and, 30
stories of (*see* Narrative)
stress and, 8–9
systems view and, 10–11
through-time motion pictures and, 250
traumatic and stressful events and, 101–21
as ugly person, 27–28
understanding of from consideration of health and disease, 252–53
  See also Identity; Physical self; Possible self
Self-beliefs, in social and behavioral analysis of health, 247
Self-concept, 25
  chronic illness and, 229–30
  health and illness behavior and, 27 (*see also* Somatoform disorders)
  physician's view of patient versus, 33–36
  race, stress and health and, 71–100
Self-definition, 249, 253
  lifestyle and, 251

Self-efficacy
  self-regulation and, 24
  well-being and, 249
Self-esteem
  physical illness and, 24
  race, stress and health and, 71–100
  well-being and, 249
Self-evaluation, initial encounter with
    chronic illness and, 194
Self-help groups, traumas dealt with
    in, 117
Self-image, 25–26
  body dysmorphic disorder and,
    27–28
  delusional disorder, somatic type
    and, 28
  health and illness behavior and, 27
    (see also Somatoform disorders)
  physical disease and, 24
Self-integration, disclosure of trau-
    matic experiences and, 114–15
Self-motives, 11
Self-regulation, 23–24, 248–49
  personality and health and, 133
  self and compliance and, 34–37
  self-efficacy and, 24
Self-regulation model, 11
  of compliance, 35
Self-reports
  disclosure of traumatic experiences
    in, 105, 107
  in personality-as-self/identity
    approach to health, 146, 147
Self-responsibility, for health, 48–52
Self-standards, 249
Self-treatment, initial encounter with
    chronic illness and, 194
Selye, Hans, 13
Semantic illness network, 56
Sex education, 175
Sexual arousal, in adolescence,
    160–61, 163
Sexual assault, inhibition of, 112
Sexual behavior, self and identity and,
    9
Sexual identity, in adolescence,
    155–82
  African Americans and, 161
  behavioral approach to, 159–62

biological and physical factors in,
    165–66, 168
  body image and, 165–66, 168,
    171–72
  gendered contexts of, 156, 159,
    168, 172–74
  health-related factors and, 156,
    160, 175
  kissing and, 161
  masturbation and, 161
  multidimensionality and, 169–71,
    175
  multiple domains and, 168
  parent-adolescent relationships
    and, 174
  peer crowds and, 167
  perceptions of others and, 168
  psychological problems and, 156
  pubertal changes and, 165–66
  research on, 168–72
  self and, 159
  self/identity approach to, 155–56,
    157, 164–72, 174–75
  sex education and, 175
  sexual arousal and, 160–61, 163
  sexual intercourse and, 160, 161,
    163, 164, 172
  sexually adventurous youth and,
    170, 171
  sexually competent youth and,
    169–71
  sexually driven youth and, 170,
    171
  sexually naive youth and, 169, 170,
    171
  sexually unassured youth and, 169,
    170, 171
  sexual self-schema scale and,
    171–72
  social relationships and, 166–67
  societal regulation and, 158–59
  tasks involved in, 158
  touching and, 161
  transitional approach to, 162–64
Sexual identity, self-regulation and,
    249
Sexual intercourse, in adolescence,
    160, 161, 163, 164, 172
Sexual self-schema scales, 171–72

Sexual trauma, health problems and inhibition of, 102
Shame, chronic illness and, 224–25
Shyness, health problems in young children and, 112
Sick role, 209–24
  acute illness and, 212–13
  blame for being in, 215
  chronic illness and, 213–16, 230, 251
  description of, 209–13
  entry into, 214–16
  lack of culpability for occupation of, 215
  noncompliance and, 214
  pain sufferers and, 214–15
  patient and, 211–12, 214, 217–18
  physical illnesses and, 30
  physician and, 212–14, 217–18
  recovery from illness and, 221–22
  self and identity and, 216–24
  social and psychological factors in absence of disease and, 6
  somatization disorder and, 31
  stigma of mental illnesses and, 30
Simple traits, personality and, 126–32, 133, 139–44, 148n. 1, 149nn. 2, 3
Skin conductance, disclosure of traumatic experiences and, 104–5, 106
Smoking. See Cigarette smoking
Social aspects, of physical health and illness, 5, 246
Social comparisons, initial encounter with chronic illness and, 194
Social environmental level, in health research, vii, viii, x, xi
Social evaluation, culture and, 44–45
Social identity, 254
  biological processes and illness and, v, vi
Social information, individual's model of a disease and, 196–97
Social networks, impact of chronic illness on self and, 199, 201–2
Social relationships
  in adolescence, 166–67
  stress-buffering effects of, 8–9

Social sciences, self and identity in, 4–5
Social support
  health and illness and, 246
  illness and traumatic events and, 103, 117
  loss of in chronic illness, 224
Society, personality and health and, 126, 132, 146, 149n. 2
Socioeconomic status (SES), health and stress and, 76–91, 92
Sociology, self and identity in, 4
Somatization disorder, 27, 28–34, 36n. 1
  culture-bound syndromes and, 56
  mechanisms of, 29–30
  prevalence of, 32
  treatment of, 33–34
  in young adults, 30–33
Somatoform disorders, 250–51
  abnormal illness behavior and, 26–34
  idiographic analysis for, 247
  prevalence of, 32
  self as sick person and, 28 (see also Somatization disorder)
  self as ugly person and, 27–28
  self-regulation and, 249
Stages of change model, 9
Story. See Narrative
Stress
  cognitive appraisal of, 8
  coping with, 8
  emotion and, 12–13
  immigration causing, 55–58
  inhibition of traumatic experiences as, 111
  pathogenic physiological changes associated with, 8–9
  personality and, 128, 129, 131, 132, 134–35, 136
  psychosocial moderators of, 8–9
  race and health and, 71–100
  response to traumatic experiences and, 101–21
  self/identity constructs and, 8–9
  somatization disorder and, 29, 30
Stroke patients, identity of, 218

Structural-functionalism, sick role and, 210

Subjective experience, of health, 6–7

Summary self-judgments, 249

Support groups, traumas dealt with in, 103, 113

Surgency or Extroversion, in Big Five approach, 127

Surveillance, Foucault and, 47

Sympathetic nervous system (SNS) activity, disclosure of traumatic experiences and, 112, 113

Symptom perception, physical self and, 253

Systems perspective, behavioral medicine and, 10–11

Talking, for disclosure of traumatic experience, 104, 105, 106–7, 109, 112, 113, 116–17

Talk therapy, stress reduction and, 117

T-helper cell growth, disclosure of traumatic experiences and, 104, 106

Thematic Apperception Test (TAT), in personality-as-self/identity approach to health, 146

Top-down processes, representation and management of chronic illness and, 192, 193, 195, 196–98, 200

Trait approach, to personality, 126–32, 133, 139–44, 148n. 1, 149nn. 2, 3

Transition, adolescent sexuality as, 162–64

Transsexualism, 37n. 2

Traumatic experiences, 101–21
disclosure and, 101–21
inhibition and, 102–3, 109, 110, 111 –13

Treatment
changes in physical self and, 190
patient's self-perceptions considered in, 6–7
personal concerns level and, 248

Tuberculosis patients, negotiations of over treatment timetables, 217

Type A individual, 8, 130, 132

Type A structured interview, in personality-as-self/identity approach to health, 146

Type B individual, 130

Type C individual, cancer and, 103

Ulcers, traumatic experiences and, 102

Ultraviolet radiation exposure, self and identity and, 9

Unfair treatment
stress and health and, 72, 73–74, 77
well-being and, 251

Upper respiratory infections, shyness in children and, 112

Victimization, cancer and, 203–4

Weight, adolescence and
body image in girls and, 166
sexual identity and, 171

Whalen, Robert, 50

Women, aging process in North America versus in Japan, 59–63, 64n. 2

Women's movement, responsibility for health and, 48–49
See also Feminist psychology

World Health Organization (WHO), health defined by, 49

Writing, for disclosure of traumatic experience, 104–9, 112, 113–16

Young adults, somatization disorder in, 30–33
See also Adolescence

Printed in the United Kingdom
by Lightning Source UK Ltd.
132440UK00002B/38/A